t TEST AND CONFIDENCE INTERVALS FOR μ

Estimated standard error of $\overline{X}$

$$s_{\overline{X}} = \frac{s}{\sqrt{N}}$$

t test for H_0 about μ

$$t = \frac{\overline{X} - \mu}{s_{\overline{X}}}$$

where $df = (N - 1)$

Confidence intervals for μ

99% CI for μ: $\overline{X} \pm t_{(.01)}(s_{\overline{X}})$

95% CI for μ: $\overline{X} \pm t_{(.05)}(s_{\overline{X}})$

z TEST FOR H_0 ABOUT POPULATION PROPORTION

$$z = \frac{p_s - p_t}{\sigma_{\text{prop}}}$$

where $\sigma_{\text{prop}} = \sqrt{\dfrac{p_t q_t}{N}}$

and p_t = proportion in H_0

DIFFERENCE BETWEEN μ_1 AND μ_2 (INDEPENDENT GROUPS)

Estimated standard error of difference
Equal N's

$$s_{\overline{X}_1 - \overline{X}_2} = \sqrt{s_{\overline{X}_1}^2 + s_{\overline{X}_2}^2}$$

Unequal N's

$$s_{\overline{X}_1 - \overline{X}_2} = \sqrt{\frac{(N_1 - 1)s_1^2 + (N_2 - 1)s_2^2}{(N_1 + N_2 - 2)}}$$

$$\times \sqrt{\left(\frac{1}{N_1}\right) + \left(\frac{1}{N_2}\right)}$$

t-test for H_0 about difference between μ's

$$t = \frac{\overline{X}_1 - \overline{X}_2}{s_{\overline{X}_1 - \overline{X}_2}}$$

where H_0: $\mu_1 - \mu_2 = 0$ and

$$df = N_1 + N_2 - 2$$

Estimated omega squared

$$\hat{\omega}^2 = \frac{t^2 - 1}{t^2 + df + 1}$$

CORRELATION

Pearson correlation coefficient (r)
Formulas for r

$$r = \frac{\sum z_X z_Y}{N} \quad \text{where } N = \text{no. of pairs, } df = N - 2$$

$$= \frac{\sum XY - \dfrac{\sum X \sum Y}{N}}{\sqrt{\sum X^2 - \dfrac{(\sum X)^2}{N}}\sqrt{\sum Y^2 - \dfrac{(\sum Y)^2}{N}}}$$

Prediction of Y from X and X from Y

$$Y_{\text{pred}} = r\left(\frac{s_Y}{s_X}\right)X + \overline{Y} - r\left(\frac{s_Y}{s_X}\right)\overline{X}$$

$$X_{\text{pred}} = r\left(\frac{s_X}{s_Y}\right)Y + \overline{X} - r\left(\frac{s_X}{s_Y}\right)\overline{Y}$$

Standard error of estimate of X and Y

$$s_{\text{est Y}} = s_Y \sqrt{1 - r^2}$$

$$s_{\text{est X}} = s_X \sqrt{1 - r^2}$$

Spearman rank order correlation coefficient

$$r_S = 1 - \frac{6 \sum d^2}{N(N^2 - 1)}$$

Fifth Edition
Elementary Statistics

JANET T. SPENCE
The University of Texas at Austin

JOHN W. COTTON
University of California at Santa Barbara

BENTON J. UNDERWOOD
Northwestern University

CARL P. DUNCAN
Northwestern University

PRENTICE HALL, Englewood Cliffs, New Jersey 07632

Library of Congress Cataloging-in-Publication Data

Elementary statistics / Janet T. Spence . . . [et al.]. — 5th ed.
   p. cm.
  Includes index.
  ISBN 0-13-260043-9
  1. Psychology—Statistical methods. 2. Psychometrics.
I. Spence, Janet T.
BF39.E46 1990
519.5—dc19   88-36482
                                       CIP

Editorial/production supervision: Marjorie Shustak/Shelly Kupperman
Interior design: Maureen Eide
Cover design: Maureen Eide
Manufacturing buyer: Ray Keating/Robert Anderson

 © 1990, 1983, 1976 by Prentice-Hall, Inc.
A Division of Simon & Schuster
Englewood Cliffs, New Jersey 07632

Printed in the United States of America

10 9 8 7 6 5 4 3 2 1

ISBN 0-13-260043-9

Prentice-Hall International (UK) Limited, *London*
Prentice-Hall of Australia Pty. Limited, *Sydney*
Prentice-Hall Canada Inc., *Toronto*
Prentice-Hall Hispanoamericana, S.A., *Mexico*
Prentice-Hall of India Private Limited, *New Delhi*
Prentice-Hall of Japan, Inc., *Tokyo*
Simon & Schuster Asia Pte. Ltd., *Singapore*
Editora Prentice-Hall do Brasil, Ltda., *Rio de Janeiro*

Contents

Preface *vii*

1 Statistics: What It's About *1*

Populations and Samples *4*
Types of Samples *5*
Parameters and Statistics *8*
Types of Data *9*
Calculators, Computers, and Statistical Analyses *12*
Definitions of Terms *13*
Problems *14*

2 Frequency Distributions *16*

Simple Frequency Distributions *17*
Grouped Frequency Distributions *18*
Stem and Leaf Display *22*
Step-by-Step Procedures *25*
Definitions of Terms and Symbols *27*
Problems *27*

3 Graphic Representations *30*

Graphic Representations of Frequency Distributions *31*
General Procedures in Constructing Histograms and Frequency Polygons *35*
Form of a Frequency Distribution *36*
Graphic Representations of Other Types of Data *41*
Definitions of Terms and Symbols *45*
Problems *46*

4 Measures of Central Tendency *49*

Arithmetic Mean *50*
Mode *58*
Median *58*
Comparison of Mean, Median, and Mode *60*
Step-by-Step Procedures *63*
Definitions of Terms and Symbols *65*
Problems *66*

5 Variability *67*

The Need for an Index of Variability *68*
Range (R) *69*
Semi-Interquartile Range *69*
Average Deviation *70*
Standard Deviation and Variance *72*
Computational Techniques *76*
A Check on Calculational Errors: Standard Deviation and the Range *87*
Step-by-Step Procedures *88*
Definitions of Terms and Symbols *94*
Problems *95*

6 Probability *97*

Sets and Probabilities *99*
Some Principles of Probability *101*
Permutations and Combinations *107*
Step-by-Step Procedures *109*
Definitions of Terms and Symbols *112*
Problems *113*

7 The Binomial and the Normal Distributions *116*

The Binomial Distribution *117*
The Normal Probability Distribution *122*
Step-by-Step Procedures *131*
Definitions of Terms and Symbols *135*
Problems *135*

8 Sampling Distributions: Single Samples *137*

Sampling Distribution of Means *138*
Means of Successive Random Samples *138*
Testing Hypotheses About μ: Large Samples *143*
Testing Hypotheses About μ: Small Samples *149*
Confidence Intervals *152*
Testing Hypotheses About Population Proportions *155*
Review of Hypothesis Testing *157*
Step-by-Step Procedures *158*
Definitions of Terms and Symbols *161*
Problems *162*

9 Sampling Distributions: Independent Samples from Two Populations   *165*

Anatomy of an Experiment   *166*

Sampling Distribution of the Difference Between Means   *168*

Testing a Hypothesis About $\mu_1 - \mu_2$:t Ratio   *171*

Another Look at the t-Ratio   *174*

The t Ratio and Small Samples   *176*

Choice of Significance Level   *179*

Power of a Statistical Test   *181*

Power and Estimated Effect Size   *185*

Step-by-Step Procedures   *186*

Definitions of Terms and Symbols   *190*

Problems   *191*

10 Correlation   *194*

Correlational Method Versus Experimental Method   *195*

The Pearson Product-Moment Correlation Coefficient (r)   *199*

Use of r in Prediction   *206*

The Rank-Order Correlation Coefficient (r_S)   *217*

Step-by-Step Procedures   *220*

Definitions of Terms and Symbols   *224*

Problems   *225*

11 Sampling Distributions: Matched Pairs   *228*

Types of Matched Pairs   *229*

Advantage of Matched Pairs   *230*

The t Test with Matched Samples   *231*

Step-by-Step Procedures   *236*

Definitions of Terms and Symbols   *239*

Problems   *239*

12 One-Way Analysis of Variance   *241*

The Purpose of Analysis of Variance   *242*

The Principles of One-Way Analysis of Variance   *244*

The Concept of Sums of Squares   *247*

The Concept of Variance or Mean Square   *255*

The F Ratio   *257*

Effect Size   *260*

A Multiple-Comparison Test Following Analysis of Variance   *261*

Step-by-Step Procedures   *263*

Definitions of Terms and Symbols *268*

Problems *269*

13 Two-Way Analysis of Variance *271*

Main Effects and Interaction in Analysis of Variance *273*

Computational Steps in Two-Way Analysis of Variance for Equal N's *278*

Step-by-Step Procedures *286*

Definitions of Terms and Symbols *292*

Problems *293*

14 Chi Square *295*

Chi Square Applied to a Single Sample *296*

Restrictions on the Use of χ^2 *299*

Testing Significance of Difference in Proportions by χ^2 *300*

Step-by-Step Procedures *306*

Definitions of Terms and Symbols *309*

Problems *310*

15 Nonparametric Tests *312*

Nonparametric Versus Parametric Tests *313*

Some Nonparametric Tests *314*

Relative Efficiency of Parametric and Nonparametric Tests *323*

Definitions of Terms and Symbols *324*

Problems *325*

16 Determination of the Appropriate Statistical Test *327*

Summary of Statistics of Inference *328*

Decision Tree *332*

Step-by-Step Procedures *332*

Problems *338*

Appendix I: The Use of Computers in Statistical Analysis *339*

Appendix II: List of Formulas *345*

Appendix III: Tables *353*

Appendix IV: Answers to Chapter Problems *365*

Index *389*

Preface

The fifth edition of *Elementary Statistics* continues in the tradition of its predecessors. As in the past, students majoring in psychology and related disciplines in the social and behavioral sciences, do not necessarily have a strong quantitative background or interest in statistics, but need to learn about statistical techniques in order to understand research articles or to conduct and analyze research projects of their own.

In the words of the preface to the previous edition, the text "was written with the conviction that statistical concepts can be described informally in clear, straightforward language, without either being oversimplified or assuming substantial mathematical sophistication on the part of the student. It also assumes that for such an audience, understanding of statistical methods as research tools can be more effectively promoted by presenting them within the context of their application to concrete data rather than as pure abstractions."

A number of additions have been made to this present edition. The final chapter summarizes the statistical tests covered in the text and presents a decision tree that allows students to select an appropriate statistical test that will answer the question posed by specific research studies. Learning what statistical technique to use is a critical but often neglected aspect of research training. Also added is an appendix, titled "The Use of Computers in Statistical Analyses." This appendix introduces students to different kinds of computers, identifies the major statistical packages used by investigators in the social and behavioral sciences, and suggests useful sources of information about computers and statistical packages. No attempt is made in the text to teach students how to use computers, a subject better taught in a separate course or in a more advanced course on statistical methods.

These days, however, students have easy access to hand held calculators. A section has been added to most chapters that outlines in step-by-step fashion the procedures used to conduct the statistical analyses discussed in the chapter and describes how to use various levels of calculators in carrying out the computations. Several new topics have been included, such as stem and leaf displays in the chapter on Graphic Representations and in later chapters, omega-squared as an index of effect size.

With one exception, the order of chapters remains the same as in the fourth edition. The chapter on correlational techniques, which previously followed the chapter on variability, now appears later in the text, preceding the chapter on sampling distributions involving matched pairs in which an understanding of correlation is required. In contrast to presenting the topic of correlation before students have been introduced to inferential statistics, this placement allows discussion of testing null hypotheses about correlation coefficients and makes explanation of the concept of the standard error of estimate more intelligible to the reader. Instructors who prefer to discuss correlation earlier in the course can easily assign this chapter (except for the section on testing the null hypothesis) out of order.

As in the previous edition, each chapter concludes with a set of problems testing students' understanding of major concepts and providing them with experience in analyzing data. Answers to these problems are given in Appendix IV.

Supplementing the text is a separate *Workbook for Elementary Statistics*, prepared by the text's senior author. The *Workbook* contains short answer questions for review, additional calculational problems, and more complex problems testing conceptual understanding. The *Workbook* also contains supplementary explanatory material, including a review of basic arithmetic operations.

Responsibility for the present edition was assumed by the first two authors. We wish to thank Corliss Cotton and Patrick Torres for their meticulous checking of formulas and computations and their editorial suggestions. Our gratitude also goes to Lou Montgomery and Susanne Douglas who skillfully and patiently typed the many drafts of the manuscript. The invaluable assistance of our production editor, Shelly Kupperman, is also acknowledged. We wish to thank the Prentice Hall reviewers for their helpful suggestions: Peter J. Rowe, College of Charleston; William H. Calhoun, University of Tennessee; and John B. Pittenger, University of Arkansas-Little Rock.

Finally, we are grateful to the Literary Executor of the late Sir Ronald A. Fisher, F.R.S., to Dr. Frank Yates, F.R.S., and to Longman Group Ltd. London, for permission to reprint Tables IV and VI from their book *Statistical Tables for Biological, Agricultural and Medical Research* (6th edition, 1974). We also thank several authors and publishers for granting us permission to abridge or reproduce their materials. The sources of these materials are acknowledged as they occur in the text.

JTS
JWC

1 Statistics: What It's About

The Collection, Classification, and Interpretation of Facts

- POPULATIONS AND SAMPLES
- TYPES OF SAMPLES
- PARAMETERS AND STATISTICS
- TYPES OF DATA
- CALCULATORS, COMPUTERS, AND STATISTICAL ANALYSES

Suppose you are driving downtown to do some shopping. You remember your tires are low, so you stop at a service station and have them brought up to 24 pounds, and while you're at it you put 10 gallons in your gas tank. In the course of your shopping you have a lumberyard cut three 5-foot planks for some shelves you are building, order a sweater in your size, buy a 40-watt lightbulb, and select a half-pound of hamburger. On your way home you glance at your watch to see if you'll make your favorite TV program.

All these commonplace activities depend on *quantification*—the assignment of *numbers* to objects or events to describe their properties. If you had attempted to express your requirements without numbers, you would have found yourself using vague verbal descriptions, gesturing a lot, and failing to communicate your exact needs. Numbers allow you to describe phenomena with considerably more precision. If numerical quantification had never been devised, it is doubtful that cars, lightbulbs, watches, and the like would even have existed.

In scientific research we attempt to describe the properties of objects and events in the universe around us and the regularities of occurrence among them. Quantification is at the heart of the scientific enterprise, and the basic data resulting from scientific research are almost invariably a set of numbers. Having collected the data, we apply statistical methods to describe and interpret them.

A look at a hypothetical investigation will show some of the statistical challenges. The instructor of an introductory course in statistics offered by the psychology department is distressed because so many of the students who take the course are afflicted by "math anxiety." He gives commonsense examples illustrating statistical principles that everyone seems to understand. But when he translates them into statistical language, many students begin to look panic-stricken. He asks students to compute a statistic by arithmetic operations no more complicated than they learned in grade school, and a number of them stare at him helplessly. They're no good at math, they say; they are convinced that statistics is beyond them. One year the instructor decides to conduct an experiment. During the first session of the class, he asks students to volunteer for a two-week therapeutic program the college counseling service has agreed to set up to help students get over their "math anxiety."* Twenty students volunteer for the program, more than can be accommodated. He picks every other person on the list to take part. These 10 students form the *experimental group*. The other 10 students serve as a *control group*—that is, they receive no special treatment. At the end of the semester, he determines the final examination scores for all the volunteers, as shown in Table 1.1.

Did the treatment program have beneficial effects? The instructor could not even begin to answer the question until he brought some sort of order to these jumbled sets of scores and described them in some way. For example, what was the average exam score in each group? In each group, how variable were the scores—that is, were they all very similar or did they vary widely?

By adding the scores together and dividing by the number of scores, the instructor determined that the average student in the experimental (treated) condition earned a score of

---

*Although this experiment is hypothetical, "math anxiety" is a real phenomenon whose origins and treatment psychologists and others have become active in investigating. [See, for example, S. Tobias, *Overcoming Math Anxiety* (New York: Norton, 1978).] The math anxious among you should take heart from the fact that this text was written so as to be comprehensible to students without extensive training in mathematics and without a high level of quantitative aptitude. To paraphrase Franklin D. Roosevelt, students should have little to fear but fear itself.

Table 1.1 Results of a Hypothetical Experiment Showing Final Examination Scores of Treated and Untreated "Math Anxious" Students

Treated		Untreated	
Student	Score	Student	Score
A.B.	74	N.K.	76
J.M.	85	E.G.	68
H.P.	77	P.F.	52
B.F.	89	K.S.	59
T.J.	72	A.V.	71
G.C.	69	L.D.	80
L.K.	77	C.R.	57
C.D.	84	M.H.	75
W.Y.	64	R.T.	69
F.L.	79	D.W.	63

77 on the final exam. For students in the control (untreated) condition, the average was 67. Does this 10-point difference mean that the treatment program was effective? Or did the treated students just happen to do better? In other words, if the instructor repeated the experiment over and over with different groups of students, is it likely that the results would turn out the same way? Before he suggests that the counseling center set up a treatment program on a regular basis, he wants to be reasonably sure the therapy is effective.

Consider another example. A doctor hears a friend of hers confidently claim that the proportion of male and female babies who are born varies according to the month of the year, with January being the high point and June the low point for boys. She bets her friend that time of year has nothing to do with a baby's sex and checks last year's birth records for these two months at the local hospital. She finds that in January 54 percent of the babies were boys, and in June 52 percent were boys. Does she lose the bet?

Simply staring at the data will not bring satisfactory answers to these questions. What is needed are methods for extracting information from the results of these studies and interpreting what they mean. This is where the science of statistics comes into play. By performing arithmetic and algebraic manipulations with the data, we can discover group trends and relationships and describe them in a precise manner. With further statistical operations, we can make inferences or guesses about the characteristics of still larger groups—for example, about the effects of treatment for math anxiety for introductory statistics students in general, not just for the particular group of students shown in Table 1.1, or for male and female babies in general, not just for the babies born during a specific year at one hospital.

In subsequent chapters we will first consider a series of *descriptive statistics*, methods that permit us to discover and describe the relationships hidden in masses of number. Then we will take up topics that are related to *inferential statistics*—techniques for making guesses about the properties of what are called *populations*, based on the data from a *sample* of individuals that has actually been observed. Before proceeding further, we will elaborate the distinction between populations and samples and introduce certain other terms and concepts that will be encountered in later chapters.

POPULATIONS AND SAMPLES

We are all familiar with national surveys in which people from all over the country are questioned about their beliefs on various topics. Should women with preschool children work outside the home? Is the president doing a good job in managing the economy? Should the death penalty be prohibited? The purpose of these surveys is to try to assess the mood of the people throughout the country. It would be both impractical and impossible to question everyone, but it *is* possible to obtain the views of a sample of individuals and to use their answers to infer the opinions of the entire population.

In still another example, a company markets a simple device that it claims will cut an automobile's gas consumption by 10 percent. If the claim is correct, the discovery is obviously of great economic significance. A testing agency equips 20 cars with the device and has each of them driven over a test course under controlled conditions. Twenty other cars that are similar except for the device are also driven over the same course, and the fuel consumption of the cars in the experimental and control groups is then compared. The testing agency is interested in the effectiveness of the device for all cars (the entire population), not just the cars in the experiment. Since testing the population of cars is impossible, the intent of the experiment is to use the results from the sample to make guesses about what *would* happen if all cars were equipped with the device.

A population consists of all members of a group of individuals who are alike on at least one specified characteristic. Populations may consist of any kind of animate or inanimate objects or events, but for illustrative purposes we will commonly refer to people. A population can be infinite or indefinitely large in number, such as all the infants who have ever been or ever will be born, or it can be finite, such as all the infants born last year in the United States. Finite populations may be large, such as all individuals enrolled in college, or they may be small, such as all majors in Greek at a given college. Populations may be real, as in the examples immediately above, or they may be hypothetical. If, for example, we were to conduct an experiment using a new drug designed to overcome psychotic depression, we would be concerned with estimating the drug's effect on the population of *all* individuals, now or in the future, who might exhibit this condition and *could* be given the drug.

Whether real or hypothetical, the population is specified by the investigator, and the aim is to find out something about it. The populations that are the subject of scientific investigation typically are large or indefinite in number, so that only a sample can be studied. *A sample is any number of cases less than the total number of cases in the population from which it is drawn.* If we have a population of 50,000, a sample might consist of 10 cases, 15,000 cases, or 49,999. Normally, however, samples consist of only a small or a very small proportion of the population being investigated.

The purpose in observing a sample, we have said, is to use the data obtained to make inferences about the characteristics of the population as a whole. We may, of course, want to study and compare the characteristics of samples from more than one population in a single study.

There are certain dangers in generalizing from sample to population data. If we were attempting to predict the outcome of a mayoral election, for example, we would be foolish to question voters from only one occupational group or income level, since these factors are likely to be related to voter preference. What we would attempt to get is a sample of voters that is a miniature picture of the population from which it is taken. If we want to reach conclusions about a population from the data of a sample, the sample ought to be *representative* of the total population from which it is drawn.

Consider a psychological experiment in which an investigator had one sample of college students solve arithmetic problems under quiet conditions and a second sample of students solve the problems while listening to a recording of the sounds of jet planes taking off and landing. The investigator could come to very erroneous conclusions about the effects of noise if members of the first group were drawn from a class in calculus and members of the second were drawn from a class in English literature. This is so because students taking calculus are very likely to be better at arithmetic problems than students in an English class. In conducting experiments, investigators must attempt to obtain samples that are initially *comparable* in order to draw appropriate conclusions about the effects of conditions on populations of individuals. Comparability implies that if the samples had been tested under the *same* conditions their performance would have been similar.

The methods by which samples are selected are therefore extremely important considerations in scientific research. A number of sampling techniques have been devised in an effort to obtain representative samples from populations. We will consider three methods: random, randomized, and matched.

TYPES OF SAMPLES

Random Samples

*Random sampling is a method of selecting a sample in such a way that each **member** of the pool has an equal probability of being selected on any given draw and each possible **sample** of members has an equal probability of being selected.* To illustrate, suppose there is a population of 20 individuals, whom we identify by the letters A through T, from which we wish to draw a sample of 5 cases. A random sample is one in which individual A has the same chance of being selected as individual B, who in turn has the same chance of being selected as individual C, and so forth. Any given set of 5 individuals—for example, individuals A, D, E, H, and S—also has the same chance of being selected as any other set of 5 individuals. If each individual has an equal chance of being selected, it almost always happens that each possible sample also has an equal chance of being selected, but there are some peculiar circumstances under which it does not.

Our intent in obtaining a random sample, we have said, is to obtain a sample whose properties are representative of the properties of the population from which the sample was selected. There is no guarantee that the measures obtained from a random sample will accurately reflect the properties of the population as a whole. However, as we will see in a later chapter, statistical theory allows us to make probability statements about how closely values obtained from random samples can be expected to agree with population values.

Sampling may be done with or without *replacement*. For example, in the instance of the 20 individuals described above, we might select the name of individual B on the first draw and after recording it, replace the individual's name in the pool before drawing a second time. This draw-and-replace procedure is continued until our desired sample of 5 has been obtained. With this replacement procedure, you will note, each individual has a 1 in 20 chance of being selected on *each* of the 5 draws.

When replacement is made, it is possible that the same individual's name will be selected more than once. For most research purposes, however, it is necessary or desirable for samples to consist of different individuals. One method of obtaining a sample or series of samples in which no individual is represented more than once is to sample *without replacement*. In this instance, the probability of being selected does not remain constant on every draw. In our group of 20, for example, the probability of any given individual being selected on the first draw is 1/20. If on the first draw we select individual B's name and do not replace it, each of the remaining 19 individuals has a probability of 1/19 of being selected on the second draw. On the third draw, the probability is 1/18, and so forth. However, the sample was still randomly selected from the population of 20 individuals because on each draw every individual remaining in the pool had an equal probability of being selected.

When several random samples are selected from a population, they are described as being *independent*. That is, the composition of a sample does not influence which individuals remaining in the pool will be selected for a subsequently chosen sample. Not all sampling methods produce independent samples, as we will see.

Table of Random Numbers.   There are a number of methods for obtaining random samples. One time-honored procedure is to put the names of all members of the population on identical slips of paper, put all the slips in a container, stir them thoroughly, pull one out, stir the slips again, choose another, and continue this process until a sample of the desired size is obtained. But since the stirring and selecting process can go awry, a more satisfactory method is to consult a table of random numbers. Modern tables of random numbers have been generated by a computer to meet the two requirements we mentioned above. A sample page from a book of random numbers is reproduced in Table A (Appendix III, page 000). For convenience, the table is set up in columns of five-digit numbers.

As an illustration* of how the table is used, suppose the Society of Comparative Psychologists has 848 members. The society's president is interested in members' opinion about whether the society should start its own scientific journal. For the sake of economy, he decides to poll a random sample of 100 individuals instead of the entire membership. The name of the first person in the Membership Directory is assigned the number 1, the second person is assigned the number 2, and so on. Next the president consults a table of random numbers. If the table has more than one page, he arbitrarily picks a page. Then he arbitrarily picks a place to start on the page, perhaps by closing his eyes and bringing the point of his pencil down. Suppose this is the fourth entry in the third column of five-digit numbers of Table A, which you can see is 29311. Since there are only 848 members of the society, he will need only the first three digits of this number. The person assigned the number 293 is the first individual in

---

*We stress that Table A contains only a single page from a large table of random numbers and therefore only a subset of all possible five-digit numbers. Table A is therefore useful only for illustrative purposes; readers interested in actually conducting research should consult a full table of random numbers. As stated in the example in the text, when the full table involves multiple pages, the process of selecting a random sample should start with selecting a page at random and then proceeding as described.

the sample. He then proceeds to consult the first three digits of the numbers that follow. Since he does not want to include anyone more than once, he writes down all numbers that do not exceed 848 until he has 100 *different* numbers: 488, 199, 60, and so forth.

As this example illustrates, the number of digits in any row that one uses for random selection depends on the size of the population. If the population consists of 50,000 cases, all five digits in each set of five would be used in selecting the sample. If the population consisted of 200,000 individuals, one would "borrow" the first digit of the five-digit number in the column to the immediate right, and so forth.

Randomized Samples

In scientific experiments, investigators test two or more groups under different conditions in an attempt to determine whether the conditions they manipulate have an effect on individuals' performance. Experimental groups could be obtained by drawing the required number of random samples from some defined population. Often, however, investigators cannot identify or do not have access to all the members of a population in which they might be interested, so they are unable to select random samples that can then be assigned to the several experimental conditions. However, often the investigator has access to a certain number of subjects and has control over what subjects are assigned to what experimental groups. For example, investigators might have a group of volunteers from their classes or a group of animals available from a biological supply house.

Such groups cannot be considered random samples from a defined population. Usually, however, members of the pool of available subjects can be assigned at random to the different conditions of the experiment. That is, an equal number of individuals can be selected for each experimental group in such a manner that each individual, and each set of individuals, have an equal chance of being assigned to a particular group. For example, the investigator might give individuals an identifying number and then consult a table of random numbers, assigning (in a two-group experiment) the individual with the first number in the table to the first condition, the second individual to the second condition, the third to the first condition, and so on. To distinguish it from random sampling, this procedure is called *randomization*—that is, randomized assignment of subject to group.

The randomized method of assigning subjects to experimental conditions also yields *independent* samples. Generally speaking, the fact that a particular individual or series of individuals has already been selected from the subject pool and assigned to a particular group does not influence the assignment of the other individuals remaining in the pool.

Matched Samples

Some techniques of selecting and assigning subjects to groups in experiments involve matched samples which are not independent. In this section we discuss a particular method of matching, the method of *matched pairs*, which is suitable for experiments in which there are only two experimental conditions or groups. In principle the method could be extended and used to obtain a larger number of groups, but for the sake of simplicity we will confine our discussion to the two-group case.

Our aim in assigning subjects to groups in an experiment, we have said, is to produce comparable groups, groups that would have performed similarly had they been observed under identical conditions. Assuming that it is done adequately, selecting matched pairs is a particularly effective method of obtaining comparable groups. In the method of matched pairs, each individual is tested under both conditions or one individual is tested under one condition and another individual who has previously been identified as being highly similar in relevant characteristics to the first individual is tested under the other condition. The result is a series of pairs of observations.

In some experimental situations, it is reasonable to test each individual under both conditions. For example, in a study of the effects on motor coordination of a drug with short-term effects, each subject might be given a well-practiced task, once while under the influence of the drug and once while drug-free. This method is particularly desirable, since individuals are obviously the best match for themselves.

Often, however, the same individual cannot legitimately take part in both conditions. It would make no sense, for example, to teach a novice violinist by one technique and then to teach the individual by another technique to find out which is more effective, since it is obviously impossible to erase what the person has learned and to start again. In such instances, other methods of matching can be used. One could randomly select pairs of identical twins, pairs of brothers or sisters, or even pairs of unrelated individuals who are similar in characteristics that are likely to affect the performance to be measured—factors such as age, sex, educational background, aptitudes, and so forth. Groups of subjects are then formed by randomly picking one member of each pair to be observed under one of the experimental conditions. The other member of each pair is then automatically assigned to the other condition. It is this feature that makes the samples nonindependent. Once one member of each pair is assigned to one group, composition of the other group is fixed.

PARAMETERS AND STATISTICS

If we had access to an entire population, we could proceed to describe its properties. For example, if we had information about how many books college graduates read last year, we could determine the average number of books read. Or if we had access to the records of all students enrolled in U.S. medical schools, we could determine the percentage who are women. The properties of populations are called population *parameters*.

Properties of samples drawn from a population can also be described. For example, the percentage of men and women in a sample of medical school students could be determined, as could the average number of books read last year by a sample of college graduates. Characteristics of samples are called sample *statistics*. To emphasize the distinction between a population parameter and the parallel sample statistic, population parameters are typically symbolized by Greek letters and sample statistics by letters from our regular alphabet.

TYPES OF DATA

Numerical Data

How tall is each person in your statistics class? How fast could each of you memorize the definitions listed at the end of this chapter? How many children would each of you like to have? Which person in the class do you think is the friendliest? Who is the next most friendly? Each of these questions asks about a property that exists along a dimension in various degrees. To answer them, we use numbers to try to express *how much* of the property each individual exhibits. We will describe two major kinds of numerical data: *magnitude* data and *rank-order* or *ordinal* data. In the case of magnitude data, each individual is given a number expressing the amount of the measured property the person possesses. In the case of rank-order or ordinal data, members of a group of individuals are ranked, 1, 2, 3, . . . , according to how much of some property each person possesses relative to others in the group.

Magnitude Data.   In the first two questions above, we asked about your classmates' *heights* and the *time* it would take them to memorize a list. In both cases, each individual could be assigned a number to express absolutely *how much* of the quantity he or she exhibits. Eric is 71 inches tall; Paula memorized the list of definitions in 12 minutes. It is obvious that the third question, "How many children do each of you want?" also calls for a number.

Numerically measurable properties are usually *continuous*. That is, objects or events may fall at *any* point along an unbroken scale of values running from high to low. In measuring the weight of objects, for example, we may have such values as 4.2681 grams, or 68.723584 grams, or any positive value we can think of. Similarly, time is continuous, as is the distance between geographic locations.

Some properties, however, are *discrete* rather than continuous. That is, they fall only at certain points along a scale. For example, students' scores on a 20-item true-false test would be whole numbers; they would fall only at certain points along a scale running from 0 to 20. Similarly, you might reasonably aspire to have 0, 1, 2, or 3 children, not 2.3 or 4.6 children.

When variables are discrete, it is possible to assign each individual an *exact* number. Daniel earned a score of exactly 19 on the true-false test and Betsy is content to have exactly 2 children. However, when the property is continuous, we can never measure objects or events exactly but only approximately within a specified degree of accuracy. Thus, in practice, the distinction between continuous and discrete measures breaks down. Depending on our purpose, for example, we might be satisfied to specify an object's age to the nearest century, the nearest year, the nearest hour, or the nearest millionth of a second. Whatever the degree of accuracy we attempt, the resulting numbers are still discrete. If we measured time to the nearest tenth of a second, for example, numbers such as .1, .3, or .8 second would be reported, but not .12, .32, or .86. If we measured to the nearest hundredth of a second, we might have .08 and .36, but not .084 or .362. Because most measurable properties are continuous, each number we assign to each object or event typically represents a range or *interval* of values, rather than an exact scale point. If length is reported to the nearest centimeter, for example, objects described as being 14 centimeters long are understood to fall someplace in a range extending from 13.5 to 14.5 and not all to be exactly 14.000. . . .

A note about rounding: It is not uncommon to record observations with greater numerical precision than we wish to report. We might have recorded our observations using two decimal places, for example, but want to report data only to the first decimal place or in whole numbers. The traditional rule is to round to the *nearest* decimal or whole number. The value 4.38, for example, would be rounded *down* to 4 if a whole number were required or rounded *up* to 4.4 if the first decimal place were to be retained. What if the number falls at the border of two adjacent intervals? For example, is 9.5 rounded to 9 or to 10? Is 2.65 rounded to 2.6 or 2.7? A convention devised for handling such situations is to round to the nearest *even* number, so that 9.5 is rounded up to 10 and 2.65 is rounded down to 2.6. This convention is intended to avoid systematic bias when a whole group of numbers is to be rounded, since it can be anticipated that about half the numbers falling on the borderline will be assigned to the lower interval and half to the upper interval.

A second situation in which rounding is desirable is one in which the result of some statistical calculation is to be reported. For example, suppose we weigh a series of 8 objects to the nearest tenth of a gram: 6.2 grams, 5.9 grams, 6.5 grams, and so forth. If the 8 objects weighed a total of 52.3 grams, we could divide 52.3 by 8 to find the average weight of the objects. The result of this calculation turns out to be exactly 6.5375 grams. Reporting this number would be misleading, because it implies that we have measured each object with greater precision than we actually have. A good rule to follow is to report the average, or other statistic, to *one or two digits beyond what has been measured directly.* In our example, the objects were measured to the nearest .1 gram. The average would therefore be rounded to 6.54 (one extra digit) or to 6.538 (two extra digits). In most of the illustrative data analyses in this text, we have retained two extra digits. Note that in carrying out the calculation, we avoid rounding or at least carry out our calculations to a number of extra digits until all stages of computation are complete. It is the *final answer* that is rounded to one or two digits beyond the original measurement.

Rank-Order or Ordinal Data.   Sometimes numbers that directly indicate how much of a given property each individual possesses are impossible or inconvenient to determine. We may instead assign *ranks* that indicate the individuals' positions relative to one another. In a foot race, for example, the contestants might not be timed but instead ranked from fastest to slowest according to the order in which they crossed the finish line. Or people might be asked to indicate how prestigious 20 occupations are by ranking them from highest to lowest. Rank orders allow objects or events to be *ordered* in terms of magnitude so we can make more than–less than statements about pairs or objects or events. For example, the occupation of physician might be ranked higher than high school teacher, which in turn might be ranked higher than auto mechanic. We can say that physicians have more prestige than high school teachers and that auto mechanics have less prestige than high school teachers. Rank order or ordinal data, however, do not indicate how much greater the difference is between ranks and therefore provide less information than do quantified data.

Categorical or Nominal Data

How many men and women are enrolled in your statistics class? How many of you are freshmen, sophomores, juniors, or seniors? How many of you have been to Europe, have smoked pot, own a car, have shoes on, are blondes, brunettes, or redheads?

Table 1.2 Percentages of Men and Women Afraid to Walk Alone at Night—1975, 1980, 1985

Year	Women			Men		
	Yes	*No*	*Can't Say*	*Yes*	*No*	*Can't Say*
1975	50	47	3	19	79	2
1980	61	36	3	22	77	1
1985	72	28	0	33	66	1

Each of these questions involves a set of two or more mutually exclusive *categories*: male *or* female; car owner *or* not; blonde, brunette, *or* redhead; and so on. It is meaningless to assign a number indicating "how much" of the property each individual has or to rank-order the individuals according to "how much" of the property each exhibits. Rather, an individual either does or does not have the property specified by each category within a given set (that is, his or her "score" is either 0 or 1). And since the categories are mutually exclusive, each individual can be assigned to one and only one of them. More than one set of categories can, of course, be used simultaneously in classifying an individual case; for example, we can identify Samantha as a female, redheaded freshman who came to class barefoot.

It is simple to describe the results of our observations when categorical data are involved. We simply sort the cases, placing each in its proper category, then count the number in each category and present the sums. For convenience, the sums may be translated into percentages. Table 1.2, for example, gives the percentages of groups of men and of women in three different years who said "yes," "no," or "can't say" about whether they were afraid to walk alone at night. The table lets us see that in each year, more women than men reported being afraid, but that both sexes were becoming more fearful over the three year periods.

Typically, each category can easily be identified or "named" by a verbal label, such as yes, no, and can't say, or blonde, brunette, and redhead. This characteristic has led categorical data also to be called *nominal* data. Sometimes it is more convenient to give each category a numerical label, such as category 1, category 2, category 3, and so forth. In this instance the numbers are also *nominal*—that is, the numbers are used as "names" to identify categories. Numbers are often used in this nominal way. For example, most people in the United States have social security numbers which are used to identify them on many kinds of forms and records.

When numbers are used merely as labels to differentiate among individuals or categorical groups, which number is assigned to which individual or which category is arbitrary. This observation serves to emphasize an important point: Categories ordinarily cannot be ordered along a continuum. For example, if people are classified by current marital status as never married, widowed, separated, divorced, or currently married, the categories could not be arranged in order according to "how much" marital status each has. With categorical data, the question we ask about each *individual* is to what category the individual belongs, not how much of some property the individual has. The question we typically have about a *set of categories* is how many individuals, or what percentage of the total number of individuals, fall into each category, not "how much" of a property is represented by a particular category in comparison to other categories in the set.

The major distinctions among the three types of data are summarized in Table 1.3.

Table 1.3 Three Types of Data and the Information Obtained about the Individual Case in Each Type

Type of Data	Information Obtained about Individual
Numerical	
Magnitude	Number indicating the amount of a property that exists along a continuum ("how much")
Rank order or ordinal	Amount of a property expressed as a rank relative to other individuals (1st, 2nd, 3rd . . .)
Categorical or nominal	Category to which individual belongs

CALCULATORS, COMPUTERS, AND STATISTICAL ANALYSES

Modern research workers almost always use computers to analyze the data they collect. In fact, when data sets are large and the statistical techniques applied to them are complex, the use of computers, with their speed and accuracy, is vital. Descriptions of various types of computers and several packages of computer programs that are particularly useful to investigators in the social and behavioral sciences can be found in Appendix I.

Hand-held calculators are also invaluable aids to research workers, even when they have access to a computer. You will also find a calculator to be useful in working through many of the problems that follow each chapter or in doing the calculational exercises in the *Workbook* designed to accompany this text. To save you from doing a lot of routine arithmetic, problems are deliberately set up with relatively few numbers and often employ numbers that are small in size. Nonetheless, you can save a good deal of tedious busywork by using a calculator.

Many calculators are on the market, varying widely in sophistication and, of course, in cost. Knowing something about the various levels of calculators may help you decide which kind to buy if you do not already own one.

The simplest level of calculator can perform only the four basic arithmetic functions and is probably not worth the investment. A second-level calculator, which can be purchased for only slightly more, has a memory, a square root key, and perhaps several other functions as well.

A third-level calculator has all the features of a second-level calculator and, in addition, has keys that will allow you to determine in one step the mean, standard deviation, and variance once the basic data have been entered. (These statistics are discussed in Chapters 4 and 5.)

A fourth-level calculator allows direct calculation of still other statistics and also is programmable. That is, you can program the calculator to carry out a series of calculations for a particular type of problem. For example, if you were an automobile salesperson, you might want to calculate the monthly payment that a buyer would need on a 36-month car loan of $8000 at 9 percent interest. Once you programmed your calculator to solve this type of problem, you could use it to find the answer to any specific problem. Many fourth-level calculators are designed for business applications, others are for general scientific use, and still others are for statistical use. Some calculators can do all three kinds of tasks effectively.

If you anticipate doing a good deal of research in the future or doing other kinds of complicated calculations, you might consider buying a fourth-level calculator. Otherwise, you will probably find a second- or third-level calculator sufficient for your needs.

Once you have purchased a calculator, study the instruction booklet to determine how to carry out certain basic operations. Particularly important for you to learn to do (assuming your calculator permits it) are the following:

1. Add a series of numbers together, e.g., $10 + 8 + 14 + 11$.

2. In one continuous operation, find the sum of the squares of a series of numbers, e.g., $10^2 + 8^2 + 14^2 + 11^2$.

3. In one continuous operation, find the sum of the products of a series of pairs of numbers, e.g., $(10 \times 2) + (8 \times 4) + (14 \times 5) + (11 \times 2)$.

4. In one continuous operation, find the sum of a series of quantities, put the sum in memory, and divide the sum by the number of quantities in the series, e.g., the sum of the 4 numbers 10, 8, 14, and 11 is 43; then divide 43 by 4.

Knowing how to perform these relatively simple operations with your calculator will save you a lot of tedious arithmetic when you are asked to calculate a number of statistics.

In the following chapters, we present various methods of describing and analyzing sets of numerical data. The final section in each chapter is titled *Step by Step Procedures*. In this section we will illustrate how to apply the statistical techniques described in the chapter to concrete sets of data. When appropriate, we will also describe how to use a calculator to minimize the amount of arithmetic that you need to do in carrying out the analysis.

DEFINITIONS OF TERMS

Population. All members of a group of individuals, objects, or events that have a specified property in common: for example, all licensed barbers in the state of Wisconsin.

Sample. A subset of cases from a population of individuals, objects, or events: for example, 100 barbers from the population of all licensed barbers in Wisconsin.

Random sample. A sample of a given size drawn from a population in such a way that each member of the population and each possible sample of that size have an equal probability of being selected.

Randomization. A technique used to assign members of an available pool of individuals to conditions in experiments involving two or more conditions. Members of the pool are assigned to condition by use of a table of random numbers or some other random procedure. The resulting groups are called *randomized samples*.

Matched pairs. A technique used in two-condition experiments in which each individual is tested twice, once under each experimental condition, or in which a series of pairs of individuals who are matched on one or more characteristics are identified prior to the experiment, one member of each pair being randomly assigned to one condition and the other member to the second condition.

Population parameter. A number representing some property of a population: for example, the average beginning salary of all assistant professors at a given university. Population parameters are typically symbolized by Greek letters.

Sample statistic. A number representing some property of a sample. Sample statistics are typically symbolized by letters from the regular alphabet.

Numerical data. Observations to which numbers have been assigned to express the absolute or relative amount of some property that exists in varying degrees. There are two major types of numerical data: magnitude data and rank-order or ordinal data.

Magnitude data. Data in which a number has been assigned to each individual to indicate the absolute amount of some property the individual exhibits: for example, the score made by a job applicant on an aptitude test.

Discrete variables. Properties existing to various degrees that in nature take only certain values along a continuum of values. For example, the number of sets won by players in a tennis match can only be whole numbers and cannot involve fractions.

Continuous variables. Properties existing to various degrees that in nature can take any possible value between an upper and lower limit: for example, the circumference of people's waists. In practice, continuous properties are measured only to a specified degree of accuracy, and the reported values thus fall only at discrete points or values. For example, length of objects measured to the nearest millimeter would take the values 1, 2, 3, etc., but not fractional values.

Rank-order or ordinal data. Data in which individuals are arranged in order according to the relative amount of some property they exhibit and assigned ranks to indicate their standing: 1st, 2nd, 3rd, and so forth.

Categorical or nominal data. Data involving a set of properties (categories), each of which a particular individual does or does not exhibit. In sets of two or more *mutually exclusive* categories, each individual falls into one and only one category, and a group of individuals is described by counting the number in each category. For example, a group of 60 children may be described as containing 28 boys and 32 girls. Numbers used to identify categories are *nominal*—that is, they are "names" of categories used in place of verbal labels. For example, boys might be called 0's and girls called 1's.

PROBLEMS

Answers to the problems in this and later chapters are given in Appendix IV.

1. For each of the following, indicate whether a *population* or a *sample* is involved and for the latter, from what population the sample was drawn.

   (a) Everyone who voted in the last U.S. presidential election.

   (b) Names of 100 individuals drawn from the residential listings of the Chicago telephone directory.

(c) The instructor ratings obtained from the students attending their introductory psychology class on the day the rating forms are distributed.

(d) Three-year-old boys.

2. For each of the following, indicate whether the sample or samples being described are *random*, *randomized*, or *matched*.

(a) Grocery store patrons fill out slips of paper with their names and addresses in a drawing for free hams. The slips are placed in a barrel and 10 are blindly selected as winners.

(b) In a study of the effects of sleeplessness on performance, a group of 10 individuals is given a simple reaction time task 3 times after members have been awake for 12, 24, and 48 hours, respectively.

(c) Two parallel forms of a vocabulary test have been prepared. The test developer arranges to give the two forms to 100 students to determine if the tests produce comparable results. Fifty form A test booklets and 50 form B booklets are arranged in random order. The first student seated in the first row is given the booklet on the top of the pile, the next student the next booklet, and so forth.

3. Twenty people have signed up for an experiment and are to be assigned to one of two experimental conditions at random. Their names have been alphabetized and then assigned a number. Starting at the sixth number in the third column of five-digit numbers in the table of random numbers in Table A, Appendix III, select a sample of 10 to serve in the first condition.

4. For each of the following, indicate whether *categorical (nominal)*, *magnitude*, or *rank-order* data are being described.

(a) The ordered list of the top 20 football teams in the country according to a poll of coaches.

(b) The current marital status of each member of a sample of 200 men.

(c) Scores on a 30-item personality test of authoritarianism.

(d) The distance each of a group of 10-year-old girls can throw a baseball.

5. Indicate for each of the following whether the property being measured is *discrete* or *continuous*.

(a) In a sample of married couples, the number of children who are living at home.

(b) The time it requires individuals to solve a set of simple arithmetic problems.

(c) The number of errors on a typing test.

(d) The birth weight of males versus females.

(e) The 12 noon temperatures yesterday at several locations in Indiana.

(f) How many times each person in your high school graduating class has been arrested.

2 Frequency Distributions

- SIMPLE FREQUENCY DISTRIBUTIONS
- GROUPED FREQUENCY DISTRIBUTIONS
- STEM AND LEAF DISPLAY

In Chapter 1 we described numerical data: the assignment of numbers that specify *how much* of some property individuals have. We might measure, for example, the performance of young children on a task designed to determine their understanding of abstract moral principles, or the ego-strength of hospitalized schizophrenics as revealed in their responses in a standardized psychiatric interview. When a group of individuals is measured, rarely do all the numbers turn out to be the same; the almost inevitable outcome is a set of numbers varying in value. In this chapter we will consider methods of ordering numerical data so that we may begin to comprehend and describe the performance of a group of differing individuals.

SIMPLE FREQUENCY DISTRIBUTIONS

One obvious method of bringing order into a collection of measures is to arrange them in order of magnitude from highest to lowest. When only a few measures are involved, this ordering is probably sufficient. But with a group of substantial size, it is no longer immediately evident how many times a particular value occurs, or whether it occurs at all. An additional step in our procedure will give us this extra information. All possible values between the highest and lowest reported measures can be listed in one column and the number of individuals receiving each value in an adjacent column, as illustrated in Table 2.1.

The numbers in the table represent scores received by a sample of 100 male psychology majors on a test of political attitudes. Scores could range from 0 to 45, with higher scores indicating more liberal political beliefs. The first column is labeled "Score." The order of highest to lowest in this column has, by custom, become the standard arrangement and should always be followed. The second column, labeled "*f*" (frequency), contains the number of cases, in this instance the number of students, receiving each score. For example, four students received a score of 43 and ten students a score of 37. At the bottom of the last frequency column you will observe the letter N, which is simply a symbol for the total number of cases

Table 2.1 Simple Frequency Distribution of Political Attitude Scores of 100 Male Psychology Majors

Score	f	Score	f	Score	f
45	2	37	10	29	4
44	2	36	9	28	2
43	4	35	6	27	3
42	2	34	7	26	2
41	4	33	5	25	1
40	6	32	5	24	0
39	5	31	6	23	2
38	8	30	5	N = 100	

in the group. In the present illustration N is 100. Such a table, in which all score values are listed in one column and the number of individuals receiving each score in the adjacent column, is called a *simple frequency distribution*.

Arranging the measures into a simple frequency distribution makes description of group performance easier. In the example in Table 2.1, the lowest score is 23 and the highest score is 45. Thus the *range* of scores—the number of score units between the highest and lowest score—is quite wide, 23 units. It can also be seen that certain scores stand out as occurring frequently and, more important, that the scores tend to be concentrated toward the high end of the scale, suggesting that as a group, these psychology majors were quite liberal in their attitudes. Collecting scores into a frequency distribution allows us to see these characteristics of group performance more easily than would just listing scores in order.

GROUPED FREQUENCY DISTRIBUTIONS

In many instances, particularly those in which the *range* of the measures (number of score units from highest to lowest) is small, a frequency distribution of the type just described yields a compact table that shows the pattern formed by a set of scores. But when the measures are scattered over a wide range, the frequency distribution is long and bulky, as in the three long pairs of columns in Table 2.1. More important, so few cases fall at each score value that the group pattern is not too clear. We can, however, simultaneously make our distribution more compact and obtain a better idea of the overall pattern of scores by bringing together the single measures into a number of groups, each containing an *equal* number of score units. Distribution (a) at the left of Table 2.2 does this with the attitude scores from Table 2.1, grouping them into blocks of two score units each. Each block or *class interval* is identified by its "class limits"—the highest and the lowest score in the interval. Thus, the top interval in the first column of Table 2.2(a) includes the scores 44 and 45 and is identified as class 44–45. The next class consists of the two scores 42 and 43 and so forth.

We can describe these intervals by saying that each has a *width* of two, since two score units are included in each. The symbol we will be using to indicate the width of the interval in any grouped frequency distribution is i. The second column again contains frequencies (f), but these are now the number of individuals falling into each class interval rather than the number receiving each separate score. The resulting distribution is an improvement over the previous one in showing group trends. We can now see quite clearly that the scores for the students tend to cluster near the high end of the scale and trail off in numbers toward the low end.

The degree of condensation obtained by grouping data is determined by the number of score units included in each class interval, since increasing the size of i decreases the number of class intervals. In Table 2.2(b) the data are again represented, but i has been increased from 2 to 5 units, thus decreasing the number of intervals and making the table shorter. A comparison of these frequency distributions, all derived from the same raw data,

Table 2.2 Two Grouped Frequency Distributions Based on the Data in Table 2.1

| (a) | | (b) | |
| i = 2 score units | | i = 5 score units | |
Class	f	Class	f
44–45	4	41–45	14
42–43	6	36–40	38
40–41	10	31–35	29
38–39	13	26–30	16
36–37	19	21–25	3
34–35	13		N = 100
32–33	10		
30–31	11		
28–29	6		
26–27	5		
24–25	1		
22–23	2		
	N = 100		

reveals an interesting fact. As the width of the class interval, i, increases, a pattern first emerges and later disappears as more and more scores are lumped together in fewer classes. We see that as far as obtaining information about group trends is concerned, a frequency distribution can be condensed too far.

A further point to be noted about grouping data is that the identity of the individual score is lost. In Table 2.2(b) for example, where i = 5, the topmost interval contains 14 men, but we do not know exactly what score each received; we know only that each person falls somewhere within the interval. As i becomes larger, the numerical value of the individual score becomes more and more obscured.

How Many Intervals?

Before a set of data can be converted into a grouped frequency distribution, we must decide how many class intervals to employ. This decision is largely arbitrary, depending on such factors as the number of cases, the range of measures, and the purpose for which the distribution is intended. As a general principle we might say that the classes should be few enough so that the resulting distribution reveals a group pattern, but not so few as to obscure a group pattern and cause great loss in the precision with which we can identify the individual score. A rule of thumb often given is that between 10 and 20 intervals should be employed, since most data can be adequately handled within these limits. However, in choosing the number of class intervals, or indeed in deciding whether the range of measures is so small that scores should not be grouped at all, we must examine each set of data individually.

How Many Units for the Class Interval?

Once the *approximate* number of class intervals has been chosen, we must determine the width of the class interval necessary to produce the desired number of intervals. We can roughly estimate the needed *i* by dividing the range of the scores (the highest minus the lowest score) by the number of intervals wanted. Thus, if a set of scores ran from 90 to 143 and about 15 intervals were to be employed, the approximate width would be 3.5 score units, since

$$\frac{143 - 90}{15} = 3.5$$

Whole numbers are more convenient than fractions for widths of intervals, especially when the original measures are themselves integers. In this example we thus have a choice of 3 or 4 units for *i*. In most situations there will be a similar choice, since dividing the range by the number of intervals wanted usually results in a fractional value.

On the basis of practical considerations, certain widths are preferable to others. When the choice is among widths smaller than 10, widths of 2, 3, 5 are often more convenient than other values. In the example above, we might therefore choose 3 as our *i* instead of 4. For interval sizes of 10 or above, multiples of 5 (10, 15, 20, and so forth) are usually selected. We are a "ten-minded" people and deal more easily with multiples of 5 or 10 than with other numbers.

When the width of the interval is a multiple of 5, the values chosen for either the lower limits or the upper limits of the classes are usually a multiple of 5 as well. For example, with *i* = 10, class intervals of 60–69, 70–79, . . . or 61–70, 71–79, . . . are more convenient to set up and interpret than, for example, 62–71, 72–81, and so forth.

In this section, we have discussed the general features of a grouped frequency distribution and what we are trying to accomplish when we arrange data in this form. At the end of this chapter, we will illustrate how to construct a grouped frequency distribution like the one in Table 2.2.

Apparent and Real Class Limits. In the frequency distribution used as an illustration up to this point, the raw measures have been whole numbers. When such data are grouped, we note that there are gaps between the upper and the lower limits of adjacent classes. Thus, if we had classes 10–12 and 13–15, the first class would go up to include (have an upper limit of) 12.0 and the next would start at (have a lower limit of) 13.0. Such values as 12.1 or 12.9, if they occurred, could not be assigned to either class as they fall in the gap between 12.0 and 13.0. When the property we have measured is continuous, these class limits with gaps in between adjacent classes are identified as *apparent limits*. By contrast, *real limits* take into account the fact that when properties are continuous, each discrete score value actually represents the *midpoint* (or middle score) of an *interval* of values. The score of 10, for example, represents the interval 9.5 to 10.5. Real limits therefore extend the upper and lower apparent limits of adjacent classes equally until they meet at the point midway between them and close the gap. For example, the real limits of the class 10–12 cited above are 9.5–12.5, and those of the adjacent class 13–15 are 12.5–15.5. The point of this distinction between the two kinds of class limits will become apparent in later chapters, where we will see that real rather than apparent limits are used in certain statistical operations.

Percent Frequencies

Sometimes there are advantages to translating the frequency of scores falling into each class interval into percent frequency. This has been done for the two grouped frequency distributions shown in Table 2.3. The data represent the scores on the first midterm examination of two sections of a statistics class taught by the same instructor and given the same examination. The % f column indicates the percent of cases, out of the total number, falling into each class interval. The sum of the percent frequencies should total 100 percent, except for rounding errors.

When two frequency distributions based on two different N's are to be compared, converting raw frequencies into percent frequencies is especially useful. By comparing the % f columns in Table 2.3, for example, we can clearly see that as a group, the 55 students in Section II (which met at 11 A.M.) did not do as well as the 48 students in Section I (which met at 8 A.M.). As the instructor had noticed this discrepancy before, he suspected that students who sign up for an early morning section are more motivated than those who sign up for a late morning section!

Table 2.3 Grouped Frequency Distributions of Test Scores for Two Statistics Classes Showing Raw Frequencies and Percent Frequencies

Class Interval	Section I		Section II	
	f	% f	f	% f
52–54	1	2.1		
49–51	3	6.2	1	1.8
46–48	2	4.2	0	0
43–45	4	8.3	4	7.3
40–42	7	14.6	5	9.1
37–39	9	18.8	9	16.4
34–36	6	12.5	8	14.5
31–33	5	10.4	10	18.2
28–30	4	8.3	7	12.7
25–27	4	8.3	6	10.9
22–24	2	4.2	3	5.5
19–21	1	2.1	1	1.8
16–18			1	1.8
	N = 48	100.0	N = 55	100.0

STEM AND LEAF DISPLAY

The conventional way to present measurement data is by means of a frequency distribution. However, another method, recently devised by the statistician John W. Tukey*, is beginning to become popular. This method is called a *stem and leaf display*. To illustrate the construction of a stem and leaf display, we will use the data in Table 2.4. The numbers represent the time (in seconds) that it took 44 army recruits to put together a disassembled rifle. For convenience, we have arranged the scores in order, although it is not necessary to do so.

In a stem and leaf display, the first one or two digits of each score is called a *stem*. For example, we might designate the first digit in the lowest score in Table 2.4 as a stem. The lowest score is 62.4, so the first stem is 6. We then go up from this number to get the remaining stems. This procedure yields stems of 6, 7, 8, 9, 10, and 11. (The highest score is 117.1, so the highest stem is 11.)

The digit next to the stem in each score is called a *leaf*. In the case of our illustrative data, the score of 83.6 has a stem of 8 and a leaf of 3, whereas the score of 106.7 has a stem of 10 and a leaf of 6. If any digits remain beyond the leaf of each score, as they do in Table 2.4, they are dropped from consideration. Thus we treat 83.6 as 83 and 106.7 as 106.

The first step in arranging a stem and leaf display is to put each different stem in a column at the left of a table, starting with the highest value at the top. This is illustrated in Table 2.5, in which we have entered the stems, 6 through 11, for the raw scores in Table 2.4. Next we enter the leaf of each score next to its stem. For example, as we have demonstrated in Table 2.5, the raw scores of 110, 111, and 117 are entered as leaves of 0, 1, and 7 next to the stem of 11. Similarly, the raw scores of 101, 101, 102, etc., are entered as leaves of 1, 1,

Table 2.4 Time (in Seconds) Taken by 44 Army Recruits to Assemble a Rifle

117.1	99.4	92.1	83.6
111.3	98.9	91.5	82.8
110.8	97.2	90.3	82.3
108.6	96.1	90.2	81.5
106.7	95.7	89.6	78.9
105.9	94.5	88.4	76.2
105.5	94.3	87.4	75.6
104.7	93.6	87.2	72.3
102.4	92.8	86.7	70.1
101.8	92.8	86.1	64.7
101.2	92.6	85.5	62.4

*J. W. Tukey, *Exploratory Data Analysis* (Reading, MA: Addison-Wesley, 1977).

Table 2.5 Stem and Leaf Display of Data in Table 2.4[a]

Raw data	Stem	Leaf	Frequency
110, 111, 117 ──────→	11	0 1 7	(3)
101, 101, 102, 104 ⎫──→	10	1 1 2 4 5 5 6 8	(8)
105, 105, 106, 108 ⎭	9	0 0 1 2 2 2 2 3 4 4 5 6 7 8 9	(15)
	8	1 2 2 3 5 6 6 7 7 8 9	(11)
	7	0 2 5 6 8	(5)
	6	2 4	(2)

[a]For purposes of illustration, raw scores for two stems and leaves are shown at the left and the frequencies of leaves for each stem are shown at the right. Each stem is the lower limit of a class with a width of 10 score units.

2, etc., next to the stem of 10. (These raw scores, remember, are the values that remain after the numbers to the right of the leaf were dropped.) We have entered the leaves attached to each stem in order of magnitude. Ordering the leaves is desirable but not strictly necessary.

A stem and leaf display produces an arrangement of scores that is quite comparable to a grouped frequency distribution. The stems are essentially the lower apparent limits of class intervals. In our illustration, the stems represent six classes whose lower limits are 60, 70, 80, and so forth. The width of each class is therefore 10 score units. The number of leaves indicate the frequency of scores within each class or stem. For demonstration purposes, we have shown these frequencies at the extreme right of Table 2.5. In a grouped frequency distribution, the identity of individual scores within each class interval is lost. One of the advantages of a stem and leaf display is that the identity of each score is retained up to the point where final digits are dropped.

A stem and leaf display has a second desirable feature. The display forms a kind of graph which shows us concretely the shape of the distribution of scores. In Chapter 3 we describe several graphic methods that are used to plot frequency distributions. A stem and leaf display has the virtue of showing the distribution of scores in a form that is itself a kind of graph.

In converting a set of scores into a grouped frequency distribution, we learned earlier, our purpose is to reveal the pattern buried in the collection of numbers. We also saw that scores could be grouped into so few class intervals that the pattern of scores is obscured. To remedy this situation we increase the number of classes by decreasing their width (number of score units within each class interval).

In stem and leaf displays the grouping can also be too coarse. This is the case in Table 2.5, in which we have assigned the scores to only six stems, each representing the lower limit of a class that is 10 score units in width. We can improve the picture revealed by the display by decreasing the width covered by each stem to 5 units. (We could reduce the number of units still further but in this instance, this would produce too many classes to reveal the pattern of scores effectively.) We have done this in Table 2.6. You can see that in preparing the display, we have entered each stem twice. The leaves for the top stem of each pair are the values 5 through 9. Following Tukey's procedure, the top stem is accompanied by an asterisk (*). The

Table 2.6 Stem and Leaf Display
of Data in Table 2.4[a]

Stem	Leaf
11*	7
11	0 1
10*	5 5 6 8
10	1 1 2 4
9*	5 6 7 8 9
9	0 0 1 2 2 2 2 3 4 4
8*	5 6 6 7 7 8 9
8	1 2 2 3
7*	5 6 8
7	0 2
6*	
6	2 4

[a]Each stem is the lower limit of a class with a width
of 5 score units.

leaves for the bottom stem of each pair are the values 0–4. Comparison of Table 2.6 with Table 2.5 shows that when the number of stems was increased, the pattern formed by the scores was revealed more clearly.

Earlier we said that the first *one or two* numbers of the raw scores could be used as stems. What would be an example of a case in which two numbers (for the smallest score) would be desirable? Consider a distribution of 60 scores ranging from 143 to 235. Using only the first digit would yield only two stems or classes (1 and 2), obviously too few. However, using the first two digits, starting with the lowest score of 143, would yield 10 stems (14, 15, 16, . . . 23), a more desirable number.

The stem and leaf display is one of a number of new exploratory techniques for arranging sets of measures that help investigators get a good "feel" for patterns in their data. As in choosing the width of class intervals for grouped frequency distributions, we have to use common sense in choosing stems when we decide to present data in a stem and leaf display. Depending on what produces the clearest picture, we could use the first digit, the first two digits, or in some cases even more digits as the stem.

When each different number is used only once as a stem, we have seen that each of the "class intervals" has a width of 10 score units. For example, in the last example, following Table 2.6, in which the stems were 14, 15, 16, . . ., the intervals created have lower apparent limits of 140, 150, 160, and so forth. We also have to examine our data commonsensically to determine whether this procedure is satisfactory or whether, as in the case of the data in Table 2.4, it would be better to set up more intervals with a narrower width by using each stem more than once and breaking down leaves into levels (e.g., 0–4, 5–9). You will find such decisions easier to make as your experience with handling sets of data increases.

Step-by-Step Procedures

In this section we discuss the steps in constructing a grouped frequency distribution for a set of data. Then we do the same for a stem and leaf display of the same data. The data we use are shown at the left of Table 2.7. The numbers represent the scores of 30 individuals on a spatial abilities test.

Constructing a Grouped Frequency Distribution

1. Find the highest and lowest score in the distribution. Then subtract them to find the range (R).
   Ex: $53 - 6 = 47$

2. Decide on the approximate number of class intervals you think will reveal the pattern most effectively. Typically, this number will be between 10 and 20. In most cases larger N's call for a greater number of classes.
   Ex: With a relatively small N of 30, 10 classes are acceptable.

3. Divide the range (R) by the number of desired classes to give an approximate width (i) for each interval. Based on the result, choose a convenient whole number for i.
   Ex: $i = 47/10 = 4.7$. Choose $i = 5$.

4. Choose apparent limits for the highest class. As all classes have the same i, these values determine the limits for all remaining classes.

Table 2.7 A Grouped Frequency Distribution and Stem and Leaf Display Based on the Data from 30 Individuals

Raw Scores			Grouped Frequency Distribution			Stem and Leaf Display	
			Class	Tally	f	Stem	Leaf
15	42	22	50–54	⌐	2	5	1 3
51	33	38	45–49		0	4*	
25	26	13	40–44	⊓	3	4	0 2 4
32	53	32	35–39	☐	4	3*	5 6 8 9
40	6	31	30–34	☒⊓	8	3	0 1 2 2 3 3 4 4
20	24	39	25–29	☒	5	2*	5 6 7 8 9
29	35	27	20–24	☐	4	2	0 1 2 4
36	21	44	15–19	⌐	2	1*	5 9
19	34	30	10–14	|	1	1	3
33	28	34	5–9	|	1	0*	6
					N = 30		

Ex: With $i = 5$, either the upper or the lower limit of each class will most conveniently be a multiple of 5. We have arbitrarily chosen the lower limit. As 53 is the highest score, the limits of the highest class are:

Class: 50–54

5. Write down the apparent class limits in a column in descending order. The lowest class should include the score with the smallest value.

   Ex: The classes are shown in Table 2.7.

6. Assign each raw score to its class, using a tally system. The number of tallies shows the number of scores falling into each class. Enter these numbers to the right of the class intervals in a column labeled f (frequency).

   Ex: Tallies and frequencies are shown in Table 2.7.

   Note: A box system, with ⬜ indicating five, has been used in Table 2.7. This method may make it easier to record scores and to read the results accurately than would the more familiar system in which ⫪ indicates five.

7. Add the frequencies, which should equal the total N. Indicate N below the f column.

   Ex: The frequencies total to $N = 30$.

Constructing a Stem and Leaf Display

1. Using the first or second digit as a stem, determine the different stems represented in the set of scores.

   Ex: As the numbers in Table 2.7 are only two digits in length, the stems have to be one-digit numbers. Stems are 0, 1, 2, 3, 4, and 5. (Numbers less than 10 can be written as 09, 08, . . ., 01. Their stems are therefore 0.)

2. Decide whether the results of Step 1 produce enough classes (stems) to reveal the group pattern. If not, each stem should be used more than once.

   Ex: There are 6 different stems (0–5). Using each stem twice would produce a more desirable number.

3. Enter the stems in a column. Then list the leaf of each raw score next to its stem.

   Ex: The stems and their leaves are listed at the right of Table 2.7. The top stem in each pair, marked by an asterisk, has leaves of 5–9 and the bottom stem has values of 0–4.

4. We have entered the leaves in order of magnitude, although it is not essential that this be done.

A final note: In this example the values of the stems, which are comparable to the lower limits of class intervals, happen to have values that are parallel to the values of the lower limits of the classes in the grouped frequency distribution, and both have widths of 5 units. The result, as you can see, is that the frequencies associated with the class intervals and the number of leaves associated with the parallel stems are the same. The outcomes of the two methods are therefore directly comparable in this instance. As you can see, however, the stem and leaf display produces a much more graphic picture of the pattern of scores than does the grouped frequency distribution.

DEFINITIONS OF TERMS
AND SYMBOLS

Score. A general expression for the number assigned to an individual to indicate the amount of some property that individual exhibits.

Range (R). The difference between the largest and smallest score in a distribution.

N. The number of cases in a group.

Frequency (f). For each score value in a distribution of scores, the number of cases in the group that has that score value.

Simple frequency distribution. A table summarizing the scores received by a group of individuals. The table lists all possible score values from the highest to the lowest obtained score and the number of individuals (frequency) receiving each of these scores.

Class interval. Collection of a subgroup of scores into a class of scores with a range of values. For example, the class interval 3–5 contains scores of 3, 4, and 5.

Midpoint. Middle score value in a class interval.

Apparent limits of class interval. The values of the highest and lowest scores in a class interval.

Real limits of class interval. For continuous properties, each score value represents the midpoint of a range of values. The real limits of a class interval reflect this range. For example, when lengths of objects are measured to the nearest millimeter (mm), the score of 8 represents objects ranging from 7.5 to 8.5 mm long. The real limits of the class of objects whose apparent limits are 8–10 mm are 7.5 and 10.5.

Width of interval (i). For continuous measures, i is the difference between the upper and lower real limits of the class interval. For most discrete measures, i is the number of integer score values in the score interval.

Grouped frequency distribution. A table listing scores grouped into class intervals of equal width (i), and the number of individuals (frequencies) falling into each class interval.

Stem and leaf display. A method of presenting the distribution of scores in which the first one or two digits of each score is designated as a stem and the digit to the right of the stem is designated as a leaf. The values of each different stem are shown in an ordered column, and next to each stem, the leaves are entered of all scores with that stem.

PROBLEMS

1. In an experiment on the effects of competitiveness, each of a group of 50 male college students was given an anagram task which he believed he was performing in competition with a female student. The times (in seconds) taken by the male students to complete the anagrams are listed below. Arrange these measures in a grouped frequency distribution, selecting a value for i that will best show the pattern of the group. Set up the distribution so that the upper limit of the highest

class interval corresponds to the largest number in the group.* Add up the frequency column to make sure you have accounted for all cases.

Be sure to use the headings "Class Interval" and "*f*" (frequency) in reporting the grouped frequency distribution you develop.

44	33	53	37	41
34	65	41	50	54
48	36	47	40	43
39	50	40	44	49
57	23	45	58	39
25	42	55	35	42
42	43	43	43	52
45	56	35	51	38
31	41	32	21	34
53	46	51	47	46

2. In a second condition of the experiment described in problem 1, members of a second group of 50 male students believed they were competing with another male student. The times to completion for these students are shown below.

Set up two grouped frequency distributions for these data, one with $i = 3$ and one with $i = 5$. Which of these distributions do you prefer? Why?

46	29	36	26	50
35	43	22	34	34
28	34	32	40	36
41	35	59	31	27
32	45	35	33	47
36	33	31	56	35
25	41	40	37	20
48	26	23	29	38
30	37	32	24	23
34	30	42	45	39

3. For the data in problem 1, determine (a) the value of the range, (R), (b) the real limits of the *lowest* class interval and of the *highest* class interval in the grouped frequency distribution you set up, and (c) the midpoint of each of these intervals.

4. In the following list, information is given about the N and the highest and lowest scores in each of six sets of data. For each set, decide whether it would be useful to arrange the data into a frequency distribution. If it would, indicate (a) the width of the interval (*i*) you would choose; (b) the approximate number of intervals that would result, assuming that the upper apparent limit of the highest interval has the value of the highest score in the distribution, (c) the real limits and the apparent limits of the *highest* class that would result from your chosen *i*; and (d) the midpoint of

---

*In the answers to the problems for this chapter, all frequency distributions were set up using this procedure. By using the same procedure, students can compare their solutions directly to those given in the answers. However, it should be noted that this procedure is neither necessary nor desirable in all data sets.

the highest interval. (*Note:* List the answers for the six sets in a table with columns labeled *i*, number of intervals, and so forth.)

	Extreme Scores	N		Extreme Scores	N
(1)	50–95	7	(4)	16–25	18
(2)	11–75	94	(5)	.38–1.52	34
(3)	100–283	65	(6)	3–34	75

5. Construct a stem and leaf display of the raw scores given in problem 1.

3

Graphic Representations

- GRAPHIC REPRESENTATIONS
  OF FREQUENCY DISTRIBUTIONS
- GENERAL PROCEDURES
  IN CONSTRUCTING HISTOGRAMS
  AND FREQUENCY POLYGONS
- FORM OF A FREQUENCY DISTRIBUTION
- GRAPHIC REPRESENTATIONS OF OTHER
  TYPES OF DATA

Most of us have seen graphs that present various types of statistical information: infant mortality rate in different countries, popularity of political candidates, the distribution of incomes, and so forth. Such graphs are used by popular writers because they are both more interesting and more easily interpreted than columns of figures. The graphic method is also employed extensively in technical articles, since the outstanding features of group performance are most readily grasped in this form.

GRAPHIC REPRESENTATIONS
OF FREQUENCY DISTRIBUTIONS

First we will discuss two methods of presenting frequency distributions: the histogram and the frequency polygon. Certain commonsense rules and ways of graphing data apply to both methods. These will be outlined after we look briefly at each type.

Histogram

Histograms are becoming a popular way to display frequency distributions because they are easily generated by computer programs. An illustration of a histogram and the data on which it is based is shown in Figure 3.1.

The grouped frequency distribution at the left of the figure represents the scores of 150 college women on a questionnaire asking about their attitudes toward men's and women's rights and roles. High numbers reflected liberal, egalitarian attitudes, with 45 being the highest possible score. These data have been plotted in the form of a histogram at the right of Figure 3.1. The width of each rectangle indicates the width of each class interval (the distance between the lower and upper real limits of the class) and the rectangle's height indicates the frequency of scores in each class. The histogram allows you to see clearly that the women tended to cluster at the upper, liberal end of the scale but that a few women were highly conservative in their sex-role attitudes.

Let us now look at the technical features of a histogram in detail. There are two axes: the horizontal baseline, also known as the X axis or the abscissa, and the vertical axis, also called the Y axis or the ordinate. The scores, in this case grouped into class intervals, are represented along the horizontal X axis, whereas the Y axis represents the frequency or percent frequency of cases. Each axis is appropriately labeled. The numbers along the Y axis refer to the frequency of cases earning each score or falling into each class interval. When simple frequency distributions are plotted in the form of a histogram, the numbers along the baseline represent each different score, from lowest to highest. When grouped frequency distributions are plotted, we have a choice of labeling the real limits or the midpoint of each class. In Figure 3.1 we have chosen to label midpoints. A rectangle or bar is erected for each score or class interval, its height being determined by the corresponding frequency.

Notice that in Figure 3.1 the boundaries of adjacent rectangles touch each other. Because

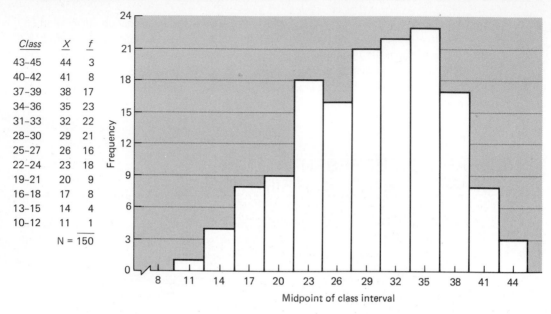

Class	X	f
43–45	44	3
40–42	41	8
37–39	38	17
34–36	35	23
31–33	32	22
28–30	29	21
25–27	26	16
22–24	23	18
19–21	20	9
16–18	17	8
13–15	14	4
10–12	11	1
	N =	150

Figure 3.1 Histogram showing sex-role attitude scores for female college students and the grouped frequency distribution from which it was plotted.*

the width of each rectangle is determined by the real class limits (reflecting the fact that a continuous property, such as attitudes, has been measured), it follows that there are no gaps between bars.

When discrete properties are plotted, however, spaces are left between rectangles to indicate that only certain values can occur. An illustration is shown in Figure 3.2. The histogram indicates the number of record albums bought last year by a group of high school students. As albums are sold whole, not in fractions, the data are discrete and the bars do not touch. Sometimes a histogram for discrete data is called a *bar graph* because it contains separated rectangles or bars. In a later section we discuss bar graphs for categorical data.

In Chapter 2 we discussed stem and leaf displays as an alternative to frequency distributions for arranging magnitude data. We also pointed out that stem and leaf displays have a graphic quality. We now can say, more particularly, that these displays resemble histograms in which the sets of leaves are comparable to the bars in a histogram. Putting stems in a column and the leaves for each stem in a row results in a histogram that is laid on its side, as it were. If this arrangement were reversed, with stems laid out horizontally at the base of the display and the leaves shown in a column above their stem, the resemblance between a conventional histogram and a stem and leaf display would become even more obvious.

*Data are representative samples taken from the 1980 groups reported in R. L. Helmreich, J. T. Spence, and R. H. Gibson, "Sex-role attitudes: 1972–1980," *Personality and Social Psychology Bulletin*, 1982, *8*, 656–63. Raw data courtesy of the authors.

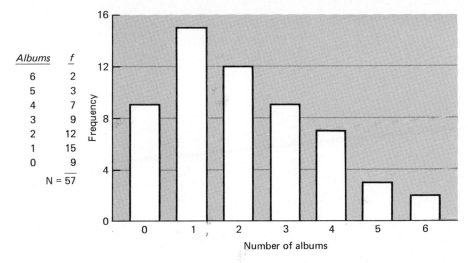

Albums	f
6	2
5	3
4	7
3	9
2	12
1	15
0	9
N =	57

Figure 3.2 Number of record albums bought by a sample of high school students in the last month.

Frequency Polygon

The method of graphing frequency distributions used most often is the frequency polygon. Two frequency polygons, along with the grouped frequency distributions from which they were derived, are shown in Figure 3.3. We have plotted both distributions in a single graph, so that we can compare them more easily.

The grouped frequency distribution at the top left of Figure 3.3 is the same distribution of sex-role attitude scores from 150 college women shown in Figure 3.1. At the top right is the distribution of attitude scores obtained from the same number of college men. You can see how much easier it is to compare the distributions of men's and women's scores by looking at the two polygons rather than by inspecting the two frequency distributions on which the polygons were based. It is clear, for example, that the men's scores are heavily concentrated around the middle of the scale. Women, in contrast, tend to cluster at the upper end of the scale, indicating that their attitudes are more egalitarian than men's.

As in a histogram, frequencies in a frequency polygon are represented along the Y axis and scores or midpoints of class intervals are represented along the baseline. To construct a frequency polygon, points are plotted over each score or midpoint, the height of each point being determined by the appropriate frequency. The polygon is completed by connecting adjacent points with a straight line. The lines should be dropped to the baseline at either end to show the upper and lower scores or class intervals at which zero frequencies begin. The exception to this rule is the case in which there are individuals who have obtained the lowest or the highest score that is possible. In Figure 3.3, for example, 3 women fall into the interval 43–45. The maximum possible score is 45, so the baseline was not extended beyond the

Women		Men	
Midpoint	*f*	*Midpoint*	*f*
44	3		
41	8	41	3
38	16	38	5
35	23	35	14
32	23	32	17
29	21	29	20
26	16	26	23
23	18	23	32
20	9	20	21
17	8	17	7
14	4	14	5
11	1	11	3

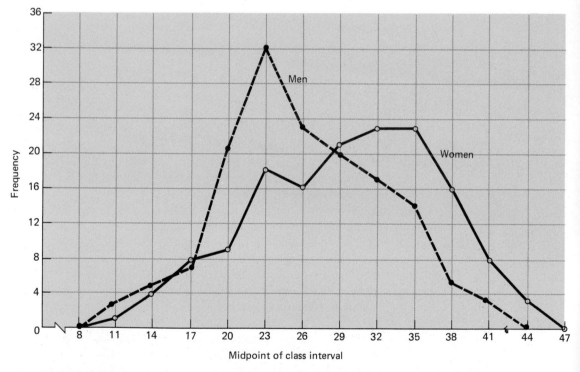

Figure 3.3 Frequency polygons showing sex-role attitude scores for male and female college students and the grouped frequency distributions from which they were drawn.*

---

*Data are representative samples taken from the 1980 groups reported in R. L. Helmreich, J. T. Spence, and R. H. Gibson, "Sex-role attitudes: 1972–1980," *Personality and Social Psychology Bulletin*, 1982, *8*, 656–63. Raw data courtesy of the authors.

midpoint of the 43–45 interval and the upper end of the curve for women was not dropped to the baseline.

GENERAL PROCEDURES IN CONSTRUCTING HISTOGRAMS AND FREQUENCY POLYGONS

With these brief descriptions of histograms and frequency polygons before us, we can now discuss certain general procedures applicable to plotting both types of graphs.

Selection of Axes and Size of Units

The horizontal baseline should represent scores or measures and the vertical axis should represent frequencies or percentages of cases. This convention should always be followed because reversal would cause confusion for those used to the customary method.

The size of each score unit on the baseline and each frequency unit on the vertical axis should be chosen in such a way that the length of the vertical axis is 60 to 75 percent of the length of the baseline. This rule may seem picayune, but there are reasons for it. Not only does the uniformity produce esthetically pleasing results, but there are practical implications as well. The latter become clearer if you examine the polygons in Figure 3.4.* Each graph gives a different impression at first glance, even though each represents the same frequency distribution. These differences have been produced by manipulating the physical distances chosen to represent scores and frequency units—or, more accurately, by changing the relationship between

Figure 3.4 Three polygons drawn from the same frequency distribution varying in ratio of X to Y axis.

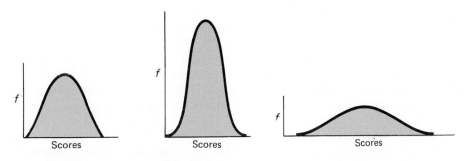

---

*Frequency polygons based on actual frequency distributions, such as shown in Figure 3.3, are almost always irregular rather than smooth, unless the samples are much larger than those for this figure. For purposes of illustration, we have drawn idealized, smoothed curves in Figure 3.4. Similar idealized curves will be used throughout the text when general principles are being discussed.

the length of the two axes. Since the reader's impression of a frequency distribution can be so easily influenced by such an arbitrary factor, the adoption of an appropriately standardized relationship between the two axes facilitates the interpretation of frequency polygons.

Labels and Titles of Graphs

Graphs should always be completely labeled. These labels include what each axis represents, such as scores, or frequencies, percentages, and the numerical values of each. The lowest values for both frequencies and scores should start at the intersection of the two axes, at the lower left of the graph. It is not necessary to indicate or number the position of every possible score along the baseline, only certain representative ones at regular intervals. Specifically, it is usually sufficient to label class limits (real or apparent) or midpoints of intervals. There is no general rule for the frequency scale; as long as enough points are identified to make interpretation easy and these are placed an equal number of units apart, labeling will be considered adequate.

Every graph should also have a concise title containing sufficient information to allow a reader to identify relevant aspects of the data, such as exactly what they measure, their source, and so forth. If several graphs are to be presented, each graph or figure should also be given its own number for further identification (for example, Figure 17). Since a graph without labels and a title is often next to meaningless, you are strongly urged to make "titling" second nature, even on statistical exercises.

FORM OF A FREQUENCY DISTRIBUTION

Frequency distributions can occur in an unlimited number of shapes and forms. Since form is often an important bit of information about a distribution, it is useful to know some of the descriptive terms used to indicate various types.

Some frequency distributions, and consequently the frequency polygons derived from them, are *bilaterally symmetrical*. That is, if the polygon is folded in half, perpendicular to the baseline, the two sides are identical in shape. A variety of symmetrical distributions is shown in Figure 3.5.

Several distributions that are not symmetrical are shown in Figure 3.6. An asymmetrical distribution in which the scores "trail off" in one direction is said to be *skewed*. Such distributions can be more exactly described in terms of degree and direction of skewness. *Degree* refers to the amount that a distribution departs from symmetry. Thus, distribution *a* in Figure 3.5 is more highly skewed than *c*. *Direction* of skewness takes account of the fact that in some asymmetrical distributions the measures tend to pile up at the lower end of the scale and to trail off, in terms of frequency, toward the upper end, while in other cases the situation is reversed. Differences in the direction of skewness are indicated by saying that the distributions are positively or negatively skewed. Both as a way of explaining which is positive and which negative and as a device for remembering the difference between the two, the lower or left end of the baseline can be pictured as the negative end (values are low) and the upper or right end as positive (values are high). If the "tail" of a distribution, where scores are relatively infrequent

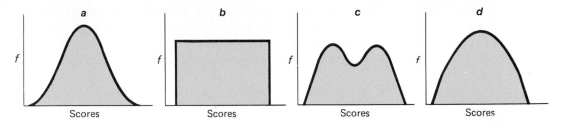

Figure 3.5 Illustrations of symmetrical frequency distributions.

in number, lies in the negative end of the scale, the distribution is negatively skewed. If the tail extends out toward the upper or positive end, the distribution is positively skewed. Curves *c* and *d* in Figure 3.6 are therefore negatively skewed, while *a* and *b* are positively skewed.

Certain distinctive forms of distributions that occur with some frequency are given special names. Curve *b* in Figure 3.6 is called a *J curve*, a curve that resembles either the letter J or its mirror image. This type is found primarily with certain types of socially conditioned behavior, such as a distribution of the number of major crimes committed by members of a large group of individuals. The vast majority have none to their credit, whereas a few members of the group are multiple offenders. In Figure 3.5, *b* is *a rectangular distribution*, the frequencies in every class interval being the same. Distribution *a* in Figure 3.5 approximates *the normal curve*, a specific form of a symmetrical bell-shaped distribution. Many phenomena, including such psychological characteristics as IQ's and certain personality traits, appear to take this form. The normal curve is of such great theoretical importance in statistics that its properties will be discussed in some detail in Chapter 8.

Finally, we call attention to distribution *c* in Figure 3.5. Unlike the rest of the frequency polygons in Figures 3.5 and 3.6, this curve has two humps rather than one. This type of curve is called *bimodal*. The other curves with single peaks are called *unimodal*.

Cumulative Frequency Curve

The cumulative frequency curve, though used less often than the frequency polygon, is preferred when we are interested primarily in specifying the position of an individual or individual score in a distribution rather than the general form of the group performance. The results from

Figure 3.6 Illustrations of skewed frequency distributions.

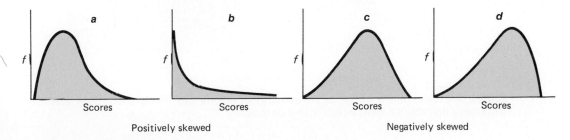

many tests of abilities, personality attributes, and the like are sometimes reported with cumulative frequencies or cumulative percentages and graphed in this fashion, since such scores are often used for individual diagnosis and evaluation. Before discussing this use of the cumulative curve, we will examine an example of a cumulative frequency curve and describe its construction.

Figure 3.7 shows a distribution of scores earned by 80 seventh-graders on a vocabulary

Class Interval	f	Cum f	Cum %
90–92	2	80	100.00%
87–89	3	78	97.50
84–86	6	75	93.75
81–83	9	69	86.25
78–80	12	60	75.00
75–77	14	48	60.00
72–74	13	34	42.50
69–71	10	21	26.25
66–68	5	11	13.75
63–65	4	6	7.50
60–62	2	2	2.50
	N = 80		

Figure 3.7 Cumulative curve of vocabulary scores for seventh-grade pupils and the frequency distribution from which it was derived.

test along with the cumulative frequency curve derived from it. The curve, which is also known as an *ogive*, shows the total number of cases earning a certain score or less. To plot a cumulative frequency curve we must first derive *cumulative frequencies* from the distribution. Looking at the distribution at the top of Figure 3.7, we find two individuals falling in the bottom interval, 60–62. The upper real limit of this class is 62.5. Thus 2 cases have a score of 62.5 *or less*. This figure (2) is entered in the cumulative frequency column. Four individuals fall in the interval that is second from the bottom; thus 2 + 4 or 6 cases have scores of 65.5 or less. This sum, 6, is entered next in the cumulative frequency column. For the next entry we determine that 11 individuals have scores of 68.5 or less (2 + 4 + 5 or 6 + 5). By successive addition, from bottom to top, of the entries in the frequency column, we get the cumulative frequencies. The entry in the topmost interval is equal to the total number of cases, since all individuals have a score equal to or less than the upper limit of this class.

A cumulative frequency curve represents the graphing of a cumulative distribution and is carried out in a manner similar to that for the frequency polygon. In this method, however, the points are plotted directly above the *upper real limits* of each interval rather than the midpoint. The upper real limits are used because cumulative frequency represents the number or percentage of cases that have scores equal to or below the value at the particular upper limit. The height of each point above the abscissa is, of course, determined by the appropriate cumulative frequency.

Inspection of the curve in Figure 3.7 shows that it is S-shaped in form. This is the shape that uniformly occurs in cumulative frequency polygons when the distribution of scores is bell-shaped. When the frequency distribution is symmetrical, so is the S in the cumulative frequency polygon; as the frequency distribution increases in skewness, the S becomes increasingly lopsided.

Cumulative Percentages and Percentiles

Cumulative frequency can also be translated into cumulative percentage. This translation has been made in the right-hand column of the frequency distribution shown in Figure 3.7. The vertical axis at the right has also been marked off in percentages, so that we may read the curve in terms of either frequencies or percentages.

Cumulative percentages are particularly useful for describing the relative position of a given score in a distribution. For example, inspection of the cumulative curve in Figure 3.7 shows that a child who earned a score of 80 is above average in vocabulary in comparison to others in the class—that is, approximately 75 percent of the children had a score of 80 or less; conversely, only 25 percent had a score of 80 or more.

Specifying an individual's standing in terms of these cumulative percentage figures often conveys more information than the raw score (how much would it mean to you, for example, simply to be told that on a 60-point examination, you scored 42; is that good or bad?) or even an individual's standing in terms of numerical rank (for example, 27th from the bottom in a class of 64). Cumulative percentages are therefore often used as alternatives to raw scores and are collectively identified as the *percentile scale*.

Using the cumulative percentage curve, we can go back and forth between the two scales. If we start with a raw score and find its equivalent on the percentile scale, we speak of the percentile rank of the score. *The percentile rank of any given score is a value indicating the percentage of cases falling at or below that score.* In Figure 3.7, for example, we can see that the percentile rank of the score 72 is approximately 27. Conversely, we can start with a percentage value and find its score equivalent. This score is called a percentile. *A percentile is the score at or below which a given percent of the cases fall.* In Figure 3.2, the 90th percentile is approximately 83. If the distinction between percentiles and percentile ranks seems confusing, don't worry. Just remember that one can go back and forth between raw scores and percentile scores and that percentiles represent the percentage that earn the score *or below*.

The percentile scale, derived from percentages, contains 100 units. A number of points along this scale are given special names. Often encountered are the *quartiles*. The first quartile, known as Q_1, is the special name for the 25th percentile, the second quartile (Q_2) is equal to the 50th percentile, and the third quartile (Q_3), to the 75th percentile. The 50th percentile is also called the *median* of the distribution. Occasionally certain percentiles are referred to as *deciles:* the first decile (or 10th percentile), the second decile (20th percentile), and so forth up to the tenth decile (100th percentile).

The percentile equivalents of raw scores can roughly be determined, we have just seen, by reading them from a graph of cumulative percentages. There are, in addition, more exact methods for calculating percentiles and percentile ranks than the estimates obtained from graphs. Once these percentage values have been determined, it is possible to represent them, as well as raw scores, in a frequency polygon.

This process is illustrated in Figure 3.8. Scores are indicated on the baseline, as usual. Below the raw-score scale we have added a *percentile scale*. We have chosen to indicate only representative percentiles. The point that is marked 50 appears below the raw score that was calculated to lie at the 50th percentile or median, the point marked 60 appears below the score that was calculated to lie at the 60th percentile, and so forth. You should notice that starting at the median and working out toward each tail, the raw-score distance between the successive

Figure 3.8 Frequency polygon with median of 20 in which both a raw-score scale and a percentile scale are indicated on the horizontal axis.

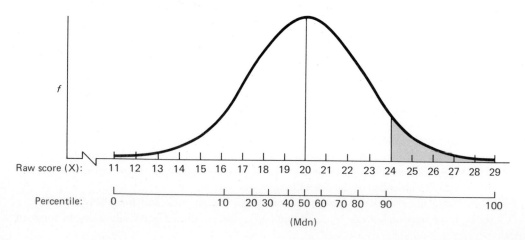

deciles becomes larger and larger. For example, the 50th percentile is 20 and the 60th percentile is 20.75, a difference of only .75 score unit. On the other hand, the scores associated with the 90th and 100th percentiles are 23.84 and 29, a difference of 5.16 score units. Why did this happen?

In answering this question, we first call your attention to the fact that the *percent frequency of cases is equal to the percent of the area under the curve.* The median, for example, is defined as that point in a distribution that divides the frequency in half, 50 percent of the cases falling at or below the point and conversely, 50 percent falling at or above the point. You can see by inspecting Figure 3.8 that the median cuts the curve in half in terms of area. The total area, of course, is 100 percent, so 50 percent of the area falls at or below the median. Similarly, the 90th percentile is that point at or below which 90 percent of the cases fall; in a polygon, 90 percent of the area also falls at or below this point, and so forth.

In a symmetrical or nearly symmetrical unimodal distribution, like the one in Figure 3.8, the scores cluster around the median and fall off, in terms of frequency, as they go away from the median toward the tails. As you can see in the figure, we have to go out only a very small distance from the median on the raw-score scale to encompass 10 percent of the area, i.e., to go from the 50th to the 60th percentile or from the 50th to the 40th percentile. On the other hand, to encompass successive slices of 10 percent of the area, we have to go further and further distances on the raw-score scale. As an illustration, we have marked off in Figure 3.8 the upper 10 percent of the area, i.e., the distance between the 90th and 100th percentiles.

There are two points that we want to emphasize before leaving this discussion. First, when frequency distributions are plotted in the form of frequency polygons (or histograms), percent area under the curve is equal to percent frequency of cases. Second, we can translate raw scores into percentiles, and vice versa, so that the percentile scale can be used as an alternative to the raw-score scale. This is comparable to saying that we can translate the length of objects back and forth from yards to meters and use the two systems of measurement as alternatives to one another.

GRAPHIC REPRESENTATIONS OF OTHER TYPES OF DATA

Up to this point we have been considering methods of graphing frequency distributions. We will now discuss very briefly how to represent several other types of data commonly encountered in psychological investigations.

Categorical Membership

Table 3.1 shows the number of men who were awarded Ph.D.'s in psychology in 1984, broken down into two types of specialties: health care provider and academic-research. The table also shows the number of women awarded their degrees in these two areas in the same year. You should note that these numbers represent categorical data: men and women, and

Table 3.1 Number of Men and Women Awarded the Ph.D. in Psychology in Two Specialty Areas, 1984

	Health Care Provider	*Academic-Research*
Men	860	362
Women	855	388

Source: Data from "The changing face of American psychology," *American Psychologist*, 1986, *41*, 1311–27.

two types of specialties. The data are plotted in Figure 3.9 in the form of a *bar graph*, the most common method for representing frequency of categorical membership. The two categorical groups for each sex are shown along the baseline, the heights of the bars indicating the number in each category. Because neither sex nor type of degree represents any sort of continuum, it makes no difference which sex appears first and within sex, which type of degree appears first on the baseline. It was also an arbitrary decision to plot the data so that the numbers for men are shown as a pair of adjacent pairs and the same for women. It would have been equally appropriate to plot the data so that a pair of bars indicating the number of men and women earning one type of degree appear first, with the pair of bars for the other type of degree appearing second. To indicate the discreteness of the categorical groups, the bars are spatially separated.

Magnitude Data from Categorical Groups

Often in research we want to compare categorical groups on some measurable property—that is, on some property that exists in various degrees. For example, we might determine the average educational aspirations of groups of eighth-grade students from several ethnic

Figure 3.9 Bar graph of data in Table 3.1 showing men and women awarded psychology Ph.D.'s in two specialty areas, 1984.

Figure 3.10 Bar graph of average number of hours per day spent on household tasks by married men, housewives, and employed married women.

backgrounds or the annual per capita consumption of beef in different Western countries. In each of these illustrations, the various groups—students or countries—represent a set of categories that do not form an ordered continuum. Unlike the section above in which our interest was in a categorical variable (in our example, type of Ph.D. degree), we are here concerned with how much of some measurable property is exhibited by the members of each group: educational aspirations in the case of students and beef consumption in the case of countries. As individuals within a group almost always differ, we use a representative number, such as the average, to characterize each group as a whole.

Magnitude data from categorical groups may be presented in the form of a bar graph to facilitate group comparisons. An illustration of a bar graph from such a study is presented in Figure 3.10. The data in the graph show the average number of hours per day spent on household tasks in the United States by married men, married women who are employed outside the home, and housewives with no paid employment. Since the groups cannot be arranged along a continuum, the order in which the bars appear on the baseline is arbitrary.

Ordered Groups

In other research, we obtain magnitude data from groups that can be ordered in some way. Our purpose is to see how performance changes with systematic increases in the value of some variable. For example, an investigator might perform an experiment in which each subject witnesses an accident under one of four conditions: alone or in the presence of 1, 2, or 3 other people. There are, let us say, 10 persons in each condition. (In actuality, the "accident" is staged and the other people are the experimenter's confederates.) It is apparent that the experimental groups are ordered along a continuum: 0, 1, 2, or 3 other witnesses. The investigator suspects that increasing the number of other bystanders will decrease the likelihood that a person will offer a victim help. She therefore determines the percent of individuals in each condition who try to help within a specified time period. Or we might obtain multiple measures

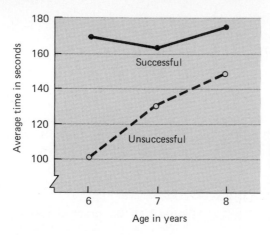

Figure 3.11 Average time in seconds spent on insoluble task by 6-, 7-, and 8-year-old children who were previously successful or unsuccessful.

from the same individual. For example, we might conduct a study of a weight reduction program designed to help people who have successfully completed the program to maintain their lower weight over a long period of time. We might therefore arrange to weigh participants once a month over a two-year period. In order to emphasize how the observed property (in our examples, helping the victim or body weight) varies with changes in the experimental variable, the results of such studies are often presented in the form of a *line graph*. The experimental groups are arranged in order along the baseline and the amount of the property is represented on the vertical axis. The average amount of the property exhibited by each group

Figure 3.12 Percentage of high school seniors using marijuana in the past year, 1979 to 1985.

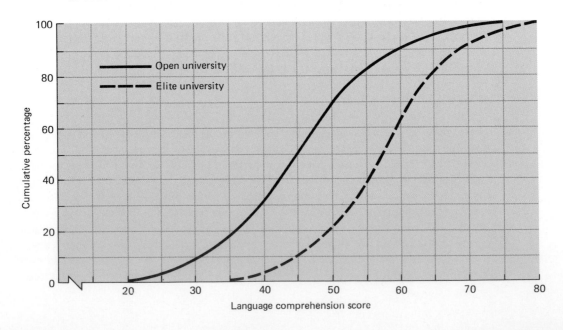

is indicated by a point rather than by a bar. The adjacent points are then connected by straight lines.

An example of a line graph is shown in Fig. 3.11. The graph shows the results of an experiment in which 6-year-old, 7-year-old, and 8-year-old children were given several tasks to perform. Half the children in each age group were told they had done much better than most other children, and the other half that they had not done as well as most children. Then all children were given a puzzle that was actually insoluble, and the time they spent on the puzzle before giving up was recorded. The line graph shows the average time spent on the puzzle by the previously "successful" children and previously "unsuccessful" children in each age group. Inspection of the graph shows that the three age groups were about equally persistent after success. At all three ages, unsuccessful children were less persistent. However, the detrimental effects on persistence of the lack of previous success became less marked as age increased.

The data from groups that can be ordered may also be plotted in the form of a bar graph. An example can be seen in Figure 3.12, which reports responses to a question about marijuana use on a national survey of high school seniors conducted annually from 1979 to 1985. The bar graph shows the percentage of students in each of these years who admitted to using marijuana in the previous 12 months. Inspection of the graph suggests that the percentages have declined since 1979 but may now have leveled off. ■

DEFINITIONS OF TERMS AND SYMBOLS

Histogram. A type of graph based on a frequency distribution. A bar is erected over each score or class interval on the baseline, the height of each bar indicating the frequency associated with each score or class interval. The width of each bar indicates the upper and lower real limits of the score or class interval, so there is no gap between adjacent bars.

Frequency polygon. A type of graph based on a frequency distribution. Scores or midpoints of class intervals are shown on the horizontal (X) axis and frequencies are shown on the vertical (Y) axis. The frequency associated with each score or class interval is indicated by a point, and adjacent points are connected by straight lines.

Cumulative frequency distribution. A distribution showing for the upper real limit of each score (or of each class interval) the total number of cases earning that score value *or less*.

Cumulative frequency polygon or ogive. A graph based on a cumulative frequency distribution. Upper real limits of scores or class intervals are shown on the horizontal axis and cumulative frequencies on the vertical axis. Adjacent points, each representing a cumulative frequency, are connected by a straight line.

Symmetrical distribution. Frequency distribution whose polygon, when bisected on the baseline, forms two halves that are mirror images of each other.

Skewed distribution. Frequency distribution whose shape is asymmetrical. When frequencies are high for high score values and tail off in the direction of low score values, the distribution is described as *negatively skewed*. When frequencies tail off in the direction of higher score values, the distribution is described as *positively skewed*.

Unimodal curve. A frequency polygon in which there is only one hump (one score value with the maximum frequency).

Bimodal curve. A frequency polygon in which there are two humps or points of maximum frequency.

Percentile rank. A raw score expressed in terms of the percentage of cases in a distribution that have that score *or less*. For example, if 35 percent of the cases score 76 or less, the percentile rank of the score 76 is 35. Percentile ranks, like percentages, range from 0 to 100.

Percentile. The score at or below which a given percentage of the cases in a distribution fall. For example, if 82 percent of the cases fall at or below a score of 110, 110 is equal to the 82nd percentile.

Median. The score at or below which 50 percent of the cases fall. The median is the same as the 50th percentile.

Quartiles. Score points that divide a distribution into quarters in terms of frequency. The first quartile (Q_1) is equal to the 25th percentile, the second quartile (Q_2) is equal to the 50th percentile or median, and the third quartile (Q_3) is equal to the 75th percentile.

Deciles. Score points that divide a distribution into tenths in terms of frequency. The first decile (D_1) is equal to the 10th percentile, the second decile (D_2) to the 20th percentile, and so forth.

Bar graph. A method of graphing data from several categorical groups or from the same individuals observed on several occasions. Groups or occasions are shown along the baseline and the results of the observations (for example, number or percent of individuals falling into each category, or average performance of the group) are indicated on the vertical axis. A bar is erected over each group or occasion on the baseline, its height being determined by the values on the Y axis associated with the group. The bars are spatially separated.

Line graph. When groups or multiple observations of the same individuals can be ordered (e.g., 1, 2, 3, or 4 days of training before a performance measure is taken), the data may be plotted by means of a line graph. The ordered groups are shown on the baseline. The performance associated with each group or occasion is indicated by a point and adjacent points are connected by straight lines.

PROBLEMS

In the problems calling for a graph, it will be most convenient for you to draw them on graph paper. For each graph, be sure to label the axes and supply a title describing what the data represent.

1. In Chapter 2, problems 1 and 2 gave data from an experiment on males' competitiveness in which the effects on performance of the sex of partner were studied. Each problem required setting up a grouped frequency distribution with $i = 3$. (These distributions are shown in the answers for Chapter 2 on page 000.)

   (a) Draw a frequency polygon for each distribution, putting both polygons in the same figure.

   (b) Which set of data shows a more skewed distribution? In what direction is it skewed?

   (c) What do the distributions suggest about the effects of sex of partner on competitiveness? Be specific.

   (d) Plot the same distributions in the form of a histogram.

2. In the first session of her class, an introductory psychology instructor gives the students a true-false test of 40 common psychological misconceptions. A grouped frequency distribution for the resulting scores is shown below.

Class Interval	f	Class Interval	f
36–40	6	16–20	6
31–35	9	11–15	0
26–30	12	6–10	3
21–25	13	1–5	1
			N = 50

(a) Find the cumulative frequency and the cumulative percentage for each class interval in the distribution.

(b) Graph the cumulative frequencies against the class intervals to produce a cumulative frequency polygon. Then give an alternative labeling of the vertical Y axis, using cumulative percentages.

(c) The *percentile ranks* of three students are shown below. Using the cumulative polygon drawn for (b), estimate each of their raw scores (X). (*Note:* Your estimates will not necessarily be whole numbers.) Student A: 70, student B: 32, student C: 20.

3. A test of language comprehension was given to freshmen students in a public university open to anyone with a high school diploma (open university) and to students in an elite private university with high admission standards (elite university). The cumulative percentage curves for the two groups are shown in the figure below.

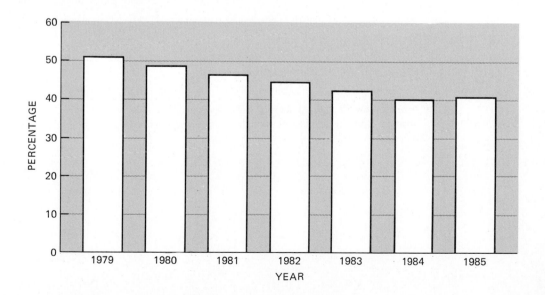

By inspecting the curves:

(a) Find the median for the open university.

(b) Find the median for the elite university.

(c) Find the 3rd quartile for the elite university.

(d) Find the 2nd decile for the open university.

(e) Mary White has a raw score of 60 and attends the open university. What is her percentile rank? What would be her percentile rank if she attended the elite university?

4. In a study of fear reduction procedures, on 10 successive days a man with a strong fear of snakes was asked to approach a glass cage containing a large but harmless snake as closely as he felt able. Shown below is the distance (in feet) from the cage at which he stopped on each day.

Day	Feet	Day	Feet
1	19	6	10
2	18	7	6
3	15	8	3
4	12	9	2
5	8	10	1

(a) Draw a line graph of these data.

(b) Describe the results of the fear reduction procedures.

5. In a particular private university, 38 percent of the students reside in the state in which the university is located, 45 percent come from other states, and 17 percent come from other countries than the United States. Draw a graph of these data.

6. From your general knowledge, sketch a frequency polygon for each set of data described below. Then describe the shape of the distribution by a label, such as symmetrical, negatively skewed, J-curve, and so on.

(a) Number of children in each of a large group of randomly selected U.S. married couples.

(b) Scores on an easy statistics exam.

(c) Number of drivers who speed up, do not change speed, momentarily slow down, or come to a full stop at a corner with a stop sign.

(d) The speed with which physically normal 10-year-old girls can run 100 yards.

(e) Attitudes toward legalized abortion on a 7-point scale (1 = strongly approve, 7 = strongly disapprove) among members of the audience attending a debate between pro- and anti-abortion groups.

4 Measures of Central Tendency

- ARITHMETIC MEAN
- MODE
- MEDIAN
- COMPARISON OF THE MEAN, MEDIAN, AND MODE

We have already seen how measures obtained from groups of individuals can be sorted to form frequency distributions that reveal group patterns and how to represent such distributions by graphing them. Typically, investigators are also interested in characterizing a group as a whole. They might have questions such as these: What is the typical beginning salary for graduates of engineering colleges? What is the average score on the Scholastic Aptitude Test for entering freshmen at a large state university, and how does it compare with the average score at an Ivy League university? What is the most popular size in men's hats?

Such questions ask for a single number that will best represent a whole distribution of measurements. This representative number will usually be near the center of a distribution, where the measures tend to be concentrated, rather than at either extreme, where, typically, only a few measures fall. From this fact comes the term *measure of central tendency*.

Although a number of measures of central tendency have been devised, we will be studying only three of them: the arithmetic mean ($\overline{X}$), the mode (Mo), and the median (Mdn). There is nothing magical about any of these measures of central tendency; each is simply a different method of determining a single representative number. As we shall see, the numbers resulting from each method usually do not agree exactly. The particular measure we compute in any instance depends on which one yields the number that best represents the fact we wish to convey. The specific situations in which each method is most appropriate will be discussed in a later section.

ARITHMETIC MEAN

Definition of the Mean

The *arithmetic mean*, popularly known as the *average*, is a measure with which most of you are already familiar. The arithmetic mean, or simply "the mean" for short, is typically represented by the symbol $\overline{X}$ (pronounced "X-bar") and is the result of the well-known procedure of adding up all the measures and dividing by the number of measures. Defining the term more formally, *the mean is equal to the sum of the measures divided by their number*. A much more compact way to express this verbal definition is by using symbols, a kind of mathematical shorthand, as shown in the formula below:

$$\overline{X} = \frac{\Sigma X}{N} \tag{4.1}$$

where $\quad \overline{X}$ = arithmetic mean

$\quad \Sigma$ = Greek capital letter sigma, meaning the "sum of" a series of measures

$\quad X$ = a raw score in a series of measures

$\quad \Sigma X$ = sum of all the measures

$\quad N$ = number of measures

Before proceeding with a discussion of the mean ($\overline{X}$), we will take time out to explain in more detail the meaning of the Greek capital letter sigma (Σ), one of the most frequently used symbols in statistics.

A Note about Summation. The presence of Σ in any formula indicates that a group of numbers is to be added or summed. Since for convenience we usually refer to any raw score in a frequency distribution as X, Σ X indicates the total obtained by adding together all the scores belonging to a distribution. Sometimes we deal with two frequency distributions—for example, scores made by business school and social science majors on a measure of political conservatism. To distinguish between the two distributions we might call one set X's (let us say, business majors) and the other Y's (the social science majors). If we wrote the symbols Σ Y, we would mean the sum of all the scores for the social science majors (the Y's). Or we might arbitrarily choose the symbol A, and then Σ A is the sum of all the A scores, whatever they happened to be, and so forth. In like manner Σf stands for the sum of all the frequencies in a frequency distribution. This sum, you should note, equals the total N in the distribution ($\Sigma f = N$).

In later chapters you will encounter such terms as ΣX^2, $(\Sigma X)^2$, ΣXY, and $\Sigma (X - \overline{X})^2$. It is important that you understand what these and other terms instruct you to do. We will use the data in Table 4.1 as an illustration of how to determine various terms (without regard to whether, in practice, these terms would be desirable to obtain for these specific data). The table shows for each of five students the days of school they missed last year because of illness (X) and their scores on a test of hypochondriasis (Y). We thus have a *pair* of scores for each student.

Consider the term ΣX^2. This instructs you to square each X score and then to sum these squares. In Table 4.1, ΣX^2 would thus be $9 + 36 + 64 + 25 + 49 = 183$. What about the term $(\Sigma X)^2$? This term involves a rule to which we should call your attention: *perform operations within parentheses first*. Following this rule, our initial step is to sum all the X's. Then we square this sum. In our example, $\Sigma X = 29$, so $(\Sigma X)^2 = (29)^2 = 841$. When you compare this value with the value of ΣX^2 we computed above, you can see that $(\Sigma X)^2$ *does not* yield the same value as ΣX^2. The two terms call for different operations and do not result in the same answer.

Next, what does the expression $\Sigma (X + Y)$ instruct you to do? Because the term X + Y is in parentheses, the first step is to add each X score to the Y score that is paired with it. Then all the X + Y scores are added together. This process is shown in Table 4.1. Another rule

Table 4.1 Number of Days Five Students Were Absent and Their Scores on a Test of Hypochondriasis

Person	Days Absent X	X²	Test Score Y	X + Y	XY
1	3	9	6	9	18
2	6	36	7	13	42
3	8	64	10	18	80
4	5	25	9	14	45
5	7	49	11	18	77
	$\Sigma X = 29$	$\Sigma X^2 = 183$	$\Sigma Y = 43$	$\Sigma (X + Y) = 72$	$\Sigma XY = 262$
	$\overline{X} = 5.8$		$\overline{Y} = 8.6$		

when pairs of numbers are to be added or subtracted from each other is that each of the terms in the parentheses can be multiplied by Σ. Thus:

$$\Sigma (X + Y) = \Sigma X + \Sigma Y$$

You can see in Table 4.1 that this is true. $\Sigma (X + Y) = 72$; $\Sigma X + \Sigma Y = 29 + 43 = 72$.

What about ΣXY? Here there are implied parentheses around XY. We are instructed to multiply each X by its corresponding Y and then to sum the products, as we have done in our illustrative table.

A formula we will encounter very shortly is $\Sigma (X - \overline{X})^2$. Here we must first determine the mean of the X scores, using Formula 4.1. In our example, $\overline{X} = 29/5 = 5.8$. Next we subtract the value of $\overline{X}$ from each X in the distribution and then square each of these differences. Lastly, we sum these squares. In our example, $(3 - 5.8)^2 + (6 - 5.8)^2 + (8 - 5.8)^2 + (5 - 5.8)^2 + (7 - 5.8)^2 = 14.8$.

One more rule is important for you to know:

$$\Sigma k = Nk$$

where k = a constant
 N = number of quantities to be summed

To understand this rule, remember that Σ indicates that N quantities in a distribution of N scores are to be added together. But a constant refers to a single value of some sort. Σk therefore means that the value of the constant (k) should be added N times. For example, if N = 3 and $k = 11$, then $\Sigma k = 11 + 11 + 11 = 33$. This sum can also be obtained by multiplying k by N, so $\Sigma k = Nk$.

The expression $\Sigma \overline{X}$ is an example of this rule. That is, in any distribution there is only one $\overline{X}$, so that in any given distribution the value of its $\overline{X}$ is a constant. To obtain $\Sigma \overline{X}$ for the data in Table 4.1, we multiply 5.8 by N: $\Sigma \overline{X} = N\overline{X} = 5 (5.8) = 29$.

When we define the mean as $\Sigma X/N$ we use X as a generalized expression for raw scores in any distribution of measures. But we sometimes deal with two (or more) distributions of scores and may use different letters to identify them. In Table 4.1, for example, we labeled the number of days students were absent as X and their scores on the measure of hypochondriasis as Y. We express the formula for the mean of the Y's as $\overline{Y} = \Sigma Y/N$. Thus $\overline{Y} = 43/5 = 8.6$.

In Chapter 5 you will encounter the formula $\Sigma x^2/N$, and in Chapter 10 you will find the formula $\Sigma z_X z_Y/N$. You do not yet know what x^2 and $z_X z_Y$ represent and it is not important at this point that you do. What *is* important for you to recognize is that each expression is a formula for a *mean*, the mean of the x^2's in one instance and the mean of the $z_X z_Y$'s in the other. Putting the matter abstractly, *the sum of a series of quantities divided by their number is always a mean, whatever the quantities happen to be.*

Alternative Definition of the Mean

Another definition or characteristic of the mean ($\overline{X}$) is important for us to state, since it contributes to an understanding both of $\overline{X}$ and of the concept of variability, a topic to be considered in Chapter 5. *The mean may be described as that point in a distribution of scores at which the algebraic*

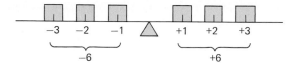

Figure 4.1 Representation of a balanced teeter-totter with "children" of equal weight placed at the distance indicated.

sum of the deviations from it (the sum of the differences of each score from $\overline{X}$) is zero. Or, expressed differently, $\overline{X}$ is a kind of "point of balance," where the sum of the deviations of the scores above $\overline{X}$ is equal in absolute value (without regard to plus or minus sign) to the sum of the deviations below $\overline{X}$. In order to clarify these statements, we will first introduce a kind of analogy.

Imagine that the horizontal line shown in Figure 4.1 is an old-fashioned teeter-totter. Suppose further that each square drawn in Figure 4.1 represents a child, each of equal weight, seated at the place indicated. We can see that the fulcrum has been placed at a point where the board balances. But why does the board balance at this particular point? First observe that we can give each child a "value" in terms of his distance from the fulcrum (-1, -2, -3, $+1$, $+2$, $+3$). These distances we will call deviations from the fulcrum. The absolute sum (that is, ignoring signs) of the deviations of the three children to the right of the fulcrum is the same as the absolute sum of the deviations of the children to its left; namely, 6 units. From painful experience, you know that the balance of the teeter-totter would be destroyed if a child were moved from one position to another, even on the same side—for example, from -1 to -3. When we disturb the values of the deviations so that their sums are not equal on both sides of the fulcrum, the balance is destroyed and the fulcrum must be moved to restore it.

Let us now relate this analogy to $\overline{X}$, which we have already said is a kind of point of balance. First, let us find $\overline{X}$ by the method of adding up the scores and dividing by N, as in the example given in Figure 4.2. Since there are 9 scores in Figure 4.2 and their sum is 450, $\overline{X}$ is 50. Next, let us find the deviation or distance each score is from $\overline{X}$. Each deviation is designated by the symbol x and is obtained by subtracting $\overline{X}$ from each score ($x = X - \overline{X}$). Obviously, scores with values greater than $\overline{X}$ will be plus deviations, those with lesser values will be minus deviations. If we now add the plus deviations, those above $\overline{X}$, and the minus deviations, those below it, as was done in Figure 4.2, we find that the absolute value of the two sums is equal;

Figure 4.2 Distribution of raw scores and deviations of these scores from $\overline{X}$, showing that the algebraic sum of the deviations is zero.

retaining signs, the two sums cancel each other so that the sum of the *total* deviations is zero ($\Sigma x = 0$).

Take as another example the numbers 5, 9, and 16. $\overline{X}$ of these numbers is 10, the sum of deviations below it is -6 [i.e., $(-5) + (-1)$] and above it $+6$; the algebraic sum of the deviations equals 0. Thus, in any distribution of scores, $\overline{X}$ is a "point of balance," comparable to the fulcrum in the teeter-totter example, in that the algebraic sum of the deviations of the scores above and below it (Σx) always equals zero.

A simple algebraic proof can also be given to demonstrate that $\Sigma x = 0$. Since $x = X - \overline{X}$, we can rewrite the statement to be proved as $\Sigma (X - \overline{X}) = 0$. As we explained earlier, we can also write:

$$\Sigma (X - \overline{X}) = \Sigma X - \Sigma \overline{X}$$

We also learned that $\Sigma k = Nk$. Since Σ directs us to add together N quantities and $\overline{X}$ is a constant, $\Sigma \overline{X}$ can be written as $N\overline{X}$. Thus:

$$\Sigma (X - \overline{X}) = \Sigma X - N\overline{X}$$

Substitute $\Sigma X/N$ for $\overline{X}$:

$$\Sigma (X - \overline{X}) = \Sigma X - N \left(\frac{\Sigma X}{N} \right)$$

Since the N's cancel:

$$\Sigma (X - \overline{X}) = \Sigma X - \Sigma X$$
$$= 0$$

We have thus proved, as intended, that Σx, the sum of the deviations from $\overline{X}$, is 0.

Methods of Computation

The basic formula that defines a statistical concept, such as that for $\overline{X}$, is usually relatively simple in appearance, but actually applying it to data often turns out to be long and tedious. To minimize effort, so-called computational formulas are usually derived from the basic one. These often look more difficult, as they involve more symbols, but are time-savers when any statistic is actually to be computed. In the following sections several computational formulas for $\overline{X}$ will be explained, in addition to the application of the basic one.

Computing $\overline{X}$ from Ungrouped Data. When $\overline{X}$ of ungrouped data is to be calculated, the basic definitional formula should be followed: the scores added and the result divided by the number of scores. An application of the basic formula is demonstrated in Table 4.2. This process is simple and should be followed if only a few scores are involved. If the number of measures is large, however, it may be prohibitively time-consuming. The use of frequency

Table 4.2 Calculation of $\overline{X}$ from Ungrouped Data

$$X$$

13
13
11
16
18
13
19
$\underline{15}$

$$\Sigma X = 118$$

$$\overline{X} = \frac{\Sigma X}{N} = \frac{118}{8} = 14.75$$

distributions, already found to be convenient for other purposes, will reduce our labor considerably in such instances.

Computing $\overline{X}$ from a Simple Frequency Distribution.   Suppose 70 children were given a perceptual judgment task to determine their susceptibility to optical illusion. The simple frequency distribution in Table 4.3 gives the number of errors these children made on the task. Note that most of the scores occur more than once. For example, two children made 9 errors and eight made 14. We could get ΣX by summing the 70 individual scores, duplicates and all—for example, adding two 9's, eight 14's. However, we could save time if we first multiplied

Table 4.3 Calculation of $\overline{X}$ from a Simple Frequency Distribution

X	f	f X	X	f	f X
28	2	56	16	4	64
27	1	27	15	5	75
26	1	26	14	8	112
25	0	0	13	6	78
24	0	0	12	5	60
23	3	69	11	3	33
22	1	22	10	3	30
21	2	42	9	2	18
20	3	60	8	3	24
19	5	95	7	1	7
18	6	108	6	0	0
17	4	68	5	2	10
				$\Sigma f = 70$	$\Sigma fX = 1084$

$$\overline{X} = \frac{\Sigma fX}{N} = \frac{1084}{70} = 15.49$$

each score by the number of individuals receiving it. Thus, 8×14 will result in the same answer as adding 14 eight times and give it to us quickly. If we then add all the products—each the result, you remember, of multiplying every X by its corresponding frequency, f—we will have the sum of all the X's with far less labor than if we had summed each raw score separately. The remaining step needed to obtain $\overline{X}$ is the usual one: dividing the sum of the scores by N.

We can express these operations symbolically by amending the basic formula for $\overline{X}$ to take account of the fact that we are now dealing with a frequency distribution. The amended formula is reproduced below and its application demonstrated in Table 4.3.

$$\overline{X} = \frac{\Sigma(fX)}{N} \tag{4.2}$$

where Σ = sum of the quantity that follows (here, all the fX's)

X = each score of different value (i.e., each value in the X column)

(fX) = a score multiplied by its corresponding frequency

N = total number of cases, equal to the sum of the frequencies (Σf)

The exact value of the mean cannot be computed from a grouped frequency distribution because the identity of individual scores is lost. However, there is a way to obtain a good approximation of the value of the mean from grouped data. Use Formula 4.2 but amend the definition of X to indicate the *midpoint* of each class interval. Therefore, each (fX) represents the midpoint of a class interval multiplied by the frequency of scores within the interval. Suppose, for example, that we had a grouped frequency distribution in which one of the class intervals was 81–83. The midpoint of the interval is 82. If 2 scores fell within the interval, then $(fX) = 2(82) = 164$. Summing the $(fX$'s) and dividing by N, the total number of cases or Σf yields a value for $\overline{X}$ that is very close to the actual value. However, there is no good reason to compute only an approximate value for $\overline{X}$ from a grouped distribution unless you are in a hurry or you do not have the raw scores. Assuming the original data are available, the use of a calculator or a computer makes it simple enough to go back to the raw scores and obtain their actual mean by summing them and dividing by N.

Population Means versus Sample Means

A population, you recall, consists of all the individuals having some specified characteristic in common, whereas a sample consists of a subset of individuals drawn from a given population. Technically speaking, the symbol $\overline{X}$ is used to refer to the mean of a sample. To distinguish the sample statistic, $\overline{X}$, from the population parameter, a different symbol is used to indicate the mean of a population. This symbol is the Greek lowercase letter μ (mu). The population μ is found in exactly the same way as $\overline{X}$; that is, it is calculated by adding all the scores together and dividing by their number. Thus:

$$\mu = \frac{\Sigma X}{N} \tag{4.3}$$

What is the relationship between the value of a population μ and the values of $\overline{X}$ for samples drawn from that population? To answer this question, suppose that each member of the population of 10,000 fifth-graders in a certain school district had been given an achievement test in mathematical reasoning and the mean score turned out to be 79.6. Now suppose that a random sample of 50 children was selected from the population and the sample mean ($\overline{X}$) was obtained. It is unlikely that $\overline{X}$ would be exactly 79.6—that is, that it would take exactly the same value as μ. However, it is quite probable that $\overline{X}$ would be close to 79.6.

Let us say that it turns out to be 78.9. We could continue to draw additional random samples of 50 cases, finding the $\overline{X}$ for each sample, until we had a very large number. We would also find that very few of these sample $\overline{X}$'s are exactly 79.6, the value of μ. These $\overline{X}$'s would also differ from each other. Some $\overline{X}$'s would be less than μ and some $\overline{X}$'s would be greater than μ, although most would be fairly close. This is illustrated in Figure 4.3. At the left we have shown the distribution of scores for the 10,000 members of the population; the mean of the population, we have said, is 79.6. At the right we have shown the $\overline{X}$'s for a series of 10 random samples, each of 50 cases, that we have drawn from the population. You can see that the values of the $\overline{X}$'s cluster around μ, some $\overline{X}$'s falling below μ and some falling above μ.

If we continued to draw additional random samples until we had measured a very large number of samples (technically, an infinite number), we would find that over the long run, the $\overline{X}$'s would fall equally above and below μ and also that the magnitudes of the differences between μ and these $\overline{X}$'s would be equal for the $\overline{X}$'s above and below μ. It follows that if we found the mean of the $\overline{X}$'s from a very large number of random samples from some population (which we would obtain by summing the $\overline{X}$'s and dividing by the number of samples), *the mean $\overline{X}$ would take the same value as the population mean (μ)*. We have shown this equality in Figure 4.3. (Note that we have shown the values of $\overline{X}$ for only the first 10 samples. The mean $\overline{X}$ is based on a much larger series of values.)

Figure 4.3 Population (N=10,000) with μ of 79.6 and $\overline{X}$'s of a series of random samples of 50 cases each drawn from the population.

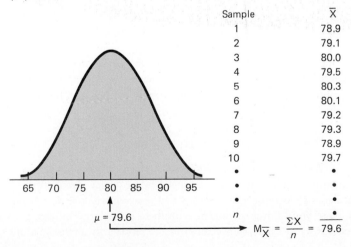

Sample	$\overline{X}$
1	78.9
2	79.1
3	80.0
4	79.5
5	80.3
6	80.1
7	79.2
8	79.3
9	78.9
10	79.7
•	•
•	•
•	•
n	•

$\mu = 79.6$

$$M_{\overline{X}} = \frac{\Sigma X}{n} = 79.6$$

Typically, we do not know the population μ and measure a sample in order to get an estimate of its value. Because we know that there is no systematic tendency for $\overline{X}$'s either to overestimate or underestimate μ, the mean of a random sample can be described as an *unbiased estimate of the population mean*. This implies that if only a single random sample is available, its mean is the best single guess that can be made about the value of an unknown population mean.

MODE

The mode (Mo) may be either computed or estimated roughly from inspection of the data. Estimation by inspection is the only method we will consider here.

In ungrouped data, the mode is defined as that score which occurs most frequently. For data grouped into class intervals, Mo is the midpoint of the interval with the greatest frequency. Thus in Table 4.3, showing a simple frequency distribution, the mode is 14, the score that occurred most frequently. In a grouped frequency distribution, the mode is the midpoint of the class interval with the greatest frequency.

When frequency distributions are plotted in the form of a frequency polygon, in most instances they turn out to have only a single hump, indicating only one point of maximum frequency or mode. These distributions, as we learned in Chapter 3, are called *unimodal*. Sometimes a frequency distribution will, like a camel, have two humps of approximately equal height, indicating two points of maximum frequency. These distributions are called *bimodal* and the peaks of both humps are identified as modes. It is more likely, however, that the peak frequency in one of the humps is not as great as in the other. Nonetheless we usually describe these distributions as bimodal to call attention to the fact that scores cluster around two points rather than only one. The value of the score occurring most frequently in the smaller hump can informally be described as a secondary mode.

MEDIAN

When scores are in the form of a frequency distribution, *the median may be defined as that score point at or below which 50 percent of the cases fall*. We have already encountered the median (Mdn) in our discussion of percentiles, as the median is just another label for the 50th percentile.

Computation of the Median and Other Percentiles

Computation from frequency distributions.   The standard procedures used to calculate the median and other percentiles from data arranged in frequency distributions involve an irksome set of calculations. As most analyses of actual research data are now being done by computer, we will spare you from involvement with these procedures. Instead, we will use a simpler method that is less exact but yields values that are satisfactory approximations for most purposes.

Table 4.4 Simple Frequency Distribution Used in Demonstrating Computation of Percentiles

X	f	cum f
95	2	80
94	5	78
93	8	73
92	11	65
91	17	54
90	14	37
89	8	23
88	7	15
87	0	8
86	3	8
85	3	5
84	2	2
	N = 80	

To illustrate the computation of the approximate value of the median, we will use the simple frequency distribution in Table 4.4. We have included a column showing the cumulative frequencies. Our first step is to determine how many of the total number of cases constitute the given percentage. In finding the median of the data in Table 4.4, we must therefore take 50 percent of N, which gives us 40 (80 × .50). The score point we want, then, is 40th from the bottom of the distribution. Going up the *cum f* column, we find that 37 cases earned scores of 90 or below, a number below the required 40. The 40th case is included among the 17 individuals who earned scores of 91 or below. The median, then, is approximately 91.

We can determine other percentiles in the same way. For example, in Table 4.4, what is the 25th percentile (which is the same as the first quartile or Q_1)? We want the score associated with the 20th case (25% of 80 = 20). Inspection of the *cum f* column shows that this score is 89.

One more example: What is the 10th percentile or first decile? Here we are interested in the 8th case (10% of 80). If you look at the *cum f* column in Table 4.4, you find that exactly 8 cases earned scores of 86 or below. But notice that no one earned a score of 87, so that it is equally true that 8 cases earned 87 or below. We defined a percentile as a *point* at or below which the given percent of cases fall. Which score value are we to pick? The most reasonable choice is to compromise and pick the midpoint of the two scores, 86 and 87. This gives us 86.5; the 10th percentile is 86.5.

When data have been arranged in a grouped frequency distribution, the identity of individual scores is lost, so the value of the median and other percentiles cannot be accurately determined. However, we can modify the procedures we just described to provide rough approximations of the value of any given percentile.

The first step, as before, is to find how many cases correspond to the median or any other percentile. We then locate the class interval in which this case is located. We give as our estimate of the percentile the *midpoint* of this class interval. If you look back at the table at the top of Figure 3.7 on page 38, for example, you will see that the median falls someplace in the class interval 75–77. The midpoint is 76, which we identify as the approximate value of the median.

Technically, this is the same method we used when determining the percentiles from simple frequency distributions. When the underlying property we are attempting to measure is continuous, each raw score represents an interval of values, e.g., the score 88 is the midpoint of the interval 87.5 to 88.5 and 89 is the midpoint of the interval 88.5 to 89.5.

Computation from Ungrouped Data.   An alternative definition of the median that is useful with ungrouped data specifies that the median is the middle score value in a set of measures arranged in numerical order. A parallel definition may be offered for any percentile by substituting the appropriate score position. With this method, scores are first ranked in order of magnitude. If the number of cases is odd, the position of the median is equal to the $(N + 1)/2$th position. The score in this position is the median. For example, in the set of five ordered numbers, 9, 11, 15, 16, and 18, $(N + 1)/2$ is equal to 3; the third score from the bottom is 15; 15 is the middle score or the median. If the number of cases is even, we count up to the cases that have the positions $N/2$ and $(N + 2)/2$ and find the average of these two scores. In the ordered set of six numbers, 3, 5, 6, 8, 12, and 13, we therefore count up to the third and fourth cases, finding the scores 6 and 8. The average of these two scores is 7, the median of the distribution.

This method of determining the median and other percentiles is not only convenient to use when data are ungrouped but also is more accurate than the method we described earlier for use with frequency distributions.

COMPARISON OF THE MEAN, MEDIAN, AND MODE

In any unimodal symmetrical distribution the values of $\overline{X}$, Mdn, and Mo are the same. This is true because the same point on the baseline occurs most frequently (Mo), divides the number of cases into the upper and lower 50 percent (Mdn), and is the point of balance ($\overline{X}$). As a curve departs from symmetry and becomes skewed, however, the values of the three measures of central tendency show differences. The relative positions of the three measures, however, will usually be the same for all single-peaked nonsymmetrical distributions, as shown in Figure 4.4. Mo in any skewed distribution occurs, of course, at the highest point of the curve. $\overline{X}$ falls someplace toward the "tail" of the distribution. This can be understood if you remember that $\overline{X}$ is a "point of balance" and is therefore very sensitive to the extreme deviations contained in the tail. Typically, in a skewed distribution the median, which divides the distribution into its upper and lower halves, is also drawn out toward the tail. The median is not drawn out as far as $\overline{X}$, which means that it lies between the $\overline{X}$ and Mo. Thus, the order of the three measures, when we start at the hump and proceed toward the tail, is (1) Mo, (2) Mdn, and (3) $\overline{X}$.

Because there is this relationship among the values of the three measures, we ordinarily can tell whether a distribution is skewed, and if so, the direction, merely by being told the

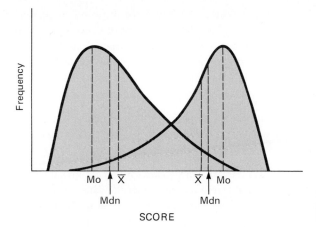

Figure 4.4 Relationship between $\overline{X}$, Mdn, and Mo in skewed distributions.

values of any two measures of central tendency. If we read that $\overline{X}$ of a distribution was 26 and that Mdn was also 26, we would infer that the distribution was probably symmetrical since in this case the measures coincide. But if we were told that $\overline{X}$ was 109 and Mo from the same distribution was 102, we would infer that the distribution was positively skewed. That is, since $\overline{X}$ always lies closest to the "tail" in a skewed distribution and in this case is greater than Mo, the tail is probably in the upper, positive end of the scale. The value of Mdn in this example could be roughly estimated—greater than 102 and less than 109—since Mdn always falls between $\overline{X}$ and Mo.

When to Use the $\overline{X}$, Mdn, or Mo

In deciding which measure of central tendency to compute, we must consider a number of factors, including how much time is available, the characteristics of the data involved, and the purpose for which the measure is intended. Some of these considerations are discussed below.

Stability of Measures. The three measures of central tendency differ with respect to their consistency or stability from sample to sample. That is, if we obtained a number of random samples from a population, the values of $\overline{X}$, as well as the values of Mdn and Mo, would vary from sample to sample. For example, we might test several samples of middle-aged businessmen to determine their cholesterol level. We would find that the mean was not the same for each group, nor was the Mdn or Mo. But we would discover that $\overline{X}$ showed less variability from sample to sample than the other two and that Mo was the least stable. That is, if we took a large number of samples from a large group and computed $\overline{X}$, Mdn, and Mo for each, we would find that the values of the $\overline{X}$'s differed less among themselves than the Mdn's and Mo's, whereas the Mo's varied the most. Since we frequently test small groups or samples in order to estimate the characteristics of the larger group or population to which the samples belong, stability is a desired virtue for a statistical measure. With respect to consistency, then, it should be remembered $\overline{X}$ is most satisfactory, Mo is least satisfactory.

Subsequent Manipulations of the Data. Of the three measures of central tendency, only $\overline{X}$ is a measure that is determined by the algebraic value of every score. This algebraic property makes $\overline{X}$ particularly useful in many further statistical operations that yield additional kinds of information about data. In contrast, once Mo and Mdn have been computed, little more can be done with them, especially Mo. Since information beyond a measure of central tendency usually is to be obtained from data, computation of $\overline{X}$ becomes almost obligatory.

Time Factors. A trivial but often practical consideration is the time taken to compute each measure. If a measure of central tendency is needed in a hurry, Mo can be rapidly obtained by inspection and would therefore be preferred over the other measures.

Characteristics of the Data. (1) *Skewed distributions*. When a distribution is markedly nonsymmetrical, it is possible to give a distorted impression of the data when reporting central tendency. Take, for example, a frequency distribution of incomes in the United States. Such a distribution is extremely skewed in a positive direction, incomes trailing off, in terms of frequency, from the modest modal point to a few fabulous incomes of millions of dollars each. The modal and median incomes will be much lower than $\overline{X}$, which is drawn far out toward the tail. It might be good capitalistic propaganda to give $\overline{X}$ as the "average income in the United States," but it would give an uninformed reader, who is likely to assume that this figure represents the most frequent income, or the income of the ordinary person, a very inflated view of our personal wealth. A Marxist, on the other hand, might select Mo to represent us, since this measure would have the smallest value. Neither way is completely honest, of course, and what is usually done in the case of extremely skewed distributions is to report all three measures. From these the reader can infer the direction and amount of skewness and interpret the data properly.

(2) *Some special cases*. In some instances, unusual characteristics of the data, other than skewness, dictate the measure of central tendency to use. A peculiarity that sometimes occurs is that one extreme of a distribution is not available for testing. For example, if we gave an intelligence test to a sample of schoolchildren in order to estimate the central tendency of IQ's of *all* children of similar age, the severely mentally retarded would not be represented in our sample, as these children are not in school.

In such a situation, computation of $\overline{X}$ would yield a distorted estimate of $\overline{X}$ for children in general, since this measure is highly sensitive to extreme deviations and these are missing at the lower end. Mo or Mdn would be more appropriate, since each would give a closer estimate of the value of central tendency that would have been obtained if the lower extremes had been available.

Occasionally, representative cases are available for testing, but exact scores cannot be obtained from cases falling in one or both extremes of the distribution. In experiments involving animals, for example, running time from one end of a path to the other may be used as a response measure. Often a few animals refuse to run and after sitting at the starting point for, say, five minutes are removed from the apparatus. Their exact running times are therefore unknown, since they might have run had they been left a second longer or they might have stayed there forever. Since $\overline{X}$ requires the exact value of every measure, it should not be computed. As long as exact values are available for more than half the animals, Mdn could be used, however, since an approximate score (five minutes plus) for the extreme cases is sufficient.

Many further examples of very special situations in which one measure is appropriate or inappropriate could be given. Instead, you will merely be reminded that every set of data should be examined to determine whether any specific problems exist and which measure of central tendency would be most appropriate.

Specific Purpose for Which Measure Is Intended. Sometimes a measure of central tendency is intended for some special use rather than as a purely scientific description of data. Such a purpose will often determine the measure to be employed, especially when a distribution is skewed so that the values of the $\overline{X}$, Mdn, and Mo disagree markedly. Occasionally, the "typical case" is wanted, thus calling for Mo. A furniture manufacturer, hoping to make money on volume of sales, might want to know the size of the typical living room, the modal dimensions, to design furniture scaled to suit the largest single consumer market. At other times, the "middle case" is desired, the median individual. Test grades are sometimes given on this basis, Mdn being the dividing line between B's and C's.

In summary, $\overline{X}$ is the most generally preferable measure of central tendency, particularly in a nearly symmetrical distribution, since it has the greatest stability and lends itself most to further statistical manipulations. Mdn is the middle case and is usually considered most appropriate when the distribution shows peculiarities: marked skewness, missing cases, and the like. Finally, Mo is utilized in situations in which a quick, rough estimate of central tendency is sufficient or the typical case is wanted. Although these are good general rules, remember that they are not exhaustive and that each set of data should be examined to see exactly which measure or measures are best in a specific situation or for a particular need.

Step-by-Step Procedures

We will illustrate how to determine the mode, mean, and median first from ungrouped data and then from a simple frequency distribution.

Ungrouped Data

To illustrate, we use the ordered set of 11 scores shown below.

$$2, 3, 4, 4, 5, 5, 5, 6, 7, 8, 10$$

Mean

The formula is $\overline{X} = \Sigma\, X/N$. The sum of the 11 numbers is 59. Thus:

$$\overline{X} = \frac{59}{11} = 5.36$$

Mode

The score of 5 occurs 3 times and all other scores occur fewer than 3 times. The mode is 5.

Median

A definition can be used that states that the median is the middle score value in an ordered set of measures.

1. When N is odd, the position of the middle case is determined by $(N + 1)/2$. In our example, $N = 11$ and $(11 + 1)/2 = 6$.
2. The sixth case from the bottom in our set of numbers has a value of 5. Thus the median is 5.

When N is an even number, the nth case is given by the average of the cases whose positions are $N/2$ and $(N + 2)/2$. In the following example, N is 6, an even number.

$$12, 14, 16, 18, 19, 24$$

$N/2$ gives us the third case and $(N + 2)/2$ gives us the fourth case. The scores associated with these positions are 16 and 18. The average of these two numbers, 17, is the median.

Simple Frequency Distribution

Computations will be based on the frequency distribution in Table 4.5.

Mode

Inspection of the f column shows that 9 individuals earned a score of 16. As this is the score that occurred most frequently, the mode is 16.

Table 4.5 Simple Frequency Distribution Used to Illustrate Computation of $\bar{X}$, Mdn, and Mo

X	f	f X	cum f
20	1	20	38
19	2	38	37
18	3	54	35
17	5	85	32
16	9	144	27
15	6	90	18
14	4	56	12
13	3	39	8
12	2	24	5
11	1	11	3
10	2	20	2
	$\Sigma f = 38$	$\Sigma f X = 581$	

Mean

The formula for computing $\overline{X}$ for a frequency distribution is:

$$\overline{X} = \frac{\Sigma f X}{N}$$

1. Multiply each X score by its corresponding frequency, as shown in Table 4.5.
2. Sum these fX products. In our example $\Sigma fX = 581$.
3. Divide ΣfX by N where N is the total number of cases:

$$\overline{X} = \frac{581}{38} = 15.29$$

Use of Calculator

Most calculators will permit you to obtain ΣfX in one operation by successive multiplication and addition. In the case of Table 4.5, you would enter $(20 \times 1) + (19 \times 2) + \cdots + (10 \times 2)$, which would yield the sum of 581. Check the instruction booklet that came with your calculator to see if it has the capacity to perform this operation and how to do it.

Median

Using the definition that the median is that point at or below which 50 percent of the cases fall, we can estimate the median.

1. Find 50 percent of N: $38 \times .5 = 19$. The median is the score of the 19th case from the bottom of the distribution.
2. Determine where the 19th case falls by consulting the *cum f* column. Inspection of Table 4.5 shows that the 19th case falls among the cases with a score of 16. The median is 16. ■

DEFINITIONS OF TERMS AND SYMBOLS

Measure of central tendency. A single number that is used to characterize an entire distribution of measures. Typically this number is at or near the center of the distribution. The mean, median, and mode are all measures of central tendency.

Mode (Mo). The score that occurs most frequently in a simple frequency distribution or the midpoint of the class interval with the greatest frequency in a grouped frequency distribution.

Median (Mdn). The median is the same as the 50th percentile and can be defined as that point in a distribution of scores at or below which 50 percent of the cases fall.

Arithmetic mean. The arithmetic mean (usually referred to simply as the mean) is obtained by summing all the measures in a distribution and dividing the result by the total number of measures. The arithmetic mean is also known as the average.

$\overline{X}$. A general expression for the mean of a sample of measures (X's) drawn from some population.

μ **(mu).** The mean of a population of measures.

Σ. The capital Greek letter sigma, meaning "the sum of." For example, Σ X is the sum of all the X's.

Deviation score (x). The difference between a score and the mean of the distribution to which the score belongs, obtained by subtracting the mean from the score. The algebraic sum of the deviation scores obtained from all scores in a distribution equals zero ($\Sigma x = 0$).

Percentile. See Chapter 3.

PROBLEMS

1. The subjects in an experiment were given two prose passages to study and after each of them were asked a series of questions about the content. The errors made by the eight subjects on each passage (labeled X and Y) are shown below. Describe what each of the following quantities represent and then find the value of each quantity for the data that are given. (a) Σ X; (b) $\overline{X}$; (c) Σ Y; (d) $\overline{Y}$; (e) $(\Sigma X)^2$; (f) ΣX^2; (g) Σx; (h) Σ XY.

Subject	X	Y	Subject	X	Y
A	4	5	E	9	8
B	1	2	F	2	2
C	7	6	G	6	5
D	4	3	H	3	1

2. A grouped frequency distribution, with N = 30, is shown below. Find the following statistics: (a) mode; (b) mean; (c) median.

Class Interval	f	Class Interval	f
21–23	3	9–11	6
18–20	2	6–8	4
15–17	5	3–5	0
12–14	7	0–2	3

3. In a random sample of 100 cases, $\overline{X}$ is calculated to be 63.4. What is your best single estimate of μ, the mean of the population from which the sample was drawn? That is, would you guess μ had the same value as $\overline{X}$, some value greater than $\overline{X}$, or some value less than $\overline{X}$? Why?

4. For ungrouped data, it is useful to define the median as the middle score value in an ordered set of numbers. Using this definition, find the median for each of the following: (a) 20, 12, 14, 10, 25, 18, 9; (b) 7, 32, 16, 25, 20, 12, 14, 24; (c) 125, 319, 238, 161, 148, 170.

5. The values of two measures of central tendency are given below for several distributions. For each distribution, estimate whether it is approximately symmetrical, negatively skewed, or positively skewed. (Assume each distribution is unimodal.) Sketch a figure showing what you expect each distribution looks like and where you expect *all three* measures of central tendency (mean, median, mode) would fall. (a) Mo = 50; $\overline{X}$ = 58; (b) Mdn = 71.4; $\overline{X}$ = 71.4; (c) Mdn = 104; $\overline{X}$ = 96.

6. Give a concrete example of data in which the (a) mean, (b) median, or (c) mode would be the most preferable measure of central tendency to report.

5

Variability

- THE NEED FOR AN INDEX
  OF VARIABILITY
- RANGE (R)
- SEMI-INTERQUARTILE RANGE
- AVERAGE DEVIATION
- STANDARD DEVIATION AND VARIANCE
- COMPUTATIONAL TECHNIQUES
- A CHECK ON CALCULATIONAL ERRORS:
  STANDARD DEVIATION AND THE RANGE

THE NEED FOR AN INDEX
OF VARIABILITY

When a group of individuals has been measured on some characteristic, it almost never happens that everyone has the same amount. In Chapter 4 we discussed several measures of central tendency, each designed to yield a representative number to describe a whole group of differing individuals. In describing a group it is useful not only to obtain a measure of central tendency but also to obtain a measure that reflects the *amount of variability* among the members of the group.

Consider the three distributions in Figure 5.1, representing three groups measured on the same characteristic. The distributions are all unimodal and symmetrical, are based on the same number of cases, and have the same mean—yet they are quite different.

Let us assume that the distributions represent the scholastic aptitude scores of freshmen at three different universities. At Apollo University some of the students look like budding geniuses, while others will probably have a tough time making it through the first semester. At Caligula University there are no such extremes; as a group the freshmen are much more alike in aptitude than those at Apollo. Bacchus University is in between; occasional freshmen are their professors' delight or despair, but most of them have a respectable, quite unexceptional degree of aptitude.

What terms might be used to describe the differences among the trio of distributions in Figure 5.1? We might say that the members of distribution C are more *homogeneous* than those in the other two distributions. Conversely, members of distribution A are more *heterogeneous* than those in the other distributions. We might also say that distribution A has a greater spread

Figure 5.1 Three hypothetical distributions, A, B, and C, differing in variability.

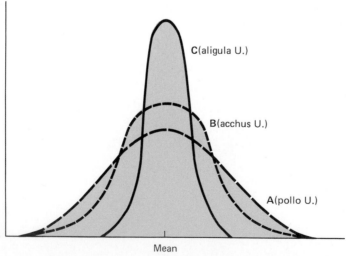

than the others—a greater scatter or dispersion or, most commonly, greater *variability*. Distribution C exhibits the least variability among the measures, and B an intermediate amount.

These examples illustrate that variability is an important characteristic of distributions. If we are to describe distributions adequately, we must include an expression that reflects the amount of variability. We shall discuss several statistics devised for this purpose.

RANGE (R)

As we learned in Chapter 2, *the range (R) is the "distance" from the lowest to the highest score in a distribution*. Or, highest score minus lowest score is R. If the lowest aptitude score in Bacchus U. is 400 and the highest 600, R is $600 - 400 = 200$.

As a measure of variability R has much the same status as Mo does as a measure of central tendency. It is useful primarily as a gross descriptive statistic, although, as we shall see later, it can form the basis for a quick and easy estimate of another statistic that requires considerable computation.

The most obvious difficulty with R as a measure of variability is that its value is wholly dependent upon the two extreme scores. This causes several problems. First, one or both of the extreme scores may be capricious, so that R will be equally capricious. This becomes quite evident when we are working with a small sample of measures, as we often do in psychological research. Suppose we had ten measures as follows: 11, 14, 14, 16, 19, 20, 21, 24, 26, 42. R is $42 - 11$, or 31. Now if we eliminate the tenth case, R becomes $26 - 11$, or 15. The elimination of one score halved the range. Of course, any measure of variability must represent changes in variability when these occur, but an ideal measure would not fluctuate so much as R does when a single score is eliminated, as in the case above.

Even if the two extreme scores are representative, there is another difficulty with R, which we may illustrate by comparing distributions A and B in Figure 5.1. Both distributions have the same R, but the bulk of the scores in distribution B cluster more closely together than those in distribution A. The R, besides being unstable, is insensitive to the shape of the distribution of the scores between the two extremes. For these reasons, R is thought of as only a rough index of variability.

SEMI-INTERQUARTILE RANGE

A measure of variability that overcomes some of the problems of the range is the *semi-interquartile range*. This measure is obtained by first calculating Q_1 and Q_3, which you recall are also the 25th and 75th percentiles. Subtracting Q_1 from Q_3 gives us the interquartile range, or the number of score units between which the middle 50 percent of the cases fall. The interquartile range is then divided by 2 to yield the semi-interquartile range. Thus:

$$\text{Semi-interquartile range} = \frac{Q_3 - Q_1}{2} \tag{5.1}$$

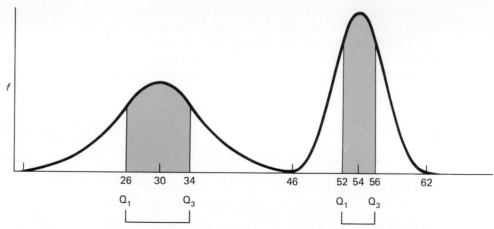

Figure 5.2 Interquartile ranges (Q_3-Q_1) for two distributions differing in variability. The shaded portions show the middle 50% of the cases.

Two distributions that differ markedly in variability are shown in Figure 5.2. The interquartile range, which encompasses the middle 50 percent of the cases, is marked off in each distribution. The value of the semi-quartile range for the distribution at the left is $(34 - 26)/2 = 4$ and for the distribution at the right it is $(59 - 55)/2 = 2$.

The semi-interquartile range is not a measure to which the exact values of all scores contribute, and for this reason its usefulness is limited. However, when the distribution of scores is extremely skewed, the semi-interquartile range is often employed as the measure of variability in conjunction with the median as the measure of central tendency.

AVERAGE DEVIATION

In Chapter 4 we discussed the deviation of raw scores from $\overline{X}$. For each raw score we can calculate a deviation score by subtracting the mean from the score ($X - \overline{X}$). Each of these deviations, you recall, is symbolized by x, so that $X - \overline{X} = x$. If all of the scores are closely clustered around the mean (if the distribution is quite homogeneous), then the raw scores deviate very little from the mean and the x's therefore are low in value. In a heterogeneous distribution in which scores are widely dispersed, on the other hand, the x's are more variable in value, since a number of scores lie far from the mean. Deviation scores, then, reflect the *variability* among a collection of raw scores. How might we capitalize on this fact to get a single number that will allow us to describe the amount of variability in a particular distribution?

We learned in Chapter 4 that the mean was a representative number used to characterize a distribution of measures of varying values. It might occur to you that we could find the mean of the x's to serve as a representative number to describe a distribution of x's. That is, add up all the deviations and divide this sum by the number of cases ($\Sigma x / N$). This is an excellent beginning, but the procedure suffers from a lethal embarrassment. The sum of the deviations from the mean, we discovered in Chapter 4, is *always* equal to zero—that is, the sums of the deviations above and below the mean are equal except for sign. Thus the mean of the deviations, $\Sigma x/N$, will also equal zero—hardly an informative figure. We could, however, disregard the signs of the deviations and treat the x's as absolute numbers. For example, for $\overline{X} = 10$, the x's of the raw scores 13 and 7 would each be treated as 3 rather than $+3$ and -3. We could then go ahead and compute the mean of these absolute x's. The resulting statistic has come to be known as the *average deviation*.

We have illustrated the computation of the average deviation in Table 5.1. (The computation of another measure of variability, to be discussed in the next section, is also illustrated in Table 5.1.) To determine the average deviation it is necessary to compute the $\overline{X}$ of the scores and then to find the deviation of each score from $\overline{X}$ ($x = X - \overline{X}$). The signs of these deviations are dropped to obtain absolute values, indicated by vertical lines ($|x|$). These absolute values are summed and the results divided by N ($\Sigma |x|/N$) to obtain the mean of the absolute deviations. This mean is the *average deviation* (AD), which in Table 5.1 was calculated to be 2.38. The average number of score units by which individuals deviated from $\overline{X}$ was 2.38.

Table 5.1 Computation of the Average Deviation and the Standard Deviation Using Deviation (x) Score Method

X	$x = (X - \overline{X})^*$	$|x|$	x^2
15	4.5	4.5	20.25
14	3.5	3.5	12.25
12	1.5	1.5	2.25
10	−.5	.5	.25
10	−.5	.5	.25
9	−1.5	1.5	2.25
8	−2.5	2.5	6.25
6	−4.5	4.5	20.25
$\Sigma X = 84$	$\Sigma x = 0.0$	$\Sigma |x| = 19.0$	$\Sigma x^2 = 64.00$

$$\overline{X} = \frac{\Sigma X}{N} = \frac{84}{8} = 10.5$$

$$AD = \frac{\Sigma |x|}{N} = \frac{19.0}{8} = 2.38$$

$$S = \sqrt{\frac{\Sigma x^2}{N}} = \sqrt{\frac{64.00}{8}} = \sqrt{8.00}$$

$$= 2.83$$

*In Table 5.1, X was not rounded. It may often be necessary or convenient to use a rounded figure for $\overline{X}$. For example, an $\overline{X}$ calculated to be 13.62358 might be reported as 13.62. If this rounded figure were used to obtain x's, slight errors would occur in each x and Σx would not be exactly zero. However, it would be very close to zero.

The average deviation provides a very satisfactory description of the amount of variability in a distribution of numbers. However, its further usefulness is limited because it is based on absolute deviations in which signs are ignored. For this reason, the average deviation is rarely used as a measure of variability. However, a few steps beyond the average deviation lead to a pair of statistics that are the preferred measures of variability, the *variance* and the *standard deviation*. These related measures represent statistical abstractions whose meaning is not easy to grasp. Our discussion of the average deviation was intended as a kind of introduction to these measures.

STANDARD DEVIATION AND VARIANCE

Like the average deviation, the variance and the standard deviation are based on the deviations of the scores in a distribution from $\overline{X}$. Unlike the average deviation, however, these measures do not ignore the signs of the deviations and therefore are algebraic.

In obtaining the variance and the standard deviation, the problem of having the plus and minus x's cancel each other is avoided by squaring each x, so that all the resulting numbers are *positive*. The squared deviations or x^2's are summed and then divided by N, thus giving the mean of the squared deviations. This mean is given a special name, the *variance*. In this section we discuss the variance of a sample of scores, which we will identify as S^2. To repeat, the *sample variance* or S^2 *is the mean of the squared deviations of the scores from* $\overline{X}$. Thus:

$$S^2 = \frac{\sum x^2}{N} = \frac{\sum (X - \overline{X})^2}{N} \tag{5.2}$$

The square root of the variance (S^2) is called the standard deviation, which is symbolized as S. The *standard deviation (S)* is thus defined as *the root of the mean squared deviation from* $\overline{X}$. Expressing this definition symbolically, we have:

$$S = \sqrt{\frac{\sum x^2}{N}} = \sqrt{\frac{\sum (X - \overline{X})^2}{N}} \tag{5.3}$$

The variance has a great deal of use in advanced statistical techniques and will be discussed in more detail in Chapter 12. Our primary emphasis until then will be on the standard deviation. An illustration of the procedures for obtaining the standard deviation is shown in Table 5.1. The deviations of each of the raw scores from $\overline{X}$ appear in the second column, as mentioned earlier, and the squares of these deviations appear in the fourth column. These squares are summed and divided by N to yield the mean of the squared deviations or the variance. In Table 5.1, the variance is $64/8 = 8$. The square root of the variance yields the standard deviation (S), which in Table 5.1 is 2.83. You will note in Table 5.1 that the average deviation (AD), whose calculation we explained earlier, is similar in value to the standard deviation, S. This is not surprising, as both are a kind of mean deviation of scores from $\overline{X}$.

Corrected Estimates of Population Variance and Standard Deviation

Recall from Chapter 4 that the symbol $\overline{X}$ is used to identify the mean of a sample of X's and the symbol μ is used to identify the mean of a population. You will also recall that $\overline{X}$'s of random samples are unbiased estimates of μ of the population from which the samples were taken. That is, in a series of random samples, $\overline{X}$'s are typically variable in value but are not systematically larger or smaller than μ. Any given $\overline{X}$ can thus be described as an unbiased estimate of μ.

We now consider the symbols used to designate the population variance and standard deviation and the relationships between these population parameters and the corresponding sample statistics. The population standard deviation is symbolized by σ, which is the Greek lowercase letter sigma. Similarly, the population variance is symbolized by σ^2 or sigma squared.

Unlike $\overline{X}$ as an estimate of μ, the sample S^2 and S are *biased estimates* of σ^2 and σ. More particularly, the S^2's and S's from a series of random samples tend to be *smaller* than the σ^2 and σ of the population to which they belong. That is, if we drew a large number of random samples from a population and found S^2 for each sample, we would find that some of the sample S^2's would be smaller than σ^2 and some would be larger than σ^2. However, there would be a greater number of S^2's whose values are less than σ^2 than S^2's whose values are more than σ^2. The same holds true for S's and σ's. This tendency of sample standard deviations and variances to be smaller than the values for the population from which the samples were selected implies that if we were to use S^2 or S from a single sample as our guess about an unknown σ^2 or σ, we would be likely to underestimate the population values. Furthermore, the amount by which sample values underestimate the population values of the variance and standard deviation tends to increase as sample N's decrease.

In explaining why the sample standard deviation and variance tend to be smaller than the population values, we will find it simpler to discuss the matter in terms of the variance. Let us consider first the components of the formula for the variance, namely Σx^2 and N. As the N of a sample increases, not only the denominator of the formula but also the numerator, Σx^2, increases. That is, as we add a case to N, we also have its x^2 to add to Σx^2. Of course, if these two components increased proportionately, the variance would remain constant. This is pretty close to what happens but not quite. As we select more and more cases, it becomes increasingly likely that extremely deviant scores will be included within our sample. For example, we would be more likely to find a man over seven feet tall—or a man well under five feet—in a group of 500 men than in a group of twenty. These extreme cases add more to Σx^2 than they do to N, simply because their deviations from the mean are bigger than those we have gotten for cases closer to the middle of the distribution. So we may expect some increase in the variance with increases in N. However, when N is relatively large to begin with, say 30 or 40 cases, we expect less change in the variance with increases in N than when it is small.

Since a sample is, by definition, smaller than the population from which it was obtained, we can now see why a sample variance tends to be smaller than the variance of its population. To obtain an unbiased estimate of the population variance from sample data, we include a *correction factor* in the basic formula for the variance by dividing the Σx^2 obtained from our sample by N − 1 rather than by N. It is customary to use the symbol s^2 to indicate an unbiased estimate of a population variance from the data of a sample.* Thus:

$$s^2 = \frac{\sum x^2}{N - 1} \qquad (5.4)$$

where, just as before, N is the number of cases in the sample and $\sum x^2$ is the sum of the squared deviations of the scores from the sample mean.

Since we lower the value of the denominator by subtracting one from the sample N, you can see that s^2, our estimate of the unknown population variance, will always be slightly larger than the variance of the sample. Further, the difference between s^2 and S^2 will be greater in samples with small N's than with large ones. This is as it should be, since the degree to which a sample variance underestimates the population variance is inversely related to sample size, so that a greater correction is required when small samples are used to estimate population variances than when large ones are used.

In order to obtain an estimate of the population σ from sample data, we simply find the square root of s^2. Thus, the preferred formula for estimating the population σ from a sample is:

$$s = \sqrt{\frac{\sum x^2}{N - 1}} = \sqrt{\frac{\sum (X - \bar{X})^2}{N - 1}} \qquad (5.5)$$

Formula 5.4 for s^2 yields a completely unbiased estimate of the population σ^2. For a rather technical mathematical reason, Formula 5.5 for s does not yield a completely unbiased estimate of the population σ. The degree of bias that remains, however, is small.

The procedure of using sample data to obtain a single estimate (or point) of the value of a population parameter, in this instance σ^2 and σ, is technically known as *point estimation*. We also call your attention to another technical concept called *degrees of freedom*, symbolized as *df*. The expression N − 1 in the denominators of the equations for s^2 and s is equivalent to the number of degrees of freedom (*df*) associated with the sample. The denominator of the equation for estimating the population variance can thus be written as *df* instead of N − 1, so that $s^2 = \sum x^2/df$. Since degrees of freedom are frequently used in the process of making inferences about population parameters, we digress at this point to explain the concept further.

---

*Statisticians are inconsistent in the symbols they use to designate the sample standard deviation and variance and the corrected estimates of the population standard deviation and variance based on sample data. In accord with the majority of advanced statistical texts, and of a committee appointed to make recommendations about statistical symbols (M. Halpern, H. O. Hartley, and P. G. Hoel. Recommended standards for statistical symbols and notations, *American Statistician*, June 1965, 12–14), we have elected to use the symbols s and s^2 to refer to the *corrected estimates* of the population σ and σ^2, in which N − 1 is used in the denominator of the definitional formulas. We have chosen the symbols S and S^2 to indicate the uncorrected *sample* values. Students who read other statistics texts should be warned to note the particular system of symbols the authors have adopted.

Degrees of Freedom

The number of values that are free to vary in a distribution, once certain requirements are placed upon the series of quantities, is known as degrees of freedom. To illustrate, assume a distribution of five numbers, 17, 18, 19, 22, and 24. The $\overline{X}$ of these numbers is 20. Assume that this value of 20 is definitely true. How many of the original set of five numbers can be changed and still meet the requirement that $\overline{X} = 20$? This question can be answered most simply by first noting that if $\overline{X}$ is to be equal to 20, the sum of the five numbers must equal 100. Suppose we change the first four numbers to 10, 15, 16, and 21. Their sum is 62. If ΣX is to be 100 and $\overline{X}$ is to be 20, as before, then the fifth number must be 38. Or suppose that we have three numbers whose $\overline{X}$ is 10. Pick any two numbers, let us say 14 and 31, and the third is fixed. In this instance it must be -15 so that $\Sigma X = 14 + 31 - 15 = 30$ and $\overline{X} = 10$. As these examples illustrate, after the mean is known we are free to vary the values of all but one score in a distribution and still obtain the specified mean. The degrees of freedom (df) in a single distribution of numbers after the mean is known is therefore $N - 1$.

A Brief Review of the Measures

By this time you may be confused by the various kinds of standard deviations we have discussed and the different symbols we have used to refer to them. As you become experienced with problems involving samples and populations, the distinctions among them should become quite clear. We can at least try to hasten the process by stating once more the three kinds of measures we have presented and the formulas for each:

A. Standard deviation of a *population* of measures (σ):

$$\sigma = \sqrt{\frac{\Sigma x^2}{N}} = \sqrt{\frac{\Sigma (X - \mu)^2}{N}} \tag{5.6}$$

where μ is the population mean and N is the number of cases in the population.

B. Standard deviation of a *sample* of measures from some population (S):

$$S = \sqrt{\frac{\Sigma x^2}{N}} = \sqrt{\frac{\Sigma (X - \overline{X})^2}{N}} \tag{5.3}$$

where $\overline{X}$ is the sample mean and N is the number of cases in the sample.

C. *Estimate* of an unknown population σ from the data of a sample (s):

$$s = \sqrt{\frac{\Sigma x^2}{N - 1}} = \sqrt{\frac{\Sigma (X - \overline{X})^2}{N - 1}} \tag{5.5}$$

where -1 in the denominator is a correction of the sample S for underestimation of the population σ.

We return now to a consideration of the standard deviation as a purely descriptive index of the amount of variability among a group of individuals whom we have actually measured. For convenience, we will assume in our discussion that we are dealing only with *samples* from some population.

COMPUTATIONAL TECHNIQUES

Computation of *S* from Raw Scores

The use of deviation scores (x) is fairly tedious and, because decimals usually result when $\overline{X}$ is subtracted from X to obtain x, inaccuracies due to rounding and calculational errors are likely to creep in. Instead of using the deviation method of computing the standard deviation, it is more convenient to use what is commonly called a raw-score formula. This is a formula that involves only the original scores (X's) rather than deviation scores (x's). Several raw score formulas can be derived from the definitional formula ($\Sigma x^2/N$). Versions you may find convenient to use are shown below. These formulas may also be used to compute σ.

$$S \text{ (or } \sigma) = \sqrt{\frac{\Sigma X^2}{N} - \overline{X}^2} = \sqrt{\frac{\Sigma X^2}{N} - \left(\frac{\Sigma X}{N}\right)^2} \qquad (5.7)$$

$$S \text{ (or } \sigma) = \sqrt{\frac{\Sigma X^2 - (\Sigma X)^2/N}{N}} \qquad (5.8)$$

Origin of Raw-score Formulas.   It will be worthwhile to see how Formulas 5.7 and 5.8 came about. Knowing this, you will have at least one set of raw-score formulas you need not take on faith and you will get a little understanding of the derivation of formulas. We start, of course, with the basic formula:

$$S = \sqrt{\frac{\Sigma x^2}{N}}$$

The first step is to square both sides of the equation, obtaining the variance $S^2 = \Sigma x^2/N$. We know that $x = X - \overline{X}$, so we substitute this to get:

$$S^2 = \frac{\Sigma (X - \overline{X})^2}{N}$$

Now, to expand the term, by squaring $X - \overline{X}$:

$$S^2 = \frac{\Sigma (X^2 - 2\overline{X} X + \overline{X}^2)}{N}$$

Placing the summation sign and N with each term gives:

$$S^2 = \frac{\Sigma X^2}{N} - \frac{2\bar{X}\,\Sigma X}{N} + \frac{\Sigma \bar{X}^2}{N}$$

Looking at the second term on the right-hand side, we see that a portion of it is $\Sigma X/N$, which we know equals $\bar{X}$. So, substituting $\bar{X}$ for $\Sigma X/N$, we get:

$$S^2 = \frac{\Sigma X^2}{N} - 2(\bar{X})(\bar{X}) + \frac{\Sigma \bar{X}^2}{N}$$

which reduces to:

$$S^2 = \frac{\Sigma X^2}{N} - 2\bar{X}^2 + \frac{\Sigma \bar{X}^2}{N}$$

Now, look at the numerator in the last term, $\Sigma \bar{X}^2/N$. We know that Σ means summation from the first to the last score in a distribution, the sum of N *scores*. Thus $\Sigma \bar{X}^2$ says that we should sum $\bar{X}^2$ together N times, so the last term may be rewritten $N\bar{X}^2/N$. If these N's are canceled, we have:

$$S^2 = \frac{\Sigma X^2}{N} - 2\bar{X}^2 + \bar{X}^2$$

and then, $-2\bar{X}^2 + \bar{X}^2 = -\bar{X}^2$, so the variance is given by:

$$S^2 = \frac{\Sigma X^2}{N} - \bar{X}^2$$

This can also be written as:

$$S^2 = \frac{\Sigma X^2}{N} - \left(\frac{\Sigma X}{N}\right)^2$$

Taking the square root of both sides produces the formulas for raw-score calculation of the standard deviation (S or σ) shown in Formula 5.7:

$$S = \sqrt{\frac{\Sigma X^2}{N} - \bar{X}^2} = \sqrt{\frac{\Sigma X^2}{N} - \left(\frac{\Sigma X}{N}\right)^2}$$

Several additional steps bring us to Formula 5.8, which in some circumstances you may find more convenient to use than Formula 5.7.

$$S^2 = \frac{\sum X^2}{N} - \left(\frac{\sum X}{N}\right)^2 = \frac{\sum X^2}{N} - \frac{(\sum X)^2}{N^2}$$

$$= \frac{\sum X^2}{N} - \frac{(\sum X)^2/N}{N}$$

$$= \frac{\sum X^2 - (\sum X)^2/N}{N}$$

Taking the square root of this formula yields the standard deviation:

$$S = \sqrt{\frac{\sum X^2 - (\sum X)^2/N}{N}}$$

Our final step is to demonstrate numerically that these raw-score formulas are the equivalent of the basic formula, $\sum x^2/N$. In Table 5.2 we have used Formulas 5.7 and 5.8 to compute S for the data shown in Table 5.1. You can see that the value of S determined by each of the raw-score formulas is the same (2.83) as we found by the deviation method in Table 5.1.

Computation of s from Raw Scores

You will recall that sample S's tend to underestimate the population sigma. Remember also that to get a less biased estimate of σ from sample data, we added a correction, -1, to the denominator of the formula for the standard deviation: $\sum x^2/(N - 1)$. This formula (shown earlier as Formula 5.5) gives us s, the corrected estimate of σ.

It is also possible to use a raw score formula to determine s. We simply modify Formula 5.8 by adding the correction, -1, to the denominator. This gives us:

$$s = \sqrt{\frac{\sum X^2 - (\sum X)^2/N}{N - 1}} \tag{5.9}$$

The application of this formula may be illustrated by the data of Table 5.2, in which $\sum X$ and $\sum X^2$ have already been determined. Entering these values into the equation, we have:

$$s = \sqrt{\frac{946 - (84)^2/8}{8 - 1}} = \sqrt{\frac{946 - 882}{7}} = \sqrt{9.14} = 3.02$$

Since the formula for s corrects for the fact that the S of a sample tends to underestimate the population sigma, the estimate of the population value we just obtained is, as expected, somewhat higher than the standard deviation of the sample found in Table 5.2 (3.02 versus 2.83).

Table 5.2 Calculation of the Standard Deviation by the Raw-Score Method*

X	X²
15	225
14	196
12	144
10	100
10	100
9	81
8	64
6	36
$\Sigma X = 84$	$\Sigma X^2 = 946$

$$\overline{X} = \frac{84}{8} = 10.5$$

$$S = \sqrt{\frac{\Sigma X^2}{N} - \left(\frac{\Sigma X}{N}\right)^2} = \sqrt{\frac{946}{8} - \left(\frac{84}{8}\right)^2}$$

$$= \sqrt{118.25 - 110.25} = \sqrt{8} = 2.83$$

OR

$$S = \sqrt{\frac{\Sigma X^2 - (\Sigma X)^2/N}{N}} = \sqrt{\frac{946 - (84)^2/8}{8}}$$

$$= \sqrt{\frac{946 - 882}{8}}$$

$$= \sqrt{\frac{64}{8}} = \sqrt{8} = 2.83$$

*The raw scores are the same as in Table 5-1.

Raw-score Formulas for Frequency Distributions

When you have arranged data in the form of a simple frequency distribution, you may find it convenient to compute S and s (as well as $\overline{X}$) from the frequency distribution rather than going back to the original raw scores. Modifications of the raw score formulas we just discussed can be used for this purpose. For S, either of the raw-score formulas can be used.

$$S = \sqrt{\frac{\Sigma fX^2}{N} - \left(\frac{\Sigma fX}{N}\right)^2} = \sqrt{\frac{\Sigma fX^2 - (\Sigma fX)^2/N}{N}} \tag{5.10}$$

where X is the value of each different score from highest to lowest.

For s, the formula is:

$$s = \sqrt{\frac{\sum fX^2 - (\sum fX)^2/N}{N - 1}} \qquad (5.11)$$

An illustration of the application of Formula 5.11 for s is worked out in Table 5.3. N is obtained by summing the frequencies. After multiplying each X by its corresponding f, we sum the fX's and enter the results in the formula. Our next task is to determine $\sum fX^2$. To do this, we first multiply each X by its corresponding fX since $(X)(fX)$ is equivalent to $(f)(X)(X)$ or fX^2. We sum these quantities to get $\sum fX^2$, which is then substituted directly into the formula. Carrying out the calculations, we find that s is 1.72.

Because the identity of individual scores is lost, S and s cannot be computed accurately from frequency distributions in which scores have been grouped into class intervals. To compute S and s, you should use the original raw scores. These may either be ungrouped or be arranged in a simple frequency distribution. However, if you have a grouped frequency distribution

Table 5.3 Calculation of S and s by Raw-score Method with Simple Frequency Distribution

X	f	f X	f X²
24	1	24	576
23	3	69	1587
22	5	110	2420
21	7	147	3087
20	8	160	3200
19	4	76	1444
18	2	36	648
17	2	34	578
	$\sum f = 32$	$\sum fX = 656$	$\sum fX^2 = 13540$

$$S = \sqrt{\frac{\sum fX^2 - (\sum fX)^2/N}{N}} \qquad\qquad s = \sqrt{\frac{\sum fX^2 - (\sum fX)^2/N}{N - 1}}$$

$$= \sqrt{\frac{13540 - (656)^2/32}{32}} \qquad\qquad = \sqrt{\frac{13540 - (656)^2/32}{32 - 1}}$$

$$= \sqrt{\frac{13540 - 13448}{32}} \qquad\qquad = \sqrt{\frac{13540 - 13448}{31}}$$

$$= \sqrt{\frac{92}{32}} = \sqrt{2.88} = 1.70 \qquad\qquad = \sqrt{\frac{92}{31}} = \sqrt{2.97} = 1.72$$

available but you do not have access to the original raw scores or you are in a hurry, you can use Formulas 5.10 and 5.11 to determine approximate values of S and s. When applied to a grouped frequency distribution, X in the formulas becomes the value of the *midpoint* of each interval. The results will usually be quite close to the actual values of S and s.

The Use of S Versus s.   We have mentioned in previous chapters that the aim of scientific research is to understand something about populations of individuals, real or hypothetical. As it is almost always impractical or impossible to test entire populations, we instead test samples of individuals and make inferences about population characteristics based on sample data. For this reason, we usually report s rather than S (that is, our corrected estimate of the population standard deviation rather than the sample standard deviation) in describing our research findings. The statistical analyses that we will present in later chapters also employ s rather than S. We will therefore refer to s rather than S in further discussion of the standard deviation and its uses.

z Scores

You now know what the standard deviation is: the square root of the mean of the squared deviations of the scores from $\overline{X}$. The standard deviation is thus a rather special kind of "average," telling us the "average" number of *score units* by which individuals deviate from the mean. You have also learned that you may use calculational formulas to find the value of the standard deviation that involve only raw scores and thus avoid the inconvenience of finding deviation scores (x's).

Once we have calculated the standard deviation of the distribution, is there any way we can picture or visualize it? Can we find any additional use for the standard deviation besides describing a distribution's variability? Again, we will work up to the answers slowly.

The distribution of final exam scores in a large biology class turns out to have a mean of 65 and s of 10. Thus, the "average" amount by which individuals deviate from $\overline{X}$ is 10 points. Lou has a score of 85. Is that good or bad? We see that Lou's score is 20 points above the mean ($x = 85 - 65 = 20$); Lou deviates from the mean twice as much as the "average" individual. With a score of 85, Lou did quite well indeed. How about Pat with a score of 67? Pat's performance was middling, slightly above the mean but deviating from it by only 2 points ($x = 67 - 65 = 2$). This deviation is far less than an "average" amount—to be precise, only $\frac{2}{10}$ of an average amount. Finally, what about Bill, with a score of 35? We can only conclude that Bill bombed biology. With a score of 30 points below the mean, three times worse than the "average" deviation, Bill's performance was obviously abysmal.

What we have done in each of these examples is to use the standard deviation as a kind of measuring unit, translating each raw score into a "standard deviation score." Lou, with a raw score of 85, had a standard deviation score exactly 2 units above the mean (a deviation of 20 points from the mean is twice the s of 10). Bill, with a raw score of 35 and x of 30 ($x = 65 - 35$), scored 3 standard deviation units below the mean. Pat's score of 67 fell $\frac{2}{10}$ of a standard deviation unit above the mean of 65. We could, of course, take *any* raw score from the distribution and express its position in standard deviation units. What we have created, then, is an alternative to the raw-score scale, using the standard deviation as the unit of measurement instead of the raw score.

This is not our first discussion of an alternative to the raw-score scale. In previous chapters we discussed using percentiles for this purpose and methods for translating raw scores (points on the raw-score scale) to percentiles (points on the percentile scale) and back again. We can also formally describe a method that permits us to go back and forth between the raw-score scale and the standard deviation scale. Before doing so, let us see how this scale can be pictured and how to lay one out.

Figure 5.3 shows a distribution whose mean has been calculated to be 25 and whose s is 5. As usual, the baseline of the polygon shows raw scores; that is, the baseline represents a *scale*, divided into steps that have a width of one raw-score unit. Below the raw-score scale we have placed a scale whose steps have a width of *one standard deviation unit*. Exactly how wide is this unit? It is, of course, as wide as s has been calculated to be for a given distribution. In Figure 5.3, in which s is 5, one standard deviation unit is therefore 5 raw-score units wide. (This is comparable to saying that a foot is 12 inches wide.)

The standard deviation scale is also known as the z scale and the scores on it as z scores. In marking off the z scale, we start at the *mean* of the distribution and work in both directions. The distribution in Figure 5.3 has a mean of 25, so we start at the point that is equivalent to 25 on the raw-score scale. As we will demonstrate shortly, the mean of a set of z scores is always 0, so this point on the z score scale has a value of 0. (This may be obvious to you if you remember that a raw score that falls exactly at $\overline{X}$ deviates 0 score units from $\overline{X}$; in this example, $x = X - \overline{X} = 25 - 25 = 0$; x^2, of course, is also 0.) The s has been calculated to

Figure 5.3 Raw-score scale and standard deviation or z-score scale for a distribution in which $\overline{X} = 25$ and $s = 5$.

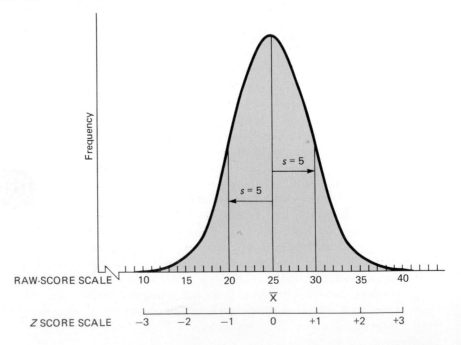

be 5 score units. In laying off the upper portion of the scale, we therefore go up from the mean to a point that is equivalent to 5 units on the raw-score scale. The distance between the mean and this point is one standard deviation unit, and the point has a value, in z units, of +1. Going up the scale the equivalent of 5 more raw-score units brings us to a z score of +2, and another 5 units to +3. The raw-score equivalents of these three z scores, we can see, are 30 ($\overline{X} + s = 25 + 5$), 35 ($\overline{X} + 2s = 25 + 10$), and 40 ($\overline{X} + 3s = 25 + 15$).

Notice in Figure 5.3 that almost all the cases that lie above $\overline{X}$ fall between the $\overline{X}$ and a z score of +3. Assuming that the total N is large, this is typically true of all symmetrical bell-shaped distributions, such as the idealized curve shown in the figure. Thus, at least when N is some finite number, approximately three standard deviations will cover all or almost all the distance between $\overline{X}$ and the highest score in the distribution.

We use the same procedure to mark off a succession of standard deviation widths below $\overline{X}$. Going 5 raw-score units below $\overline{X}$ brings us to a z score of −1, 10 units to a z score of −2, and 15 units to −3. Since the distribution is symmetrical, we are not surprised to find that three standard deviations also cover the distance between $\overline{X}$ and the lowest raw score in this sample of measures.

We are now aware that the standard deviation is a unit of width that is some multiple of the raw-score width. For any given distribution, the standard deviation is a calculable value of fixed size, but it may vary from one distribution to another. Now, we are accustomed to think of our measuring scales for linear dimensions such as width to be fixed and unalterable. A yard is a yard and a meter is a meter, and neither varies in size. In the case of the standard deviation as a width measure, however, we must change this conception. To repeat, the standard deviation is a given value for a specific distribution, but may vary from distribution to distribution.

Finding z from X

We are now ready to discuss the procedures we use to translate back and forth between the scales, finding the z-score equivalent of raw scores and vice versa. Take first a simple and familiar example: If we want to translate feet into yards, we divide the number of feet by 3. If we want to change ounces to pounds, we divide the number of ounces by 16. In the same fashion, if we want to change a raw score into a z score, we find the distance that score is from $\overline{X}$ and divide it by the standard deviation. In Figure 5.2, for example, where $\overline{X} = 25$ and $s = 5$, what is the z-score equivalent of a raw score of 28? This score lies 3 raw-score units above $\overline{X}$ (28 − 25 = +3); dividing this distance by the s of 5 gives us a z score of +.60. If we put these steps into equation form, we have:

$$z = \frac{X - \overline{X}}{s} \qquad (5.12)$$

But, since $X - \overline{X}$ is the definition of x, we can also write the formula as:

$$z = \frac{x}{s}$$

Let's work out a few examples from a distribution with a mean of 42 and *s* of 8. For a raw score of 54:

$$z = \frac{X - \overline{X}}{s} = \frac{54 - 42}{8} = \frac{12}{8} = +1.5$$

If the raw score is below $\overline{X}$, the z score takes a minus value. For example, in the same distribution, what is the z score of a raw score of 36?

$$z = \frac{36 - 42}{8} = \frac{-6}{8} = -.75$$

Finding X from z

We have just seen how to translate a raw score into a z score. We can reverse this procedure, so that if we know a z score we can obtain a raw score. We could use exactly the same formula as before and solve for an unknown raw score. However, it is more convenient to rearrange the formula so that the raw score X becomes the unknown on the left-hand side of the equation. This formula is:

$$X = \overline{X} + z(s) \tag{5.13}$$

For example, with $\overline{X} = 42$ and $s = 8$, what is the raw-score equivalent of a z score of -1.5? Applying Formula 5.13, we find:

$$X = 42 + (-1.5)(8) = 42 - 12$$
$$= 30$$

We do not change raw-score distances into z scores and back again merely to get practice in arithmetic. These z scores have very definite uses. For example, the need sometimes arises to compare the same persons with themselves in two different distributions of scores. If a group of people take a test of clerical aptitude and a test of mechanical aptitude, we might want to know the relative standing of an individual on both tests. If both tests have the same $\overline{X}$ and s, and the distributions are similar in shape, the raw scores can be compared directly. This would be a rare case. More likely, the two distributions will have different $\overline{X}$'s and s's. Thus, a particular raw score on one test will probably mean something quite different from the same raw score on another.

One satisfactory way of comparing an individual across distributions is by comparing ranks. This, in effect, is what a percentile rank is. If a person has a percentile rank of 78 on one test and of 62 on the other, we know the person has done better on the first test than on the second. We may use z scores for this same purpose of comparing two scores in distributions in which the $\overline{X}$'s and s's are different. Suppose that a group is given the mechanical and clerical aptitude tests as suggested above, with the following result:

Test	$\overline{X}$	s
Mechanical	100	10
Clerical	60	6

A man gets a raw score of 69 on the clerical test and 75 on the mechanical test. His z score for the former is:

$$z = \frac{x}{s} = \frac{9}{6} = +1.5$$

and for the latter:

$$z = \frac{-25}{10} = -2.5$$

He is much worse on the mechanical aptitude test than on the clerical test, even though his raw score is higher for the mechanical test. That is, his z score on the mechanical test is nearly at the bottom of the distribution, whereas it is considerably above $\overline{X}$ on the clerical test. The pattern of aptitude shown by this individual suggests that he might do well in a job requiring clerical skills but ought to leave anything mechanical to other people.

Properties of z Scores. It is useful to know certain properties of a set of z scores. First, the *mean of a set of z scores is always zero*. This relationship is expressed as

$$\bar{z} = \frac{\Sigma z}{N} = 0 \tag{5.14}$$

This relationship can be verified by considering the z score formula: $z = (X - \overline{X})/s$. When X takes the same value as $\overline{X}$, this equation can be rewritten: $z = (\overline{X} - \overline{X})/s$. Since the numerator is 0, it follows that the z of a score that falls at $\overline{X}$ is 0. This in turn implies that the mean of the z scores is zero.

The second property concerns the variance and standard deviation of a set of z scores. *The value of the variance and the standard deviation of a set of z scores is always one.* Thus:

$$s_z^2 = s_z = 1 \tag{5.15}$$

This value can be demonstrated mathematically by first rewriting the general formula for s^2, $\Sigma (X - \overline{X})^2/(N - 1)$, to indicate that we are now dealing with z scores: $\Sigma (z - \bar{z})^2/$

(N − 1). Since $\bar{z} = 0$, this reduces to $\Sigma z^2/(N − 1)$. It can be demonstrated by a proof we will not show here that Σz^2 is equal to $N − 1$. Thus:

$$s_z^2 = \frac{\Sigma z^2}{N − 1} = \frac{N − 1}{N − 1} = 1$$

and

$$s_z = \sqrt{1} = 1$$

To restate these properties, the mean of a set of z scores is always equal to 0, and the standard deviation and variance are always equal to 1. These relationships are illustrated in Figure 5.3, in which it is shown graphically that $\overline{X}$ has a z score equivalent of 0 and the scores one sigma unit from $\overline{X}$ have z score equivalents of ± 1.00.

z Scores from Populations.   In the preceding discussion, we defined z in terms of $\overline{X}$ and s, which are estimates of the population mean and standard deviation based on sample data. However, when the μ and σ of a population are known, we can define z more precisely:

$$z = \frac{X − \mu}{\sigma} \tag{5.16}$$

In the next section, in which we discuss standard scores, you will see an instance in which Formula 5.16 is used.

Standard Scores

A z score is also called a standard score because it indicates relative standing in a distribution of measures without regard to the particular units of measurement in the original set of observations. A z score of $+.50$, for example, indicates a score that is somewhat above average, whether the distribution represents the heights of a group of individuals measured in inches, their weights in pounds, or their performance on an 80-item personality test.

Other types of standard scores based on z scores are often used to report the results of widely used tests, such as clinical tests of personality or nationally used tests of academic achievement. Typically, the distribution of raw scores from which the z scores are derived involves extremely large samples so that, for all practical purposes, the mean and standard deviation of the raw scores can be considered to be population values.

One type of standard score derived from z is known as the T score. T scores are obtained by multiplying each z score by 10 and then adding 50 to each of the resulting scores:

$$T = 10(z) + 50$$

This procedure removes decimals and negative numbers and results in a distribution with a mean of 50 and a standard deviation of 10. That is, when $z = 0$, $T = 10(0) + 50 = 50$, and when $z = \pm 1.00$, $T = 10(\pm 1) + 50 = 40$ or 60.

A second system of standard scores that is often used multiplies each z by 100 and adds 500 to the result: 100(z) + 500. The outcome is a distribution of scores with a mean of 500 and a standard deviation of 100.

As may be inferred from these examples, it is possible to transform any set of z scores into a set of standard scores in which the mean (μ) and the standard deviation (σ) each take any value that one specifies beforehand. A general formula can be given in which we identify the transformed score as U, the specified mean of the distribution of transformed scores as μ_U, and the specified standard deviation as σ_U. Thus:

$$U = (\sigma_U)(z_X) + \mu_U \tag{5.17}$$

where z_X is the z-score value of a given raw score (X).

The method we just described makes it necessary to convert raw scores (X's) into z scores before they can be transformed into standard scores with a new μ and σ. A calculational formula can be derived from Formula 5.17 that avoids the necessity of computing z scores. This formula is more convenient to use when the entire distribution of raw scores is to be changed into standard scores with a different μ and σ. This formula is:

$$U = \frac{\sigma_U(X)}{\sigma_X} - \frac{(\sigma_U)(\mu_X)}{\sigma_X} + \mu_U \tag{5.18}$$

where μ_X and σ_X are the mean and standard deviation, respectively, of the distribution of raw scores. We will illustrate the use of Formula 5.18 later in the Step by Step Procedures section.

In all such conversions, the shape of the original distribution of scores is retained and the interpretation of the scores remains the same as for z scores. For example, a z score of −2.00 indicates a performance that is much below average. The equivalent score T is 30; that is, with a standard deviation of 10 and a mean of 50, 30 is two standard deviation units below the mean. If the standard deviation had instead been set at 50 and the mean at 200, the equivalent standard score would be 100, still a score that is two standard deviation units below the mean.

A CHECK ON CALCULATIONAL ERRORS: STANDARD DEVIATION AND THE RANGE

In discussing z scores, we noted that the sizes of the range (R) and the standard deviation are related. This suggests that we can check on computational errors by comparing the calculated s with the range of scores in the distribution. We have already seen that in a sample with a large N and a symmetrical bell-shaped distribution, such as the one in Figure 5.3, all or almost all the scores are encompassed by six standard deviation units, three on either side of the mean. For large samples that approximate this curve shape, therefore, you can check your calculated s to see if it is approximately one-sixth of R. After you have calculated several s's you will begin to get the "feel" of them in relationship to the distribution of scores from which they have been calculated. You will quickly find out that if R of your distribution is 24 and your calculated s is 25, something is wrong with your calculations, since s is larger than R. Or, if you have R of 24 and you obtain s of 1, something also is wrong.

But we must stress now, and stress emphatically, that we do not calculate s by taking one-sixth of R; rather, *after* we have calculated s we check to see if its value is approximately one-sixth of R. This provides only a very crude check, unless the number of measures is very large and the distribution quite symmetrical and shaped like Figure 5.3. However, so many sets of data are distributed like those of Figure 5.3 that the check has considerable usefulness.

Step-by-Step Procedures

Computation of Standard Deviation

We will illustrate the procedures used to compute S, σ and s from an ungrouped set of raw scores and from raw scores arranged in a simple frequency distribution.

Computations from Ungrouped Data

Calculations will be based on the sample of scores shown in Table 5.4.

Calculation of S or σ

Either Formula 5.7 or 5.8 may be used to calculate S, the standard deviation of a sample drawn from some population. The same formulas are used to calculate σ, the standard deviation of a population. These formulas are shown below:

$$\sigma \text{ or } S = \sqrt{\frac{\Sigma X^2}{N} - \left(\frac{\Sigma X}{N}\right)^2}$$

$$\sigma \text{ or } S = \sqrt{\frac{\Sigma X^2 - (\Sigma X)^2/N}{N}}$$

1. In both formulas, the basic ingredients are N, ΣX, and ΣX^2. The first step, then, is to find N (by counting the number of cases), ΣX (by adding the X's together), and ΣX^2 (by squaring each X and summing the squares). These quantities are shown in Table 5.4.

2. Once N, ΣX, and ΣX^2 have been found, their values are entered into the formula. The calculations specified by the formula are then performed. Calculations for both Formulas 5.7 and 5.8 are also shown in Table 5.4. Because the scores constitute a sample rather than a population, the resulting standard deviation is identified as S rather than σ. As expected, the two formulas produce the same value for S. (Rounding errors, however, can sometimes produce slight discrepancies between the answers provided by the two methods of calculating S.)

Table 5.4 Computation of S and s from Ungrouped Data

S#	X	X²	S#	X	X²
1	29	841	6	22	484
2	26	676	7	20	400
3	25	625	8	19	361
4	23	529	9	17	289
5	22	484	10	16	256

$$\Sigma X = 219 \quad \Sigma X^2 = 4945$$

$$S = \sqrt{\frac{\Sigma X^2}{N} - \left(\frac{\Sigma X}{N}\right)^2} = \sqrt{\frac{4945}{10} - \left(\frac{219}{10}\right)^2}$$

$$= \sqrt{494.5 - 479.61} = \sqrt{14.89} = 3.86$$

OR

$$S = \sqrt{\frac{\Sigma X^2 - (\Sigma X)^2/N}{N}} = \sqrt{\frac{4945 - (219)^2/10}{10}}$$

$$= \sqrt{\frac{4945 - 4796.1}{10}} = \sqrt{\frac{148.9}{10}} = \sqrt{14.89} = 3.86$$

AND

$$s = \sqrt{\frac{\Sigma X^2 - (\Sigma X)^2/N}{N - 1}} = \sqrt{\frac{4945 - (219)^2/10}{9}}$$

$$= \sqrt{\frac{148.9}{9}} = \sqrt{16.54} = 4.07$$

Calculation of s

The standard deviations of samples (S) tend to underestimate the value of the population sigma. A corrected estimate of the population sigma, s, is given by Formula 5.9, in which −1 in the denominator represents the correction factor. This formula is shown below.

$$s = \sqrt{\frac{\Sigma X^2 - (\Sigma X)^2/N}{N - 1}}$$

Note that this formula is identical to Formula 5.8 for S, except for the addition of the correction factor to the denominator. Except for using N − 1 rather than N in the denominator, the procedures for computing s are therefore the same as for computing S using Formula 5.8. The procedures used to determine s are illustrated in Table 5.4.

Use of Calculator

Calculators designed to perform statistical analyses (third or fourth level) are preprogrammed to compute S (or σ), s, or both, directly after the basic data (raw scores) are entered. This is accomplished by pressing special keys. Pressing other keys will give you the components on which the calculations were based, that is, N, ΣX and ΣX^2, and perhaps $\overline{X}$, s^2, and S^2 as well. These values may be useful for other purposes.

If your calculator permits you to calculate s or S by pressing a special key, it is important that you identify which statistic you want to compute and what you are actually computing. If your calculator allows you to compute only S directly, you can convert S to s by use of the following formula:

$$s = S\sqrt{\frac{N}{N-1}} \qquad (5.19)$$

For example, in Table 5.4, in which N = 10, we calculated S to be 3.86. Thus:

$$s = 3.86\sqrt{\frac{10}{9}} = 3.86\sqrt{1.054} = 4.07$$

You will observe that this value, 4.07, is the same as we obtained in Table 5.4 by using the raw-score formula for s.

With less sophisticated calculators, the best you may be able to do, in addition to finding ΣX, is to find ΣX^2 in one continuous operation [e.g., $(29 \times 29) + (26 \times 26) + \cdots + (16 \times 16) = 4945$]. Some calculators may allow you to find ΣX and ΣX^2 simultaneously.

Computations from Simple Frequency Distributions

Formulas 5.10 and 5.11, used to determine S and s from frequency distributions, are as follows.

$$S = \sqrt{\frac{\Sigma fX^2 - (\Sigma fX)^2/N}{N}}$$

$$s = \sqrt{\frac{\Sigma fX^2 - (\Sigma fX)^2/N}{N-1}}$$

In these formulas X is the value of each different score from the highest to the lowest and f is the frequency with which each of these X values occurs. In Table 5.5, for example, two individuals had a score of 15.

1. In the formulas, the basic ingredients are N, ΣfX, and ΣfX^2. N, the total number of cases, is obtained by summing the frequency column (N = Σf). To obtain ΣfX, each value of X is

Table 5.5 Calculation of *s* from a Simple Frequency Distribution

X	f	f X	f X²
16	1	16	256
15	2	30	450
14	0	0	0
13	3	39	507
12	3	36	432
11	4	44	484
10	3	30	300
9	2	18	162
8	1	8	64
7	1	7	49
	$\Sigma f = 20$	$\Sigma fX = 228$	$\Sigma fX^2 = 2704$

$$S = \sqrt{\frac{\Sigma fX^2 - (\Sigma fX)^2/N}{N-1}} = \sqrt{\frac{2704 - (228)^2/20}{20-1}}$$

$$= \sqrt{\frac{104.8}{19}} = \sqrt{5.52} = 2.35$$

multiplied by its corresponding frequency and the sum of these fX values is obtained. After we have found each fX, the simplest way to obtain ΣfX^2 is, first, to multiply each X by its corresponding fX, which yields fX^2. For example, in Table 5.5 the fX for X = 12 is 36 and 12(36) = 432. These fX^2 values are then summed, as shown in Table 5.5.

2. The values of ΣfX^2 are entered into each formula. Then the calculations called for by the formula are carried out. We have illustrated these procedures in Table 5.5 only for *s*.

Use of Calculator

If your calculator allows you to compute *s* or *S* directly from ungrouped data, it may also allow you to compute these statistics with the data from a frequency distribution. Check your instruction booklet.

With lower-level calculators, you may be able to determine ΣfX^2 in one continuous operation by adding successive terms for (f) (X) (X). For example, in Table 5.5 [(1 × 16 × 16) + (2 × 15 × 15) + · · · + (1 × 7 × 7)] = 2704.

Calculation of *z* scores

We will use the data in Table 5.5 to illustrate how to translate raw scores into *z* scores, and vice versa. From Table 5.5:

$$\overline{X} = \frac{228}{20} = 11.4 \quad s = 2.35 \quad N = 20$$

z-score equivalent of a raw score

The formula for z is:

$$z = \frac{X - \overline{X}}{s}$$

Suppose that we want to translate the scores 15 and 9 into z scores. We enter the values of X, $\overline{X}$, and s into the z formula.

For X = 15:

$$z = \frac{15 - 11.4}{2.35} = \frac{3.6}{2.35} = 1.53$$

The score of 15 is 1.53 sigma-units above the mean.

For X = 9:

$$z = \frac{9 - 11.4}{2.35} = \frac{-2.4}{2.35} = -1.02$$

The score of 9 is 1.02 sigma-units below the mean.

Raw-score equivalent of a z score

We may have questions of the following sort. A z score of +2.00 has a raw-score equivalent of what? What is the raw-score equivalent of z = −1.5? The formula we use is:

$$X = \overline{X} + z(s)$$

For z = 2.00:

$$X = 11.4 + 2.00(2.35) = 11.4 + 4.70 = 16.1$$

For z = −1.5:

$$X = 11.4 + (-1.5)(2.35) = 11.4 - 3.52 = 7.88$$

Computation of Standard Scores

Standard scores based on z scores, you recall, are often used with widely used tests that have been given to very large numbers of individuals. The mean and standard deviation of the group of scores can for all practical purposes be considered to be the μ and σ of the population.

Raw scores can be translated into z scores for a population by Formula 5.16: $z = (X - \mu)/\sigma$. These z scores can in turn be translated into standard scores, which have identified as U scores, in which the mean (μ_U) and standard deviation (σ_U) of the distribution of U scores take any values that one specifies. This can be done by means of Formula 5.17:

$$U = (\sigma_U)(z_X) + \mu_U$$

A more convenient formula, Formula 5.18, uses only raw scores:

$$U = \left(\frac{\sigma_U}{\sigma_X}\right)(X) - \frac{(\sigma_U)(\mu_X)}{\sigma_X} + \mu_U$$

Procedures for computing two popular kinds of standard scores are shown below. The examples are based on a population of scores in which:

$$\mu_X = 112 \quad \text{and} \quad \sigma_X = 14$$

and in which the raw score of 133 is to be translated into a standard score.

Mean of 50 and σ of 10

Standard scores with a μ specified as 50 and a σ specified as 10 are known as T scores. Translating raw scores into T scores by Formula 5.17 involves finding their z-score equivalents and entering these z scores into Formula 5.17 along with the specified mean and σ.

$$\text{For } X = 133, z_X = (133 - 112)/14 = 1.5 \text{ and:}$$

$$T = 10(1.5) + (50) = 65$$

Using Formula 5.18 instead, we have

$$T = \frac{10}{14}(X) - \frac{10(112)}{14} + 50 = .714(X) - 80 + 50$$

$$= .714(X) - 30 = .714(133) - 30 = 64.83$$

Except for a slight rounding error, we obtain the same answer as with Formula 5.17. Note how easy it is to find additional T scores with Formula 5.18. For example, for X = 82,

$$T = .714(82) - 30 = 28.55$$

Mean of 500 and σ of 100

We follow the same procedures as for T scores but change to a mean of 500 and σ of 100.
By Formula 5.17 for X = 133:

$$U = 100(1.5) + (500) = 650$$

By Formula 5.18:

$$U = \frac{100}{14}(133) - \frac{100(112)}{14} + 500$$

$$= 7.143(133) - 800 + 500 = 950.02 - 300 = 650.02 \quad\blacksquare$$

DEFINITIONS OF TERMS AND SYMBOLS

Semi-interquartile range. A measure of variability obtained by finding $(Q_3 - Q_1)/2$, half the score distance from the first quartile to the third quartile.

Deviation (x). The difference between a given score and the mean of the distribution to which it belongs: $(X - \overline{X})$.

Average deviation. A measure of variability obtained by finding the mean (average) of the *absolute* deviations of the scores in a distribution from $\overline{X}$: $\Sigma |x|/N$.

Variance. A measure of variability obtained by finding the mean of the *squared* deviations of the scores from $\overline{X}$: $\Sigma x^2/N$.

Standard deviation. The square root of the variance.

σ and σ^2. Symbols for the standard deviation and variance of a population.

S and S^2. Symbols for the standard deviation and variance of a *sample* of measures. S and S^2 tend to underestimate the standard deviation and variance of the parent population and are referred to as uncorrected estimates of the population values.

s and s^2. Corrected estimates of the population standard deviation and variance based on sample data, obtained by the formulas $\sqrt{\Sigma x^2/(N-1)}$ and $\Sigma x^2/(N-1)$. The formula for s^2 yields an unbiased estimate of σ^2—that is, on the average, s^2 will equal σ^2. A slight bias remains in s.

Degrees of freedom (df). Number of scores in a distribution whose values are free to vary when the total set of scores meets some constraint, such as the value of the mean. After the mean is known, the number of degrees of freedom in a single distribution of raw scores is $N - 1$.

z score. A score expressed in standard deviation units. A z score is obtained by finding the deviation of the score from the mean of the distribution and dividing the result by the standard deviation. For a sample, $z = (X - \overline{X})/s$ and for a population, $z = (X - \mu)/\sigma$. The mean of a distribution of z scores is 0, and the variance and standard deviation are each 1.

Standard scores. Standard scores are z scores or scores based on z scores in which the transformed distribution has a specified mean and standard deviation and the score corresponding to each z is obtained by the formula: (specified standard deviation) (z) + (specified mean). Standard scores are so named because they indicate relative standing in a distribution without regard to the unit of measurement in the original raw scores.

PROBLEMS

1. A series of pairs of distributions is presented below. For each pair, indicate whether distribution 1 or 2 is *more* variable.

   (a) Dist. 1: 5, 6, 7, 7, 8, 9; Dist. 2: 7, 9, 10, 11, 12, 14.

   (b) Dist. 1: 16, 21, 25, 30, 35, 44; Dist 2: 144, 146, 149, 153, 154, 160.

   (c) Dist. 1: 23, 25, 27, 31, 32, 34; Dist 2: 5, 26, 28, 29, 30, 33.

   (d)

Dist. 1		Dist. 2	
X	f	X	f
62	1	28	1
61	2	27	1
60	2	26	4
59	5	25	7
58	9	24	11
57	7	23	7
56	4	22	6
55	5	21	2
54	3	20	0
53	2	19	1
	$\Sigma f = 40$		$\Sigma f = 40$

2. For each of the distributions above, determine the range (R).

3. For the pairs of distributions in problem 1(c) and (d), compare the values of R. What do these comparisons tell you about the limitations of R as a measure of variability?

4. Determine the semi-interquartile range for distribution 1 in problem 1(d).

5. What do the following trios of symbols represent: σ^2, S^2, and s^2; and σ, S, and s?

6. Find the variance (S^2) and standard deviation (S) for the distribution of scores below, using raw scores and Formula 5.7: 1, 2, 4, 5, 5, 7, 7, 8, 10, 11.

7. For the distribution in problem 6, find the standard deviation (S) using Formula 5.8. Check to see if this is the same value as you obtained in problem 6. If they are not the same (except for possible rounding errors), one or both of your calculations is in error.

8. For the distribution in problem 6, find s using Formula 5.9.

9. Find s for the simple frequency distribution shown below.

X	f	X	f
15	1	11	4
14	2	10	3
13	3	9	2
12	3	8	2

10. Students were given data from several frequency distributions, each of which had a large N and was close to being symmetrical and bell-shaped, and asked to compute s for each distribution. The

answers of one student, along with the range (highest minus lowest score), are given below. Based on your knowledge of the relationship between R and s in symmetrical, bell-shaped distributions, determine for each distribution whether the student's calculated s is probably accurate, too small, or too large.

(a) $R = 99 - 51; s = 8.5$.

(b) $R = 34 - 13; s = 7.2$.

(c) $R = 105 - 46; s = 9.3$.

(d) $R = 49 - 3; s = 3.8$.

(e) $R = 149 - 106; s = -3.6$.

11. A physical anthropologist administers a battery of tests to 200 male high school seniors. The means and standard deviations of these students for a test of reaction time (RT) and a test of lung capacity (LC) are shown below. Each distribution was approximately symmetrical and bell-shaped ($N = 200$).

$$\overline{X}_{RT} = 34 \quad \overline{X}_{LC} = 193$$

$$s_{RT} = 4 \quad s_{LC} = 20$$

(a) Sketch a figure for each distribution, marking off on the baseline the raw-score values of $\overline{X}$ and the raw scores that are one, two, and three standard deviations above and below $\overline{X}$. Below this raw-score scale, add a z-score scale showing the corresponding z values for the raw-score values you have plotted.

(b) The raw scores for three of the men are shown below. For each of these scores, find the z-score equivalent.

	RT	LC
Alex	39	210
Max	31	183
Perry	42	155

(c) On the graphs drawn for (a), show where each student fell in the distribution and compare the relative standing of each student on the two tests.

(d) Three other males received the following z scores. What are their raw scores? Sam: $z_{RT} = +2.50$; Jim: $z_{RT} = -1.75$; Boris: $z_{LC} = +.25$.

12. An arithmetic test has been administered to a very large national sample of fourth-grade students. The mean for the group has been found to be 65 and the standard deviation to be 15.

(a) If raw scores were changed into T scores, what is the T-score equivalent of 80?

(b) If raw scores were converted into standard scores with a mean of 500 and a standard deviation of 100, what are the score equivalents of raw scores of 41 and 93? Use Formula 5.18.

6

Probability

- SETS AND PROBABILITIES
- SOME PRINCIPLES OF PROBABILITY
- PERMUTATIONS AND COMBINATIONS

In observing samples of individuals, we have noted, our scientific aim is to discover something about the properties of populations as a whole. Even if samples are selected randomly or in some other unbiased manner, the statistics obtained from a number of independent samples seldom agree exactly. For example, in the case of categorical data, the same percentage of individuals does not fall into any given category in all samples. Nor, in the case of measurement data, are all sample means identical.

Since the samples differ, no single sample can automatically be assumed to reflect exactly the properties of the population. Most samples are reasonably similar in their properties to the population, but on occasion they may be highly deviant.

Consider the following example. If a perfectly balanced coin is tossed a very large number of times—technically, an infinite number of times—a head (H) will come up half the time and a tail (T) the other half. That H and T occur equally often is in fact our *definition* of a perfectly balanced or *fair* coin. Now, suppose that instead of obtaining the entire *population* of tosses of a fair coin (possible only in theory anyway, since the population is infinitely large), we obtain a *sample* of only 10 tosses, tallying the total number of H and T for the series of 10. We repeat this procedure over and over again, gathering data on a substantial number of samples of 10 each. What do we expect the number of H and T to be in these samples? Our best *single* guess is 5 H and 5 T. But we wouldn't be at all surprised to find unequal splits, such as 6 H and 4 T or 3 H and 7 T, occurring quite frequently. Very occasionally, samples as deviant as all H or all T may occur. Samples, then, do not always mirror faithfully the population from which they were drawn.

But statistical theory does permit us, given certain facts about the population, to state the exact frequency with which events can be expected to occur. These same theoretical principles also permit us to describe the likelihood or *probability* of occurrence of some event or series of events. For example, if you toss an unbiased, balanced coin a single time, what is the probability of occurrence of H? Conversely, what is the probability of T? You know that these two events are *equally likely*, so you might describe H and T as having a 50-50 chance of occurring. Setting the sum of the probabilities of all possible events at 1.00, we therefore can describe the probability of H as .50 and of T as .50. Suppose you are about to toss the coin 5 times. What is the probability of getting 3 H and 2 T? You will discover in later discussion that, over the long run, 3 H and 2 T can be expected to occur 10 times out of 32 or approximately 31 percent of the time. The theory of probability allows us to state that the probability of getting 3 H and 2 T in a *single* series of 5 tosses therefore is .31.

Now consider another example. We have a coin of unknown origin and ask whether it is a balanced, unbiased coin or a biased one. That is, we want to know whether an infinite number of tosses of the coin (the entire population of tosses) would produce half H and half T, or some other ratio. Not having infinite patience or time, we obtain instead a sample of only 50 tosses, finding 22 H and 28 T. Is the coin unbiased? No conclusive answer can be given, but we can make a reasonable guess by determining the probability that a sample with this H-T split or an even more extreme split would occur *if the coin were in fact unbiased*. If the probability is low—that is, the likelihood is very small that a sample this different from an even split would occur if the coin were unbiased—then we reject our assumption about the coin's fairness and conclude instead that it is biased. Conversely, if the probability is high of getting a result this extreme or more so with a fair coin, we conclude that this particular coin is likely to be unbiased. What we have done in this example is to use probability theory to *test a hypothesis* about a population characteristic and to reach some conclusion about it. Probability theory thus permits us to make reasonable guesses or inferences about populations, based on the data from samples.

In this chapter we will review some of the elementary principles of probability to lay the foundation for discussion in later chapters of hypothesis testing and the statistics of inference. It is a time-honored tradition in discussing probability to use simple, understandable examples such as coins, dice, cards, or balls in a bowl, and we have already begun our discussion in this way. Although these illustrations may be of interest only to gamblers, they are useful explanatory devices. With occasional exceptions, we will therefore continue to employ them throughout the chapter.

Before beginning our discussion, it is important to mention that in this chapter we will be considering principles of probability that are applicable to *categorical* data, rather than to *numerical* data. You will recall from Chapter 1 that some properties exist in varying degrees, which means that in describing individuals, we measure the amount of the property that each individual exhibits. These measurements give us numerical data. Categorical data, on the other hand, involve a set of two or more discrete properties, each of which the individual does or does not exhibit. When each individual can fall into only one category in the set, the categories are said to be *mutually exclusive*. For example, when we toss a coin, there is a set of two mutually exclusive outcomes (categories): heads or tails. We do not measure how much "headness" or "tailness" each coin exhibits; rather, we ask whether it came up heads or tails. Similarly, if an airline offers its passengers a choice of chicken, beef, or fish as a dinner entrée, there are three categories and each dinner tray can be classified as belonging to one and only one category. To repeat, the principles of probability we will discuss in this chapter involve mutually exclusive categorical data.

SETS AND PROBABILITIES

We start with an example: Take five balls and number them 1, 2, 3, 4, and 5. These numbered balls constitute what is called a *set* and the individual balls the *elements* of the set. In this example the elements of the set are mutually exclusive. That is, each ball has a single number on it, so that if we put the balls in a bowl, mix them thoroughly, and then draw one out, only one number can occur. If the ball we select has a 3 on it, for example, it cannot simultaneously have any other number. Some events are *not* mutually exclusive. For example, suppose a group of individuals is asked whether they used public transportation or some other means of getting to work yesterday. Some might say they had used a combination of both, such as driving their car to the railroad station and taking a train from there. Use of one form of transportation on the way to work did not preclude use of other forms. Similarly, each of our five balls could have more than one number on it from the set of numbers from 1 to 5. If we wished to classify each ball as having the property 1, 2, 3, 4, or 5, a ball having the numbers 2 and 3, for example, could be simultaneously classified as having the property 2 and 3; the set of properties in this instance is not mutually exclusive.

Returning to our mutually exclusive set of five numbered balls—that is, the balls with single numbers on them—suppose we went many, many times through the procedures of drawing a ball, replacing it, mixing up the balls, and drawing again. How frequently would we expect each ball to be selected? Before answering, we should note an additional characteristic of this procedure that is critical: *On any occasion, each element is equally likely to occur.* That is, except for the numbers, the balls are identical; and if we scramble them thoroughly no ball is any more likely than another to come to hand when we draw. It can therefore confidently be stated that over the long run, each ball will be selected $\frac{1}{5}$ of the time. It can also be said that on the average each ball will be selected 20 percent of the time, or that the average *proportion* of the time it will be selected is .20.

Now if we draw a single ball, how likely (how probable) is it that a given number will occur? What is the probability that the ball is, say, a 4? The answer follows from our conclusion that each ball will be selected $\frac{1}{5}$ of the time. That is, over repeated occasions, we expect a 4 to occur $\frac{1}{5}$ of the time. For a single draw, therefore, there is one chance in five of getting a 4; alternatively, we can say that a 4 will occur 20 percent of the time on the average, or that it has a *probability* of occurrence of .20. What is the probability that in a single draw from our set of five balls we will pick a ball with an *even* number—that is, a ball from the *subset* of balls numbered 2 and 4? We have 2 chances out of 5 of drawing an even number, so the answer is $\frac{2}{5}$ or .40. What is the probability of *not* drawing an even number? We have divided the set into two nonoverlapping subsets, two balls with even numbers and three with odd numbers. The probability of drawing noneven (that is, odd) numbered balls is therefore $\frac{3}{5}$ or .60. What about the probability of a ball with either an odd number *or* an even number? Since the question encompasses all elements of the set, the probability has to be unity: $\frac{5}{5}$ or 1.00.

We offer one more example. Suppose we have ten balls, five of them numbered 1, three of them 2, and two of them 3. Each of the individual *balls*—that is, each of the elements of the set, has an equal probability of being selected on a single draw $(\frac{1}{10})$, but what about each *number*? Since there are five balls numbered 1, $\frac{5}{10}$ or half of them fall into this "1" category; the probability of drawing a 1 therefore is .50. Similarly, the probability of a 2 is $\frac{3}{10}$ or .30, and of a 3, $\frac{2}{10}$ or .20.

Probability Defined

With these examples before us we can now offer a definition of probability *for equally likely events*. When a single, random observation from a set of mutually exclusive, equally likely events is to be made, the *probability of an event from a specific subset of events is the ratio of the number of events belonging to that subset to the total number of possible events*. This definition can be expressed in a simple formula, in which n_A stands for the number of events belonging to subset A and N for the total number of all possible events:

$$p(A) = \frac{n_A}{N} \tag{6.1}$$

To illustrate the application of this formula, suppose we had six objects, three of them yellow, two of them red, and one of them blue. In this example, N is 6. What is the probability of selecting a red object on a single draw? There are two red objects, so n_A is 2, and the probability of selecting a red one is $\frac{2}{6} = .33$.

We can also express N as $n_A + n_{\overline{A}}$, where $\overline{A}$ stands for all categories of the elements in the set that are *not* in the A category. $\overline{A}$ is technically called the *complement* of A. Thus, we can also write:

$$p(A) = \frac{n_A}{n_A + n_{\overline{A}}} \tag{6.2}$$

The probability that A will not occur—that is, $p(\overline{A})$—is given by:

$$p(\overline{A}) = \frac{n_{\overline{A}}}{n_A + n_{\overline{A}}} \tag{6.3}$$

The two probabilities, $p(A)$ and $p(\overline{A})$, must add up to 1.00. In our example of six objects, the probability of selecting one of the two red (R) objects or $p(R)$ is $\frac{2}{6}$ and the probability of *not* selecting a red object or $p(\overline{R})$ is $\frac{4}{6}$, and $p(R) + p(\overline{R})$ is $\frac{2}{6} + \frac{4}{6} = 1.00$.

Notice that the definition above is of the probability of *equally likely events*. The condition of equal likelihood does not always hold. Take the simple case of a "loaded" coin—a coin that does not have perfect balance so that H and T do *not* come up equally often. For example, a coin may be biased in a manner that results in 60 percent H and 40 percent T over an infinite number of tosses. The likelihood of H on a given occasion thus is greater than the likelihood of T, specifically .60 versus .40. We may give a more general definition of probability that holds for this as well as for the equal likelihood case. *The probability of a random event of a certain type occurring on a given occasion is the proportion of times it would occur on an unlimited number of occasions.* Our subsequent discussion of the principles of probability, however, will be limited to examples of equally likely events.

SOME PRINCIPLES OF PROBABILITY

The Addition Rule

We have a deck of 52 well-shuffled cards and pick one at random. The probability of selecting an ace of hearts is $\frac{1}{52}$; similarly, the probability of selecting a king of spades is $\frac{1}{52}$. What is the probability that the card will be either an ace of hearts *or* a king of spades? The answer is the sum of the probabilities of the two individual events, $\frac{1}{52} + \frac{1}{52}$, or $\frac{1}{26}$. Similarly, what is the probability of selecting an ace or a king of any suit? Since there are four aces and four kings in the deck, the answer is $\frac{4}{52} + \frac{4}{52}$ or $\frac{2}{13}$. These examples are illustrations of the *addition rule: In a set of mutually exclusive random events the probability of occurrence of either one event or another event (or subset of events) is the sum of their individual probabilities.* For the three-event case, this rule may be expressed as:

$$p(A \text{ or } B \text{ or } C) = p(A) + p(B) + p(C) \tag{6.4}$$

For example, the probability that a card drawn at random would be an ace, king, or jack therefore is $\frac{4}{52} + \frac{4}{52} + \frac{4}{52} = \frac{3}{13}$.

The Multiplication Rule for Independent Events

In the previous section we were concerned with specifying the probability that on a single occasion one of two or more mutually exclusive events or subsets of events will occur—for example, an ace *or* a king. We now consider the probability of occurrence of a *series* of events. Suppose we toss a fair coin two times; what is the probability that on the first toss a head will turn up and on the second a tail? Observe first that in two tosses four equally likely patterns are possible: HH, HT, TH, TT; over the long run, two tosses of the coin will produce our specified pair of events, HT, $\frac{1}{4}$ of the time. The probability of obtaining HT on a single pair of tosses therefore is $\frac{1}{4}$ or .25. Similarly, what is the probability of obtaining HTH, in that order, in three tosses? With three tosses eight different patterns are possible: HHH, HTH, HHT, HTT, THH, TTH, THT, TTT. The probability of HTH is therefore $\frac{1}{8}$. For four tosses there are 16 possibilities, so that the probability of any one of them is $\frac{1}{16}$, and so on.

Application of the *multiplication rule* allows us to determine these probabilities without having to figure out and then count all the possibilities. This rule states that *the probability of two or more independent events occurring on separate occasions is the product of their individual probabilities*. For the case of three independent events, this rule can be expressed as:

$$p(A, B, C) = p(A) \times p(B) \times p(C) \tag{6.5}$$

where $p(A, B, C)$ is to be read as the probability of A, B, and C occurring.

Let's see how the rule works. In the case of a coin, H and T each have a probability of $\frac{1}{2}$ on a single toss. The pattern HT about which we inquired should thus occur $\frac{1}{2} \times \frac{1}{2} = \frac{1}{4}$ of the time. For three tosses the probability of a given pattern is $\frac{1}{2} \times \frac{1}{2} \times \frac{1}{2} = \frac{1}{8}$, and so on. How about this example: What is the probability of drawing from a deck of 52 cards a 2-spot, followed (after replacing our first card in the deck) by a heart? Since a 2 has a probability of $\frac{4}{52}$ or $\frac{1}{13}$ and a heart a probability of $\frac{13}{52}$ or $\frac{1}{4}$, the answer is $\frac{1}{13} \times \frac{1}{4} = \frac{1}{52}$.

Note that our definition of the multiplication rule states that the events whose probability of occurrence we are specifying must be *independent*. By independent we mean that the occurrence of one event does not change the probability of the occurrence of any other event. Tossing a fair coin, for example, and observing a head does not mean that on the next toss a second head is any more or any less likely to occur; its probability remains $\frac{1}{2}$.* This independence can be demonstrated by tossing a coin many times and comparing the proportion of heads following heads and following tails. The proportion of H following both H and T, you will discover, remains $\frac{1}{2}$.

---

*We are here denying what is known as the *gambler's fallacy*. Many gamblers believe, for example, that if a head has occurred with unusual frequency, a tail is "overdue" and therefore has a higher probability of occurrence than .50. In actual fact, no matter how many heads happen to come up in a row—5, 10, or 200—the probability of a tail on the next toss of a fair coin stubbornly remains at .5.

Conditional Probability

Independent Events.   Suppose we have one hundred balls, numbered 1 through 100. We draw a ball numbered 3 and replace it. We now inquire about the probability that on the next draw we will select the ball numbered 68. This type of question concerns a *conditional probability*: the likelihood that an event will occur, given the fact that another event or series of events *has already occurred*. A conditional probability is indicated by the expression $p(B|A)$, which is read as "the probability of B given A." In our example, 3 is event A and 68 is event B.

The answer to our question above is that $p(B|A) = \frac{1}{100}$. With replacement of each ball before drawing another to keep the N at 100, the probability of selecting a specific ball remains $\frac{1}{100}$, no matter what ball or how many balls have previously been selected. That is, as we discussed in the section above, the events are independent; when we replace each ball before drawing another, the probability of the individual event remains constant whatever prior events have occurred. When events are independent, you notice, the probability of B given A [$p(B|A)$] reduces to $p(B)$. When events are *not* independent, $p(B|A)$ is *not* equal to $p(B)$, as we shall see in the next section.

Nonindependent Events.   We now turn to the conditional probabilities of nonindependent events. Suppose, to relieve the tedium of our previous examples, we imagine that six men on a hunting trip find themselves trapped in a mountain cabin by a snowstorm. Three of them happen to be lawyers, two are physicans, and one is an architect. One of them, they decide, should go for help, and they decide to draw lots for the honor. The man chosen is one of the lawyers (the most likely event, since the probability of selection of the architect is $\frac{1}{6}$, of one of the physicians $\frac{2}{6}$, and of one of the lawyers $\frac{3}{6}$). After days of waiting, the five remaining men decide to send out a second messenger. What is the probability that the person selected by their second lottery will be a lawyer? With one of the lawyers gone and the group diminished to 5, the probability of another lawyer's being selected as the second man is $\frac{2}{5}$. If, instead, the *architect* had gone first, the probability of a lawyer's going second would be $\frac{3}{5}$. Or suppose that we were concerned with the probability that a *physician* went second, given that a physician had also gone first. In this instance the probability would be $\frac{1}{5}$.

These are examples of *conditional probabilities for nonindependent events*. Questions are being asked about $p(B|A)$, the likelihood of B given A, in a situation in which event A is not replaced in the original set before selection of B (the first man didn't come back). Without replacement, the probability of B *is* influenced by what has gone before. The reasoning by which $p(B|A)$ is determined is no different from that by which $p(A)$ is determined, except that we must take into account the change in the set brought about by prior events that have not been replaced. For example, if the balls numbered 2 and 4 are removed from a set numbered 1 through 100 and are not replaced, what is the probability that any particular ball of the remaining 98 will be selected on the next draw? The answer is $\frac{1}{98}$. Since the balls that were removed were both even, the probability of an *even* number on the next draw is $\frac{48}{98}$, and so on.

Multiplication Rule for Dependent Events.   In the example of the hunters above, what is the probability that the first and the second men will both be lawyers? In a set of balls numbered 1 through 10, what is the probability, assuming nonreplacement, that the first ball will be 2, the second 4, and the third 5? These questions about a series of events are subject to the same sort of *multiplication rule* governing independent events. This rule, we recall, states that the joint probability of a series of events is the product of the probabilities of the individual events. Our previous statement of this rule, however, has to be modified to take into account that the probability of event B is conditional upon event A, C is conditional upon A and B, and so on. Thus, for three events (A, B, C) we have: $p(A, B) = p(A) \times p(B \mid A)$, so that $p(A, B, C) = p(A, B) \times p(C \mid A, B)$ and:

$$p(A, B, C) = p(A) \times p(B \mid A) \times p(C \mid A, B) \tag{6.6}$$

where $p(A)$ is the probability of A, $p(B \mid A)$ is the probability of B given A, and $p(C \mid A, B)$ is the probability of C given A and B in that order.

The answer to our question about the two hunters being lawyers is therefore $(\frac{3}{6})(\frac{2}{5}) = \frac{1}{5}$ or .20. The probability of drawing balls 2, 4, and 5 in that order without replacement from the set of 10 is $(\frac{1}{10})(\frac{1}{9})(\frac{1}{8}) = \frac{1}{720}$ (or .0014), and so on.*

Conditional Probabilities and Joint Events

We now extend our discussion to consider conditional probabilities in situations in which each member of a group has been categorized according to two characteristics rather than one. Suppose, for example, that you are trying out as a ship's recreation director on a weekend cruise for "singles." You have been told that if the cruise is a success, you can have the job permanently. Quickly you size up the 80 men and 120 women who are on the cruise and assign each to one of three groups: Swingers, who are going to have a good time anyway, Duds, for whom little can be done, and Eagers, who are ready to enjoy themselves, given a little encouragement. You decide to concentrate your efforts on the Eagers. For convenience, we will assume the validity of your judgments. We will also assume that for your purposes—getting the job—the group of 200 constitutes a complete *population* of individuals. The results of your assignments are shown in Table 6.1.

Members of the group, you will notice, have been classified according to *two* characteristics: first, their enjoyment potential, in which each of the 200 individuals is assigned to one of three mutually exclusive categories (A_1, A_2, A_3), and second, their sex, in which each is assigned to one of two mutually exclusive categories (B_1, B_2). The entries in the cells of the table indicate the number of individuals exhibiting each pair of characteristics. The $B_1 A_3$ cell, for example, shows that 25 of the 80 men are classified as Duds. These numbers can also be expressed as the *proportion* of the total group exhibiting each pair of characteristics. The frequency data for the group of 200 men and women just reported, when translated into proportions, yield the values shown in Table 6.2.

---

*When A, B, C, and so forth are used as general terms to identify specific events or subset of events, order of events is unimportant. In the two-event case, for example:

$$p(A, B) = p(A) \times p(B \mid A) = p(B) \times p(A \mid B)$$

To illustrate, the probability of a heart and a black card (club or spade) drawn from a deck of cards, one after the other or as a pair, is $p(H, B) = \frac{13}{52} \times \frac{26}{51} = \frac{26}{52} \times \frac{13}{51} = .13$.

Table 6.1 Number of Men and Women Classified in the Three Enjoyment-Potential Groups

	Swingers (A₁)	Eagers (A₂)	Duds (A₃)	Total
Men (B₁)	25	30	25	80
Women (B₂)	25	60	35	120
Total	50	90	60	200

Table 6.2 is also a *probability table*. For example, the probability that an individual drawn at random will be a woman (fall in the B_2 category) is .60, the sum of the three A entries for B_2. Similarly, the probability that an individual chosen at random is a Swinger (A_1) is .25, the sum of the two B entries of A_1. We could also inquire about the probability that an individual will jointly exhibit a given pair of characteristics. For example, what is the probability that a randomly selected individual will be both female *and* a Swinger (will be classified as A_1B_2)? We can read this probability directly from the table by locating the entry in the appropriate cell; we find it is .125.

Now we ask a somewhat different question. Given that an individual selected from the population of 200 is a *woman* (belongs to category B_2), what is the probability that she is an Eager (belongs to category A_2)? You will recognize this question as inquiring about a *conditional* probability, in this instance $p(A_2 | B_2)$ or the probability of A_2 given B_2. In attempting to determine this conditional probability, let us first go back to the frequencies in Table 6.1. There are 120 women in the group, 60 (50 percent) of whom are classified as Eager. Given that an individual is a woman, the probability that she falls into the Eager category is therefore .50. Among the males, the probability that a man is a Dud is $\frac{25}{80}$, and so on.

This type of conditional probability can also be determined by the following formula, using the probability values shown in Table 6.2:

$$p(A \mid B) = \frac{p(A, \, B)}{p(B)} \tag{6.7}$$

Table 6.2 Proportion of the 200 Individuals Falling into Each Category

	Swingers (A₁)	Eagers (A₂)	Duds (A₃)	Total
Men (B₁)	.125	.150	.125	.400
Women (B₂)	.125	.300	.175	.600
Total	.250	.450	.300	1.000

Table 6.3 Conditional Probabilities, $p(A|B)$, of the Individual's Being in Each Enjoyment-Potential Category, Given the Individual's Sex

	Swingers (A₁)	Eagers (A₂)	Duds (A₃)	Total
Men (B₁)	.3125	.3750	.3125	1.00
Women (B₂)	.2083	.5000	.2917	1.00

Note that this formula is a rearrangement of a multiplication rule: $p(A, B) = p(B) \times p(A|B)$, obtained by dividing both sides of the latter equation by $p(B)$. As an illustration of the application of this formula, we again consider the probability of being Eager, given an individual who is a woman, $p(A_2|B_2)$. We first find, by inspecting Table 6.2, the probability that the individual is both A_2 *and* B_2. This $p(A_2, B_2)$ value we find to be .30. Next we determine, from examining the column at the far right of the table, that the probability of B_2 is .60. This $p(A_2, B_2)$ value is then divided by $p(B_2)$, giving us $\frac{30}{60}$ or .50, the same figure for the conditional probability $p(A_2|B_2)$ that we obtained earlier.

What about $p(A_3|B_1)$, the probability of being a *Dud*, given a *man*? The joint probability of A_3 and B_1, Table 6.2 shows, is .125, and the probability of B_1 is .40; the conditional probability of A_3 given B_1 therefore is $\frac{.125}{.40}$ or .3125. Application of this formula to all combinations of $A|B$—that is, probabilities of the three Enjoyment categories given the individual's sex—yields the conditional probabilities shown in Table 6.3. Note that for each B category the probabilities total 1.00; each man or each woman falls into one of the Enjoyment categories, so that the probabilities in the three Enjoyment groups must add up to unity in each sex.

Conditional probabilities can also be found for B, given A, by a parallel formula:

$$p(B|A) = \frac{p(A, B)}{p(A)} \tag{6.8}$$

For example, given an individual who is a Swinger (A_1), what is the probability that the

Table 6.4 Conditional Probabilities, $p(B|A)$, of the Individual's Being a Man or Woman, Given the Individual's Enjoyment Potential

	Swingers (A₁)	Eagers (A₂)	Duds (A₃)
Men (B₁)	.50	.33	.417
Women (B₂)	.50	.67	.583
Total	1.00	1.00	1.000

individual is male (B_1)? From the joint probabilities in Table 6.2 we determine that the A_1B_1 probability is .125 and that $p(A_1)$ is .25; $p(B_1|A_1)$ is therefore .125/.25 or .50. The complete set of $p(B|A)$ values is shown in Table 6.4. Again you will see that for a given class of A (enjoyment potential) the two categories of B (sex) account for all cases of that A; the two B probabilities therefore total 1.00 for each A.

PERMUTATIONS AND COMBINATIONS

Permutations

A budding art collector has four paintings, which he displays on his living room walls. The wall hooks are fixed, but he regularly changes the places where each painting hangs. How many different spatial arrangements or orders of the four paintings are possible? This question concerns the number of different sequences or *permutations* a set of discrete objects can take. With two objects two orders or permutations are possible: AB and BA; with three objects, A, B, and C, six permutations are possible: ABC, ACB, BAC, BCA, CAB, and CBA. With four objects there are 24 permutations—an answer we could have figured out by jotting down and counting all the possibilities. We can determine the answer more easily by recognizing that the number of permutations (P) a set of N objects can take is equal to the product of the integers from N to 1. The product is called N *factorial* or N!.* Thus:

$$P_N = N! = N(N - 1)(N - 2) \cdots (1) \tag{6.9}$$

Application of this formula to three objects gives us $3 \times 2 \times 1 = 6$, and to four objects $4 \times 3 \times 2 \times 1 = 24$.

The reason that the number of orders N objects may take is equal to N! is as follows. There are N ways to choose the first object or event. For example, in a set of four objects, A, B, C, and D, any one of the four may be chosen first. For each of these ways, there are $N - 1$ ways to choose the second object. For example, if B is chosen first from the set of four, A, C, or D may be chosen second. This gives $N(N - 1)$ possible orders so far. For each of these possibilities, there are then $N - 2$ ways to choose the third object and $N(N - 1)(N - 2)$ possible orders. Continuing this argument to its end yields N! ways to arrange the set of N things.

In Formula 6.9, you will note that P has a subscript, N. This subscript indicates that we are trying to determine the number of possible permutations for N objects taken N at a time. But we may also be interested in N objects taken *r* at a time, where *r* is some number less than N. For example, our art collector may have increased his holdings to nine paintings but have room to display only five of them at one time. How many arrangements or permutations of

---

*Occasionally, the number may turn out to be 0 or 1. Both 0! and 1! take the value 1.

these nine paintings, hung five at a time, are possible? The formula that permits us to answer this question is:

$$P_r^N = \frac{N!}{(N - r)!} \tag{6.10}$$

where the subscript r attached to P indicates that we are seeking the number of permutations for r objects at a time, rather than the entire set. On the right side of the equation the numerator is the same N factorial as above, while the denominator indicates that r is to be subtracted from N and the factorial of the resulting number found—that is, the product of the integers from $(N - r)$ to 1. If six objects are taken two at a time, then the number of permutations is determined by $6!/(6 - 2)!$ or $(6 \times 5 \times 4 \times 3 \times 2 \times 1)/(4 \times 3 \times 2 \times 1)$. The result of these calculations is 30.

You may understand Formula 6.10 better if you again notice that in this example of 6 objects taken two at a time, there are 6 ways of choosing the first object and, for each of these possibilities, 5 ways of choosing the second object, thus yielding 6×5 or 30.

Combinations

Our art collector with nine paintings that he wants to hang in all possible orders of five at a time faces an almost impossible task, since $9!/(9 - 5)!$ yields 15,120 permutations. He would have a better chance of succeeding if he contented himself with all possible *combinations* of his paintings. Combinations refer to the number of different subsets of r objects each that we can select from a set of N objects *without regard to sequence*. For example, three objects taken two at a time permit six sequential arrangements or permutations: AB and BA, AC and CA, BC and CB. If we disregard order (for example, treat AB and BA as the same), we see that there are three different subsets of objects; therefore the number of unordered subsets or *combinations* of three objects taken two at a time is 3. The formula for determining this number is as follows:

$$C_r^N = \frac{N!}{r!(N - r)!} \tag{6.11}$$

The number of ways that nine paintings can be displayed five at a time, ignoring the particular arrangement of a given subset of five on the walls, is therefore $9!5!(9 - 5)!$. This equals 126, a more manageable number than 15,120.

Knowledge of permutations and combinations also allows us to make probability statements about sets of events. One example will suffice. Four sisters were left 8 pieces of jewelry by their grandmother, her will stating that to avoid quarrels, each was to receive 2 pieces to be determined at random. One of the sisters had her eye on a topaz ring and a sapphire pin. What is the probability she will get her wish? Application of Formula 6.11 shows that there are 28 combinations of 8 things taken two at a time. She has only 1 chance out of 28, or a probability of only .036, to get both the pieces she covets.

The principles of probability will also help us to understand binomial probability distributions and the normal probability distribution, discussed in the next chapter.

Step-by-Step Procedures

In Table 6.5 we have reproduced the formulas for the various principles of probability that we have discussed and for permutations and combinations. Illustrations of their application to concrete sets of data appear below.

Probability of equally likely events

A total of 700 lottery tickets have been sold. On the basis of a random drawing, one first prize of $50, 5 second prizes of $20, and 10 third prizes of $10 are to be awarded. You have bought a single ticket.

1. What is your probability of getting a third prize? There are 10 third prizes. Therefore:

$$p(A) = \frac{n_A}{N} = \frac{10}{700} = \frac{1}{70} = .014$$

Table 6.5 Summary of Formulas for Principles of Probability and for Permutations and Combinations

Type	Formula	Formula Numbers
Probability of equally likely events	$p(A) = \dfrac{n_A}{N} = \dfrac{n_A}{n_A + n_{\overline{A}}}$	(6.1), (6.2)
	$p(\overline{A}) = \dfrac{n_{\overline{A}}}{n_A + n_{\overline{A}}}$	(6.3)
Addition rule	$p(A \text{ or } B \text{ or } C) = p(A) + p(B) + p(C)$	(6.4)
Multiplication rule for independent events	$p(A, B, C) = p(A) \times p(B) \times p(C)$	(6.5)
Multiplication for dependent events	$p(A, B, C) = p(A) \times p(B\|A) \times p(C\|A, B)$	(6.6)
Conditional probabilities and two joint events	$p(A\|B) = \dfrac{p(A, B)}{p(B)}$	(6.7)
	$p(B\|A) = \dfrac{p(A, B)}{p(A)}$	(6.8)
Permutations	$P_N = N!$	(6.9)
	$P_r^N = \dfrac{N!}{(N - r)!}$	(6.10)
Combinations	$C_r^N = \dfrac{N!}{r!(N - r)!}$	(6.11)

2. What is your probability of *not* getting a prize? Sixteen prizes are to be awarded. Therefore:

$$p(\overline{A}) = \frac{n_{\overline{A}}}{n_A + n_{\overline{A}}} = \frac{684}{16 + 684}$$

$$= .977$$

Addition rule

A pair of tickets to a basketball game is to be given away and there are 12 people who want them, including two friends, Alex and Bill. The winner is to be chosen at random. What is the probability that either Alex or Bill will be chosen to get a pair of tickets?

$$p(A \text{ or } B) = p(A) + p(B) = \frac{1}{12} + \frac{1}{12} = \frac{2}{12} = \frac{1}{6} = .167$$

Multiplication rule for independent events

Someone puts a coin (A) in a slot machine whose probability of a payoff (of any amount) is $\frac{1}{6}$ and then puts another coin (B) in another machine whose probability of a payoff is $\frac{1}{5}$. What is the probability of a payoff on both machines?

$$p(A, B) = p(A) \times p(B) = \frac{1}{6} \times \frac{1}{5} = \frac{1}{30} = .033$$

Multiplication rule for dependent events

A nursery school teacher has a bag of hard candies with 10 pieces of orange, 5 pieces of lemon, and 10 pieces of grape. She hands out a piece of candy to each child as a treat. Assuming she chose the candy at random, what is the probability that the first child received orange, the second child lemon, and the third child orange?

$$p(O, L, O) = p(O) \times p(L|O) \times p(O|O, L)$$

$$= \frac{10}{25} \times \frac{5}{24} \times \frac{9}{23} = \frac{450}{13800} = \frac{3}{92} = .033.$$

Conditional probabilities and joint events

The 45 female and 35 male students in a university history class came from three colleges: Liberal Arts, Natural Sciences, and Business. The breakdown by sex and college is shown on the next page.

	Liberal Arts (A1)	Natural Sciences (A2)	Business (A3)	Total
Men (B1)	20 (.250)	10 (.125)	5 (.062)	35 (.438)
Women (B2)	25 (.313)	5 (.062)	15 (.188)	45 (.562)
Total	45 (.563)	15 (.187)	20 (.250)	80 (1.000)

1. Translate numbers in each category to proportions. The table shows that of the 80 students, 20 are men in Liberal Arts. Therefore, $20/80 = .25$ are men in Liberal Arts. Similarly, $25/80 = .31$ are women in Liberal Arts. Continuing in this way, we generate the probabilities shown above in parentheses. (*Note:* Each proportion has been calculated separately. Totals do not always have exactly the same value as those obtained by adding cell values due to rounding errors. For example, the proportion of students in Natural Sciences is $\frac{15}{80} = .188$, and the proportions of men and women in this college are .125 and .062 = .187.)

2. Given category A, determine the probability of a person falling into a particular B category. For example, given that a student is in Liberal Arts (A1), what is the probability that the student is female (B2)? We use Formula 6.8:

$$p(B2 \mid A1) = \frac{p(A1, B2)}{p(A1)} = \frac{.313}{.563} = .556$$

3. Given category B, determine the probability of a person falling into a particular A category. For example, given that a student is male (B1), what is the probability that he is in Natural Sciences (A2)? The formula and procedures are parallel to those we used in problem 2. Thus by Formula 6.7:

$$p(A2 \mid B1) = \frac{p(A2, B1)}{p(B1)} = \frac{.125}{.438} = .285$$

Permutations

Number of permutations (P_N)

The research staff of an opinion polling organization has designed a 6-part questionnaire to be administered to a large national sample. They are concerned that a person's answers to questions in one part might influence their answers to questions in a later part. They therefore decide to vary the orders in which the parts are given. How many possible orders of the 6 parts are there?

This question calls for determining the number of permutations of 6 things. Therefore:

$$P_N = N!$$

$$P_6 = 6! = (6)(5)(4)(3)(2)(1) = 720$$

Number of permutations of N things taken r at a time (P_r^N)

In a certain state, all automobile license plates end with 4 numerals. How many different orders of the 10 numerals, 0–9, are there? The question calls for the number of permutations of 10 things taken 4 at a time. According to Formula 6.10:

$$P_r^N = \frac{N!}{(N - r)!}$$

$$P_4^{10} = \frac{10!}{(10 - 4)!} = \frac{10!}{6!}$$

$$= \frac{(10)(9)(8)(7)(6)(5)(4)(3)(2)(1)}{(6)(5)(4)(3)(2)(1)} = (10)(9)(8)(7) = 5040$$

(*Note:* To reduce the amount of arithmetic, first cancel terms in the numerator and denominator.)

Combinations

Five audiotapes have been prepared for a study of auditory perception. Each subject in the experiment is to be presented with three tapes, selected from the set of 5. If all possible combinations are used, what is the minimum number of subjects that is needed? We calculate the number by Formula 6.11:

$$C_r^N = \frac{N!}{r!(N - r)!}$$

$$C_3^5 = \frac{5!}{3!(5 - 3)!} = \frac{(5)(4)(3)(2)(1)}{(3)(2)(1)(2)(1)} = \frac{(5)(4)(3)}{2} = (5)(2)(3) = 30 \quad ■$$

DEFINITIONS OF TERMS AND SYMBOLS

Set. A collection of objects or events. For example, a deck of cards represents a set of 52 objects.

Elements. The individual members of a set of objects or events.

Equally likely events. The probability of occurrence of a single element on any given occasion is equally likely for each element in a set.

Mutually exclusive events. Two or more events that cannot possibly occur together. For example, a person is either alive or dead and cannot be both.

Independent events. The probability of an event remains unchanged whether or not some other event occurs.

Nonindependent events. The probability of an event is different when some other event occurs than when it does not occur.

Probability of equally likely events. In a set of N mutually exclusive events that are equally likely to occur, the likelihood of occurrence of any one event on a single occasion is $1/N$. The likelihood of occurrence of a subset of events (n) is the ratio of the number of events belonging to the subset to N, the total number of events: n/N.

Addition rule. In a set of mutually exclusive random events, the probability of occurrence of either one event or another event (or subset of events) is the sum of their individual probabilities. In the two-event case, this rule is expressed as $p(A \text{ or } B) = p(A) + p(B)$.

Multiplication rule for independent events. The probability of two or more independent events or subsets of events occurring on separate occasions is the product of their individual probabilities. In the two-event case, this rule is expressed as $p(A, B) = p(A) \times p(B)$.

Conditional probability of successive events. The probability that an event will occur, given the fact that another event or series of events has already occurred. In the instance of the probability of B occurring, given that A has already occurred, this probability is expressed as $p(B \mid A)$.

Multiplication rule for dependent events. The probability of two or more dependent events occurring is the product of their individual probabilities, with the probability of each event after the first being a conditional probability. In the case of the probability of event A accompanied by event B, this rule is expressed as $p(A, B) = p(A) \times p(B \mid A) = p(B) \times p(A \mid B)$

Joint events. Events are classified according to more than one set of mutually exclusive categories. For example, in a group of N people, each person could be classified by sex (male or female) and by marital status (married or not married). The probability of an individual having a given combination of characteristics (e.g., married and female) is the ratio of the number of individuals in the group having that combination to the total number in the group.

N factorial (N!). Multiplication of every integer from 1 to N by every other integer. Thus, $N! = N(N - 1)(N - 2) \cdots 1$

Permutations of N things (P_N). The number of orders or sequences that N discrete objects or events can take. $P_N = N!$

Permutations of r things out of N (P_r^N). The number of possible orders of a specified number (r) of objects selected from a larger set of N objects. $P_r^N = N!/(N - r)!$

Combinations (C_r^N). The number of different subsets of r objects that can be selected from N objects without regard to sequence. $C_r^N = N!/r!(N - r)!$

PROBLEMS

1. In each of the following, indicate whether the individuals or events have been classified into mutually exclusive (ME) or non-mutually exclusive (NME) categories. Explain your choice.

   (a) The recorded crimes committed in Travis County last year are categorized according to the type of offense (for example, murder, armed robbery, attempted rape, and so forth), and the totals for each category of offense are reported.

   (b) The number of undergraduate students in a state university who are enrolled in the College of Liberal Arts, College of Sciences, College of Business, and College of Engineering.

   (c) The instructor in a course in freshman English determines the number of students who were given course grades of A, B, C, D, and F.

2. In each of the following, indicate whether the samples or series of events being described are independent (I) or nonindependent (NI).

   (a) In a study of the effects of two types of diet on young rats, an investigator selects two males from each of 20 litters of pups. One pup in each pair is selected at random and assigned to one diet condition and the other pup is assigned to the second diet condition.

   (b) Students' grade point averages over three successive semesters.

   (c) The number of aces in each of a person's bridge hands over the course of three rubbers.

3. In a group of 200 individuals, 60 do not wear glasses, 50 wear glasses all the time, and 90 wear glasses only for reading. For purposes of this question, identify these subgroups as A, B, and C, respectively.

   (a) What is the probability that an individual randomly selected from the group of 200 never wears glasses?

   (b) What is the probability of selecting someone who wears glasses either all or some of the time?

   (c) If the answer to (a) is identified as $p(A)$, how can the answer to (b) be identified?

   (d) What is the probability of randomly selecting a person who wears glasses only for reading, followed by a person who wears glasses all the time, *assuming replacement*?

   (e) What is the probability of randomly selecting three people in a row who never wear glasses, again assuming replacement?

4. A nationally distributed magazine stages a prize lottery in which a contestant is first chosen from each of the 50 states. From these 50, three are chosen at random, the first drawn receiving the grand prize, the second drawn the second prize, and the third the third prize. No contestant may receive more than one prize.

   (a) What is the probability that the grand prize winner will be from Alaska or Hawaii?

   (b) What is the probability that the grand prize winner will come from one of the original 13 states?

   (c) Suppose that the grand prize winner comes from Texas. What is the probability that the second prize winner will come from California?

   (d) What is the probability that the first prize winner will come from Iowa, the second from Maine, and the third from Wyoming?

5. In a study of the development of the principle of conservation, a psychologist studies groups of 3-year-old, 5-year-old, and 8-year-old children. Each child is shown a glass half full of colored water. Then the child watches as the water is poured into a taller glass of smaller diameter. The child is next asked whether the amount of water in the second glass is less than, the same as, or more than the amount that was in the first glass. The children's responses are shown below.

	Less	Same	More	Total
3-year-olds	1	2	6	9
5-year-olds	0	5	5	10
8-year-olds	0	9	2	11
Total	1	16	13	30

   (a) Construct a table, similar to the one above, in which the *proportions* of the total group of 30 are shown instead of frequencies.

   (b) What is the probability that a child responded "same"?

(c) Set up a conditional probability table of the child's being in each response category, given the child's age.

(d) Given a 5-year-old child, what is the probability that the child responded "same"?

(e) Given a 3-year-old, what is the probability that the child responded "more"?

6. A psychologist intends to give subjects a battery of four personality tests. She is uncertain whether the order in which the tests are given will influence subjects' responses and decides to vary order among subjects. How many possible orders are there?

7. In a psychophysical experiment, an investigator prepares 10 cylinders that are identical in appearance but form a finely graded series in weight. Each subject is to be presented two cylinders at a time, one placed in the right hand and the other placed in the left hand, and asked to judge which one is heavier.

(a) If subjects were presented with all possible permutations of pairs, how many pairs would be involved?

(b) If subjects were presented with all possible combinations of pairs, how many pairs would be involved?

7

The Binomial and the Normal Distributions

- THE BINOMIAL DISTRIBUTION
- THE NORMAL PROBABILITY DISTRIBUTION

THE BINOMIAL DISTRIBUTION

In Chapter 6 we discussed the application of several principles of probability to data involving mutually exclusive categories. That is, our observations consist of a set of events (as they are called), each event falling into one and only one of two or more categories. The binomial distribution also deals with mutually exclusive categorical data. We start our discussion of this distribution by presenting an example.

A wine-loving friend of yours claims his palate is so sensitive that he can discriminate between two wines of the same type produced in the same year by neighboring vintners. He happens to have two bottles of wine that meet this description, and you challenge him to prove his boast. On each of ten "trials" you have him sip from each of two unmarked glasses and then announce which wine is which. On eight of the ten trials his identification is correct. At first you're impressed; eight out of ten is a pretty good hit rate, you think to yourself. But then it occurs to you that if he couldn't discriminate at all, he would be expected to be "right" half the time by chance alone. Was it pure luck he guessed correctly 80 percent of the time, or is it likely that he really can discriminate above the chance level?

This example illustrates a *binomial experiment*. In the binomial situation, one of two possible outcomes occurs on each of a number of independent occasions. The wine-taster was given 10 independent opportunities to judge which of the two wines was which and on each occasion was either *right or wrong*. To answer the question the experiment was designed to test, we must know something about a theoretical distribution called the *binomial probability distribution*.

In the binomial situation, we have said, one of two possible outcomes occurs on each occasion. Assume, for purposes of illustration, that each outcome has a probability of occurrence of $\frac{1}{2}$. For example, we might be tossing a fair coin in which H and T have an equal probability of turning up. Or the subject in our wine-tasting experiment might be unable to discriminate between the two wines and therefore be equally likely to be right as wrong. If we call the occurrence of a head or of a correct guess a "hit," and a tail or a wrong guess a "miss," we can determine by applying the multiplication rule the number of possible patterns of hits and misses on a given number of occasions and the probability of occurrence of each. If we toss a coin three times, for example, eight equally likely patterns of hits and misses are possible (HHH, HHM, HMM, HMH, MHH, MHM, MMH, MMM) and the probability of each is $(\frac{1}{2})^3$. That is, the probability of each is $\frac{1}{2} \times \frac{1}{2} \times \frac{1}{2}$ or $\frac{1}{8}$. Similarly, with five occasions there are 32 possible outcomes, each having a probability of $(\frac{1}{2})^5$ or $\frac{1}{32}$.

Now suppose that for the five-trial case we write out the 32 possible patterns of hits and misses. For each pattern we then count the number of *hits*, ranging from five out of five to zero. We find that five hits occur in only *one* of the 32 possible outcomes, but there are five patterns in which four hits occur (HHHHM, HHHMH, HHMHH, HMHHH, MHHHH), ten patterns in which three hits occur, and so on. A complete frequency distribution of the various numbers of hits, from five to zero, is shown in Table 7.1. In the final column of the table is the probability of occurrence of each number of hits. This list of probabilities is known as a *binomial probability distribution*.

Table 7.1 Theoretical Frequency Distribution of Number of "Hits," Where Number of Occasions = 5 and p = .50

Hits	Frequency (f)	prob (Hits) = $\frac{1}{\Sigma f}(f)$
5	1	.03125
4	5	.15625
3	10	.31250
2	10	.31250
1	5	.15625
0	$\underline{1}$	.03125
	$\Sigma f = 32$	Σ prob (Hits) = 1.00000

The binomial probabilities in the table were obtained by applying the addition rule, discussed in Chapter 6. That is, each of the *individual* patterns of hits and misses has a probability of $\frac{1}{32}$ or .03125. Five hits occur only once among the 32 patterns, so its probability is .03125. Four hits occur in *five* of the patterns; adding .03125 together five times gives .15625, and so on. [Instead of adding, we could get the same answer for each number of hits by multiplying .03125 by the frequency associated with the given number of hits, e.g., for 4 hits, $5(.03125) = .15625$.]

The Binomial Expansion

In explaining the binomial distribution above, we suggested writing down all the possible patterns of the two events that could occur on N occasions and then counting the number of patterns containing N of the specified ("favored") event, N − 1 of the favored event, and so forth down to (N − N) or 0. We can determine the distribution more efficiently by expanding the binomial:

$$(p + q)^N$$

where p is the probability of obtaining the favored event on a given occasion, q is the probability of the nonfavored event, and N is the number of independent occasions or observations. The expansion takes the general form:

$$(p + q)^N = p^N + Np^{N-1}q + \frac{N(N-1)}{1 \times 2} p^{N-2}q^2$$

$$+ \frac{N(N-1)(N-2)}{1 \times 2 \times 3} p^{N-3}q^3 + \cdots + q^N \tag{7.1}$$

For example, for $p = \frac{1}{2}$ and $N = 5$ we thus have:

$$\left(\frac{1}{2} + \frac{1}{2}\right)^5 = \left(\frac{1}{2}\right)^5 + 5\left(\frac{1}{2}\right)^4\left(\frac{1}{2}\right) + 10\left(\frac{1}{2}\right)^3\left(\frac{1}{2}\right)^2$$

$$+ 10\left(\frac{1}{2}\right)^2\left(\frac{1}{2}\right)^3 + 5\left(\frac{1}{2}\right)\left(\frac{1}{2}\right)^4 + \left(\frac{1}{2}\right)^5$$

Note the coefficients in each term in the expansion. The coefficient for the first term, $\left(\frac{1}{2}\right)^5$, is understood to be 1, and the remainder are 5, 10, 10, 5, and 1. These coefficients correspond to the frequencies in Table 7.1, while the terms themselves correspond to the probabilities listed in the table. For example, the probability of four hits is given by the second term, $5\left(\frac{1}{2}\right)^4\left(\frac{1}{2}\right)$; the value of this term equals .15625, the same figure we obtained earlier by the addition rule.

General Expression for Each Term of the Binomial Expansion. Each term in the binomial expansion can also be obtained by calculating:

$$C_r^N p^r q^{N-r}$$

where C_r^N is the combination of N things taken r at a time, as we discussed in Chapter 6. Since, according to Formula 6.11, C_r^N is equal to $N!/r!(N-r)!$, we can write:

$$C_r^N p^r q^{N-r} = \frac{N!}{r!(N-r)!} p^r q^{N-r} \tag{7.2}$$

As an example of the application of this equation, we determine the probability of obtaining three hits in a sample of five observations, where $p = \frac{1}{2}$:

$$C_3^5 p^3 q^2 = \frac{5!}{3!(5-3)!}\left(\frac{1}{2}\right)^3\left(\frac{1}{2}\right)^2 = 10\left(\frac{1}{32}\right) = .3125$$

The coefficient (10) and the probability (.3125) agree, you will observe, with the term for three hits in the expansion of the binomial equation and the entries in Table 7.1.

Combining Probabilities. Tables like Table 7.1 allow us to state for a given N the probability of obtaining patterns with a specific number of hits. They also allow us to answer questions of the following sort: What is the probability of obtaining patterns with the given number of hits or more? For example, with $N = 5$ and $p = .50$, what is the probability of getting 3 *or more* hits? To answer this question, we apply the addition rule and sum the probabilities for 3, 4, and 5 hits. Looking at Table 7.1, we find that these probabilities are .31250, .15625, and .03125. Their sum is .50; the probability of patterns with 3 or more hits is .50. What is the probability of 1 *or fewer* hits? Adding together the probabilities in Table 7.1 for 1 and 0 hits, we find that the answer is .18750.

Example Where p ≠ .50. So far we have discussed the situation in which the probability of the favored event (*p*) is .50 and the probability of the nonfavored event (*q*) is therefore also .50. Let us consider an illustration of the application of Formula 7.2 in which *p* and *q* are unequal.

If we rolled four dice, we could determine the probability of getting various numbers of, let us say, six-spots. Sixes could come up on all four dice, on only three of them, two of them, and so on. Since the probability of rolling a six-spot in a single die is $\frac{1}{6}$ and of rolling any other number $\frac{5}{6}$, we could determine the probability of these various numbers of six-spots in four rolls by expanding the binomial $(p + q)^N = (\frac{1}{6} + \frac{5}{6})^4$. What if we wanted to know only the probability of obtaining *two* sixes among the four dice? We could expand the binomial and use the appropriate term, or we could apply Formula 7.2. The latter procedure gives us:

$$C_2^4 p^2 q^2 = \frac{4!}{2!(4-2)!}\left(\frac{1}{6}\right)^2\left(\frac{5}{6}\right)^2 = 6\left(\frac{25}{1296}\right) = .116$$

Before concluding this section, we return briefly to the results of the wine-tasting experiment with which we started. The would-be expert, you recall, succeeded in guessing correctly on eight of ten occasions. If he could not discriminate at all, how likely is it that he would get eight or more correct out of ten by chance? If he cannot discriminate, the probability of a correct guess (a hit) on each trial is $\frac{1}{2}$. Expansion of the binomial shows us that with $p = \frac{1}{2}$ and N = 10, the frequencies of eight, nine, and ten hits are 45, 10, and 1, respectively. (In Figure 7.1, we have shown the frequencies of all numbers of hits from 0 to 10 in both graphic and

Figure 7.1 Binomial frequency distribution in which *p* = .50 and N = 10 and a superimposed normal distribution with the same mean and σ.

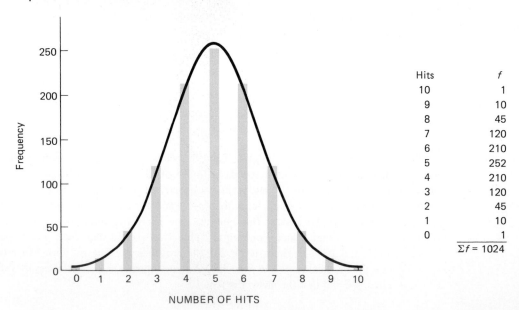

Hits	f
10	1
9	10
8	45
7	120
6	210
5	252
4	210
3	120
2	45
1	10
0	1
	Σf = 1024

tabular form.) We then sum these frequencies and divide the sum by the total number of outcomes (or Σf). This gives us $\frac{56}{1024} = .0547$. This result is the probability of being correct 8 or more times by chance. Alternatively, we could have first calculated the probabilities of eight, nine, and ten hits (by dividing each f by Σf or by applying Formula 7.2) and then summing these probabilities. This gives us .0439, .0098, and .0010, whose sum equals .0547.

With a probability as small as this, it is unlikely that your friend guessed correctly as often as he did by pure dumb luck; very probably he *can* discriminate above the level of chance. The kind of reasoning we have just gone through involves setting up and testing a hypothesis about some state of affairs, and then coming to some conclusion about the validity of the hypothesis. In the next chapter, we will discuss the topic of hypothesis testing in more detail. We return now to describing the binomial distribution.

The Mean and Standard Deviation of the Binomial Distribution

It is possible to calculate the mean and standard deviation of a binomial distribution, just as we learned to do for any other kind of distribution. If you look at Table 7.1, for example, where $p = .50$ and $N = 5$, what is the mean number of hits? Since the distribution is perfectly symmetrical, the mean falls at the midpoint of the range, which we observe to be 2.5. We could also calculate the mean in the ordinary way by multiplying each hit by the corresponding p (which is essentially percent frequency), summing these products, and dividing by Σp. Σp, of course, equals 1. If you were to carry out these operations, you would find that the mean turns out to be 2.5, just as it should be. The formula for the mean of the binomial can be reduced to a simpler form that considerably lessens our calculational labors:

$$\mu_b = Np \qquad (7.3)$$

where N is the number of observations and p the probability of the favored event. In our example μ_b therefore equals $5(.5)$ or 2.5. You will observe that we are dealing with a theoretical population of values, so the symbol we use for the mean is μ(mu). The subscript, b, indicates that we are referring to the mean of the binomial distribution.

We can determine the variance and the standard deviation of a binomial distribution in the usual way by finding the squared deviations of the "scores" from μ_b, finding the mean of these squared deviations, and so on. But just as in the case of μ_b, simpler formulas can be used. The *variance* of the binomial is given by:

$$\sigma_b^2 = Npq \qquad (7.4)$$

and the *standard deviation* by:

$$\sigma_b = \sqrt{Npq} \qquad (7.5)$$

where $q = 1 - p$.

Thus, in our example, we have for the standard deviation:

$$\sigma_b = \sqrt{(5)(.5)(.5)} = \sqrt{1.25} = 1.118$$

Shape of the Binomial Distribution When $p = \frac{1}{2}$

When $p = \frac{1}{2}$, the binomial distribution is always symmetrical. As N, the number of possible occurrences, becomes larger and larger, the shape of the binomial distribution with $p = \frac{1}{2}$ becomes increasingly similar to another theoretical distribution. This is the *normal probability distribution*, a particular member of the family of bell-shaped curves based on continuous rather than discrete measures. The similarity is illustrated in Figure 7.1, in which $p = \frac{1}{2}$ and N = 10. On the baseline we have indicated the number of "hits"—for example, number of heads coming up in a toss of ten coins. On the Y axis is shown the frequency, out of the 1024 possible patterns of hits and misses, with which each *number* of hits could be expected to occur. These frequencies, you recall, correspond to the coefficients of the terms in the binomial expansion. The frequencies have been plotted as bars to emphasize that the measures are discrete. That is, they take the values 0, 1, 2, 3, and so on; intermediate values such as 1.54 hits or 3.791 do not occur. Superimposed on the bar graph for the binomial distribution is a normal probability curve whose mean and standard deviation have the same values as those of the binomial. Since continuous measures (those that can take any value) are represented, the curve is unbroken.

You will observe that the two shapes are highly similar. As the N in a binomial increases toward infinity, the size of the "steps" between adjacent bars becomes smaller and smaller, and the distribution increasingly resembles the continuous normal distribution. Thus, we can state that the *limit of the binomial distribution*, where $p = \frac{1}{2}$ and N is infinitely large, is the *normal probability distribution*.

The similarity between the two distributions often leads us to substitute the normal distribution for the binomial distribution when we are evaluating binomial data like those in our wine-tasting experiment. When $p = \frac{1}{2}$, this substitution may safely be made when N is relatively small—as low as 10, let us say. As p departs from $\frac{1}{2}$ toward 0 or 1, the normal curve may provide a satisfactory approximation but N must be increasingly larger for the normal curve to be used. We shall discuss this use of the normal curve more specifically in the next chapter. We devote the rest of this chapter to describing the properties of the normal curve.

THE NORMAL PROBABILITY DISTRIBUTION

The binomial distribution, we have said, is based on situations in which one of two categorical outcomes (one of which is labeled a hit or favored event) occurs on each of a number of independent occasions. The binomial distribution itself is composed of a discrete number of hits or favored events, i.e., 0, 1, 2, 3, 4; and so forth. The normal probability distribution, on the other hand, is based on properties that exist along an unbroken continuum of values, e.g., height, weight, temperature, or time. Like the binomial distribution, the normal probability distribution is a theoretical mathematical model, based on a population of measures that is infinite in size.

The normal curve is a specific member of a family of curves that is shaped like a bell and can be described by a mathematical equation that is unique to it. But there is an infinite variety of curves based on continuous measures, and by choosing the appropriate mathematical equation we can plot and describe the properties of any of them we wish. Why, then, are we giving so much emphasis to this particular curve? The primary reason has to do with statistical theory. We have already seen that the binomial distribution approaches this form as N increases, and we shall see in later chapters that other theoretical sampling distributions also take this form.

A second reason why the normal curve is of interest is that many empirical distributions—those obtained by actually measuring some characteristic—are approximately normal in shape. That is, if we attempt to fit an idealized mathematical shape to the data we obtain, the equation for the normal distribution is an appropriate model. By applying our knowledge of the properties of the normal curve to an empirical distribution, we can answer many types of questions about the distribution.

In explaining the properties of normal curves, we will use only empirical distributions for illustrative purposes, deferring discussion of the curve's theoretical uses until later chapters.

Characteristics of the Normal Curve

The normal curve is shown in Figure 7.2. Since it is a plot of a theoretical distribution and not of actual data, the units of measurement along the baseline are expressed in z scores. We should also recall that the distribution is based on an infinite number of cases, which can take any z-score value. The curve therefore is not dropped to the baseline at either end and can be understood to reach it only at z values of $\pm\infty$.

The most obvious characteristic of the normal curve is its shape, somewhat like a bell, rising to a rounded peak in the middle and tapering off symmetrically at both tails. The half of the curve below μ is shaped like an elongated S ($\mathcal{S}$) and the half above μ is the reverse of this shape ($\leftharpoonup$). The vertical lines erected from the baseline at distances of $+1\sigma$ and -1σ

Figure 7.2 The normal distribution curve.

SIGMA DISTANCES FROM μ

both intersect the curve as its "inflection point"—the point at which the S and its mirror image each change directions, from being concave to being convex or vice versa.

The total *area* under the curve—the area between the curve and the baseline—is taken as 100 percent. We can also mark off portions of the curve and describe their areas as a percent of the total. In Figure 7.2, for example, we have dropped lines from the curve to the baseline at μ and at one σ above μ. Now in *any* curve, normal or any other shape, the portion of the total area under the curve between μ and the point that is one σ above μ is always the same for *that particular curve*. In other words, for any single curve, regardless of its shape, there is a fixed relationship between distance along the baseline measured in z scores, and area under the curve. In the *normal* curve the area under the curve between μ and $+1\sigma$ turns out to be 34.13 percent of the total area. *The percent area is the same as the percent frequency*; therefore, we know immediately that in the normal curve 34.13 percent of the total frequency is included between μ and the point that is one σ above μ. *When distance along the baseline is measured in σ units, percent area under the normal curve between μ and any other point is the same as percent frequency.* Recall that σ units are z scores; the score that is one σ above the mean is the score where $z = +1.00$. Thus, we can restate what we have just said in z-score terms: In the normal curve the percent frequency between μ and the point where $z = +1.00$ is 34.13.

Since the normal curve is symmetrical, another 34.13 percent of the frequency lies between μ and the point one σ below μ, between μ and $z = -1.00$. Therefore, 68.26 percent of the cases fall between $z = -1.00$ and $z = +1.00$. From μ to the point two σ's from μ is 47.72 percent of the frequency, so 95.44 percent fall between $z = -2.00$ and $z = +2.00$. Between μ and three σ's is 49.87 percent. Thus, three σ's above and below μ, six σ's in all, include 99.74 percent, or almost all, of the total frequency.

Let us illustrate what we have stated. If the weight distribution for a sample of 10,000 men were exactly normal, 3413 men (34.13 percent of N) would fall between the mean weight and the weight that was one σ above the mean. If the mean were 170 and σ 15, then 68.26 percent or 6826 of them could be expected to weigh between 155 and 185 (170 $\pm$ 15, the scores where $z = \pm1.00$). About 95% of the men would achieve scores between 140 and 200 ($\mu - 20$ and $\mu + 20$). Almost all men in the group would score between 110 and 230, that is, between $z = -3.00$ and $z = +3.00$.

Probability and Percent Area

We have discussed the percent of the total area in a normal curve that lies between representative points on the baseline, and the relationship between these percent areas and percent frequencies. For example, approximately 34 percent of the area, and hence about 34 percent of the total number of cases, fall in the interval between μ and one σ above μ. These percentages could instead be expressed as proportions. For example, the proportion of cases falling between μ and $z = 1.00$ is approximately .34.

These area values also reflect *probabilities*. For example, the probability that an individual selected at random from a normal distribution will fall between μ and one σ above μ (will have a z score ranging from 0 to $+1.00$) is .34.

When we were discussing equally likely categorical events in the last chapter, such as the outcome of coin tossing or drawing cards from a deck, we defined probability as the ratio of the number of times the specified event can occur to the total number of possible events. The normal curve, however, involves continuous rather than discrete categorical variables. Therefore, we must employ a somewhat different definition of probability for events randomly sampled from a normal distribution. This definition states that probability in the normal curve is the *ratio of the area under the specified portion of the curve to the total area*. This definition, you will observe, states formally what we have said in the paragraph above.

The Normal Curve Table

The percent area under the normal curve, and therefore the percent frequency, between μ and various σ distances from μ is shown in Table B at the end of the book. This table will be used repeatedly from now on. Let us examine the table and determine how to read it. The left-hand column, labeled x/σ, gives deviations from μ in σ or z-score units.

The values in the x/σ column in Table B are given to one decimal place; the second decimal place is shown in the top row of the table. The values in the body of the table are the *percent area* or *percent frequency* between μ and the point x/σ distance from μ. For example, if we wished to determine the percentage of the total frequency between μ and the point where $z = 1.96$, we would first find the value of 1.9 in the x/σ column, then go along that row to the column headed .06 and read off the percent frequency, which in this case is 47.50 percent.

Note that the table gives percentages only on *one* side of μ—that is, for only one-half of the normal curve—so none of the values in the table is larger than 50 percent. Because the normal curve is symmetrical, it is not necessary to print another table of the percentages for the other half of the curve; the percent frequency between μ and any x/σ value is the same whether the x/σ value is above or below μ, whether the z score is plus or minus.

Using the Normal Curve Table to Solve Problems

Let us now take up some problems involving real data and show how the normal curve table can be used to solve them. To avoid terminological confusion, we will assume that each group that has been measured constitutes a population of some sort, even if only a highly artificial one. Therefore, we will assume that the means and standard deviations of the obtained distributions are population values and refer to them, respectively, by the symbols μ and σ.

It may be helpful to state our general procedure first. If our empirical distribution is normal, or approximately so, the relation shown in Table B between percent frequency and z scores in the normal curve also holds for the empirical distribution. But the raw scores in an empirical distribution may be in any kind of units, such as feet, seconds, letters canceled per four minutes, and the like. In the normal curve the units are z scores, x/σ values. Therefore, we shall have to convert the raw score from the empirical distribution, given us in the problem, into a z score or x/σ value, and then immediately Table B becomes applicable. Let us see how this works.

In a study dealing with various athletic skills, 90 nine-year-old boys were measured as to how far they could throw a softball.* The mean was 79.06 feet, the standard deviation was

---

*Data courtesy of Dr. Robert Malina.

19.87 feet, and the distribution sufficiently approximated the normal distribution to allow us to assume normality. With this information, we are in a position to answer all sorts of questions. For example, what percentage of the boys threw 109 feet or more? How many threw 45 feet or less? Any boy who qualifies among the top 10 percent must be able to throw at least how far? What is the probability that a boy picked at random from the group threw somewhere between 59 and 99 feet? What distances are so extreme that they were thrown by only 1 percent of the boys? What extreme distances were thrown by only 5 percent?

Since it will not affect the method we are illustrating, we will make the data more convenient to handle by rounding off μ to 79 feet and σ to 20 feet, although we would not do this in actual practice. We also will assume, for purposes of illustration, that the data were normally distributed. The first question we asked concerning this distribution was, What percentage of the boys could throw 109 feet or more? This problem is shown graphically in Figure 7.3. We are interested in determining the percentage of the group falling at or above 109 feet in their scores, the shaded upper portion of the curve. To determine this percentage, the raw score of 109 feet must first be converted to a z-score value:

$$z = \frac{X - \mu}{\sigma} = \frac{x}{\sigma} = \frac{109 - 79}{20} = \frac{30}{20} = 1.50$$

From Table B, we find that 43.32 percent of the frequency in a normal distribution falls between μ and $z = 1.50$. We are interested, however, in the percentage that falls *beyond* $z = 1.50$. Since the total percent frequency above μ is 50 percent, we determine that $50 - 43.32 = 6.68$ percent of the boys throw 109 feet or more.

The second question asked was, *How many* threw 45 feet or less? Note carefully that this question asks about the *lower* extremes of the curve, scores of 45 feet or *less*, and about the raw frequency rather than percent frequency. Although we will not show this problem graphically, it might be helpful for you to draw a normal curve and mark off the portion

Figure 7.3 Percentage of boys throwing 109 feet or more, assuming normality of distribution.

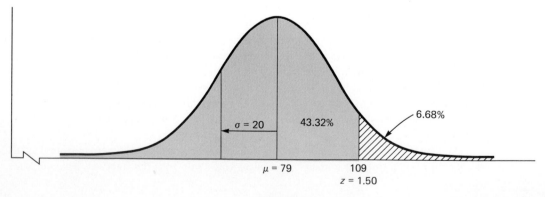

SCORES

of the curve in which we are interested. Our first step is to convert 45 feet to a z score: $z = (45 - 79)/20 = -34/20 = -1.70$. Table B shows us that 45.54 percent of the area lies between μ and $z = -1.70$; $50 - 45.54$ or 4.46 percent of the area lies below this z score. Since the questions ask about raw frequency, we must now find the number of boys, out of 90, that correspond to the percentage we have just determined. We find that $(4.46)(90/100)$ gives us 4.014. Rounding off this number, 4 boys threw 45 feet or less.

The third question asks: Any boy who qualifies among the top 10 percent must be able to throw at least how far? Note the difference between this question and the previous ones. Instead of being given a raw score and ending up with a percent frequency or a raw frequency, we are here given a percent frequency and asked for a raw score. We must go through the same steps as before, but in the opposite direction. Remember that a total of 50 percent of the area of the normal curve lies at or above μ. We want to find the z score that divides the percentage area above μ into two portions: 40 percent between μ and the z score and 10 percent beyond the z score. Since Table B gives the percent area between μ and a given z score, we look in the *body* of the table for 40 percent; this will give us the z score *beyond* which 10 percent remains. The closest value to 40 percent we can find in Table B is 39.97 percent, which corresponds to $z = 1.28$. We now know that the top 10 percent of the boys have z scores of $+1.28$ or more. But the question asks for a raw score, so we must convert the z of 1.28 into a raw score. Recall that the formula for this conversion is $X = \mu + z(\sigma)$ and that in our problem, $\mu = 79$ and $\sigma = 20$. Thus $X = 79 + 1.28(20) = 79 + 25.6 = 104.6$. The top 10 percent of the boys threw 104.6 feet or more.

The fourth question asks, What is the probability that a boy threw somewhere between 59 and 99 feet? This problem has been shown pictorially in Figure 7.4. Observe that 59 feet lies below μ and 99 feet lies above μ and that the question inquires about the probability of falling between these two values, the shaded portion of Figure 7.4. To find this probability, we must first convert both raw scores to z scores. As it turns out, both fall one σ unit from μ:

Figure 7.4 Percentage of boys throwing between 59 and 99 feet, assuming normality of distribution.

$z = (59 - 79)/20 = -1.00$ and $z = (99 - 79)/20 = +1.00$. Our next task, then, is to find the percent frequency between $z = \pm 1.00$. Looking at Table B, we find that 34.13 percent of the frequency falls between μ and $z = +1.00$ and the same percent between μ and $z = -1.00$. Thus 34.13×2 or 68.26 percent of the boys fall between z scores of ± 1.00 or between raw scores of 59 and 99 feet. This percentage can also be expressed as a proportion by moving the decimal points two places to the left: The proportion of the boys falling between the raw scores of 59 and 99 feet is approximately .68. This proportion reflects the *probability* that the score of a single boy, selected at random, fell between these two values, which is what our question asked. The answer to our question is thus .68.

The fifth question asks, What distances are so extreme that they are thrown by only 1 percent of the boys? This question, unlike the previous questions, does not specify whether it is the upper or the lower extreme that is of concern. Therefore, it should be assumed that the question refers to *both* extremes, the top $\frac{1}{2}$ percent plus the bottom $\frac{1}{2}$ percent, for a total of 1 percent. The problem we are working on may be clearer if we restate the question as follows: What scores (distances of throw) deviate from μ in either direction to such an extent that the *total* frequency of scores beyond these values is 1 percent? The problem is also shown graphically in Figure 7.5.

Our first step is to find the z score *above* which $\frac{1}{2}$ percent of the cases fall, the z score that divides the upper half of the curve into two portions with respect to area or percent frequency: 49.5 percent between μ and the z-score point, and .5 percent beyond this point. Looking in the body of Table B, we find that the number 49.5 percent lies midway between $z = 2.57$ and 2.58, so we may choose either one. We decide to select 2.58; thus we may state that $\frac{1}{2}$ percent of the cases lie above $z = +2.58$. Correspondingly, $\frac{1}{2}$ percent lie below $z = -2.58$. We now have the answer to our question in z-score terms: the extreme 1 percent of the cases have z scores of ± 2.58 or greater. Our final step is to convert these two z-score values into their raw-score equivalents, using the formulas $\mu + z(\sigma)$ and $\mu - z(\sigma)$. Filling in the appro-

Figure 7.5 Baseball-throwing scores that occur 1 percent of the time or less, assuming normality of distribution.

priate values, we thus have $79 + 2.58(20) = 79 + 51.6 = 130.6$, and $79 - 51.6 = 27.4$. The extreme 1 percent of the cases, then, have scores of 27.4 or less and 130.6 or greater.

The problem we have just solved was chosen to illustrate something we will now emphasize. The problem asked for the deviation beyond which a certain percent frequency occurs *without specifying the direction of the deviation*. As we will find in later chapters, this type of problem occurs often. We may state as a general rule that whenever the direction is *not* specified in a problem, you always assume the deviation in both directions is meant. In other words, when you are given a percent frequency and have to find the deviation corresponding to it, *unless it specifically states otherwise* the problem means that the deviation be such that half the percent frequency remains beyond it at each end of the curve.

Another reason why the above problem was chosen is that in the next chapter, when we take up the important problem of testing hypotheses, we will find that the frequency of 1 percent, one-half percent under each tail of the curve, has special significance. You should memorize the fact that 1 percent of the frequency in a normal distribution lies beyond $z = \pm 2.58$.

The final question asked the distances that could be thrown by the extreme 5 percent of the boys. This question is of the same type as the one we have just answered. It inquires about both extremes of the distribution, 2.5 percent at one end and 2.5 percent at the other. We must look in Table B for the z score that includes 47.5 percent of the area between μ and that z. (We obtain 47.5 by subtracting 2.5 from 50.) Doing so, we find the z of 1.96; 2.5 percent of the cases have a z of $+1.96$ or greater and 2.5 percent of the cases have a z of -1.96 or less. We next convert these z scores to raw scores: $79 \pm 1.96(20) = 39.8$ and 118.2. The extreme 5 percent of the cases have scores of 39.8 or less or 118.2 or more. The frequency of 5 percent—2.5 percent under each tail of the curve—also has special significance when we test hypotheses about populations. You should memorize that 5 percent of the cases in a normal distribution equal or exceed z scores of ± 1.96.

Percentiles from the Normal Curve

Table B is also useful for determining percentile ranks for raw scores from normally distributed data. It must be emphasized, however, that percentile ranks determined from Table B will not be accurate unless the raw scores are distributed normally or very nearly so. Recall that the percentile rank of a given score is the percentage of the total number of cases, the percent frequency, lying *below* that score. To illustrate, assume a normal distribution with a mean of 121 and a standard deviation of 20. What is the percentile rank of the raw score 141? As usual, we have to get the z score corresponding to the raw score; in this case $z = +1.00$. From Table B, 34.13 percent fall between this z-score value and μ. Therefore, the raw score 141 is above this 34.13 percent of the cases plus the 50 percent that are below μ, so the percentile rank is 84 (rounded). As you can see, we have merely found the total percent frequency falling below the given raw score. In other words, to use Table B to find the percentile rank for a raw score from normally distributed data, we have only to perform the usual step of converting the raw score to a z-score value and then, using Table B, find the total percent frequency falling below the z.

Let us also illustrate how to find the raw score corresponding to a known percentile rank; for example, what score in the distribution above (where $\mu = 121$ and $\sigma = 20$) corresponds to the 31st percentile? This must be the score below which 31 percent of the cases fall, which means 19 percent of the cases are between that score and μ. From Table B we find that .50 is the z score most closely corresponding to 19 percent. We now know that the raw score we are looking for is (.50)(20) score units below μ; therefore the 31st percentile corresponds to a score of 111.

We have now considered a variety of normal curve problems; before going further it may be helpful to point out how similar they are. You should find the solution of normal curve problems easier if you keep in mind that all problems give some information expressed in one kind of unit, and that to answer the problem the given information will have to be translated into some other kind of unit. Specifically, the problem will give us at least one of the following units: a raw score, a z score or x/σ value, a percent frequency, or a raw frequency. Answering the problem will require translating from one to another of these units. Perhaps the diagram below will make this clearer. The top row shows the general procedure in all problems: We are given one kind of unit and we translate into another kind of unit. The two-headed arrows indicate that we can translate in either direction. Note, however, that whether we are translating from left to right or right to left, *we cannot skip a step*. To get from X to % f we have to go from X to z, then from z to % f; to get from f to X, we must first convert f to % f, then % f to z, then z to X.

$$X \longleftrightarrow z \longleftrightarrow \%\,f \longleftrightarrow f$$

$$\frac{X - \mu}{\sigma} = z \longrightarrow \text{Table B} \longrightarrow \frac{\%\,f(N)}{100} = f$$

$$X = z\sigma + \mu \longleftarrow \text{Table B} \longleftarrow \%\,f = \frac{f}{N}(100)$$

The other two rows of the diagram show the specific steps to take. Thus, suppose a problem gives a raw score (X) and asks for the percent frequency (% f), or raw frequency (f), above or below that score. For example, how many boys scored below 50 feet in the baseball-throwing distribution? We would proceed from *left to right* in the top row of the diagram and we would also go through the steps shown in the *second* row.

On the other hand, suppose the problem gives a percent frequency or raw frequency and asks for either a z score or raw score. As an example, the top 30 boys are above what score in the baseball distribution? In this case we would go from *right to left* in the top row of the diagram and would also go through the steps shown in the *bottom* row.

The point we want to make is that there are really not several different kinds of normal curve problems. All normal curve problems are essentially the same; they only look different because they can be stated in so many different ways. One more thing: we strongly advise drawing a graph for each problem. You often will find that if you express graphically the information given in a problem, it will help you get started answering it.

Step-by-Step Procedures

Binomial Distribution

Example 1 ($p = \frac{1}{2}$)

In our first example, assume that there is a set of 6 independent events and that on each occasion, the probability of the favored event (or hit) is .50 ($p = \frac{1}{2}$). The probability of the nonfavored event (or miss) is therefore .50 ($q = 1 - p = \frac{1}{2}$).

1. In the set of N events, determine how many different patterns of hits and misses there are and the probability of occurrence of each unique pattern. The number of patterns is equal to 2^N and the probability of each is $(\frac{1}{2})^N$. In our example in which N = 6:

$$2^6 = 64 \quad \text{and} \quad \left(\frac{1}{2}\right)^6 = \frac{1}{64} = .016$$

2. Determine the frequency of patterns (out of the total number) that have a specific number of hits. Also determine the probability of obtaining a pattern with the specified number of hits. The answers to these questions may be obtained by applying the appropriate term in the expansion of the binomial equation (Formula 7.1). A simpler method is to use the generalized expression for each term in the binomial expansion. This expression, found in Formula 7.2, is as follows:

$$C_r^N p^r q^{N-r} = \frac{N!}{r!(N - r)!} p^r q^{N-r}$$

The first part of the formula, C_r^N (the combination of N things taken r at a time), is the coefficient and gives the frequency of the patterns in which the specified number of hits (r) appear. The term as a whole gives the corresponding probability.

In our example in which N = 6 and $p = \frac{1}{2}$, find the frequency (out of 64) and probability of patterns with 3 hits:*

$$\frac{6!}{3!(6 - 3)!} \left(\frac{1}{2}\right)^3 \left(\frac{1}{2}\right)^3 = \frac{(6)(5)(4)(3)(2)(1)}{(3)(2)(1)(3)(2)(1)} \left(\frac{1}{2}\right)^3 \left(\frac{1}{2}\right)^3$$

$$= 20\left(\frac{1}{8}\right)\left(\frac{1}{8}\right) = \frac{20}{64} = .3125$$

Thus 20 of the 64 patterns have 3 hits and the probability of a pattern with 3 hits occurring is .3125.

---

*You can cut down arithmetic labor by canceling terms in the numerator and denominator of the coefficient before you start to multiply.

3. Find the mean and standard deviation of the binomial frequency distribution. By Formulas 7.3 and 7.4:

$$\mu_b = Np \qquad\qquad \sigma_b = \sqrt{Npq}$$

$$= 6\left(\frac{1}{2}\right) = 3 \qquad = \sqrt{6\left(\frac{1}{2}\right)\left(\frac{1}{2}\right)} = \sqrt{\frac{6}{4}} = 1.22$$

Example 2 ($p \neq \frac{1}{2}$)

In our second example, there are again 6 events but $p = \frac{2}{3}$ and $q = \frac{1}{3}$.

1. Determine the probability of obtaining a pattern with two hits.

$$\frac{6!}{2!(6-2)!}\left(\frac{2}{3}\right)^2\left(\frac{1}{3}\right)^4 = 15\left(\frac{4}{9}\right)\left(\frac{1}{81}\right)$$

$$= 15\left(\frac{4}{729}\right) = .0823$$

Suppose that in this example, you had calculated the probabilities for *all* numbers of hits, from 6 − 0, with the following results.

Hits	p	Hits	p
6	.0878	2	.0823
5	.2634	1	.0165
4	.3292	0	.0014
3	.2194		1.000

2. Determine the probability of a specified number of hits *or more* (or a specified number of hits *or less*). The answer is obtained by adding the probabilities with the specified number and greater numbers of hits (or with the specified number and lesser numbers of hits). In our example, find the probability of 4 hits or more and of 2 hits or less.

4 hits or more: .3292 + .2634 + .0878 = .6804
2 hits or less: .0823 + .0165 + .0014 = .1002

Note: If you examine the probabilities in the preceding table for our example in which $p = \frac{2}{3}$, you will see that unlike the situation in Table 7.1 in which $p = \frac{1}{2}$, the binomial distribution is not symmetrical. This is particularly apparent in the last example, in which the probability of 4, 5, or 6 hits is .6804 and the probability of 2, 1, or 0 hits is only .1002. The departure of the binomial distribution from symmetry becomes increasingly marked as p departs (in either direction) from $\frac{1}{2}$, particularly with small N's.

Normal Probability Distribution

Illustrations of normal curve problems are broken down into two types: problems in which a z score or a raw score is given and a percentage, probability, or number of cases is to be found, and problems in which a percentage, probability, or number of cases is given and a z score or raw score is to be found.

The solutions to the first set of problems require going from left to right in the steps outlined in the diagram below, whereas the solutions to the second set require going from right to left.

$$X \longleftrightarrow z \longleftrightarrow \% \, f \, (\text{Table B}) \longleftrightarrow f$$

In all problems, assume a normally distributed population of scores in which:

$$\mu = 60$$
$$\sigma = 8$$
$$N = 5000$$

Problems in Which z or X Is Given

1. What is the probability of a z score of 1.5 or more? As shown in the graph at the left, the problem asks for the area above $z = 1.5$. The % area between μ and this z is 43.32 (Table B). The area above 1.5 is $50 - 43.32 = 6.68$ percent; $p = .0668$.

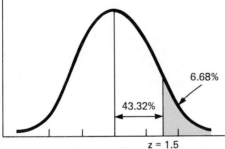

6.68%

43.32%

z = 1.5

2. How many of the 5000 cases score $z = 1.5$ or above? Translate the percent of cases found in problem 1 to a number:

$$6.68\% \text{ of } 5000 = 334$$

3. How many of the 5000 cases score 72 or above? The first step is to translate the raw score into a z score.

$$z = \frac{X - \mu}{\sigma} = \frac{72 - 60}{8} = 1.5$$

The next step is to determine the percent of cases at or above 72. This has already been done in problem 2, in which it was found that 6.68% of the cases had z scores of 1.5 or above.

The last step is to translate the percent of cases into a number. This has already been done in problem 2. The answer is 334 cases.

4. How many cases deviate 16 or more points in either direction from μ? As shown in the graph, the question asks about the two tails of the distribution. First, translate the given raw score

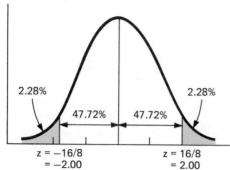

deviation ($X - \mu = \pm 16$) into z scores: z's = $(X - \mu)/\sigma = \pm 16/8 = \pm 2.00$. Second, find from Table B that 47.72% of the cases lie between μ and $z = +2.00$ and $50 - 47.72 = 2.28\%$ beyond it. As both tails are required, $2 \times 2.28\% = 4.56\%$. The final step is to translate the percent into a number of cases: 4.56% of 5000 = 228.

Problems in Which Number or Percentage of Cases Is Given

1. What score is equal to the 70th percentile? The 70th percentile divides the area under the curve into the lower 70% and the upper 30%. This means that 20% of the area lies between μ and the

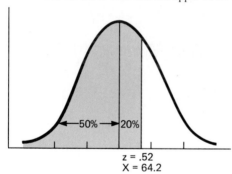

z equal to the 70th percentile. We look in the body of Table B and find that it is associated with a z of approximately .52. The final step is to translate this z into a raw score.

$$X = \mu + z(\sigma) = 60 + .52(8) = 64.2$$

The 70th percentile is the score 64.2.

2. The extreme 10% of the cases have raw scores of what or greater or what or less? The question asks about both tails of the distribution, 5% at either end. This means that for both extremes, 45% of the area lies between μ and the z score associated with the extreme 5%. Looking at the

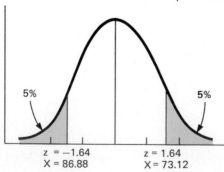

body of Table B, we find that these z's are approximately ± 1.64. Translating these z's into raw scores: $\mu \pm z(\sigma) = 60 \pm 1.64(8) = 60 \pm 13.12$. The extreme 10% of the cases had scores of 46.88 or less or 73.12 or greater.

3. What raw scores are associated with the extreme 500 cases? Translating number into percent, we find that 500 cases is 10% of 5000. As no direction is specified, it may be assumed that both extremes are meant, 250 or 5% at either end. The raw scores associated with these percentages were calculated in problem 2. ■

DEFINITIONS OF TERMS AND SYMBOLS

Binomial probability distribution. Theoretical distribution giving the probability of each possible number of hits (or favored event) and misses (or nonfavored event) when N independent attempts are made. The probability of a hit is p, and the probability of a miss is $q = 1 - p$.

Binomial expansion. Expansion of the binomial $(p + q)^N$ to give the probability of each number of hits, r. This probability is given by:

$$\frac{N!}{r!(N - r)!} p^r q^{N-r}.$$

Mean of binomial (μ_b). Mean of the binomial distribution. $\mu_b = Np$, where N is the number of observations and p is the probability of the favored event.

Standard deviation of binomial (σ_b). This standard deviation is given by $\sigma_b = \sqrt{Npq}$, where N is the number of observations, p is the probability of the favored event, and q is the probability of the favored event not occurring, with $q = 1 - p$.

Normal probability distribution. A particular theoretical probability distribution, based on continuous measures, of an infinite number of scores. The shape of the normal distribution is symmetrical and somewhat like a bell, rising to a rounded peak in the middle and tapering off symmetrically at both tails. The percentage of the area under the normal curve between μ and each sigma (z score) distance from μ is fixed and unique to the normal curve.

Inflection point. Point on a curve such as a normal curve where the curve changes direction from being concave to convex, or vice versa. In a normal curve, the inflection points occur at $z = \pm 1$.

PROBLEMS

1. As a promotional gimmick, a grocery store gives each customer at the checkout counter a card with four coated lines on it. The customer is to pick one line and scrape off the coating. Behind one of the lines is the name of an item of merchandise that the customer wins if he or she picks that line. Nothing is printed on the other lines, and the customer who chooses one of these lines "loses." The cards have been printed so that one-fourth of them have the "winner" on each line. One customer accumulates three cards before making her choice of a line for each card.
   (a) On these three cards, how many *different* patterns of "winners" and "losers" are possible and what is the probability of each?

(b) Expand the binomial (Formula 7.1) to find the probabilities of obtaining 0, 1, 2, and 3 winners on the three cards.

(c) Determine the probability of getting two losers and one winner by Formula 7.2. Check to see if your answer agrees with the probability value you calculated for one winner in (b).

(d) What is the probability of having two *or* three winners?

(e) What is the mean and the standard deviation of the distribution of number of losers in the set of three cards?

2. A test measuring knowledge of the U.S. Constitution has been given to a national sample of 5000 high school seniors. The distribution of scores closely approximates the normal curve and has a mean of 75 and a standard deviation of 12.

(a) What percentage of those tested scored 63 or below?

(b) What percentage scored between 63 and 87?

(c) *How many* of the 5000 individuals scored between these score values?

(d) What percentage scored between 81 and 93?

(e) A raw score of 66 has a percentile rank of what?

(f) What is the raw-score equivalent of the 67th percentile?

3. The 5000 high school seniors were also given a test of their knowledge of current events. This distribution also closely approximated the normal curve and had a mean of 58 and a standard deviation of 10.

(a) What is the probability that a senior chosen at random would earn a score of 62 or below?

(b) What is the probability that a randomly chosen student would have a score that deviated 5 or more score units *in either direction* from the mean?

(c) The extreme 5 percent of the seniors (2.5 percent at either end) earned raw scores of what and above or what and below?

8

Sampling Distributions:

Single Samples

- SAMPLING DISTRIBUTION OF MEANS
- MEANS OF SUCCESSIVE RANDOM SAMPLES
- TESTING HYPOTHESES ABOUT μ: LARGE SAMPLES
- TESTING HYPOTHESES ABOUT μ: SMALL SAMPLES
- CONFIDENCE INTERVALS
- TESTING HYPOTHESES ABOUT POPULATION PROPORTIONS
- OVERVIEW OF HYPOTHESIS TESTING

In Chapter 7 we discussed the binomial distribution—the distribution expected from a large number of samples of events in situations in which each event has one of two possible outcomes. For example, in Figure 7.1 we plotted the relative frequency, in an infinite number of samples of 10 coin tosses each, with which samples with 0 to 10 heads would theoretically occur. Although we did not then describe it as such, Figure 7.1 represents what is called a *sampling distribution*. A sampling distribution is a theoretical distribution, based on a mathematical model, that represents the *distribution of values of a statistic that would be obtained from an infinite number of random samples of a given size.*

In this chapter we extend our discussion of sampling distributions to include the distribution of sample *means*. Means, you recall, are derived from a group of scores, each based on the measurement of some property that exists in varying amount. We will consider the use of sampling distributions in making inferences about population characteristics.

SAMPLING DISTRIBUTION OF MEANS

When we measure the amount of some characteristic that each member of a random sample exhibits, one of the statistics we compute from the sample data is $\overline{X}$. Our purpose in determining $\overline{X}$ is not merely to describe the individuals in the sample, but also to get an idea about the value of the population mean. The likelihood is very small that this $\overline{X}$ has *exactly* the same value as μ of the population from which the sample was selected. That is, if we measured a large number of samples from the population, we would discover that the values of the sample $\overline{X}$'s were varied and that few were exactly the same as μ. If we were to use any given $\overline{X}$ as an estimate of μ, then, our estimate would be likely to contain a certain degree of inaccuracy. This fact is known as the *sampling error* of $\overline{X}$'s with respect to μ.

In Chapter 4 we said that the value of $\overline{X}$ was the best *single* guess we could make about the value of μ. But if $\overline{X}$ is not expected to be the same as μ, how can we use the sample $\overline{X}$ as indicative of the population mean? The best answer is, first, that sample means show no systematic tendency to be either larger or smaller than μ and hence can serve as an unbiased estimate of μ. Second, the mean of a truly random sample rarely deviates far from the population mean, particularly if the sample is large, so that $\overline{X}$ is usually a fairly close approximation of μ. In practice, however, we seldom use $\overline{X}$ to assign a precise value to μ; instead we use the sample data to test some specific hypothesis about the value of μ or to make estimates about a range of values that might reasonably be expected to contain μ. We will go on now with further elaboration of this important problem.

MEANS OF SUCCESSIVE RANDOM SAMPLES

Strictly speaking, the steps in reasoning we are going through now are based upon the assumption that we are drawing an infinite number of samples from an infinite population. However, it is quite satisfactory for illustrative purposes to go through the statistical logic with a finite population and a finite number of samples. We will follow this procedure for the clarity it affords.

Suppose that we have been able to measure all the members of a very large population. We have calculated μ to be 90 and σ to be 7.5. Now we draw a random sample of 225 cases from the population and determine its $\overline{X}$. Then we replace the sample and randomly draw another sample of the same size and determine its $\overline{X}$. We continue in this way until we have drawn, let us say, 5000 samples, each of 225 cases. The result is a set of 5000 numbers, each of which represents the mean of a sample. We can describe these 5000 numbers in the same way we describe raw scores. That is, the mean of the 5000 $\overline{X}$'s can be determined by adding them up and dividing by 5000. Similarly, the same procedures used with raw scores (X's) can be used to determine the standard deviation of the set of 5000 $\overline{X}$'s. And, of course, we can order the 5000 $\overline{X}$'s and cast them in the form of a frequency distribution. This frequency distribution is given a special name: *the sampling distribution of $\overline{X}$'s.*

Shape of the Sampling Distribution of $\overline{X}$'s.   The sampling distribution of $\overline{X}$'s can also be presented graphically as a frequency polygon, the values of $\overline{X}$'s being placed along the baseline (X axis) and the frequencies on the ordinate (Y axis). When the size of each of the samples is relatively large, the frequency distribution of $\overline{X}$'s approximates a *normal distribution* even if the distribution of measures (X's) in the population is not normal. We have plotted the normal distribution that would be approximated by our 5000 sample $\overline{X}$'s in Figure 8.1.

Mean of the Sampling Distribution of $\overline{X}$'s.   What do we expect the mean of this distribution of $\overline{X}$'s to be? Recall that $\overline{X}$'s are *unbiased estimates* of μ. That is, overall the $\overline{X}$'s are not systematically larger or smaller than μ. Further, errors of overestimation of a given size occur equally as often as errors of underestimation of μ. The mean of a sampling distribution of $\overline{X}$'s,

Figure 8.1 Sampling distribution of $\overline{X}$'s of 225 cases each from a population in which $\mu = 90$ and $\sigma = 7.5$.

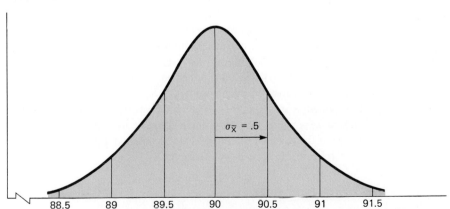

therefore, can theoretically be expected to take the *same value as μ for the population*. In our illustration, we have said that μ is 90. In Figure 8.1, the mean of the sampling distribution of $\overline{X}$'s can be seen to take this same value. Thus another way of defining lack of bias in $\overline{X}$ as an estimate of μ is to say that the average $\overline{X}$ in a sampling distribution is equal to μ, that is, the population parameter that is parallel to the statistic obtained for each sample.

Standard Deviation (Standard Error) of the Sampling Distribution. In addition to calculating the mean of the sampling distribution of $\overline{X}$'s, we could also calculate its standard deviation by treating each $\overline{X}$ as if it were a raw score and applying the procedures described in Chapter 5. The standard deviation of the sampling distribution of $\overline{X}$'s is given a special name, the *standard error of the mean*, and is symbolized as $\sigma_{\overline{X}}$. The word "error" is used to label this particular standard deviation because each $\overline{X}$ in the distribution that differs from μ incorporates a sampling error and is not an accurate estimate of μ.

Before proceeding with a discussion of how to compute the standard error of the mean, we will consider its value, relative to the value of the standard deviation of the population from which the samples were drawn. In our example, you recall, $\mu = 90$ and $\sigma = 7.5$, from which we may infer that the scores vary from approximately 67.5 to 112.5 ($\mu \pm 3\sigma$), a range of 22.5 points above μ and below μ. We know that the mean of our collection of 5000 sample $\overline{X}$'s (each based on 225 cases) is 90, the same value as the mean of the population. But what about the variability among the $\overline{X}$'s? Would you expect the $\overline{X}$'s to vary over the same range as the raw scores? Put another way, would you expect the value of $\sigma_{\overline{X}}$ to be greater than, equal to, or less than 7.5, the value of σ?

If you think about it, you will realize that it would be extremely unusual for a sample of 225 people to be so different from the population as a whole that their *mean* would differ from μ by as much as 7.5 points, let alone as much as 22.5 points above or below μ. Common sense tells us that most of our sample $\overline{X}$'s would fall very close to 90, the μ of the population. The variability among our 5000 $\overline{X}$'s, then, would be much smaller than the variability among the raw scores belonging to the population. This implies, of course, that $\sigma_{\overline{X}}$, the standard deviation of the sampling distribution of $\overline{X}$'s, would be smaller than σ, the standard deviation of the distribution of raw scores. How much smaller depends on the N within each sample. If samples are as large as 225 (for example), their $\overline{X}$'s all closely resemble μ so their standard deviation, $\sigma_{\overline{X}}$, is much smaller than σ. On the other hand, if the samples consisted of, let us say, only 5 cases each, we would not be surprised to find occasional $\overline{X}$'s that deviated considerably from μ; $\sigma_{\overline{X}}$ would still be smaller than σ but not as much smaller as with larger samples.

The standard error of the mean of our 5000 $\overline{X}$'s, we have said, could be calculated directly. However, an alternative method is available. Statisticians have demonstrated that the value of the standard error of the mean, $\sigma_{\overline{X}}$, has a constant relationship to the standard deviation of the population from which the samples were obtained and to the size of each of the samples. The exact relationship is given by the formula:

$$\sigma_{\overline{X}} = \frac{\sigma}{\sqrt{N}} \tag{8.1}$$

where N = sample size.

We specified earlier that the σ of our population is known to be 7.5. Since each sample N is 225, $\sigma_{\overline{X}}$ can be calculated as:

$$\sigma_{\overline{X}} = \frac{7.5}{\sqrt{225}} = .5$$

The sampling distribution in Figure 8.1 therefore has a mean of 90, the same value as μ, and a standard deviation or standard error of .5.

Inspection of Formula 8.1 shows that as sample N's grow larger, $\sigma_{\overline{X}}$ grows smaller. This reflects the fact that as the size of the individual samples is increased, the $\overline{X}$'s of the samples are increasingly likely to be close to μ and hence to the mean of the sampling distribution.

To repeat, as sample size is increased, $\overline{X}$'s cluster closer and closer around μ. As sample size is increased, the distribution of $\overline{X}$'s also increasingly resembles the normal probability distribution. These relationships with sample size comprise what is known as the *central limit theorem.*

Knowing the shape of the sampling distribution and its mean and standard deviation, we are in a position to make probability statements about $\overline{X}$'s. In Chapter 7, we discovered that a case drawn at random from a normal distribution has a probability of approximately .68 of falling between the points established by $+1\sigma$ and -1σ—that is, between z scores of ±1. Similarly, we determined from Table B that an individual has a probability of .05 of falling at or beyond the point established by a z of $+1.65$. Since for all practical purposes our sampling distribution of $\overline{X}$'s can be assumed to be normal when N is large, we can make similar probability statements about a single sample $\overline{X}$. Thus, for example, the probability that an $\overline{X}$ will fall within the interval bounded by a z of ±1 in the sampling distribution is .68.

We now ask a more concrete question about the distribution in Figure 8.1. What is the probability that a $\overline{X}$ will deviate from the μ of 90, *in either direction*, by 1 or more points? That is, what is the probability of obtaining $\overline{X}$'s of 91 or greater or of 89 or less? We first must convert this deviation into a z score, defined, you recall, as the score minus the mean of the distribution, divided by its standard deviation.

The "score" in this instance is $\overline{X}$; the mean of the sampling distribution takes the value of the μ of the population; and the distribution's standard deviation is $\sigma_{\overline{X}}$. Thus:

$$z = \frac{\overline{X} - \mu}{\sigma_{\overline{X}}} = \frac{x}{\sigma_{\overline{X}}} \tag{8.2}$$

Filling in the values for our example, $\pm1/.5$ is equal to a z of ±2.00. Consultation with Table B shows that approximately 2.28 percent of the area under the normal curve lies at or beyond a z of $+2.00$. The same percent lies at or beyond a z of -2.00. Thus 4.56 percent of the area lies at or beyond $z = \pm2.00$. The probability of drawing a random sample whose $\overline{X}$ is 91 or greater or 89 or less is therefore .0456.

Our aim, however, is not to learn how to make probability statements about obtaining sample $\overline{X}$'s of certain values, given the values of the population μ and σ. If we had this information about the population, there would be little purpose in measuring samples. Our goal is the reverse: to make inferences about the unknown μ, given data from a single random sample. If we knew the standard error of the sampling distribution of $\overline{X}$'s, we would be able to make these inferences about μ. Unfortunately, when we do not know the population μ, we also do not know the standard error of the mean, $\sigma_{\overline{X}}$. We can, however, calculate an *estimate* of $\sigma_{\overline{X}}$ from the data of a sample. Recall from Chapter 5 that estimating a single value for a population parameter from the data of a sample is known as *point estimation*.

A Point Estimate of the Standard Error of the Mean

The $\sigma_{\overline{X}}$ of a sampling distribution, we have seen, can be determined by dividing σ, the standard deviation of the population, by the square root of N, the number in each sample. This formula is used as a basis for estimating the standard error of the mean from the data of a single sample by substituting for the unknown σ an *estimate* of σ. We recall that s is our preferred estimate of σ and is determined by the formula:

$$s = \sqrt{\Sigma x^2/(N - 1)}$$

Our estimate of the standard error of the mean, symbolized as $s_{\overline{X}}$, is obtained by substituting s for σ in Formula 8.1. Thus:

$$s_{\overline{X}} = \frac{s}{\sqrt{N}} \qquad (8.3)$$

where $s = \sqrt{\dfrac{\Sigma x^2}{N - 1}}$

N = sample size

Before proceeding further, let us state once more what $s_{\overline{X}}$ represents. It is an *estimate*, based on the data from a single sample, of the *standard deviation of a distribution of randomly drawn sample means*. This estimated standard deviation is given a special label, the *standard error of the mean*. In other words, $s_{\overline{X}}$ is an estimate of the *variability* of the sampling distribution of $\overline{X}$'s and thus reflects the *errors* in the distribution of $\overline{X}$'s in estimating μ.

We can now demonstrate the calculation of $s_{\overline{X}}$. We have a random sample of 25 cases with s of 15. Thus:

$$s_{\overline{X}} = \frac{s}{\sqrt{N}} = \frac{15}{\sqrt{25}} = 3.00$$

Suppose that we increased our sample N from 25 to 100 cases, but again found $s = 15$. In this instance, we calculate $s_{\overline{X}}$ to be $15/\sqrt{100}$ or 1.5. This value is considerably smaller than the one calculated above; in fact, it happens to be just half the size of $s_{\overline{X}}$ where N = 25. This example illustrates the implications of the central limit theorem: as sample N's increases, $\overline{X}$'s in a sampling distribution become less and less variable, clustering closer and closer around μ.

We now have before us the statistical logic that will permit us to make inferences about population μ's from sample data. Several approaches are open to us. Sometimes we wish to test a hypothesis that the μ of a population is some particular value and collect data from a sample of individuals so that we may evaluate how likely it is that the hypothesis is true. On other occasions we have no prior hypothesis about the value of μ. We could make a point estimate, specifying that the $\overline{X}$ of the sample we have measured is our best estimate of μ. However, when we have no prior hypothesis, we typically make what is known as an *interval estimate*, in which we establish a range or interval of values within which μ probably falls. Interval estimation will be discussed further in the section on confidence intervals later in the chapter.

TESTING HYPOTHESES
ABOUT μ: LARGE SAMPLES

We conduct a study to determine the beliefs of American middle-class adults about people who are impoverished. One of the questions asks for a rating, on a 7-point scale, of the relative interest of the poor and nonpoor in having material things. A scale point of 1 indicates that the poor are very much *less* materialistic than the nonpoor, and 7 that the poor are very much *more* materialistic; a scale point of 4 indicates that the two are equally materialistic.

Before we test a random group of middle-class adults, we set up two rival hypotheses. The first hypothesis we choose to set up is that in the population as a whole, the mean scale point that would be chosen is 4.00—the hypothesis that in the population of middle-class adults, the poor and nonpoor are believed to be equally materialistic. (From a statistical point of view we could have selected any value from 1 through 7 for our hypothesis, but for other reasons we explain later we have chosen 4.) This hypothesis, which *always specifies an exact value for* μ, is known as the *null hypothesis* or H_0. The second hypothesis, called the *alternative hypothesis* and symbolized as H_1, is typically more general and specifies that μ is some value other than the one specified in the null hypothesis.*

The H_1, or alternative, hypothesis can be either *bidirectional or unidirectional*. That is, we may hypothesize merely that the true value of μ is not equal to the value specified in the null hypothesis ($\mu \neq$ value in H_0). This is called a bidirectional hypothesis because it specifies that μ is some value either above or below the value specified in H_0. Or we may specify the *direction* in which we expect the difference; for example, μ is some value *less*, but not greater, than the one specified in H_0 ($\mu <$ value in H_0). This is called a unidirectional hypothesis. The importance of the distinction between a unidirectional and a bidirectional alternative hypothesis will become clear later when we discuss the procedures used to evaluate H_0. We will see that we

---

*The alternative hypothesis could be a specific value, let us say in our example a value of 2.00. However, it is more common to set up a more general H_1, specifying that μ may be *any* value that differs from H_0 in a given direction (unidirectional hypothesis) or in either direction (bidirectional). For example, if H_0 states that $\mu = 64$, a unidirectional H_1 might be that μ is some value greater than 64; the bidirectional H_1 would state that μ is some value greater *or* smaller than 64.

normally use a so-called *two-tailed* test when H_1 is bidirectional but may use a *one-tailed* test when H_1 is unidirectional.

Returning to our example, let us suppose that if the poor and nonpoor are *not* believed to be equally materialistic by middle-class adults—that is, if H_0 that $\mu = 4.00$ is not true—we have no sound reason for guessing which group would be judged to be more materialistic. Our H_1 would therefore be bidirectional. Our two hypotheses are therefore:

$$H_0: \mu = 4.00$$

$$H_1: \mu \neq 4.00$$

After stating H_0 and H_1, we test 121 individuals and find that the mean scale point chosen is 3.91 and that the *s* of the sample ratings is .70. We now proceed to evaluate the null hypothesis that $\mu = 4.00$.

What we want to do first is to determine what the sampling distribution of $\overline{X}$'s would look like if $\mu = 4.00$ and we had tested not one but a very large number of random samples of 121 cases each. We know that if $\mu = 4.00$, then the mean of the sampling distribution of $\overline{X}$'s would also equal 4.00. We must now inquire about the shape of the sampling distribution and the value of the standard error of the distribution, $\sigma_{\overline{X}}$. Since we do not know the value of σ, we have no way of calculating $\sigma_{\overline{X}}$. But we may obtain an *estimate* of the standard error, which we have agreed to symbolize as $s_{\overline{X}}$, by using the sample *s* given above:

$$s_{\overline{X}} = \frac{s}{\sqrt{N}} = \frac{.70}{\sqrt{121}} = .06$$

The standard error of the sampling distribution, we thus estimate, is .06.

With a sample as large as the one we have obtained, the *shape* of our distribution of sample means is close enough to normal to permit us to assume the normal distribution. Our hypothetical sampling distribution of $\overline{X}$'s under H_0, then, is normal in shape, has a mean of 4.00, and an estimated standard error of .06. This hypothetical distribution is shown in Figure 8.2. The figure also shows where our obtained $\overline{X}$ of 3.91 falls in this sampling distribution.

Ordinarily, our next task would be to find the *z* score of our obtained $\overline{X}$ value by dividing the quantity $(\overline{X} - \mu)$ by the standard error of the distribution. However, since we can only estimate the standard error, we can only estimate *z*. The estimated *z* is identified as *Student's t* or simply *t*. ("Student" was the nom de plume of the statistician who did the original work on the distribution of estimated *z* or *t*.) The formula for this estimated *z* or *t* score is as follows:

$$t = \frac{\overline{X} - \mu}{s_{\overline{X}}} \tag{8.4}$$

This formula, of course, is the same one we used earlier for *z* (see Formula 8.2), except that we have substituted for the unknown standard error, $\sigma_{\overline{X}}$, our estimate of its value, $s_{\overline{X}}$. Applying this *t* formula to our data, we find:

$$t = \frac{\overline{X} - \mu}{s_{\overline{X}}} = \frac{3.91 - 4.00}{.06} = -1.50$$

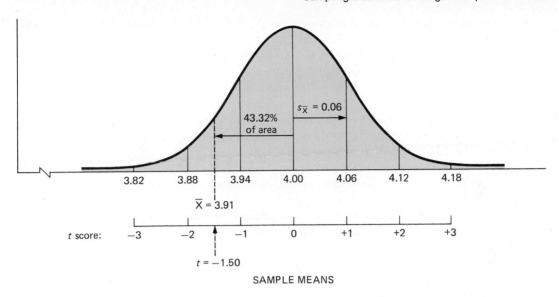

Figure 8.2 Visual test of the hypothesis that μ = 4.00 when $\overline{X}$ = 3.91 and $s_{\overline{X}}$ = .06.

Our obtained $\overline{X}$, then, falls 1.50 $s_{\overline{X}}$ units below μ. Since with a sample as large as ours the sampling distribution of t can be assumed to be normal, we can treat this value as if it were a z score and determine from Table B the percentage of the area lying between μ and z = -1.50. Table B indicates that 43.32 percent of the area under the curve lies between μ and -1.50, and that 6.68 percent of the area lies *beyond* -1.50. Since our alternative hypothesis, H_1, is bidirectional, we must be concerned with the other end of the distribution as well. We therefore state that if the null hypothesis, H_0, were correct, the probability of obtaining by chance a sample $\overline{X}$ that deviated from μ *this much or more in either direction* would be .134 (.0668 × 2 = .1336). In other words, if the study were repeated over and over and over again, sample $\overline{X}$'s that deviated this much or more in either direction from μ = 4.00 would be expected approximately 13 percent of the time.

Significance Levels

We now face a decision: is H_0, the hypothesis that μ = 4.00, a reasonable one? Or should we conclude that it is unreasonable and that H_1, the bidirectional hypothesis that μ is some value other than 4, is more likely to be correct? We need some decision rule, some cutoff point, that will allow us to reach a conclusion. One of two probability levels, .01 or .05, is typically used in scientific research for this purpose. We have determined in our example that if H_0 were true, the probability is .13 that we would obtain a $\overline{X}$ that deviated as much or more from the hypothesized μ as our obtained $\overline{X}$. Since this probability is greater than either .01 or.05, we conclude that our null hypothesis that μ = 4.00 is a *reasonable* one.

When used to evaluate null hypotheses, the .01 and .05 probability levels are commonly called the .01 (or 1%) and .05 (or 5%) *significance levels*. The particular significance level an investigator decides to use in reaching a decision about the null hypothesis is called the *alpha* (α) level.

If the investigator decides to use the 1% or .01 significance level as the cutoff point in evaluating H_0, $\alpha = .01$. It is stated that if $\overline{X}$ would be obtained only 1% or *less* of the time by chance alone if H_0 were true, H_0 will be *rejected* as being unreasonable. In other words, instead of concluding that H_0 is correct and that this unusual an $\overline{X}$ has occurred by chance, the investigator decides that H_0 is probably false and that H_1, the hypothesis that μ is some other value, is more reasonable. If, on the other hand, $\overline{X}$ could be obtained *more* than 1 percent of the time if H_0 were correct, the investigator does not reject H_0, deciding instead to retain it as a reasonable hypothesis about the value of μ. In stating a conclusion about whether H_0 is accepted or rejected, the investigator should also indicate the α level that was used to reach a decision.

The 5% significance level sets a less stringent criterion than the 1% level for rejecting the null hypothesis about μ. If investigators set α at .05, they will *reject* H_0 if a difference as great as or greater than the difference between the obtained $\overline{X}$ and μ would occur by chance only 5 percent of the time or less if H_0 were true. Conversely, if a $\overline{X}$ this extreme would occur *more* than 5 percent of the time by chance, the investigators will retain H_0 as a reasonable hypothesis at the 5% significance level.

Now we take a slightly different approach to our study of beliefs about poverty. Suppose we had decided beforehand to use the 5% significance level in reaching a decision about the hypothesis that $\mu = 4.00$. We therefore will reject as unlikely any null hypothesis that would result in a sample $\overline{X}$ as different from μ as the one we have obtained 5 percent of the time or less by chance alone. We remind you that we have specified that H_1 is bidirectional; that is, we are concerned about deviations that occur 5 percent or less of the time in *either* direction from μ. In a normal distribution, 5 percent of the cases are expected to fall at or beyond a z of ± 1.96 with 2.5 percent at either extreme. With large samples, the distribution of estimated z scores or t's can be assumed to be normal. When the α level is .05 and H_1 is a bidirectional hypothesis, the critical values of t that we use to assess H_0 are ± 1.96. If the t we have computed for our obtained $\overline{X}$ is greater in absolute value than the critical value of 1.96, we *reject* H_0. We reject H_0 because there are only 5 chances in 100 or less that we would get a $\overline{X}$ that deviated this much or more from μ if H_0 were correct. Conversely, if our computed t has an absolute value that is less than 1.96, we retain H_0. In our example, t was determined to be -1.50. The absolute value of this t is less than 1.96. We therefore do not reject, at the 5% significance level, the null hypothesis that $\mu = 4.00$.

These procedures are illustrated in Figure 8.3, which shows a t distribution based on large samples and which we therefore have assumed to be normal. In this figure a center portion of the curve, bounded by t's of $+1.96$ and -1.96, is marked off. If the value of any $\overline{X}$, expressed in $s_{\overline{X}}$ units (t score), falls within this area, we do not reject H_0; we accept H_0 as reasonable. If, on the other hand, the t score for $\overline{X}$ falls in either tail, we reject H_0. We saw above that our sample $\overline{X}$ fell only -1.50 $s_{\overline{X}}$ units from μ. We see in Figure 8.3 that this result falls within the "don't reject" area. We therefore retain, at the 5% significance level, the null hypothesis that $\mu = 4.00$; we conclude that H_0 is a reasonable one.

We could, of course, prepare a figure similar to Figure 8.3 for evaluating a bidirectional H_1 using the 1% alpha level. The extreme one-half percent of the area at either end of a normal

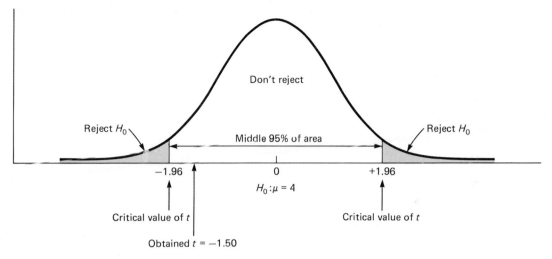

Figure 8.3 Illustration of a two-tailed significance test for μ at $\alpha = .05$ with normal curve values.

curve falls at or beyond ± 2.58. The two tails of the distribution at or beyond t's of ± 2.58 thus define the area of rejection.

When H_1 is bidirectional and we consider both extremes of the z or t distribution in evaluating H_0, we are using a *two-tailed* test. When we have good reason to believe before collecting the sample data that any deviation of $\overline{X}$ from the null hypothesis will be in a specific direction, we may elect to set up an H_1 that is unidirectional and to employ a *one-tailed* test, one that considers the probability of $\overline{X}$'s falling at only one extreme of the distribution. For example, suppose that in investigating beliefs about poverty we also ask our sample of 121 to compare the ability of the poor and the nonpoor to manage their money effectively. Again, our subjects use a 7-point scale, with 1 indicating that the poor are much less able to manage their money, 4 that the poor and nonpoor are equal, and so on. We also choose again to test the null hypothesis that $\mu = 4.00$. We suspect, however, that the poor will be rated as *less* able to manage money than the nonpoor; that is, we believe μ will be less than 4. Our hypotheses are therefore:

$$H_0\text{: } \mu = 4.00$$

$$H_1\text{: } \mu < 4.00$$

(where $<$ means less than).

Suppose that the $\overline{X}$ turned out to be 3.75 and s to be .81. The $\overline{X}$, you will notice, is in the direction specified by H_1. Suppose also that we had decided to use $\alpha = .01$ instead of .05 as in the example above. The extreme 1 percent of the cases falling at *one* end of a normal distribution, we find in Table B, lie at or beyond a z of 2.33. Since H_1 specifies that $\mu <$

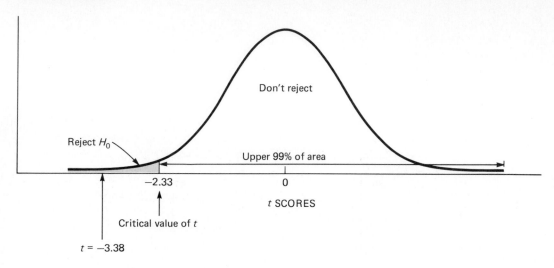

Figure 8.4 Illustration of a one-tailed significance test for μ at $\alpha = .01$ with normal curve values.

4.00, the critical value of t that is used to assess our null hypothesis is -2.33. We calculate t for our $\overline{X}$ of 3.75 as follows:

$$t = \frac{\overline{X} - \mu}{s_{\overline{X}}} = \frac{3.75 - 4.00}{.07} = -3.57$$

where $s_{\overline{X}} = s/\sqrt{N} = .81/\sqrt{121} = .07$.

The t for our $\overline{X}$ falls far beyond -2.33. If H_0 were true, we would obtain an $\overline{X}$ this different from μ less than 1 percent of the time. As is illustrated in Figure 8.4, we therefore *reject* the null hypothesis that $\mu = 4.00$ and accept as more reasonable the unidirectional alternative hypothesis that μ is less than 4.*

Statistical vs. Experimental Hypotheses

The example above may have puzzled you. If we had good reason to expect that middle-class individuals believe that the poor manage their money less well than the nonpoor, why did we test the particular null hypothesis that we did—that they are judged, by middle-class individuals as a group, to be *equally* capable? That is, why did we test the hypothesis that $\mu = 4$ rather than a value less than 4? The answer is that we suspected that μ has *some* value less than 4 but

---

*What if the difference between $\overline{X}$ and the μ specified in H_0 turns out to be in the *opposite* direction as specified in a unidirectional H_1? Obviously, H_1 can be rejected without further ado. Unfortunately, it is not legitimate to test H_0 by changing H_1 to a bidirectional form after the fact and performing a two-tailed significance test or to change the direction of H_1 to correspond to the results.

had no basis for predicting how much less. The null hypothesis, however, must be assigned an exact value. We therefore chose to select 4.00 (no difference between poor and nonpoor) as the null hypothesis to test, with the hope that we could *reject* this hypothesis and accept, instead, the more general H_1 hypothesis that μ is *some* value less than 4.00.

The null hypothesis that we test, then, may sometimes be picked only for statistical reasons. Our actual *experimental* hypothesis—our guess about the true state of affairs that we conducted the study to evaluate—may not always correspond to the null hypothesis. Of course, there are instances in which our experimental hypothesis specifies an exact value for μ, rather than a range of values, such as less than 4. In these instances the statistical null hypothesis we test is the same as our experimental hypothesis.

One-Tailed vs. Two-Tailed Tests.   When the null hypothesis an investigator tests statistically does not coincide with the experimental hypothesis, the investigator typically has predicted beforehand the direction in which $\overline{X}$ is expected to differ from the μ specified in H_0. There is some controversy among statisticians as to whether a unidirectional H_1 should be set up and H_0 evaluated by means of a one-tailed test when the investigator has predicted the outcome or whether all tests of H_0 should be two-tailed. We will not attempt here to discuss the reasons for the controversy. We will say only that one-tailed tests are sometimes used when the investigator has good reason to set up a unidirectional H_1. Despite the fact that investigators usually have unidirectional experimental hypotheses, bidirectional *statistical* hypotheses are much more common. It typically is assumed that H_1 is bidirectional and that a two-tailed significance test has been performed, unless a unidirectional H_1 and a one-tailed test are specifically mentioned. (We will follow this practice in all subsequent discussions.) In reporting the results of our statistical analyses, then, we should always specifically mention the use of a one-tailed probability figure if we have employed this procedure.

Unidirectional H_1's could be discussed in connection with other kinds of significance tests introduced in later chapters. We have chosen not to do so, however, both because no new principles are involved and because they are used less frequently than bidirectional H_1's.

TESTING HYPOTHESES ABOUT μ: SMALL SAMPLES

The central limit theorem, we have learned, states that as samples increase in size, the shape of the sampling distribution of $\overline{X}$'s approaches the normal curve. When the sample N is large, the sampling distribution of t so closely approximates the normal curve that for practical purposes we may treat it as if it were normal. In our previous examples, all of which involved large samples, we therefore used the z-score values found in the normal curve table in testing hypotheses about μ using the 1% and 5% significance levels.

The t values obtained from small samples are *not* normally distributed. Assuming that the measured characteristic is normally distributed in the population from which the samples were drawn, the distribution of small sample t's is, however, *symmetrical* and its exact shape varies systematically with the degrees of freedom associated with the samples. Degrees of freedom (*df*), as explained in Chapter 5, refers to the number of values in a distribution of measures that are free to vary and still yield the original value of $\overline{X}$. The *df* associated with t for single samples is N − 1, the number of cases in the sample minus one.

$$df = N - 1 \tag{8.5}$$

As sample *df*'s become smaller, the shape of the sampling distribution of t becomes increasingly flatter than the normal curve, with the peak being lower and the tails of the distribution being "pulled out" farther along the baseline. This increasing flatness means that we must go farther and farther along the t scale on the baseline to encompass the same area.

The upshot of all of this is that when samples are small, we cannot use normal curve values in assessing hypotheses about μ. In making decisions about H_0 at a given α level, we must instead use the critical values of t at $\alpha = .05$ or .01 that are associated with the t distribution for the particular *df* associated with our sample. Special tables have been prepared that list these critical values; one such is Table C in Appendix III. At the left of Table C is a column labeled *df* (degrees of freedom). In the other columns are listed the t values for each *df* that are required at the 10%, 5%, 2%, and 1% significance levels for a two-tailed test, and at the 5%, 2.5%, 1%, and 0.5% significance levels for a one-tailed test.

As we described earlier, as sample N and therefore sample *df* decrease, the critical value of t associated with a given α level increases. Inspection of the second page of Table C shows, for example, that with *df* = 120, the value of t at $\alpha = .05$ for a two-tailed test is 1.9799; this figure is very close to the normal curve value of 1.9600. With *df* = 50, the corresponding value is 2.0086 and with *df* = 10, it is 2.2281.

As an example of the use of Table C, assume that an investigator has hypothesized that μ is 80 and has specified a bidirectional H_1. To test this hypothesis, the investigator has measured 25 individuals, finding $\overline{X} = 84$ and $s = 8$. Thus:

$$H_0: \mu = 80$$

$$H_1: \mu \neq 80$$

$$t = \frac{\overline{X} - \mu}{s_{\overline{X}}} = \frac{84 - 80}{1.6} = 2.50$$

where

$$s_{\overline{X}} = \frac{s}{\sqrt{N}} = \frac{8}{5} = 1.60$$

$$df = N - 1 = 25 - 1 = 24$$

Consultation of Table C shows that the two-tailed values of t needed at $\alpha = .05$ and .01 for *df* = 24 are 2.06 and 2.80. Since the calculated t is 2.50, H_0 can be rejected at the 5% but not at the 1% significance level.

How Small Is Small? We have emphasized that when the sample N is small, we must use the values in the t table associated with the sample *df* in evaluating the significance of a calculated t. But we have not stated how large a sample must be before we may reasonably assume the normal distribution and use the values in Table B or, conversely, how small a sample must be before we use the values listed in Table C. There is no precise answer to this question, but inspection of the bottom entries in Table C shows that with $df = 120$, the critical value of t at a given α level is very similar to the parallel value in a normal curve, obtained with an infinite df. Thus we have chosen to assume the normal distribution in all sampling distributions of t in which df is greater than 120.

Two Types of Error

Let us repeat once more what we have done when we reject a null hypothesis about μ at a given α level. For example, we reject a hypothesis at the 5% level. We say that if H_0 is correct, a difference between $\overline{X}$ and the hypothesized μ as large as or larger than the one we have obtained would occur by chance 5 percent of the time or less. Rather than concluding that by chance our sample happened to deviate this much from μ, we decide instead that the null hypothesis we tested is faulty. But we could be wrong. In fact, we know that the probability of being wrong is .05. If H_0 were *true* and we repeated our study over and over again, we would get $\overline{X}$'s that differed this much or more from μ 5 times out of 100 purely by chance. Thus, in rejecting the null hypothesis on a given occasion, we run the risk of labeling as false a hypothesis that is in fact true. Rejecting a true null hypothesis is known as a *Type I error*. The Type I error also is identified as an α error.

How might we reduce the likelihood of making a Type I error? The answer is simple enough: we set a more stringent α level for rejecting H_0. If we used $\alpha = .01$, we would demand that a deviation between $\overline{X}$ and μ occur by chance no more than 1 time in 100, thus cutting down the probability of rejecting a true hypothesis to .01. We would be even surer of avoiding a Type I error by using the .001 α level (only 1 chance in 1000 of obtaining the results by chance), and so on. However, while we reduce the risk of a Type I error by lowering our α level, we simultaneously *increase* the likelihood of making what is called a *Type II error*. In a Type II error (also called a *beta* or β error), we retain (fail to reject) a hypothesis that is actually *false*. We can lower the risk of a Type II in exactly the *opposite* way as we minimized a Type I error: by *raising* the α level. If we use the 5% level of significance, for example, we will reduce Type II error—that is, fail to reject false hypotheses less often than if we used $\alpha = 1\%$—and reduce this error even more if we raise α to 10 or 20%.

Although changing our α level has opposite effects on the likelihood of Types I and II errors, the probabilities of the two errors are not mathematically the exact complement of each other. That is, if α is 5%, the probability of a Type I error is .05 when we reject a hypothesis but may be *higher* than .05 for a Type II error when we fail to reject a hypothesis. You may begin to appreciate the reason why Type II errors may be more frequent when you consider the following. Suppose we postulate μ to be 52 and find $\overline{X}$ to be 53. After testing this H_0, we conclude at a given α level that it is tenable. But we could have set H_0 as $\mu = 53$ or $\mu = 54$, among other values, and we would have concluded that these hypotheses are also tenable. In short, a whole *range* of null hypotheses would be acceptable at a given α level. When we retain a null hypothesis, all we are saying is that it is *one* of a number of acceptable hypotheses. For this reason, investigators prefer not to speak of "accepting" the null hypothesis; they are more likely to be cautious and say they have *failed to reject* the null hypothesis.

As noted above in the section on statistical versus experimental hypotheses, investigators often set up null hypotheses to evaluate statistically that they hope to be able to reject. As a result, investigators have a special concern with the ability of their statistical tests to detect false null hypotheses. This ability is known as the *power* of the test. The topic of power will be discussed in detail in the next chapter. We will note here only that one of the factors affecting the power of a test is the sample N. That is, we are more likely to detect null hypotheses that are false, thus reducing the incidence of Type II errors, when the sample size is large than when it is small. This relationship can be understood by recalling that the formula for $s_{\overline{X}}$ is $s/\sqrt{N}$.

Assume, for example, that we have incorrectly hypothesized that $\mu = 122$ when it actually has some other value. Testing a sample of two, we obtain $\overline{X}$ of 119 and s of 10. Thus, $s_{\overline{X}}$ would be 7.07 and t under H_0: $\mu = 122$ would be $3/7.07$ or .424. We would thus *fail* to reject the false hypothesis that $\mu = 122$. Increasing N to 100, on the other hand, and continuing to assume $\overline{X} = 119$ and $s = 10$, $s_{\overline{X}}$ is calculated to be 1.00 and t is calculated to be 3.00; thus with N = 100, we would *reject* the false null hypothesis that $\mu = 122$ beyond the 1% significance level.

CONFIDENCE INTERVALS

In working with research data, we often do not have hypotheses about specific values of μ that we wish to test. Suppose, for example, that we were interested in the satisfaction of assembly line workers with their jobs and were able to persuade a random sample of 144 workers to take a test that measured job satisfaction. We have no prior hypothesis about how satisfied the average worker is and, in fact, have done the study to find out what workers' feelings are like. It would be possible to use the $\overline{X}$ of the sample as an exact estimate of the population μ. However, rather than making this kind of point estimate, it is more common to make what is known as an *interval estimate*. That is, we establish a range of values within which we may reasonably assert that μ lies. The assertion that μ falls somewhere within a specific range or interval of values has a certain probability of being correct; we make it with a certain degree of confidence. When we establish such a range, it is commonly spoken of as a *confidence interval*. In research reports two confidence intervals are used most frequently: the *99% confidence interval* and the *95% confidence interval*.

Ninety-Nine Percent Confidence Interval

You will remember that if we were testing a hypothesis about μ using $\alpha = .01$ (and a bidirectional H_1), we would reject any H_0 that would make an absolute difference between μ and $\overline{X}$ as large as or larger than the one we have obtained occur 1 percent of the time or less by chance alone (that is, a positive difference between μ and $\overline{X}$ of the size we have obtained or larger would occur by chance one-half percent of the time or less and a negative difference of this size or larger one-half percent of the time or less). Conversely, we would retain as reasonable *any* H_0 that would make the difference between $\overline{X}$ and μ occur by chance more than 1 percent of the time. As we indicated in an earlier discussion, there is a whole range of reasonable or acceptable hypotheses at a given α level. If $\alpha = 1\%$, the range of acceptable hypotheses for μ establishes what is known as the *99% confidence interval* for μ. That is, we assert that μ

falls someplace within this range of values, 99% of such statements being correct, and conversely, 1% of such statements being incorrect. Let us now demonstrate how to go about establishing the 99% confidence interval.

If we were testing a bidirectional hypothesis about μ, we would convert $\overline{X}$ into a t score and using $\alpha = .01$, we would reject the hypothesis if the absolute value of our obtained t were greater than the critical value of t associated with the 1% significance level for the sample *df*. Conversely, if our obtained t were smaller than this critical value, we would accept the hypothesis.

Given $\overline{X}$ and s computed from our sample, how large could our hypothesis and μ be and still be accepted at $\alpha = .01$? We could answer this question by setting t at the value associated with $\alpha = .01$ and our *df* and then entering our obtained $\overline{X}$ and $s_{\overline{X}}$ into the right-hand side of the t equation. Finally, we solve for μ:

$$t_{.01} = \frac{\overline{X} - \mu}{s_{\overline{X}}}$$

and by rearrangement:

$$\mu = \overline{X} + t_{.01}(s_{\overline{X}})$$

Suppose that for the 144 workers to whom we gave a test of job satisfaction, $\overline{X}$ was 73 and s was 18, yielding $s_{\overline{X}} = 1.5$. With a sample this large, we use the normal curve figure, 2.58, as the critical value of $t_{.01}$. Thus the largest acceptable hypothesis about μ at $\alpha = .01$ is:

$$\mu = 73 + 2.58(1.5) = 73 + 3.87 = 76.87$$

We can find the smallest acceptable hypothesis about μ by setting $t_{.01}$ at a minus value and again solving for μ:

$$\mu = \overline{X} - t_{.01}(s_{\overline{X}})$$

In our example, the smallest value of μ that would be acceptable at $\alpha = .01$ is therefore:

$$\mu = 73 - 3.87 = 69.13$$

If we generalize from this series of steps, we see that the range of acceptable values for μ at $\alpha = .01$, which we identify as the 99% confidence interval, is given by:

$$99\% \text{ CI: } \overline{X} \pm t_{.01}(s_{\overline{X}}) \tag{8.6}$$

In our example, the 99% confidence interval is thus 73 ± 3.87 or 69.13 to 76.87. When we assert that the unknown μ falls within this range of values, 99% of such assertions will be correct.

One more example. We have tested 36 cases, and have calculated $\overline{X}$ to be 105 and $s_{\overline{X}}$ to be 1.78. Before we can determine the 99% confidence interval for μ, we must find the critical value of t for a two-tailed test at $\alpha = .01$. The df of our sample is 35—that is, $36 - 1$. In Table C, the value of t associated with $df = 35$ is 2.72. Therefore:

$$99\% \text{ CI: } \overline{X} \pm t_{.01}(s_{\overline{X}}) = 105 \pm (2.72)(1.78) = 105 \pm 4.84 = 100.16 \text{ to } 109.84$$

Ninety-Five Percent Confidence Interval

The 95% confidence interval establishes the range of acceptable hypotheses for μ with $\alpha = .05$. We determine the 95% confidence interval exactly as we did the 99% interval, except that we now use the value of t associated with $\alpha = .05$. The formula for the 95% confidence interval is:

$$95\% \text{ CI: } \overline{X} \pm t_{.05}(s_{\overline{X}}) \tag{8.7}$$

In our example in which $\overline{X}$ for 36 cases was 105 and $s_{\overline{X}}$ was 1.78, we first determine from Table C the value of t associated with 35 df for a two-tailed test. This value is 2.03. Thus:

$$95\% \text{ CI: } 105 \pm (2.03)(1.78) =$$

$$105 \pm 3.61 = 101.39 \text{ to } 108.61$$

You will note that the range of values established for the 95% confidence interval is narrower than the range of values established for the 99% confidence interval, which we calculated to be 100.16 to 109.84.

In using the 95% confidence interval to specify a range of values within which the mean of a population may lie we are less sure of including the true μ than with the 99% interval, but for the sake of greater specificity many research workers are willing to take the chance that μ does not fall beyond the limits set up by the 95% interval. The 95% confidence level, however, is usually considered the minimum probability value that should be used in setting up a range of values for μ. We could, for example, set up the 90% confidence interval. But then there would be 10 chances in 100, or 1 in 10, that μ lies outside this interval, and this probability of error is generally agreed to be too high. One could set up confidence intervals that fall between the 99 and 95% intervals, such as a 97% confidence interval. As a matter of custom, however, the 99 and 95% confidence intervals are commonly used as reference values. Similar remarks can be made about the use of the 5% and 1% significance levels in testing hypotheses about μ. Under ordinary circumstances the maximum α and thus the minimal significance level that should be used is 5%. If we go much beyond this level—for example, to the 10% level—we make the risk unacceptably high that we will commit a Type I error; that is, we will too frequently reject hypotheses about μ that are true.

The use of significance levels, which allow us to reject or not reject hypotheses with a stated probability, simplifies our writing our research reports. We merely state which one of the two α levels we are using and reject any hypothesis that exceeds this level. It is important to note once more that we must always state whether we are using the 5% or 1% α level in deciding to reject or not reject a hypothesis, so that there will be no misunderstanding. When we wish to establish a confidence interval for μ rather than to test a specific hypothesis about its value, we must also be sure to state whether it is the 99% or 95% interval we have determined.

TESTING HYPOTHESES ABOUT POPULATION PROPORTIONS

Formulas are available that allow us to obtain standard errors for the sampling distributions of other statistics than the mean and hence to test hypotheses about their population parameters. We will discuss here only one such technique, a test of a hypothesis about a population proportion.

Suppose we are investigating the biases that may influence choice behavior. It has been shown, for example, that in predicting heads or tails in the toss of a coin, people tend to pick heads; in guessing what number from 1 to 10 someone is thinking of, they tend to pick an even number; in a choice between right and left, they tend to choose right, and so on. We give a random sample of 50 individuals a novel series of tests, one of which involves asking them to guess whether the nonsense statement. "The sagem is bep," is true or false. If there is no bias, we expect that 50 percent of the subjects would choose true and 50 percent false. The null hypothesis (H_0) that we decide to test, then, is that the percentage choosing true is 50. We find that the actual numbers are 32 choosing true and 18 choosing false—percentages of 64 and 36. What should we conclude?

By this time we are wise enough not to jump to the conclusion that H_0 is false and that there is a bias for choosing true simply because more than half the sample chose this alternative. There are sampling errors involved, and the question we really need to ask ourselves is this: "If there is no bias—that is, if the population proportion choosing true is .50—how likely is it that we would obtain a proportion as high as .64 with 50 cases?"

It is critical that you recognize we are no longer dealing with measurement data—that is, the property we have observed in the individual case does not differ in amount. Rather, each individual has been assigned to one of two mutually exclusive categories according to the answer, true or false, to the test item. More particularly, we are discussing a binomial sampling distribution in which we determine, in each sample, the proportion of individuals choosing true, which we will identify as p, and the proportion of individuals choosing false, which we will identify as q, where $p + q = 1.00$.

In Chapter 7 we saw that when $p = .5$, the normal distribution provides a good approximation of the binomial distribution with moderate N's or greater, say 10 or more. It would be somewhat more precise to utilize the binomial distribution to answer our question, but it is usually more convenient to use the normal distribution.

If we drew a very large number of random samples of the same size from a population in which $p = .5$ and for each obtained a proportion, we may thus assume, if N is large enough, that these sample proportions would be distributed normally. If we calculated the standard deviation of this distribution, we could make statements of probability about where any sample would fall. (If these statements have a familiar ring, it is because we used the same language in discussing the sampling distribution of $\overline{X}$.) Thus, we need to know the standard deviation of the distribution of sample proportions—that is, the standard error of the proportion, σ_{prop}.

We recall from Chapter 7 that in a binomial sampling distribution in which we specify the frequency of a certain event out of a total of N occasions, the standard deviation, which is the standard error of the distribution of frequencies or σ_f, is given by $\sqrt{Npq}$. However, we are looking for the standard error of a distribution of sample *proportions*. Since proportion is determined by dividing frequency by N, σ_{prop} may be obtained by dividing the expression for σ_f by N: $\sqrt{Npq}/N$. This may be reduced to $\sqrt{pq/N}$. Thus:

$$\sigma_{prop} = \sqrt{\frac{p_t q_t}{N}} \qquad (8.8)$$

where p_t = true population proportion
$q_t = 1 - p_t$
N = sample size

It is important to note that p in the formula for σ_{prop} is not the obtained *sample* proportion; it is the *true* proportion in a known or hypothesized population.

The question we ask in our bias experiment, we repeat is, "If the true population proportion is .50, is it likely that our obtained proportion, .64, occurred by chance?" In answering the question, we first calculate σ_{prop}:

$$\sigma_{prop} = \sqrt{\frac{p_t q_t}{N}} = \sqrt{\frac{(.5)(.5)}{50}} = \sqrt{\frac{.25}{50}} = .071$$

We can visualize our hypothetical sampling distribution and determine where our obtained proportion falls. This has been done in Figure 8.5. We can see by inspection that it would be quite unusual to get a sample proportion of .64 if the true proportion were .50. However, we need a more precise probability statement and must therefore convert our sample proportion (p_s) into a z score. Since we know σ_{prop} of the distribution, note that we can calculate the actual z rather than an estimate of it. The mean of the sampling distribution of sample proportions takes the same value as the value of the population proportion specified in our null hypothesis. The standard deviation or standard error of the sampling distribution is σ_{prop}. Thus the z formula may be written:

$$z = \frac{p_s - p_t}{\sigma_{prop}} \qquad (8.9)$$

where p_s = sample proportion and p_t = hypothetical true proportion specified in H_0. In our example, we thus have:

$$z = \frac{.64 - .50}{.071} = 1.97$$

If we had set α at .05 and our H_1 were bidirectional—that is, our alternate hypothesis to H_0 is $H_1: p_t \neq .50$—we would reject any null hypothesis that would result in a z score, for our p_s, of ± 1.96 or greater. We use ± 1.96 as cutoff points, of course, because these are the values associated with the extreme 5 percent of the area in a normal distribution, 2.5 percent at each tail. Our z was calculated to be 1.97. We therefore reject the null hypothesis that $p_t = .50$; we conclude that the difference between p_s and p_t is significant at the .05 level. More concretely, we conclude that people are probably biased in favor of "true."

It might seem that for any problem in which we obtain a proportion we could test any hypothesis about the true proportion for a given N, using the kinds of procedures we have just

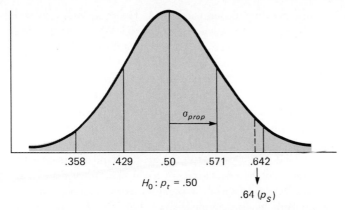

$H_0: p_t = .50$

Figure 8.5 Visual test of the hypothesis that the true proportion is .50 when the obtained sample proportion is .64.

illustrated. A word of caution is in order, however. The binomial distribution, we remind you, generally approaches the normal distribution as N grows larger, doing so most rapidly when p_t is .50. We therefore should not test hypotheses about p_t based on the normal curve assumption unless N is some reasonable size, 10 at a minimum. As our hypothesis about p_t departs from .5, the sample N should be even larger than this minimum. If we test extreme hypotheses about true proportions, about .80 or greater or .20 or smaller, use of the normal curve may lead to serious errors of interpretation, when N's are not large, because the sampling distributions will be markedly skewed. Under this circumstance we can, however, fall back on the less convenient but more exact binomial distribution discussed in Chapter 7.

OVERVIEW OF HYPOTHESIS TESTING

In this chapter we have presented techniques for testing two types of null hypotheses, one about a population μ (based on measurement of properties varying in amount), and the other about a population proportion (based on data involving two mutually exclusive categories). The general logic of both tests is the same and also underlies tests of still other hypotheses we have not yet discussed.

In this section we will review the logic in general terms, as a way both of summarizing the tests discussed in the present chapter and of introducing tests of hypotheses about other population parameters. The basic notion to grasp concerns the nature of a sampling distribution. A very large number (theoretically, an infinite number) of random samples can be drawn from a population and a statistic of some kind derived from each sample. The values of the statistic determined from each of the samples constitute a sampling distribution.

Like other distributions, a sampling distribution has a mean, obtained by adding up all the sample values and dividing the sum by the number of samples. Statistical theory tells us that *this mean takes the same value as the value of the population parameter parallel to the sample statistic.* Thus the mean of a distribution of sample *proportions* (sample statistics) takes the same value as the population *proportion* (population parameter). The mean of a distribution of $\overline{X}$'s takes the same value as μ, the population parameter parallel to $\overline{X}$. We could also determine for each sample whose $\overline{X}$ we calculated the value of s; the mean of the sampling distribution of s's takes the same value as the population σ. In a later chapter, we obtain a pair of measures from each of a sample of individuals and derive from the sample of paired measures a statistic called a correlation coefficient, symbolized as r; the mean of the sampling distribution of r's takes the same value as the population r, and so forth. To repeat what we said earlier, the mean of the sampling distribution of some statistic takes the same value as the parallel population parameter.

Formulas are also available that allow us to calculate the standard error (standard deviation) of the sampling distribution of various statistics or to calculate an estimate of the standard error, based on sample data. Statistical theory also allows us to determine the shape of the sampling distribution of a statistic, given the sample size.

In practice, we obtain data from a single sample and use our theoretical knowledge about sampling distributions to test a null hypothesis (H_0) and an alternative hypothesis (H_1) about the population parameter. If H_0 is true, we know the value of the mean of the hypothetical sampling distribution, namely, the value of the population parameter specified in H_0. We can also determine the standard error of the sampling distribution or estimate its value from the sample data. Armed with knowledge about the mean and standard error and about the shape of the hypothetical sampling distribution, we are able to translate our sample value into a z or estimated z (or t). We then are able to make probability statements about the obtaining of our sample statistic if H_0 were true. If the probability is less than a specified α level (typically .05 or .01), we reject H_0.

Step-by-Step Procedures

Test H_0 about μ

We have listed below the steps in testing a null hypothesis about μ. We have then applied them to a concrete set of data.

1. Set up a null hypothesis about the value of μ and an alternative hypothesis:

$$H_0: \mu = \text{some specific value}$$

$$H_1: \mu \neq \text{value in } H_0 \text{ (bidirectional hypothesis)}$$

or

$$H_1: \mu > \text{value in } H_0 \text{ (unidirectional hypothesis)}$$

or

$$H_1: \mu < \text{value in } H_0 \text{ (another unidirectional hypothesis)}$$

2. After testing a random sample of individuals and determining $\overline{X}$ and s, compute $s_{\overline{X}}$, t and df.

$$t = \frac{\overline{X} - \mu}{s_{\overline{X}}} \qquad df = N - 1$$

where $\quad s_{\overline{X}} = \dfrac{s}{\sqrt{N}}$

$$\mu = \text{value specified in } H_0$$

3. Look up the critical values of $t_{.05}$ and $t_{.01}$ in Table C for the calculated df. If H_1 is bidirectional, these are the values associated with a two-tailed test. If H_1 is unidirectional, these may be the values associated with either a one-tailed or a two-tailed test.

4. Compare the calculated t with the critical value of t at a given α level. When a two-tailed test is being conducted and the calculated t is *larger* in absolute value than the critical value, reject H_0 at that α level. If the calculated t is *smaller* in absolute value than the critical value, retain H_0.

    If a one-tailed test is being conducted, H_0 is rejected when the calculated t is larger than the critical value of t in the direction specified by H_1; that is, the obtained t must be *negative* in sign when H_1 specifies that μ is *less than* the value stated in H_1 or must be *positive* in sign when H_1 specifies that μ is *greater than* the value stated in H_0. If the obtained t has the sign predicted by H_1 but is less than the critical value at the given α level, *or*, whatever its absolute value, if t has the sign opposite to that predicted in H_1, H_1 is rejected and there is no choice but to retain H_0.

5. In stating the conclusion about H_0, the α level and df should be specified. If a one-tailed test has been used, this should be stated. It will otherwise be assumed that a two-tailed test was conducted.

Example.   An industrial psychologist speculates that the average worker can absorb 35 pieces of information about a new procedure in a two-hour training period. He decides to put the hypothesis to the test by training a group of 16 workers and later gives them a test about the information they have retained. The $\overline{X}$ turns out to be 31.0 and s to be 5.

1. Set up H_0 and H_1.

$$H_0: \mu = 35$$
$$H_1: \mu \neq 35$$

2. Compute $s_{\overline{X}}$, t, and df.

$$s_{\overline{X}} = \frac{s}{\sqrt{N}} \qquad\qquad t = \frac{\overline{X} - \mu}{s_{\overline{X}}} = \frac{31.9 - 35}{1.25}$$

$$= \frac{5}{4} = 1.25 \qquad\qquad = \frac{3.1}{1.25} = 2.48$$

$$df = N - 1 = 16 - 1 - 15$$

3. Determine critical value of t at $\alpha = .05$ and $.01$. For $df = 15$, $t_{.05} = 2.13$ and $t_{.01} = 2.60$ (Table C).

4. Evaluate H_0. The calculated t of 2.48 is larger than $t_{.05} = 2.13$. Reject at $\alpha = .05$ (but not at $\alpha = .01$).

5. State conclusion. The H_0 that $\mu = 35$ is rejected at the 5% significance level. The investigator concludes that workers, on average, absorb less than he hypothesized.

Set Up Confidence Interval for μ

An entomologist has discovered a new variety of insect and measures the length of each member of a sample he has collected, with the following results.

$$\overline{X} = 9.25 \text{ mm} \qquad s = .20 \qquad N = 25$$

He decides to set up a confidence interval for the population mean, as he has no basis on which to hypothesize that μ takes a specific value.

95% CI: $\overline{X} \pm t_{.05}(s_{\overline{X}})$

$$s_{\overline{X}} = \frac{s}{\sqrt{N}} = \frac{.20}{5} = .04 \qquad df = N - 1 = 24$$

For $df = 24$, $t_{.05} = 2.06$.

$$95\% \text{ CI: } 9.25 \pm 2.06(.04) = 9.25 \pm 0.82 = 9.168 \text{ to } 9.332$$

The investigator asserts that μ lies within this range of values, with a 95 percent chance of being correct.

He could be even more certain of including μ by setting up the 99% confidence interval.

99% CI: $\overline{X} \pm t_{.01}(s_{\overline{X}})$

For $df = 24$, $t_{.01} = 2.80$,

$$99\% \text{ CI: } 9.25 \pm 2.80(.04) = 9.25 \pm .112 = 9.138 \text{ to } 9.362$$

Note that although the investigator can be more certain that μ is within this interval than with the 95% interval, the 99% CI is broader.

Test Hypothesis about Population Proportion

This test is applied to the binomial situation in which each object or event falls into one of two categories. For example, a child psychologist wants to select two toys that are equally preferred by 4-year-old boys for an experiment she is going to conduct. She picks out a pair of toys, a train and a truck, she thinks are equally attractive but decides to test this hypothesis. She presents the pair of toys to each of 30 boys and tells the child that he may pick the one with which he wants to play. She finds that 16 pick the truck (call it the favored toy, p) and 14 pick the train (call it the nonfavored toy, q).

1. Set up H_0 and H_1.

$$H_0: p_t = .50 \quad \text{where } p_t = \text{true population proportion}$$
$$H_1: p_t \neq .50$$

2. Convert number of choices to proportion.

$$p = \frac{16}{30} = .53 \quad q = \frac{14}{30} = .47$$

3. Compute z. With an N of this size, the binomial distribution for categorical data approximates the normal curve for continuous data. Instead of using the binomial expansion, we can therefore treat the sampling distribution of proportions as a normal curve. As the σ_p of the sampling distribution under H_0 can be determined exactly, we can convert our obtained proportion into a z score (rather than an estimated z or t).

$$z = \frac{p_s - p_t}{\sigma_{\text{prop}}} = \frac{.53 - .50}{.091} = .33$$

$$\text{where} \quad \sigma_{\text{prop}} = \sqrt{\frac{p_t q_t}{N}} = \sqrt{\frac{(.5)(.5)}{30}} = .091$$

4. Evaluate H_0. The critical value for z at $\alpha = .05$, two-tailed test, is 1.96. Our calculated z of .33 falls short of this value. The investigator retains H_0, concluding that the toys are equally preferred by 4-year-old boys. ■

DEFINITIONS OF TERMS AND SYMBOLS

Samping distribution. A theoretical distribution of values of a statistic such as $\overline{X}$, obtained from an infinite number of random samples of a given size.

Standard error of $\overline{X}$ ($\sigma_{\overline{X}}$). The standard deviation of a sampling distribution of $\overline{X}$'s.

Estimated standard error of $\overline{X}$ ($s_{\overline{X}}$). An estimate of $\sigma_{\overline{X}}$ based on the data from a single random sample. $s_{\overline{X}} = s/\sqrt{N}$.

Central limit theorem. The theorem that as sample size increases, the shape of the sampling distribution of $\overline{X}$'s increasingly resembles the normal probability distribution and the values of the $\overline{X}$'s cluster closer and closer to μ—that is, $\sigma_{\overline{X}}$ becomes increasingly smaller.

Null hypothesis (H_0). The hypothesis that a specified population parameter, such as the mean of a population (μ), takes some specified value. The null hypothesis is evaluated by the data from a single random sample.

Alternative hypothesis (H_1). The hypothesis that a population parameter, such as μ, has some value other than the value specified in H_0. A bidirectional H_1 merely states that the population value is unequal to the value stated in H_0. A unidirectional H_1 states the direction of the difference: either that the population parameter has some value greater than the one specified in H_0 or that it has some value less than the value specified in H_0.

Student's *t* (*t* ratio). The estimated value of z for a sample statistic in a sampling distribution of that statistic under a given H_0 about the parallel population parameter. In the case of a sampling distribution of $\overline{X}$'s, the *t* for an observed sample $\overline{X}$ is given by $t = (\overline{X} - \mu)/s_{\overline{X}}$.

Significance level (α level). The probability level that an investigator decides to use as a critical value in evaluating H_0. Investigators typically use either $\alpha = .05$ or $\alpha = .01$.

Two-tailed test. Both extremes of the *t* or z distribution are considered in evaluating H_0. A two-tailed test must be used to test H_0 when H_1 is bidirectional.

One-tailed test. Only one extreme of the *t* or z distribution is considered in evaluating H_0. A one-tailed test can be used only when H_1 is unidirectional. The extreme to be considered (upper or lower) is specified in H_1.

Type I (α) error. Rejecting a null hypothesis (H_0) as false when it is true. The Type I error is also identified as an *alpha* (α) error.

Type II (β) error. Failing to reject H_0 when it is false. The Type II error is also identified as a *beta* (β) error.

Confidence interval. The range of acceptable values for a population parameter at a given α level, determined from the data of a single sample. When $\alpha = .01$, the 99% confidence interval is established. When $\alpha = .05$, the 95% confidence interval is established.

Confidence interval for μ. The 95% confidence interval for μ is given by $\overline{X} \pm t_{.05} (s_{\overline{X}})$. The 99% confidence interval for μ is given by $\overline{X} \pm t_{.01}(s_{\overline{X}})$.

Standard error of proportion (σ_{prop}). The standard deviation of a binomial sampling distribution of sample proportions. $\sigma_{prop} = \sqrt{p_t q_t / N}$ where *p* is the population proportion of the favored event and q_t is $1 - p_t$.

PROBLEMS

1. Scores are available for all individuals who have taken a particular Civil Service examination over the past five years. These scores can be said to constitute a population of measures. The distribution of scores is found to be approximately normal. The mean and the standard deviation have the following values: $\mu = 78$, $\sigma = 10$.

   (a) If an infinite number of random samples of 25 cases each were drawn from the population and $\overline{X}$ determined for each sample, what would the resulting distribution of $\overline{X}$'s be called?

   (b) What numerical value would the mean of the distribution of $\overline{X}$'s be expected to take?

   (c) What is the standard deviation of the distribution of $\overline{X}$'s called? With samples of 25 cases each, what value would this standard deviation be expected to take?

   (d) If, instead, an infinite number of random samples of 49 cases each were drawn from the population and their $\overline{X}$'s determined, what numerical values would the mean and the standard deviation of this sampling distribution of $\overline{X}$'s be expected to take?

   (e) What would the standard deviation be if the samples consisted of 100 cases each?

   (f) Using the calculations you performed above, sketch three normal distributions of sample $\overline{X}$'s for 25, 49, and 100 cases each in a *single* graph. Show values of $\overline{X}$'s along the baseline and the mean and standard deviation in each distribution. (*Suggestion:* Mark off the baseline in one-score units ranging from 72 to 84.)

(g) After inspecting the figure in (f), describe how the variability in the distribution of $\overline{X}$'s changes as sample N's increase. As sample N's increase, $\sigma_{\overline{X}}$ approaches what value?

2. For a normally distributed population of scores, $\mu = 150$ and $\sigma = 16$. A single sample of 64 cases is drawn at random from the population.

(a) What is the probability that the $\overline{X}$ of this sample of 64 cases is 153 or *greater*? (In answering this and the following questions, it might be helpful to draw first the sampling distribution of $\overline{X}$'s to be expected for an infinite number of samples with N = 64.)

(b) What is the probability that this $\overline{X}$ deviates 4 or more units *in either direction* from the population μ?

(c) The probability is .05 that the $\overline{X}$ of this single sample will have a value of what or above?

(d) Suppose that the population μ and σ were unknown to you and that for a sample of 64 cases, $s = 17$. Using the sample data, estimate the standard error of the mean. Where does the discrepancy between $s_{\overline{X}}$ and the true $\sigma_{\overline{X}}$ come from?

3. A study of sex stereotypes about occupations is conducted in which 144 16-year-old girls are given a list of occupations, each accompanied by a 7-point rating scale. Point 1 is labeled "much more appropriate for men," point 4 is labeled "equally appropriate for men and women," and point 7 is labeled "much more appropriate for women." For the occupation "salesclerk," the following data were obtained: $\overline{X} = 4.15$, $s = 1.20$, N = 144.

(a) What is $s_{\overline{X}}$ for the sampling distribution of $\overline{X}$'s?

(b) A sex stereotype is said to exist if it is believed that an occupation is more appropriate for one sex than another. In determining whether there is a sex stereotype among 16-year-old girls about salesclerks, what null hypothesis should you test? After specifying H_0, set up a bidirectional alternative hypothesis.

(c) Test H_0, using $\alpha = .05$. What do you conclude about this hypothesis? State your conclusions specifically, in terms of the stereotype about salesclerks.

(d) Your conclusion in (c) could be in error. Describe this error verbally and identify which type (I or II) it is.

(e) If you wanted to minimize this type of error, would $\alpha = .05$ or $\alpha = .01$ be preferable?

4. In the study of stereotypes described in problem 3, the following data were obtained from 25 16-year-old boys for the occupation of lawyer: $\overline{X} = 3.12$, $s = 1.50$, N = 25.

(a) Specify H_0 and a unidirectional H_1. Explain your choice of H_1.

(b) Test H_0 against H_1, using $\alpha = .01$. What do you conclude? Be specific.

5. Assuming that the shape of the distribution in the population from which samples were drawn is normal, describe the shape of the sampling distribution of t as df's based on the sample N's go from low to high.

6. A manufacturer claims that its lightbulbs will last for an average of 500 hours. A consumer organization tests this claim, with the following results: $\overline{X} = 480$, $s = 50$.

(a) If the sample had consisted of 9 bulbs, what would you conclude about the validity of the manufacturer's claim? In conducting your test, set up a bidirectional H_1 and use $\alpha = .05$.

(b) If the sample had consisted of 16 bulbs and $\overline{X}$ and s were the same as above, what would you conclude?

   (c) What would you conclude if the sample consisted of 49 bulbs?

   (d) After examining your answers in (a), (b), and (c), state how sample size affects the power of the *t* test to detect a false null hypothesis at a given α level.

7. The waist circumferences of 144 20-year-old women are measured in centimeters, with the following results: $\overline{X} = 78.4$ cm, $s = 7.5$.

   (a) What are the values that define the limits of the 95% confidence interval for the μ of the population of 20-year-old women?

   (b) What are the values that define the limits of the 99% confidence interval?

8. An investigator is planning a study in which subjects are to be given pairs of words and to learn which arbitrarily chosen member of each pair has been designated as "correct." The investigator wants to select word pairs for which there is no initial selection bias among subjects and does a pilot study in which 40 subjects are shown a number of pairs and for each asked to guess which is "correct." On one pair, "grass-table," 22 pick "grass" and 18 pick "table." Perform a statistical test that will allow the investigator to conclude whether there is equal or unequal initial preference for the two words. Be sure to specify the α level you have used in reaching your conclusion. (Be sure to note in answering this question that the data involve two mutually exclusive categories and not measurement of some property.)

9. Each child in a sample of 20 5-year-old children was given a set of 9 objects consisting of 3 squares, 3 circles, and 3 triangles. For each shape, one object was yellow, one was blue, and one was red. The child was instructed to sort the objects, putting those together that belonged together. Of the 20 children, 15 sorted by color and 5 sorted by form. Is there an equal or unequal preference for form versus color?

9

Sampling Distributions:

Independent
Samples from
Two Populations

- ANATOMY OF AN EXPERIMENT
- SAMPLING DISTRIBUTION OF THE
  DIFFERENCE BETWEEN MEANS
- TESTING A HYPOTHESIS
  ABOUT $\mu_1 - \mu_2$: t RATIO
- ANOTHER LOOK AT THE t RATIO
- THE t RATIO AND SMALL SAMPLES
- CHOICE OF SIGNIFICANCE LEVEL
- POWER OF A STATISTICAL TEST
- POWER AND ESTIMATED EFFECT SIZE

ANATOMY OF AN EXPERIMENT

Psychologists have shown that under some circumstances, giving people tangible rewards for doing tasks they find enjoyable lessens their interest in these tasks and may also result in poorer task performance. An investigator who is interested in this topic gives second-grade children an attractive jigsaw puzzle to put together. The children, each of whom is seen individually, are randomly assigned to one of two conditions. In one condition, the child is given a bag of candy after completing the puzzle. In the other condition, no reward is given. Then each child is given a second puzzle, and the time the child takes to complete it is recorded.* The mean time taken to complete the second puzzle is 73 seconds for the children in the rewarded group and 62 seconds for the children in the nonrewarded group. Should the investigator conclude that reward subsequently leads to poorer performance? In this chapter, we consider techniques for answering this question.

Before getting to the statistics of the matter, we will discuss some of the features of the study just described and introduce some terminology. The study is an illustration of a basic two-group experiment. In such an experiment, the investigator manipulates the conditions under which subjects are tested, treating members of one group in one way and members of another group in another. In our example, there was an *experimental group* given a reward and a *control group* given no reward.

Although we will discuss in this chapter only two-group experiments, more than two conditions can be studied in the same investigation. For example, in our illustrative study, the investigation might include, as a second experimental condition, a group of children who are praised after completing the first puzzle for having done it so well. Techniques for analyzing experiments in which more than two conditions are manipulated are discussed in a later chapter.

The conditions the investigator manipulates are identified as the *independent variable*. The observations the investigator gathers from each subject are known as the *dependent variable*. The purpose of the experiment is to determine whether the variations in experimental condition, the independent variable, bring about variations in the dependent variable.† In our example, the investigator wished to find out whether the independent variable, reward condition, results in differences in the dependent variable, time to completion on the second puzzle.

To reach a reasonable conclusion, investigators must attempt to make the values of all variables that could affect performance equal in the two groups, except for the variable under study. In our example, the children were all tested in the same room, given the same instructions, treated the same by the experimenter except for the reward, and so forth. Investigators must also try to obtain initially comparable groups—that is, groups that, if treated alike, would have behaved alike. In our example, an effort was made to obtain comparable groups by

---

*Although this study is hypothetical, it is modeled after a number of actual experiments showing that under certain conditions, tangible rewards often have deleterious effects. See M. R. Lepper and D. Greene (eds.), *The Hidden Costs of Rewards: New Perspectives on the Psychology of Human Motivation* (Hillsdale, N.J.: Lawrence Erlbaum, 1978).

†In this section we are discussing true experiments—that is, research in which the investigator systematically varies the conditions under which groups of subjects are observed in order to determine whether the conditions have a differential effect on some measure. Investigators may also be interested in comparing on some dependent variable groups of individuals who differ in some preexisting property—for example, sex, age, occupation, or personality characteristics. The statistical techniques discussed in this chapter are appropriate for both types of research.

randomly assigning the children to the two conditions. This technique of forming groups was earlier identified as randomization.

When we say that experimental conditions have differential effects on the dependent variable, we imply that the μ's of the hypothetical populations would not be the same. For example, if giving children a candy reward actually does lead to poorer performance on an interesting puzzle than no reward, the μ of the hypothetical population of all children who could be tested under the reward condition would be less than the μ of the population of all children who could be tested under the nonreward condition. When μ's differ, it is also likely that the $\overline{X}$'s of samples of children tested under the two conditions would show a similar difference.

On the other hand, when experimental conditions have *no* differential effects on the dependent variable, the μ's of the hypothetical populations from which the samples were drawn would be equal. If investigators were able to obtain perfectly comparable samples and, with the exception of the independent variable, tested the two samples under exactly the same conditions, then not only the means of the populations but also the means of the samples would be the same. However, these goals are rarely if ever perfectly achieved, and as a result, the $\overline{X}$'s may differ purely because of chance factors the investigator is unable to identify or control. For this reason, a statistical technique is needed that allows investigators to come to a reasonable conclusion about the difference between the $\overline{X}$'s of their experimental groups—to decide whether the difference is due simply to sampling error or whether, instead, the population μ's differ and the obtained difference between $\overline{X}$'s reflects this fact. The conclusion that μ's differ implies that the experimental conditions *do* differentially influence the dependent variable.

The procedures used to assess these rival hypotheses—that the conditions are and are not differential in their effects—involve an extension of the logic used to test a hypothesis about the μ of a single population from the data of a single sample.

As we learned in Chapter 8, we first set up the null hypothesis (H_0) that μ is some specific value and an alternative hypothesis (H_1) that the value of μ is not the same as specified in H_0. Based on our theoretical knowledge about the sampling distribution of $\overline{X}$'s and on the assumption that H_0 is correct, we translate our obtained $\overline{X}$ into a t score (an estimated z). Then we determine the probability of obtaining a t of this size or greater if H_0 were correct. If the probability is small enough (typically .05 or less), we reject H_0; otherwise, we retain H_0 as reasonable.

We will follow parallel procedures in assessing the difference between the means of two groups drawn from different populations. We first set up a null hypothesis about the difference between the μ's of the populations. For reasons we explain in a later section, the H_0 we almost always test is that the two μ's are equal so that $\mu_1 - \mu_2 = 0$. The H_1 may either be bidirectional ($\mu_1 - \mu_2 \neq 0$) or unidirectional ($\mu_1 - \mu_2 > 0$ or $\mu_1 - \mu_2 < 0$). We obtain data from a pair of samples, one from each population, and translate our obtained difference between $\overline{X}$'s ($\overline{X}_1 - \overline{X}_2$) into t. Our last step is to determine the significance of the t we have calculated and to decide whether to reject or retain the H_0 that the samples came from populations with the same means.

With this brief overview before us, we will first discuss the nature of the sampling distribution of the difference between $\overline{X}$'s and then proceed to a detailed description of how to test a null hypothesis about the difference between μ's.

SAMPLING DISTRIBUTION OF THE DIFFERENCE BETWEEN MEANS

For purposes of illustration, suppose that we were able to test all the members of two populations on some common measure and have found that $\mu_1 = 60$ and $\mu_2 = 57$. The $\mu_1 - \mu_2$ difference, then, is $+3$ points. Now suppose that we selected a pair of random samples

Figure 9.1 Hypothetical distribution of differences between sample $\overline{X}$'s when the difference between population μ's $(\mu_1 - \mu_2)$ is 3.00 and the standard error is 1.5. For the first pair of samples in which $\overline{X}_1 - \overline{X}_2 = 1.6$, the deviation from the mean of the distribution is 1.4 score units $(1.6 - 3.0 = -1.4)$.

Sample #	$\overline{X}_1$	$\overline{X}_2$	$(\overline{X}_1 - \overline{X}_2)$
1	60.2	58.6	1.6
2	59.9	56.7	3.2
3	60.3	59.8	0.5
4	59.6	57.1	2.5
5	61.1	57.5	3.6
6	59.4	56.5	2.9
7	63.1	58.9	4.2
8	62.5	60.3	2.2
9	58.2	57.1	1.1
10	60.2	55.9	4.3
⋮	⋮	⋮	⋮
∞	⋮	⋮	⋮

$$M_{\overline{X}_1 - \overline{X}_2} = \overline{3.0}$$

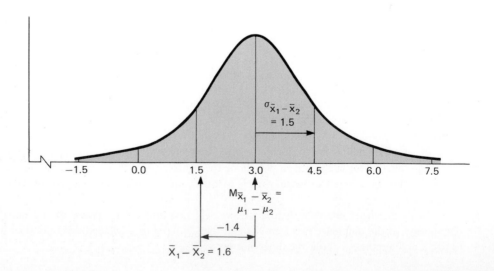

of equal size, one from each population, found the $\overline{X}$ for each sample, and then found the difference between them. We then select another pair of samples and find the difference between their $\overline{X}$'s ($\overline{X}_1 - \overline{X}_2$), until we have measured a very large number of pairs. (Technically, we should measure an infinite number, something that is humanly impossible, but as this is an exercise in statistical theory, we can imagine that we have done so.) The result is a series of numbers, each representing the difference between a pair of $\overline{X}$'s ($\overline{X}_1 - \overline{X}_2$).

These numbers can be arranged to form a frequency distribution in the ordinary way and can be plotted graphically as a frequency polygon. Assuming that each of the populations from which the samples were drawn are normally distributed or that the size of the samples is relatively large, we expect the shape of this sampling distribution of differences between $\overline{X}$'s to approximate a normal distribution, just as in the case of the sampling distribution of $\overline{X}$'s from a single population.

Such a distribution has been plotted graphically at the bottom of Figure 9.1. At the right, we have shown the results for the first 10 of the infinite number of pairs of samples we ultimately test. They were drawn, you recall, from populations in which $\mu_1 - \mu_2 = 3$.

The mean of the sampling distribution could also be obtained in the ordinary way. What value will this mean take? Remember that we said in Chapter 8 that the *mean of a sampling distribution of some statistic takes the same value as the parallel population parameter*. The population parameter we are now discussing is $\mu_1 - \mu_2$, which in our example is 3. The mean of the sampling distribution of the statistic ($\overline{X}_1 - \overline{X}_2$) is therefore 3. This equivalence is also shown in Figure 9.1.

The standard deviation of the sampling distribution could also be computed. The standard deviation of a sampling distribution, you remember, is called a *standard error*, in this case, the standard error of the difference between means, symbolized as $\sigma_{\overline{X}_1 - \overline{X}_2}$. With this information about the shape of the sampling distribution, and its mean and standard deviation, we are able to determine the probability of obtaining any given difference between $\overline{X}$'s of a given size or larger.

Standard Error of the Difference Between Means

We noted that the standard error of the difference, $\sigma_{\overline{X}_1 - \overline{X}_2}$, could be computed directly from the actual distribution of differences between $\overline{X}$'s. However, a constant relationship has been demonstrated between this standard error and the standard error of the mean ($\sigma_{\overline{X}}$) of each of the populations from which the samples are drawn; $\sigma_{\overline{X}}$ is in turn related to the σ of the population and the sample N, as we learned earlier. This relationship is shown in the following formula.

$$\sigma_{\overline{X}_1 - \overline{X}_2} = \sqrt{\sigma_{\overline{X}_1}^2 + \sigma_{\overline{X}_2}^2} \tag{9.1}$$

where

$$\sigma_{\overline{X}_1}^2 = \frac{\sigma_1^2}{N_1} \quad \text{and} \quad \sigma_{\overline{X}_2}^2 = \frac{\sigma_2^2}{N_2}$$

Using Formula 9.1, we can determine $\sigma_{\overline{X}_1 - \overline{X}_2}$, the standard error of the difference between $\overline{X}$'s, if we know the σ of each population and the sample sizes, N_1 and N_2.

Suppose in our illustration, in which $\mu_1 - \mu_2 = 3$, $\sigma_{\overline{X}_1 - \overline{X}_2}$ turns out to be 1.5, as shown in Figure 9.1. The difference between the $\overline{X}$'s of the first pair of samples we measured, we see at the right of Figure 9.1, is 1.6. The deviation (x) between the mean of the sampling distribution (which takes the same value as $\mu_1 - \mu_2$) and the difference between $\overline{X}$'s in this pair of samples is thus -1.4 (x = score − mean = $1.6 - 3.0 = -1.4$). How common is this event? That is, how probable is it that in a single pair of $\overline{X}$'s, we would obtain a difference between $\overline{X}$'s that deviates 1.4 or more points in either direction from the mean of the sampling distribution? We can see from Figure 9.1 that our obtained $(\overline{X}_1 - \overline{X}_2)$ value lies quite close to the mean of the distribution. A deviation of ± 1.4 or more score points from the mean would be a quite probable event. We can determine the probability more exactly by computing a z score for our obtained difference between $\overline{X}$'s and by then consulting the normal curve table. We define z as a score minus the mean of the distribution from which it came, divided by the standard deviation of the distribution. Thus the formula for determining z in sampling distributions of differences between means is:

$$z = \frac{(\overline{X}_1 - \overline{X}_2) - (\mu_1 - \mu_2)}{\sigma_{\overline{X}_1 - \overline{X}_2}} \tag{9.2}$$

thus yielding for our example:

$$z = \frac{1.6 - 3.0}{1.5} = \frac{-1.4}{1.5} = -.93$$

Looking at Table B, we find that 32.38 percent of the area in a normal curve falls between the mean and a z of .93 and 17.62 percent beyond this point; z scores exceeding $\pm .93$ therefore will occur approximately 35 percent of the time (17.62% × 2).

Estimating the Standard Error of the Difference

We rarely know μ and σ for a single population, let alone for two populations. Therefore, we cannot obtain either $(\mu_1 - \mu_2)$ or $\sigma_{\overline{X}_1 - \overline{X}_2}$. However, if we had some way to estimate $\sigma_{\overline{X}_1 - \overline{X}_2}$, we would be able to test hypotheses about the difference between μ's, based on the data from a single pair of samples. Fortunately, we can arrive at such an estimate by using, in place of each $\sigma_{\overline{X}}$, estimated standard errors of the mean ($s_{\overline{X}}$), which we learned to calculate in Chapter 8.

The formula for estimating the standard error of the difference between $\overline{X}$'s parallels Formula 9.1 given above for determining $\sigma_{\overline{X}_1 - \overline{X}_2}$. Thus:

$$s_{\overline{X}_1 - \overline{X}_2} = \sqrt{s_{\overline{X}_1}^2 + s_{\overline{X}_2}^2} \tag{9.3}$$

where $s_{\overline{X}_1}^2 = \dfrac{s_1^2}{N_1}$ and $s_{\overline{X}_2}^2 = \dfrac{s_2^2}{N_2}$

The calculation of $s_{\overline{X}_1} - \overline{x}_2$ is illustrated in the following section.

TESTING A HYPOTHESIS
ABOUT $\mu_1 - \mu_2$: t RATIO

We perform an experiment with laboratory animals to determine whether a diet deficient in protein affects their general activity level. One group of 60 animals is fed a low-protein diet for six months; another group of 60 is given a normal amount of protein. Near the end of this interval members of both groups are tested for activity level. The $\overline{X}$ of the normal group turns out to be 97.51, and s is 13.7; for the deficient group $\overline{X}$ is 91.36 and s is 14.2.

Our purpose in testing these samples is to make an inference about *populations*—populations of animals given diets that are normal or deficient in protein. We decide to test the hypothesis that the μ's of the two populations are the *same*; in other words, our null hypothesis for this study is $\mu_1 - \mu_2 = 0$. Our alternate hypothesis is the bidirectional hypothesis that the difference is some value other than zero. Thus:

$$H_0: \mu_1 - \mu_2 = 0$$

$$H_1: \mu_1 - \mu_2 \neq 0$$

Which population is identified as 1 and which is 2 is purely arbitrary; in our example, 1 will refer to the normal diet condition and 2 to the deficient.

To test the hypothesis, we first must calculate the estimated standard error of the difference by Formula 9.3:

$$s_{\overline{X}_1 - \overline{X}_2} = \sqrt{s_{\overline{X}_1}^2 + s_{\overline{X}_2}^2} = \sqrt{\frac{s_1^2}{N_1} + \frac{s_2^2}{N_2}}$$

$$= \sqrt{\frac{(13.7)^2}{60} + \frac{(14.2)^2}{60}} = \sqrt{3.13 + 3.36}$$

$$= \sqrt{6.49} = 2.55$$

If our null hypothesis that $\mu_1 - \mu_2 = 0$ is true, we know that the mean of the sampling distribution of differences between $\overline{X}$'s is also zero. The standard deviation of the distribution, we estimate, is 2.55. The difference between $\overline{X}$'s in the two samples we actually measured is $97.51 - 91.36 = 6.15$. Now we ask ourselves the following question. If $\mu_1 - \mu_2 = 0$, how probable is it that the difference between a pair of sample $\overline{X}$'s would deviate from zero as much as or more in either direction as occurred in our samples? In order to answer this question, we must first determine the estimated z score of our obtained difference between $\overline{X}$'s. We recall from Chapter 8 that the estimated z is identified as t. To obtain the estimated z or t, we simply substitute $s_{\overline{X}_1 - \overline{X}_2}$ for $\sigma_{\overline{X}_1 - \overline{X}_2}$ in Formula 9.2. Thus, the t formula for the difference between means is:

$$t = \frac{(\overline{X}_1 - \overline{X}_2) - (\mu_1 - \mu_2)}{s_{\overline{X}_1 - \overline{X}_2}} \tag{9.4}$$

In our example we proposed the null hypothesis that $\mu_1 - \mu_2 = 0$. When this particular H_0 is being tested, the expression $(\mu_1 - \mu_2)$ can be omitted from the numerator, so that the formula for t becomes:

$$t = \frac{\overline{X}_1 - \overline{X}_2}{s_{\overline{X}_1 - \overline{X}_2}} \qquad (9.5)$$

where

$$H_0: \mu_1 - \mu_2 = 0.$$

Application of Formula 9.5 to the data from our groups of laboratory animals gives us:

$$t = \frac{97.51 - 91.36}{2.55} = \frac{6.15}{2.55} = 2.41$$

Significance Levels of t. As we described in Chapter 8 when discussing the testing of hypotheses about μ, we evaluate the null hypothesis about the difference between means by comparing our obtained t with the t associated with a predetermined α level. As before, α typically is either the 5% or the 1% level. When the obtained t equals or exceeds the t associated with our specified α level, we conclude that our t is *significant*. We *reject* the null hypothesis that we have set up about the difference between μ's and conclude that our alternate hypothesis is more reasonable.

When the sample N's are large, the sampling distribution of t may be assumed to be normal. The values associated with the 5% and 1% significance levels are therefore those found in the normal curve table. We also remind you that when H_1 is bidirectional, these values are 1.96 and 2.58 for the 5% and 1% levels, respectively.

In our example, the samples of 60 each are large enough to permit us to assume the normal distribution. If α were set at the 5% level, we would reject the null hypothesis that $\mu_1 - \mu_2 = 0$, since the calculated t of 2.41 is greater than the critical value of 1.96, as illustrated in Figure 9.2. We would conclude, at the 5% level, that our obtained difference between $\overline{X}$'s was significant—that in the population as a whole, prolonged protein deficiency leads to lowered activity level.

We could, of course, use $\alpha = .01$ to evaluate H_0. The critical value of t, assuming a bidirectional H_1, is 2.58. When the t we have calculated is ± 2.58 or greater, we may reject our H_0 at the 1% significance level. In our illustrative experiment, $t = 2.41$. We can reject the null hypothesis at $\alpha = .05$ but not at $\alpha = .01$.

Choice of the Null Hypothesis

If investigators anticipate that the experimental conditions they study have no differential effects on the dependent variable, they assume that the two population μ's are the same. Therefore, it is understandable that the null hypothesis that is tested is $\mu_1 - \mu_2 = 0$. In most experiments, however, investigators expect that the conditions they study *do* differentially affect the dependent variable; they conduct the study because they suspect the population μ's are *not* equal.

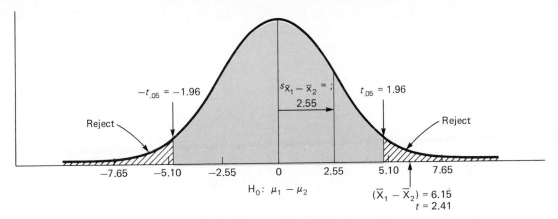

Figure 9.2 Illustration of significance test for H_0: $\mu_1 - \mu_2 = 0$, and H_1: $\mu_1 - \mu_2 \neq 0$ at $\alpha = .05$ where $(\overline{X}_1 - \overline{X}_2) = 6.15$, $s_{\overline{X}_1 - \overline{X}_2} = 2.55$, and $t = 2.41$.

If investigators have reason to hypothesize that the population μ's differ by some *specific* amount, they will probably choose to test this hypothesis. For example, an investigator may have a theoretical model that leads to the prediction that $\mu_1 - \mu_2 = 6$ and therefore sets H_0 at this value. In computing t, the investigator uses Formula 9.4, inserting 6 as the value of $\mu_1 - \mu_2$.

However, even when investigators have firm grounds for postulating not only a difference between μ's but also the direction of the difference, they rarely have a basis for predicting the *exact* value of this difference. But the logic of hypothesis testing, we noted previously, demands that H_0 be assigned a precise value. The solution is to approach the matter backwards, as it were. For *statistical* purposes, the investigator sets up the null hypothesis that $\mu_1 - \mu_2 = 0$, thus specifying an exact value for the difference. The investigator then sets up a more general alternative hypothesis (H_1) that states that the difference between μ's is some unspecified value other than zero. The investigator's expectation is that it will be possible to *reject* H_0 and to accept instead the alternative hypothesis that the μ's are different, that the experimental conditions *do* have a different effect.

Thus, whatever the investigators' experimental hypothesis, the statistical hypothesis they almost always test is H_0: $\mu_1 - \mu_2 = 0$. This procedure is so common that the expression "the null hypothesis" often is used synonymously with the specific hypothesis that the difference between μ's is zero, and the formula for t is frequently the one shown in Formula 9.5, in which the term ($\mu_1 - \mu_2$) is omitted.

We have said that the null hypothesis an investigator sets up to test statistically may or may not correspond to the *experimental* hypothesis. That is, in some instances, investigators predict beforehand that the null hypothesis that the two μ's are equal will be shown to be reasonable and thus will be retained. In other instances, they predict that it will be shown to be unreasonable and thus will be rejected. Whatever their intent, investigators are left in more doubt when they accept the null hypothesis than when they reject it. Perhaps the simplest way to explain this statement is to take a different approach to the difference between $\overline{X}$'s obtained in a single pair of samples; to use the sample data to set up a confidence interval for $\mu_1 - \mu_2$, in the same manner as we set up a confidence interval for μ in Chapter 8. For $\alpha = .05$, this confidence interval is defined as

$$95\% \text{ CI: } (\overline{X}_1 - \overline{X}_2) \pm t_{.05}(s_{\overline{X}_1 - \overline{X}_2})$$

Now suppose that $(\overline{X}_1 - \overline{X}_2)$ for a pair of large samples is 7.0 and $s_{\overline{X}_1 - \overline{X}_2}$ is calculated to be 3.0. Since the samples are large, $t_{.05}$ takes the normal curve value of 1.96. Thus:

$$95\% \text{ CI: } 7 \pm 1.96(3) = 7 \pm 5.88 = 1.12 \text{ to } 12.88$$

At the 95% confidence level, we assert that the value of $\mu_1 - \mu_2$ falls someplace within the interval of 1.12 to 12.88. Suppose instead that we had used the sample data to test H_0: $\mu_1 - \mu_2 = 0$. We find $t = 7/3 = 2.3$ and, with $\alpha = .05$, reject H_0. This conclusion corresponds to what is indicated by the 95% confidence interval: the range of values established for $\mu_1 - \mu_2$ *does not* include zero.

But now suppose instead that $(\overline{X}_1 - \overline{X}_2)$ had turned out to be 2. Assuming $s_{\overline{X}_1 - \overline{X}_2}$ to be the same, the 95% confidence interval for $(\mu_1 - \mu_2)$ turns out to be:

$$95\% \text{ CI: } 2 \pm 1.96(3) = 2 \pm 5.88 = -3.88 \text{ to } +7.88$$

At the 95% confidence level, we assert that $\mu_1 - \mu_2$ falls someplace in the interval -3.88 to $+7.88$. If we had used the sample data to test H_0: $\mu_1 - \mu_2 = 0$, we would find that $t = 2/3 = .67$ and would accept H_0 at the 5% level. But inspection of the range of values established for the 95% confidence interval shows that the hypothesis $\mu_1 - \mu_2 = 0$ is but one of many hypotheses that would be acceptable at $\alpha = .05$. In fact, *any* H_0 between -3.88 and $+7.88$ would be acceptable at this α level.

As these examples illustrate, rejecting H_0 with a statistical test is a relatively clean process, but accepting H_0 leaves investigators in greater uncertainty. For this reason, as we have noted before, investigators are reluctant to describe a null hypothesis as having been "accepted" because it connotes a positive conclusion. When the computed t falls short of the critical value of t at a specified α level, it is preferable to be cautious and to conclude instead that H_0 has *not been rejected*.

ANOTHER LOOK AT THE t RATIO

We have said that when we test the null hypothesis that the difference between μ's is zero $(\mu_1 - \mu_2 = 0)$, we convert our observed difference between $\overline{X}$'s $(\overline{X}_1 - \overline{X}_2)$ into an estimated z score in the hypothetical sampling distribution of differences between $\overline{X}$'s that would obtain if H_0 were true. This we do by dividing $\overline{X}_1 - \overline{X}_2$ by our estimate of the standard deviation of the sampling distribution (standard error of the difference between $\overline{X}$'s). This estimated z we call t. If the probability of obtaining our calculated t by chance alone is small, e.g., less than .05, we reject H_0 as being unreasonable.

There is another useful way of looking at the t ratio. By way of illustration, assume that we have tested two groups of 60 each and have found $\overline{X}$ and s for each group. We could also combine the data from the two groups into a single group of scores whose variability we could also describe. Where does this variability come from? Part of the variability in the total group of scores comes from the fact that scores within each of the two independent groups are not alike. This source can be called *within-groups* variability. The remainder of the variability in the total group comes from the fact that the two group means are not alike. This source can be called *between-groups* variability. These two sources of variability, between groups and within groups, are associated, respectively, with the numerator and denominator of the t ratio. That is, if the denominator, $\overline{X}_1 - \overline{X}_2$, is small, we can say that there is little variability between groups; if $\overline{X}_1 - \overline{X}_2$ is large, we can say that there is considerable variability between groups. The denominator of the equation, $s_{\overline{X}_1 - \overline{X}_2}$, can be described as reflecting the *variability within groups*. That is, holding the N's of the groups constant, the size of $s_{\overline{X}_1 - \overline{X}_2}$ is determined by the size of the s's of the two groups (and s, of course, reflects the amount of variability within a group). When the variability between groups is sufficiently large in comparison to the variability within groups, with the result that t is large, the null hypothesis that the samples were drawn from populations with the same means is rejected.

We can also approach the t ratio from another perspective. Suppose that we were to combine the two groups of scores into one large group of scores. The variability among the total group of scores comes from two potential sources: *systematic differences between groups* and *error*. The systematic source of variability is reflected in the difference between $\overline{X}$'s. That is, when population μ's differ, the differences between pairs of samples means will show a systematic tendency to mirror these differences in direction and magnitude (as illustrated, for example, in Figure 9.1). On the other hand, the standard error of the difference between $\overline{X}$'s reflects *error*. That is, the variability within each group comes from a variety of unknown, uncontrolled factors—variations in the experimental procedures or in environmental conditions, differences among the subjects, and so forth. Ideally, we would like to minimize the variability within groups, down to zero if it were possible, so that all the variability between groups, that is, between $\overline{X}$'s, could be attributed to the systematic source, a difference between μ's. In the sense that it comes from unwanted, uncontrolled sources, within groups variability is an "error." Of course, the same kind of uncontrollable factors may also contribute to the difference between $\overline{X}$'s. In fact, when it is true that $\mu_1 = \mu_2$, any difference between $\overline{X}$'s is due to sampling errors. So, before we reject the H_0 that $\mu_1 - \mu_2 = 0$ and conclude that the observed difference between $\overline{X}$'s is due to the fact that the μ's differ (the systematic source), we demand that the difference between $\overline{X}$'s be sufficiently larger than $s_{\overline{X}_1 - \overline{X}_2}$, the error source of variability.

In Chapter 12 we introduce a statistical technique, one-way analysis of variance, that is used to analyze data from studies comparing any number of conditions or groups, not merely two. As you will discover, the new descriptive terms we have introduced in this section serve as an introduction to this technique.

THE t RATIO AND SMALL SAMPLES

Standard Error of Difference and Unequal N's

In our discussion of t thus far, we have dealt only with relatively large samples—samples that have 60 to 70 members or more. We make several modifications in our procedures when we wish to determine the significance of the difference between the means of small samples. First, we should use Formula 9.3 for $s_{\bar{X}_1 - \bar{X}_2}$ *only if the N's for the two samples are equal.* To repeat this formula and the conditions under which it is used in comparing small samples:

$$s_{\bar{X}_1 - \bar{X}_2} = \sqrt{s_{\bar{X}_1}^2 + s_{\bar{X}_2}^2} \quad \text{(small samples with equal N's)}$$

where

$$s_{\bar{X}_1}^2 = \frac{s_1^2}{N_1} \quad \text{and} \quad s_{\bar{X}_2}^2 = \frac{s_2^2}{N_2}$$

In this formula, observe that the $s_{\bar{X}}^2$ of each sample, which in turn is based on the s^2 of each sample, contributes equally to the estimate of the standard error of the difference. When the sample N's are not equal, we must amend our formula so that the contribution of the data from each sample to our estimate of the standard error of the difference is weighted according to the sample N. This modification, shown below, *must* be used for small samples with unequal N's but also may be used when N's are the same, since in this instance it yields the same value as Formula 9.3.

$$s_{\bar{X}_1 - \bar{X}_2} = \sqrt{\frac{(N_1 - 1)s_1^2 + (N_2 - 1)s_2^2}{(N_1 + N_2 - 2)} \left(\frac{1}{N_1} + \frac{1}{N_2} \right)} \tag{9.6}$$

(small samples with equal or unequal N's)

A raw-score formula also may be used:

$$s_{\bar{X}_1 - \bar{X}_2} = \sqrt{\frac{(\sum X_1^2 + \sum X_2^2) - (N_1\bar{X}_1^2 + N_2\bar{X}_2^2)}{(N_1 + N_2 - 2)} \left(\frac{1}{N_1} + \frac{1}{N_2} \right)} \tag{9.7}$$

Note that when sample N's *are* equal, these formulas produce exactly the same answer as does the simpler formula based on the addition of the two $s_{\bar{X}}^2$'s. Thus, as we have noted, the use of these modified formulas always is appropriate, whether the sample N's are the same or different.

Use of the *t* Table

A second difference in the procedures we employ with small samples has to do with interpreting the *t* that we have calculated. As we discussed earlier, the *t* values obtained from large samples approximate the normal distribution. Thus, in interpreting large-sample *t*'s, we use Table B, the normal curve table. You will recall from Chapter 8 that the *t* values obtained from small samples are *not* normally distributed. However, assuming that the populations from which the samples were drawn are normally distributed, the distributions of small sample *t*'s are symmetrical, their shape being related to the degrees of freedom (*df*) associated with the samples.

The *df* associated with a single sample, it will be recalled, is equal to N − 1. In evaluating a hypothesis about the difference between μ's, the calculated *t* is based on the data from two samples, each with N − 1 *df*. The *df* that is used in evaluating *t* is therefore the sum of the *df*'s for the two samples:

$$df = (N_1 - 1) + (N_2 - 1) = N_1 + N_2 - 2 \qquad (9.8)$$

If we draw two independent samples where N is 10 each, the *df* is 18 (i.e., 10 + 10 − 2). If we have two samples, one of 7 and the other of 9 cases, the *df* is 14.

Having calculated *t*, we consult the *t* table, Table C, to find the critical values of *t* at the 5% and 1% significance levels that are associated with the *df* for our pair of samples. If the calculated *t* exceeds the critical value of *t* at a given α level, we reject the null hypothesis that $\mu_1 - \mu_2 = 0$. If, on the other hand, the calculated *t* falls short of the tabled value, we conclude we cannot reject the null hypothesis at the given α level.

An Example

We can now demonstrate how to go about testing the significance of the difference between $\overline{X}$'s of small samples. Our example comes from a study in which the perceptual-motor performance of individuals with a certain type of brain injury was tested. We wish to compare the mean performance of a group of 12 persons whose injury was unilateral—on only one side of the cortex—with the performance of a group of 5 whose injury was bilateral. We may suspect that bilateral injuries result in poorer performance than unilateral injuries. The null hypothesis we test, however, is that the two types of damage have equal effects on performance; the alternative hypothesis is that they do not. Therefore:

$$H_0: \mu_{Bi} - \mu_{Uni} = 0$$

$$H_1: \mu_{Bi} - \mu_{Uni} \neq 0$$

We have reported below the mean score obtained by each of the two groups on the task. (Higher scores indicate better performance.) We have also reported the s^2 we have calculated from the data of each sample. Notice that the two groups do not have the same number of cases. We must therefore use the formula appropriate for unequal N's when computing $s_{\bar{X}_1 - \bar{X}_2}$.

Unilateral	Bilateral
$N_1 = 12$	$N_2 = 5$
$\bar{X}_1 = 49.19$	$\bar{X}_2 = 38.43$
$s_1^2 = 74.65$	$s_2^2 = 49.28$

$$s_{\bar{X}_1 - \bar{X}_2} = \sqrt{\frac{(N_1 - 1)s_1^2 + (N_2 - 1)s_2^2}{(N_1 + N_2 - 2)}\left(\frac{1}{N_1} + \frac{1}{N_2}\right)}$$

$$= \sqrt{\frac{11(74.65) + 4(49.28)}{12 + 5 - 2}\left(\frac{1}{12} + \frac{1}{5}\right)}$$

$$= \sqrt{\frac{821.15 + 197.12}{15}(.083 + .200)} = \sqrt{19.21}$$

$$= 4.38$$

$$t = \frac{\bar{X}_1 - \bar{X}_2}{s_{\bar{X}_1 - \bar{X}_2}} = \frac{49.19 - 38.43}{4.38}$$

$$= \frac{10.76}{4.38} = 2.46$$

$$df = 12 + 5 - 2 = 15$$

For $df = 15$, $t_{.05} = 2.13$ and $t_{.01} = 2.95$ (Table C). Conclusion: Assuming that α was set beforehand at .05, $H_0: \mu_1 - \mu_2 = 0$ is rejected at the 5% level, since the calculated t of 2.46 is greater than the critical value of 2.13. As low scores reflect poor performance, it is concluded at the 5% level that bilateral brain injury results in poorer perceptual-motor performance than unilateral injury. However, if α had been set at .01, the null hypothesis would *not* be rejected, since $t = 2.46$ is less than $t_{.01} = 2.95$.

Assumptions Underlying t

We mentioned earlier, but did not emphasize, that the theoretically derived t distributions are based on the assumption that the characteristic being measured is normally distributed in the populations from which the samples were drawn. Use of the t ratio to test a hypothesis about the difference between population means also assumes that the population σ's are the same. It has been demonstrated, however, that t tests may be used without noticeably distorting our conclusions even when these assumptions are not met, as long as the σ's are not markedly different or the distributions do not depart radically from normal. If one or more of these assumptions is seriously violated, one procedure that is open to us is to use an alternate type of statistical test that makes no assumptions about population parameters such as distribution shapes or σ's. Some of these *nonparametric techniques*, as they are called, are discussed in Chapter 15.

In the procedures for calculating and evaluating t that have been discussed in this chapter, a final assumption is that the two samples are both randomly drawn from their respective populations and are independent of each other. Techniques are also available for calculating t from the data of samples that have not been independently selected but instead have been deliberately matched. This topic is discussed in Chapter 11.

In practice, investigators almost never have access to all the members of a population and hence are unable to select and test random samples in their experiments. As we noted in Chapter 1, the most common procedure is to use *randomized* groups. That is, a pool of individuals is available, sometimes called a *sample of convenience*, and individuals in the pool are randomly assigned to experimental conditions. Strictly speaking, statistical tests based on the assumption of randomized assignment of subjects to groups should be used in analyzing the data from experiments using this type of design. However, statistical theory is far better developed for situations involving random sampling than for those involving randomization. Primarily for this reason, the results of investigations using the randomization design are almost always treated as though the groups had been obtained by random sampling and analyzed by statistical tests, such as t, based on the random-sampling assumption. Fortunately, the significance level given by t appears to be quite close to that yielded by a more exact test when both are applied to randomized data.

CHOICE OF SIGNIFICANCE LEVEL

Statisticians advise investigators to specify beforehand the α level they will use to decide whether or not to reject the null hypothesis they have designed their study to test. This procedure makes the decision-making process automatic and invulnerable to the investigator's biases or wishful thinking. The investigator does, however, have a choice of significance level, which raises a question about the factors that determine this choice. We begin our discussion of this problem by presenting two examples.

The research division of a drug company has discovered a new drug for the treatment of a specific medical disorder. It is not known whether the drug differs in its therapeutic effectiveness from the standard remedy, but it is known that the two drugs are otherwise comparable in cost, ease of administration, side effects, and so on. An experiment is therefore planned to compare the two drugs' therapeutic effectiveness. The null hypothesis the investigators decide to test is that the two drugs have equal effects ($\mu_1 = \mu_2$); the alternate hypothesis they set up is the unidirectional hypothesis that the new drug is *better*. If the new drug turns out to be significantly better than the old, the company will put it on the market. In considering which α level to use, the researchers ponder the possible kinds of decisions that could result. The H_0 is either true or false, and, after assessing H_0 statistically, they will either accept or reject it. Thus, there are four possibilities, two of them involving ways to come to a *correct* conclusion: the investigator can reject H_0 when it is in fact false and can accept H_0 when it is in fact true. Similarly, there are two ways to come to an *incorrect* conclusion: the investigator can erroneously reject H_0 when it is in fact true (Type I error) and can accept H_0 when it is in fact false (Type II error). These possibilities and the probabilities of each are shown in Table

Table 9.1 The Four Possible Outcomes in Evaluating H_0 at a Given α Level and Probabilities of Each

		Correctness of H_0	
		True	*False*
	Accept H_0	Correct $1 - \alpha$	Error (Type II) β
Conclusion			
	Reject H_0	Error (Type I) α	Correct $1 - \beta$

9.1. Recall from Chapter 8 that the probability of making a Type I error at a given α level is equal to that α, while the probability of a Type II error takes a value somewhat higher than α and is identified as β.

The researchers must weigh the hazards of the two types of errors. If the new drug is better than the old and they accept the false hypothesis that $\mu_1 - \mu_2 = 0$, the drug will not be marketed and those who suffer from the disorder will be deprived of a more potent therapeutic agent. On the other hand, if the new drug is no better than the old and they incorrectly *reject H_0*, the company will waste time and money marketing the new product. Marketing expense, however, is quite minimal, and they decide that a Type I error, concluding that the new drug is more effective when it isn't, would be less costly than a Type II error, concluding that the new drug is equally effective as the old when it is better. Therefore, they decide to use a relatively large value of α, 5 percent or perhaps even 10 percent, to minimize the probability of a Type II error.

Another example: a new method of teaching eighth-grade biology has been devised that would be quite expensive to implement, requiring new books, special laboratory equipment, and retraining of teachers. Before deciding whether or not to introduce the method into a large elementary school, the principal asks that an experiment be conducted in which the exam scores of a group of pupils taught by this method are compared with those of a group taught in the regular way. Because of the expense involved, an α level of 1 percent or even smaller might be used to assess H_0. Setting a more stringent criterion for rejecting the null hypothesis minimizes the probability of a Type I error—that is, lessens the probability that the H_0 will be incorrectly rejected when in fact the new method does not produce better performance than the old. The principal also might insist that the new method produce results not only *better* than the old, but *substantially superior*. A technique that would help in this decision is described later in this chapter.

In both these examples a practical decision is to be based on the conclusion drawn from the experimental data. The α level chosen for assessing the null hypothesis is adjusted up or down, depending on the investigator's judgment about the relative risks of a Type I or Type II error. In purely scientific research the acceptance or rejection of the null hypothesis usually does not have consequences as immediate and as obvious as those in our examples. Nonetheless, errors can be costly. Promising ideas can be abandoned or investigators' time and energy wasted in pursuit of false trails as a consequence of an incorrect decision about H_0. In general, however, scientists prefer to be conservative about rejecting hypotheses and consider a rule that would permit the occurrence of a Type I error more than 5 percent of the time to be unacceptable. Therefore, the highest α value conventionally used is .05. On the other hand, setting α lower than .01 results too often in failure to detect a false H_0 (Type II error) to be acceptable. One therefore finds the 1% and 5% levels used almost exclusively in research reports.

Since there usually is little pressure on anyone to take direct action based on an investigator's decision about the correctness of H_0, most investigators report their data as being significantly different from the null hypothesis if it can be rejected at the 5% level or less. If it is possible to reject H_0 at the 1% level, or at some level lower than 5%, this is the significance level that is actually reported.

POWER OF A STATISTICAL TEST

In their concern not to make Type I errors, scientists have specified relatively stringent criteria for rejecting the null hypothesis, the 5% and 1% significance levels. They are also concerned about minimizing Type II errors and hence about the probability that a statistical test will detect false hypotheses, as noted in Chapter 8. This probability, known as the *power* of the test, is determined by the following formula:

$$\text{Power} = 1 - p(\text{Type II error}) \tag{9.9}$$

We have noted that the probability of a Type II error is symbolized by the Greek letter β (beta). Thus we may also write:

$$\text{Power} = 1 - \beta$$

What the formula indicates, we repeat, is the probability that H_0 will be rejected when it is in fact false.

We will discuss power for the simple case in which we test H_0: $\mu_1 - \mu_2 = 0$ and know the values of μ and σ. We can illustrate the method of calculating power by the following example involving two populations. For the first population μ is 93 and for the second μ is 89; both populations have a σ of 8.

We test a random sample of 10 cases from each population and set up the null hypothesis that $\mu_1 - \mu_2 = 0$. Note that the true difference is $93 - 89$ or 4 and H_0 is false. For convenience, we will assume that our alternative hypothesis, H_1, is the unidirectional hypothesis that $\mu_1 > \mu_2$. The α level we decide to use in evaluating H_0 is .05.

Since we know the population σ, we are able to compute the z score for the difference between our sample $\overline{X}$'s rather than having to obtain t, an estimate of z. The formula we use is this:

$$z = \frac{(\overline{X}_1 - \overline{X}_2) - (\mu_1 - \mu_2)}{\sigma_{\overline{X}_1 - \overline{X}_2}}$$

Looking at the normal curve table, we see that 45% of the area lies between μ and $z =$ 1.64 and 5% above this value of z. Thus with $\alpha = .05$, $H_0: \mu_1 - \mu_2 = 0$ and $H_1: \mu_1 > \mu_2$, we will reject the null hypothesis of no difference between μ's if we obtain a z of 1.64 or greater. We know that H_0 is false; that is, our null hypothesis states that the difference is zero but the true difference, in our illustrative example, is 4.

The power of our test, which we have defined as the probability of detecting a false null hypothesis, is thus equal to the probability of obtaining a z of 1.64 or greater. We proceed to determine this probability by first determining $\sigma_{\overline{X}_1 - \overline{X}_2}$. Since each σ equals 8:

$$\sigma_{\overline{X}_1 - \overline{X}_2} = \sqrt{\sigma_{\overline{X}_1}{}^2 + \sigma_{\overline{X}_2}{}^2} = \sqrt{\frac{8^2}{10} + \frac{8^2}{10}}$$

$$= \sqrt{\frac{128}{10}} = 3.58$$

Next we substitute in the z formula the critical value of z, the value of $(\mu_1 - \mu_2)$ under H_0, and the value of $\sigma_{\overline{X}_1 - \overline{X}_2}$; we then solve for $(\overline{X}_1 - \overline{X}_2)$:

$$1.64 = \frac{(\overline{X}_1 - \overline{X}_2) - 0}{3.58}$$

so that

$$(\overline{X}_1 - \overline{X}_2) = 1.64(3.58) = 5.87$$

We have now determined that if we test two samples of 10 cases each, we will reject H_0 at $\alpha = .05$ whenever the $\overline{X}_1 - \overline{X}_2$ difference is 5.87 or greater. When we reject H_0 we will accept instead our H_1 that $\mu_1 > \mu_2$. This is illustrated in Figure 9.3. Our next step is to determine the probability of getting a difference between $\overline{X}$'s of +5.87 with the *actual* sampling distribution of difference between means with $\mu_1 = 93$ and $\mu_2 = 89$. We first compute z:

$$z = \frac{5.87 - (93 - 89)}{3.58} = \frac{5.87 - 4.00}{3.58} = .52$$

Looking at Table B, we find 19.85 percent of the area lies between μ and $z = .52$, and 30.15 percent beyond it. Thus, the probability of rejecting the false H_0 is .3015. This probability is equal to $1 - \beta$, *the power of the test*. We can also see that β, the probability of making a Type II error, is $1 - .3015$ or .6985. We add that a power of .3015 is usually considered too low a value to have in a well-designed experiment. Therefore, an experimenter faced with this set of calculations would seek a new research procedure with a higher value of $1 - \beta$ (power).

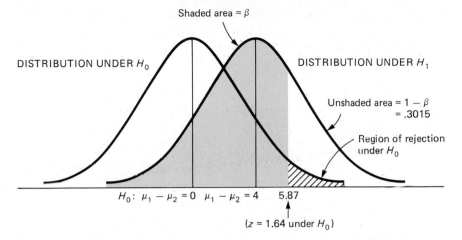

Figure 9.3 Illustration of determination of the power of a test to detect that H_0: $\mu_1 - \mu_2 = 0$ is false when $\mu_1 - \mu_2 = 4$. The power of the test is equal to $1 - \beta$.

Our example has illustrated the calculation of the power of a test when H_0 concerns the difference between μ's. The same general logic is used in determining the power of a test of other types of hypotheses. For example, in testing a hypothesis about μ we would use the z formula $(\overline{X} - \mu)/\sigma_{\overline{X}}$ and follow the same steps outlined above.

Factors Affecting Power of a Test

If you examine the z formula and the steps for determining the power of a test, you will see that the values of the mean and standard error of the sampling distribution (in our example, $\mu_1 - \mu_2$ and $\sigma_{\overline{X}_1 - \overline{X}_2}$, respectively), as well as the value of z itself, all affect the probability figure we obtain. We will consider each of these terms and their implications for power one at a time. Again, we will use the two-population case as an illustration.

In our example the mean of the sampling distribution specified by the false H_0 is zero. The power of the test to detect this false hypothesis increases as the discrepancy between this mean and the true mean of the sampling difference, determined here by $\mu_1 - \mu_2$, increases. We can see this by examining Figure 9.3. If the $\mu_1 - \mu_2$ difference is small, close to the value specified by H_0, the true sampling distribution will show considerable overlap with the distribution under H_0. The value of β will therefore be high and $1 - \beta$, which defines the power of the test, correspondingly low. As $\mu_1 - \mu_2$ grows larger, the true sampling distribution is displaced further and further along the baseline and overlaps less and less with the distribution under H_0. Area β thus approaches a zero value and $1 - \beta$ approaches one. As the difference between H_0 and the true state of affairs increases, then, the probability of rejecting the false H_0 approaches unity.

The second factor affecting power is the standard error of the sampling distribution, in our example $\sigma_{\bar{X}_1 - \bar{X}_2}$, which is equal to:

$$\sqrt{\sigma_{\bar{X}_1}^2 + \sigma_{\bar{X}_2}^2} \quad \text{or} \quad \sqrt{\frac{\sigma_1^2}{N_1} + \frac{\sigma_2^2}{N_2}}$$

The basic components of the standard error formula, we can see, are N, the number of cases in each sample, and σ, the standard deviation in each population. Consider first the implications of variations in the N's. As an N increases, the value of the corresponding $\sigma_{\bar{X}}^2$ and hence of $\sigma_{\bar{X}_1 - \bar{X}_2}$ will *decrease*. Picture what would happen to the sampling distributions in Figure 9.3 as N increased from 10 per sample to larger numbers. The means of the distributions would remain the same, but with less variability (a smaller $\sigma_{\bar{X}_1 - \bar{X}_2}$), the distributions would each become taller and thinner. This in turn would reduce the overlap of the two sampling distributions. Reduction in overlap, we have already seen, increases $1 - \beta$, the power of the test. Large N's, then, make it less difficult to reject false hypotheses than small N's.

The second component affecting the standard error of sampling distributions is σ, with the standard error decreasing as σ decreases. In designing experiments, therefore, investigators try to minimize the influence of extraneous factors that may result in increased variability among their subjects and hence reduce the power of their test of significance.

To summarize our discussion so far, the formula for z in the two-population case is:

$$z = \frac{(\bar{X}_1 - \bar{X}_2) - (\mu_1 - \mu_2)}{\sqrt{\frac{\sigma_1^2}{N_1} + \frac{\sigma_2^2}{N_2}}}$$

The value of z, and hence the power of the test to detect a false H_0, will increase as (1) the difference between μ's increases, (2) the size of σ's decreases, and (3) sample N's increase.

Another factor affecting power is the α level we have chosen, which in turn determines z. We indicated earlier that the lower we set α, the less the probability of committing a Type I (α) error and the greater the probability of committing a Type II (β) error. Since power is defined by $1 - \beta$, this implies that the lower the α, the smaller the power of the test. We can demonstrate this by considering z. With a one-tailed test, as we saw in our example, the z associated with $\alpha = .05$ is 1.64. The value of $(\bar{X}_1 - \bar{X}_2)$ permitting us to reject H_0 was thus 1.64 $(\sigma_{\bar{X}_1 - \bar{X}_2})$ or 1.64(3.58) = 5.87. We determined that the probability of getting a difference of this size or greater in the true sampling distribution was .3015. The power of the test was thus .3015. If we had set α at .01, z would have been 2.33 and the critical value of $(\bar{X}_1 - \bar{X}_2)$ would have been 2.33(3.58) = 8.34. By finding the z-score equivalent of 8.34 in the true distribution $[(8.34 - 4.00)/3.58 = 1.21]$, we determine from Table B that only 11.31 percent of the area falls beyond this point. We can see that the power of the test for $\alpha = .01$ is .1131, less than when we used the higher α level of .05.

The final factor affecting the power of a test is the nature of H_1. At a given α level the value of z is less when H_1 is unidirectional and evaluated by a one-tailed test than when a bidirectional H_1 and two-tailed test are used—for example, 1.64 vs. 1.96 for $\alpha = .05$; 2.33 vs. 2.58 for $\alpha = .01$. We have just seen that, other things being equal, the lower the value of this z, the greater the power of the test. Unidirectional H_1's evaluated by one-tailed tests therefore are more powerful than bidirectional H_1's.

POWER AND ESTIMATED
EFFECT SIZE

Imagine that there are two populations, A and B, that both have σ's of 10 but have different means: $\mu_A = 85$ and $\mu_B = 74$. Now imagine two other populations, C and D, whose σ's also equal 10 but with $\mu_C = 91$ and $\mu_D = 89$. In the first pair of populations, the difference between μ's is 11 points ($85 - 74 = 11$), whereas in the second pair, the difference between μ's is 2 points ($91 - 89 = 2$). If these pairs of μ's were unknown to us and we did an experiment testing the null hypothesis that the difference between μ's is zero, it is quite likely that we would reject H_0 in the case of a pair of samples drawn from populations A and B even when we tested relatively small samples. However, we are unlikely to reject H_0 in the case of samples drawn from populations C and D unless the samples are quite large. That is, as we have just shown, the power of a test to reject H_0 when it is false is affected by the magnitude of the difference between μ's. It is also affected by sample size. Holding $\sigma_{\bar{X}_1 - \bar{X}_2}$ constant, we therefore have to employ considerably larger samples to get a significant t when the difference between μ's is small than when the difference between μ's is large.

The fact that even a small difference between μ's can be detected when sample N's are large enough illustrates an important point. Even when t is statistically significant, leading us to reject the null hypothesis that the variables whose influence we are investigating have no differential effects, the magnitude of these effects may be trivial, having little or no importance. Statistical significance, then, does not necessarily imply scientific or practical significance. When we have performed a t test and have rejected H_0: $\mu_1 - \mu_2 = 0$, it is therefore useful to get an estimate of the magnitude of the effect of the variable we are studying, or as it is technically called, the *effect size*.

One of the most commonly used estimates of effect size is symbolized as $\hat{\omega}^2$. The letter ω is the Greek lowercase letter omega. The "hat" over the ω, called a circumflex, is used to indicate that we are estimating the value of omega squared from sample data. (The expression ω^2 is reserved for the *population* value.) The formula for $\hat{\omega}^2$ is:

$$\hat{\omega}^2 = \frac{t^2 - 1}{t^2 + df + 1} \tag{9.10}$$

where $df = N_1 + N_2 - 2$ and t^2 is the squared value of the t we have calculated. The formula yields an estimate of the proportion of the variability in scores on the dependent variable that can be accounted for or explained by the independent variable.

The upper limit on the proportion of explained variability is, of course, 1.00 and this is the maximum value that $\hat{\omega}^2$ can be expected to take. It is relatively rare in psychology and other behavioral sciences that differences in a single variable account for a substantial proportion of the variability, and some statisticians* describe $\hat{\omega}^2$ values of .15 to .20 or greater as "strong."

A word of caution is in order. When sample N's are large and we compute $\hat{\omega}^2$ for every experiment and not just significant ones, our estimated effect size, $\hat{\omega}^2$, is probably quite close

---

*See, for example, J. Cohen, *Statistical Power Analysis for the Behavioral Sciences*, rev. ed. (New York: Academic Press, 1977); D. M. Lane and W. P. Dunlap, "Estimating effect size: Bias resulting from the significance criterion in editorial decisions," *The British Journal of Mathematical and Statistical Psychology*, 1978, *31*, 107–12.

to the true effect size, ω^2. However, for small samples—let us say 10 or less—we are less confident about the accuracy of $\hat{\omega}^2$. Whatever the sample size, if we calculate $\hat{\omega}^2$ only in experiments in which t is significant, we will substantially overestimate ω^2.*

To illustrate the application of $\hat{\omega}^2$, we refer to the results of a hypothetical experiment in which the effectiveness of a new bonus system in increasing worker satisfaction was studied in a large manufacturing company in which morale was low. Fifty individuals were assigned to the experimental group (bonus) and another 50 individuals served as a control group (no bonus). After the bonus system had been in effect for three months, both groups were given a questionnaire assessing their job satisfaction. Possible scores on the questionnaire ranged from 0 to 45. Analysis of the data produced the results below, which allowed H_0 to be rejected at the 5% level.

$$\overline{X}_E = 28.1 \qquad \overline{X}_C = 25.7 \qquad t = 2.13$$

$$df = 50 + 50 - 2 = 98, t_{05} = 1.99.$$

Omega squared was estimated to be:

$$\hat{\omega}^2 = \frac{t^2 - 1}{t^2 + df + 1} = \frac{(2.13)^2 - 1}{(2.13)^2 + 98 + 1} = \frac{3.54}{103.54} = .034$$

Although the bonus system significantly increased worker satisfaction, the size of its effect was quite small. We estimate that only about 3 percent of the variability in satisfaction scores can be accounted for by differences in the treatment of the experimental and control groups. It seems possible that the benefits of the bonus system were not worth the expense of implementing it and that the company would decide to discontinue the system.

Step-by-Step Procedures

Example with Equal N's

Subjects worked in pairs on a series of problem-solving tasks and could use both cooperative and individualistic strategies. Half the pairs of subjects had a 15-minute "get acquainted" session before beginning the task (experimental group) and the other half did not (control group). There were 25 pairs in each group. The experimenter suspected that the pretask inter-

---

*For this and other reasons there is some controversy about the use and interpretation of $\hat{\omega}^2$ and other measures of effect size. Before using this technique in their own studies, serious research workers should consult more advanced treatments such as G. Keppel, *Design and Analysis: A Researcher's Handbook*, 2nd ed. (Englewood Cliffs, N.J.: Prentice-Hall, 1982), pp. 89–96.

action would lead the pairs to use more cooperative strategies. Number of cooperative strategies was the dependent variable.

$$H_0: \mu_E - \mu_C = 0$$

$$H_1: \mu_E \neq \mu_C \quad \text{(bidirectional)}$$

or

$$\mu_E > \mu_C \quad \text{(unidirectional)}$$

If a unidirectional H_1 is selected, it should reflect the investigator's experimental hypothesis, in this case that prior interaction should increase cooperative strategies.

Basic Data

Determine for each distribution ΣX, ΣX^2, and N (in this example, number of pairs of subjects) From these data, compute $\overline{X}$ and s. The relevant statistics for our example are:

$$\overline{X}_E = 28.3 \qquad \overline{X}_C = 23.5$$

$$s_E = 3.4 \qquad s_C = 3.2$$

$$N_E = 25 \qquad N_C = 25$$

Compute t by Formula 9.5:

$$t = \frac{\overline{X}_1 - \overline{X}_2}{s_{\overline{X}_1 - \overline{X}_2}}$$

1. $\overline{X}_E - \overline{X}_C = 28.3 - 23.5 = 4.8$

2. By Formula 9.3:

$$s_{\overline{X}_1 - \overline{X}_2} = \sqrt{s_{\overline{X}_1}^2 + s_{\overline{X}_2}^2} = \sqrt{.46 + .41} = \sqrt{.87}$$

$$= .93$$

$$\text{where} \quad s_{\overline{X}_E}^2 = \frac{s_E^2}{N_E} \qquad\qquad s_{\overline{X}_C}^2 = \frac{s_C^2}{N_C}$$

$$= \frac{(3.4)^2}{25} = .46 \qquad\qquad = \frac{(3.2)^2}{25} = .41$$

3. Find t

$$t = \frac{4.8}{.93} = 5.16$$

Evaluate H_0:

$$df = N_E + N_C - 2 = 25 + 25 - 2 = 48$$

For $df = 48$, $t_{.01} = 2.69$ for a two-tailed test and $t_{.01} = 2.41$ for a one-tailed test (Table C). (*Note:* $df = 48$ is not tabled in Table C; use the nearest tabled df below the obtained df to find the critical value of t.) The obtained t is greater than these values.

State Conclusion:

The null hypothesis that the two groups came from populations with the same means is rejected at $\alpha = .01$. It is concluded that prior interaction increases cooperation. (*Note:* In this example, this conclusion can be drawn with both a bidirectional H_1 and a unidirectional H_1 that $\mu_E > \mu_C$.)

Estimate Effect Size by Computing $\hat{\omega}^2$

By Formula 9.10:

$$\hat{\omega}^2 = \frac{t^2 - 1}{t^2 + df + 1}$$

$$= \frac{(5.16)^2 - 1}{(5.16)^2 + 48 + 1} = \frac{25.63}{75.63} = .34$$

We estimate that the introduction of an initial interaction period accounted for 34 percent of the variability in cooperation scores. The estimated effect size is quite large.

Example with Unequal N's

Five years ago 16 men and 11 women were awarded Ph.D.'s in chemistry from Big City University. This year the graduates, all of whom were working in the field, were sent a survey that included a question about the number of scientific papers they had published. Was there a difference between men and women?

Set up H_0 and H_1:

$$H_0: \mu_M - \mu_W = 0$$

$$H_1: \mu_M - \mu_W \neq 0$$

Basic Data

Determine for each distribution ΣX, ΣX^2, $\overline{X}$, and s. These data are reported below.

	Men	Women
ΣX	128	71
ΣX^2	1220	617
$\overline{X}$	8.00	6.45
s	3.61	3.98
N	16	11

Compute t:

1. $\overline{X}_M - \overline{X}_W = 8.00 - 6.45 = 1.55$

2. By Formula 9.6:

$$s_{\overline{X}_1 - \overline{X}_2} = \sqrt{\frac{(N_1 - 1)s_1^2 + (N_2 - 1)s_2^2}{(N_1 + N_2 - 2)}\left(\frac{1}{N_1} + \frac{1}{N_2}\right)}$$

$$= \sqrt{\frac{(16 - 1)(3.61)^2 + (11 - 1)(3.98)^2}{16 + 11 - 2}\left(\frac{1}{16} + \frac{1}{11}\right)}$$

$$= \sqrt{\frac{15(13.03) + 10(15.84)}{25}(.15)}$$

$$= \sqrt{\frac{195.45 + 158.40}{.25}(.15)}$$

$$= \sqrt{\frac{353.85}{25}(.15)} = \sqrt{14.15(.15)}$$

$$= \sqrt{2.12} = 1.46$$

or, by Formula 9.7:

$$s_{\overline{X}_1 - \overline{X}_2} = \sqrt{\frac{(\Sigma X_1^2 + \Sigma X_2^2) - (N_1\overline{X}_1^2 + N_2\overline{X}_2^2)}{(N_1 + N_2 - 2)}\left(\frac{1}{N_1} + \frac{1}{N_2}\right)}$$

$$= \sqrt{\frac{(1220 + 617) - [16(8.00)^2 + 11(6.45)^2]}{16 + 11 - 2}\left(\frac{1}{16} + \frac{1}{11}\right)}$$

$$= \sqrt{\frac{1837 - 1481.63}{25}(.15)}$$

$$= \sqrt{\frac{355.37}{25}(.15)} = \sqrt{14.22(.15)}$$

$$= \sqrt{2.13} = 1.46$$

3. $t = 1.55/1.46 = 1.06$ $df = N_1 + N_2 - 2$.

For $df = 16 + 11 - 2 = 25$, $t_{.05} = 2.06$ for the two-tailed test.

State Conclusion:

Our calculated t is less than the critical value at $\alpha = .05$ and H_0 is retained. We conclude that there is a nonsignificant difference between the average number of publications of men and women.

DEFINITIONS OF TERMS
AND SYMBOLS

Independent variable. The condition the investigator manipulates in an experiment.

Dependent variable. The observations the investigator gathers from each subject in an experiment. The purpose of the experiment is to determine whether the conditions of the experiment (values of the independent variable) differentially affect the dependent variable.

Sampling distribution of differences between means. A theoretical frequency distribution consisting of an infinite number of differences ($\overline{X}_1 - \overline{X}_2$) between pairs of random sample means, the samples in each pair having been drawn from population 1 and population 2, respectively.

Standard error of the difference between $\overline{X}$'s ($\sigma_{\overline{X}_1 - \overline{X}_2}$). The standard deviation of the sampling distribution of differences between $\overline{X}$'s.

Estimated standard error of the difference between $\overline{X}$'s ($s_{\overline{X}_1 - \overline{X}_2}$). An estimate of $\sigma_{\overline{X}_1 - \overline{X}_2}$ based on the data from a single pair of samples.

Null hypothesis (H_0) about difference between μ's. A statistical hypothesis about the specific value of the difference between μ's that is evaluated by means of a t test. Typically, H_0 is that $\mu_1 - \mu_2 = 0$.

t ratio. An estimated z for ($\overline{X}_1 - \overline{X}_2$), defined as $[(\overline{X}_1 - \overline{X}_2) - (\mu_1 - \mu_2)]/s_{\overline{X}_1 - \overline{X}_2}$. In this formula, ($\overline{X}_1 - \overline{X}_2$) is determined from the data of the pair of samples that have been observed, ($\mu_1 - \mu_2$) is the value specified in H_0, and $s_{\overline{X}_1 - \overline{X}_2}$ is the estimated standard error of the sampling distribution of differences. The numerator of the t ratio reflects variability between groups (systematic source) and the denominator reflects variability within groups (error source).

Estimated omega squared ($\hat{\omega}^2$). A statistic providing an estimate of effect size expressed as the estimated proportion of the variability in scores on the dependent variable that can be accounted for by the independent variable.

Degrees of freedom (df). For a pair of independent random samples, $df = N_1 + N_2 - 2$.

Assumptions underlying t test. The logic of the t test for evaluating a hypothesis about the difference between μ's described in this chapter assumes that (a) the characteristic that has been measured is normally distributed in each of the populations from which the samples were drawn, (b) the population σ's are equal, and (c) the two samples are each randomly selected and independent of each other. If any of these assumptions is seriously violated, use of the t test may lead to inappropriate conclusions about H_0.

Type I and Type II errors. See Chapter 8.

Power of a statistical test. Power refers to the ability of a statistical test to detect false null hypotheses and is defined as $1 - \beta$, where β is the probability of a Type II error. The power of a test of a hypothesis about $\mu_1 - \mu_2$ (a) increases with the magnitude of the $\mu_1 - \mu_2$ difference, (b) decreases with the size of the population σ's and (c) increases with the size of the sample N's.

PROBLEMS

1. Three studies are described below, each of which compares two groups on some measure. For each study, identify the independent variable and the dependent variable. Then describe verbally the specific null hypothesis that would be evaluated in conducting a t test of the data.

   (a) Students who seek help at their college counseling service because they are anxious and upset are assigned at random to one of two types of treatment programs, insight therapy and cognitive therapy. Six months after their first therapeutic session, all students are given a test that evaluates their current emotional status.

   (b) Two groups of students, one high and one low in self-esteem, are allowed to succeed at a task and then asked to attribute their success to their ability or their effort on a 5-point scale ranging from "primarily my ability" to "primarily my effort."

   (c) Two groups of infant monkeys were reared in a cage with their mother, isolated from other monkeys. Those in one group were also placed in a cage with other young monkeys for 30 minutes several times a week, whereas those in the other group were not given this social experience. When they were 3 months old, each animal was placed in a cage alone and the amount of fear each displayed when a strange mechanical windup toy was placed in the cage was recorded.

2. Assume that information is available on the heights of all men inducted into the U.S. Army during World War I and World War II and the following results (in inches) are obtained for the two populations. WWI: $\mu = 65$, $\sigma = 3$; WWII: $\mu = 68$, $\sigma = 3$.

   (a) If a very large number of random samples of 100 men each were drawn from each population, what would be the value of the standard deviation (standard error of the mean) of each sampling distribution of $\overline{X}$'s?

   (b) Suppose the random samples of 100 had been drawn in independent pairs, one from the men in WWI and the other from WWII, and the difference between $\overline{X}$'s, in the order $\overline{X}_{WWII} - \overline{X}_{WWI}$, was determined for each pair. What would be the value of the mean of the resulting distribution of differences between $\overline{X}$'s?

   (c) What is the standard deviation of the sampling distribution of differences called? What would be its value?

   (d) What is the probability of drawing a pair of samples of 100 cases each in which the $\overline{X}$ for the WWII sample is 4 or more score units higher than the $\overline{X}$ for the WWI sample? (Drawing a sketch of the sampling distribution of differences and showing its mean and standard error may help you figure out how to answer this question.)

Note: The following problems call for the conduct of a t test. In each problem, specify the H_0 and H_1 you are testing, the α level you select, and df.

3. Assume that you have available data from a single pair of random samples of 70 men each, drawn from the populations described in problem 2, and that you do not know the population μ's and σ's. The sample $\overline{X}$'s and s's turn out to be:

$$\text{WWI: } \overline{X} = 65.8, s = 3.1; \text{ WWII: } \overline{X} = 67.2, s = 2.9.$$

   Your interest in these sample data is in estimating whether or not men inducted into the army in the two wars differed in height.

   (a) Set up the null hypothesis that you will test and a bidirectional alternate hypothesis. Explain your choice of H_0.

(b) If you were to test H_0 against a unidirectional H_1, what specific alternative hypothesis would you select? (Use your general knowledge about factors related to height to answer this question.)

(c) Test the H_0 (with the bidirectional H_1) you set up in (a).

(d) What do you conclude? State your conclusion in terms of the specific research question the study was designed to answer.

4. A university counseling psychologist finds that students who complain they are lonely also say they would like someone to talk to and confide in. He wonders whether, if given an opportunity to disclose something about themselves, they would be more likely to do so than others because they have greater need or would be less likely to disclose because they are inhibited or lack the skills. He performs an experiment in which women students who receive high scores or low scores on a loneliness questionnaire are asked by a trained interviewer to talk about a series of moderately intimate topics. Their taped responses are later rated by judges for degree of intimacy of self-disclosure. The results are shown below, with high scores indicating more self-disclosure.

	Lonely	Nonlonely
$\overline{X}$	43.2	47.7
s	4.1	3.6
N	20	20

After conducting the appropriate statistical test, come to some conclusion about loneliness and self-disclosure.

5. A medical researcher has identified a new drug that animal investigations suggest may be a more effective treatment for a genetic defect apparent at birth that results in mental retardation. She is able to find 15 cases of the disorder, but because the drug is scarce and expensive, can treat only 5 of the infants. With parental consent, 5 infants are selected at random for the experimental treatment and the remainder are given a standard drug treatment. When the children are 2 years old, they are given a test of cognitive development. The results are shown below. (High scores indicate high development.)

	Experimental	Standard
$\overline{X}$	58.4	52.6
s	5.6	5.2
N	5	10

In testing H_0, set up a bidirectional H_1 and use $\alpha = .05$. What can be concluded about the relative effectiveness of the two drugs? In conducting your t test, be sure to use Formula 9.6 for calculating $s_{\overline{X}_1 - \overline{X}_2}$ for unequal N's.

6. The investigator described in problem 5 was later able to repeat the experiment with two treatment groups of 25 cases each. The following results were obtained.

	Experimental	Standard
$\overline{X}$	58.9	53.1
s	5.5	5.3

$$s_{\overline{X}_E - \overline{X}_S} = 1.53$$

(a) Using $\alpha = .05$, what do you conclude about the effectiveness of the experimental drug?

(b) If your calculations are correct, your conclusion is different from your conclusion in problem 5. Explain the discrepancy, referring to the concept of power.

7. The results of two experiments are described below. For each, compute $\hat{\omega}^2$ and describe your conclusions about this estimated effect size.

(a) Subjects were shown a list of words, one at a time, so rapidly that all they could report seeing was a dark blur. For half of the subjects the words described a positive emotional state (Pos) and for the other half, they described a neutral object (Ne). All subjects were then presented with a list of words describing positive emotional states and for each, they rated on a 7-point scale how much it described their current mood. (High scores indicated high agreement.)

$$\overline{X}_{Pos} = 53.2 \qquad \overline{X}_{Ne} = 51.3$$

$$N_{Pos} = 36 \qquad N_{Ne} = 36 \qquad t = 2.18$$

(b) During their pregnancy and after the birth of their litters of pups, female rats were fed standard lab food to which a substance with a distinctive taste and odor had been added. After they had been weaned, half of the pups were fed standard lab food (St) and the other half were fed this food plus the substance given to their mothers (St +). The amount eaten by each animal during the first week was determined.

$$\overline{X}_{St} = 114.2 \qquad \overline{X}_{St+} = 118.5$$

$$N_{St} = 15 \qquad N_{St+} = 15 \qquad t = 2.98$$

10

Linear Correlation and Regression

- CORRELATIONAL METHOD VERSUS EXPERIMENTAL METHOD
- THE PEARSON PRODUCT-MOMENT CORRELATION COEFFICIENT (r)
- USE OF r IN PREDICTION
- THE RANK-ORDER CORRELATION COEFFICIENT (r_S)

CORRELATIONAL METHOD
VERSUS EXPERIMENTAL METHOD

Scientific problems are usually attacked experimentally if it is possible to do so. For example, many charities solicit contributions by telephone, and we might be interested in whether a "hard sell" or a "soft sell" approach would be more effective in persuading people to make a pledge. We could train one group of solicitors in one technique and another group in the other technique and then compare the number of pledges obtained by members of each group in 50 phone calls. However, there are many phenomena that we are unable to manipulate experimentally and still others that for ethical reasons we would not manipulate even if it were possible. For example, we might suspect that children reared in certain ways by their parents would suffer long-term deleterious effects but we would never try to induce a group of parents to rear their children in these ways in order to test our suspicions. When experimentation is not feasible, we often turn to correlational techniques. Consider the following questions.

Are the political attitudes of college men related to their fathers' attitudes? That is, do students who are liberal or conservative in comparison to their peers tend to have fathers whose attitudes are liberal or conservative for members of their generation? Do more highly educated women tend to have more or fewer children than less highly educated women? Two professors independently read the essay exams of a class of 10 students and rank them from best to worst. How strongly do they agree in their judgments? Each of these questions asks about the relationship or *correlation* between two variables—*the degree to which the variables are associated or covary*.

Correlational problems, it is important to note, involve distributions of paired scores. In Table 10.1, for example, we have shown the scores of 15 college men on a political attitudes questionnaire and, for each student, the score of his father on the same questionnaire. We can examine the relationship between the two sets of scores by graphing them as shown in Figure 10.1. This type of graph is called a *scatter plot* because it shows how the scores scatter over a range of possible scores.

Every point in a scatter plot represents two values, an individual's score on one variable, identified as X, and the same or a paired individual's score on a second variable, identified as Y. Both variables are plotted on the same graph because we are interested in the relationship between them. As we established in Chapter 3, values of the X variable are always displayed along the horizontal axis and values of the Y variable are always displayed along the vertical axis. In Table 10.1, for example, the sons' scores are identified as X and their fathers' scores as Y. The first pair of scores is $X = 12$ and $Y = 14$. In preparing the scatter plot, we went across the horizontal X axis to a score of 12 and up the Y axis to a score of 14. As illustrated in Figure 10.1, we placed a point at the intersection of the vertical and horizontal lines erected from these score values at right angles to the X and Y axes. This point represents the pair of scores, $X = 12$ and $Y = 14$. We proceeded in this fashion until the points for all pairs were plotted. Examination of the resulting scatter plot, shown in Figure 10.1, indicates that as the sons' scores go up, their fathers' scores tend to go up, and vice versa. We say that there is a tendency for fathers' and sons' attitudes to be related or *correlated*.

Correlations between variables vary in direction. In the case of fathers and sons, the correlation between their attitudes is *positive*. That is, conservative fathers tend to have conserv-

Table 10.1 Scores of 15 College Men and their Fathers on a Test of Political Attitudes

Pair	Son (X)	Father (Y)
1	12	14
2	11	18
3	13	16
4	14	17
5	12	15
6	7	8
7	22	19
8	13	11
9	10	16
10	14	23
11	17	15
12	12	19
13	18	17
14	10	12
15	2	6

Figure 10.1 Scatter plot of scores of 15 father–son pairs on a test of political attitudes. (The data are from Table 10.1.)

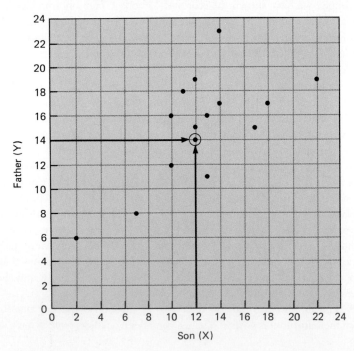

ative sons and liberal fathers tend to have liberal sons. Suppose instead that we determined people's scores on a test of extroversion and their estimate of the number of hours they typically spend alone each week. We wouldn't be surprised to find that people who are highly extroverted tend to spend very *little* time by themselves, whereas those who are low on this personality dimension tend to spend a *good deal* of time by themselves. In this instance, high goes with low and low goes with high; there is a *negative* correlation between the two variables. The third possibility is that there is no relationship between two variables. For example, we might show that tall people are neither more likely nor less likely to read a lot than are short people. In this case, there is a *zero* correlation between the variables.

Hypothetical examples of these three classes of correlations, positive, negative, and zero, are shown in the three scatter plots of Figure 10.2. Figure 10.2(a) shows the relationship between scores on a measure of self-esteem (X) and a measure of assertiveness (Y). This scatter plot shows that amount of self-esteem is related to amount of assertiveness; individuals with high scores on one measure tend to have high scores on the other, and those with low scores on one tend to have low scores on the other. This, of course, is an example of a *positive* correlation. The next graph, Figure 10.2(b), shows the relationship between high school students' grade point average and average amount of time per week spent watching television. In this scatter plot there is a tendency for students with *high* X scores to have *low* Y scores and vice versa. We therefore say that there is a *negative* correlation between X and Y; those who spend a lot of time watching TV tend to have a low grade point average and those with a good average tend to spend little time watching TV.

Figure 10.2(c) shows a scatter plot of two variables with virtually no relationship between them. Each X score represents the time taken to complete an introductory psychology test, and the Y score represents the same person's grade on that test. Examination scores do not vary consistently in relation to the length of time spent by the students taking the examination. We describe this lack of relationship as reflecting an essentially *zero* correlation between X and Y.

We have just seen that the data of Figure 10.2(a) and 10.2(b) exhibit different *directions* of correlation—positive and negative, respectively. When we look at the graphs carefully, we note another difference. In Figure 10.2(a) we have drawn a straight line in such a way that it falls close to as many points as possible. Most of the points do not lie far from the straight line, which indicates a very strong positive relationship between the two variables. If the relationship were perfect—that is, could not be improved upon—all the points would fall exactly along a straight line.* Similarly, all the points in a perfect negative correlation would fall along a straight line, except that high scores on the X measure would be paired with low scores on Y, and vice versa.

If we look at Figure 10.2(b), however, we observe that the straight line drawn through the points describes them fairly well, but that a number of points lie at quite a distance from that line. The two variables, we see, are not as strongly correlated as in Figure 10.2(a). In Figure 10.2(c), no straight line would be particularly successful. The relationship between the variables is essentially zero. Thus, the second way in which scatter plots may differ is with

---

*We actually are discussing here correlations that are *linear* in nature. That is, a straight line describes the points in the scatter plot better than a curved line. [See pages 203–204 for a discussion of curvilinear correlation and Figure 10.4(b) for an example.] With a perfect *linear* correlation, all points fall along a straight line.

(a) An example of high positive correlation

(b) An example of moderate negative correlation

(c) An example of an approximately zero correlation

Figure 10.2 Scatter plots showing three types of correlations between X and Y.

respect to the amount or *degree* of correlation. Correlations may go from a perfect relationship, in which all the points lie on a straight line, to a zero relationship, in which the points are so scattered that no X shows a greater tendency to be paired with one Y more than any other, and vice versa.

Correlation and Causation

The demonstration that two variables are correlated demonstrates *only* that they covary, that changes in the values of one tend to be associated with changes in the other. We cannot infer from the correlation alone that one of these variables has caused or brought about the other.

There are, of course, instances in which additional evidence suggests that variations in X do have some causal effect on Y. For example, the time since individuals last ate (X) is correlated with how hungry they report they are (Y). We know that hunger pangs are brought about by lack of food, so it is plausible to assume that X causes Y but not the reverse: changing your report about how hungry you feel does not affect when you last ate. But as this example illustrates, the causal path may not be direct or immediately obvious. A host of physiological events are taking place over time to affect the sensation of hunger. We do not know from the correlation, then, exactly how deprivation of food (X) brings about changes in reported hunger (Y).

Unfortunately, it is often tempting to infer a cause-effect relationship from no more than the correlation itself. For example, you may have seen an ad for a vocabulary-building program that stated (correctly) that people with large vocabularies tend to have higher incomes than those with smaller vocabularies. Enlarging your vocabulary, the ad promises, will increase your chances of getting a better-paying job. What the ad assumes, of course, is that the size of a person's vocabulary directly affects the nature of the job that he or she is able to get. However, vocabulary is related to other characteristics, such as general intelligence and amount of education, that are more likely than vocabulary to have a causal link to the type of job people obtain. These factors will not change when people purposefully set out to expand their vocabulary. We could even argue that having a better-paying, high-level job causes people to enlarge their vocabularies. That is, such jobs may bring them into daily contact with better-educated individuals with large vocabularies or require that they read material written at a higher level than they have been used to. What this example illustrates is that interpreting the meaning of a correlation in terms of causal links is very tricky business. Understanding how a correlation comes about requires much more information than the correlation itself.

Although correlation coefficients do not show what factors are responsible for the relationship between two variables, correlational techniques are nevertheless valuable for describing such relationships. The primary purpose of this chapter is to describe two of the most frequently used correlational techniques and to show how to make predictions of one variable from another when the correlation between the two is known. The latter technique enables us to do such things as predicting students' success in college from their entrance test scores or the adult heights of children from their heights at age 6. Predictions of some accuracy are possible in these instances, because the pairs of variables are known to be correlated.

THE PEARSON PRODUCT-MOMENT CORRELATION COEFFICIENT (*r*)

Earlier in this chapter we developed in a general way the meaning of the terms positive and negative correlation and of relationships that are high, relatively low, or zero in magnitude. We also saw how, by inspecting a scatter plot, we often can specify the direction of the correlation between X and Y and make some kind of statement about its magnitude. Descriptions based on observing scatter plots, however, are not very precise. To overcome this deficiency we introduce a new concept, the *correlation coefficient*. This coefficient will have a specific numerical value for any given set of paired data. Positive values will correspond to what we have called positive correlation, negative values to negative correlation. Furthermore, high values of the coefficient, regardless of whether they are positive or negative, will correspond to what we have called high correlation, and low values to low correlation. What would be called zero correlation when seen on a scatter plot may not in fact have a correlation coefficient of exactly zero, although the value will surely be near zero.

In practice, statisticians use several different correlation coefficients, depending on the type of data involved. In this chapter we will discuss two coefficients that describe the linear (straight line) correlation between variables. The first correlation coefficient we will discuss is used with magnitude data—that is, numerical scores indicating the amount of the characteristic each individual exhibits. The technical name of this coefficient is the *Pearson product-moment correlation coefficient*, named in honor of Karl Pearson, one of the great pioneers of statistics, and symbolized as *r*. Because product-moment correlation coefficient is a highly technical term whose meaning is not essential to the research worker, we will not explain its origin. The three expressions—Pearson correlation coefficient, product-moment correlation coefficient, and *r*— will be used interchangeably in this chapter.

Basic Formula for *r*

The Pearson correlation coefficient, *r*, is defined as the *mean of the products of the z scores for the X and Y pairs*. The mean of any series of quantities, you recall, is equal to the sum of the quantities divided by their number. Thus, the definition of *r* is stated algebraically as:

$$r = \frac{\sum z_X z_Y}{N} \tag{10.1}$$

$$\text{where } z_X = \frac{X - \overline{X}}{S_X}$$

$$z_Y = \frac{Y - \overline{Y}}{S_Y}$$

$$N = \text{number of pairs}$$

In determining *r*, we first calculate the z score for each X and for its paired Y. Next we multiply each z_X score by its z_Y score, giving us a ($z_X z_Y$) product for each pair of scores. Then we add up all these cross-products (that is, find $\sum z_X z_Y$) and divide by N. Thus, as we stated above, *r* is the mean of the z-score cross-products.

Now that we have a definition of *r*, it is appropriate to ask if the *r* values we obtain with this definition will have the same size and direction that our early statements about correlation suggest. We have said, for example, that a positive correlation will occur if relatively high X's and Y's tend to be paired and if relatively low X's and Y's tend to be paired. Can we say that *r* will be positive when these conditions are met? To answer this question, we will study how the value of *r* changes for different arrangements of z scores.

Four scatter plots are shown in Figure 10.3, the first showing a correlation that is close to zero, the second showing a moderate positive correlation, the third a high negative correlation, and the fourth showing a perfect positive correlation. The points that are plotted represent z scores and each plot is marked off into quadrants, indicating scores above and below the mean ($z = 0$) on X and on Y.

When both X and Y in a pair of scores are above the mean, both of their z scores are positive and the point indicating their joint value falls into the upper right quadrant. The

Figure 10.3 Scatter plots of z scores showing signs of z-score cross-products in each quadrant.

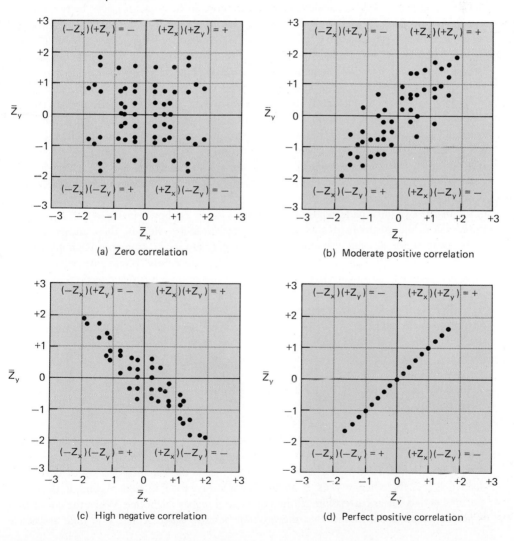

(a) Zero correlation

(b) Moderate positive correlation

(c) High negative correlation

(d) Perfect positive correlation

z-score cross-products ($z_X z_Y$) of all the pairs falling into this quadrant will also be positive, as indicated in the graphs in Figure 10.3. When both X and Y are below the mean, both of their z's are negative and the point indicating their joint value falls into the lower left quadrant. Because a negative number multiplied by a negative number yields a positive number, all the z-score cross-products for pairs falling into this quadrant are positive. In the two remaining quadrants one of the z scores in each pair is positive and the other is negative, so the resulting z-score cross-products for pairs falling into these quadrants are all negative.

In Figure 10.3(a), which represents a correlation near zero, we see that the points are quite evenly distributed among the four quadrants. When the cross-products are added together, the negative cross-products will cancel out the positive products, and the sum will be very close to zero. The mean of the cross-products, r, will also be approximately zero. In Figure 10.3(b), which represents a moderate positive correlation, most of the points fall into the two positive quadrants but quite a few fall into the two negative quadrants. The sum of the cross-products will therefore be positive in sign but, because of the frequency of negative cross-products, rather low in magnitude. Correspondingly, the mean of the cross-products, r, will also be positive but low in value. In Figure 10.3(c), almost all the points fall into the two negative quadrants. The sum and the mean of the cross-product will therefore be negative in sign and higher in absolute value than in the case of Figure 10.3(b). Finally, Figure 10.3(d) shows a perfect positive correlation. A perfect linear correlation, you recall, is one in which all the points in the scatter plot fall along a straight line. When the pairs are plotted in z scores, the line described by the points passes through the intersection of the quadrants (where z_X and $z_Y = 0$) at a 45° angle. The line on which the points fall goes from the lower left to the upper right quadrant when the correlation is positive and from the upper left to the lower right quadrant when the correlation is negative.

In the case of a perfect positive correlation, such as shown in Figure 10.3(d), all the points fall in the quadrants that yield positive cross-products. Because there are no negative cross-products, the absolute value of $\Sigma\, z_X z_Y$ is higher than in the case of correlations that are less than perfect. (The sign of $\Sigma\, z_X z_Y$, and hence r, is, of course, positive.) Similarly, when there is a perfect negative correlation, the $\Sigma\, z_X z_Y$ is higher (in a negative direction) than when the correlation is less than perfect.

We have seen that r, the mean of the z-score cross-products, is positive when the relationship between a pair of variables is positive and negative when the relationship is negative. We have also seen that the value of r is zero when there is no relationship and increases in absolute value as r approaches perfect positive or perfect negative.

Value of a Perfect Positive and a Perfect Negative Correlation

The value of r for a perfect positive correlation is always $+1.00$ and the value of r for a perfect negative correlation is always -1.00. In order to show you why this is so, we first remind you of two things. First, as we discussed in Chapter 5, the variance of a set of z scores is defined as $\Sigma\, z^2/N$, where $z = (\overline{X} - X)/S_X$, and is always equal to 1.00. Second, in the scatter plot of a perfect linear correlation, all the points lie along a straight line. When the correlation is perfect positive, this implies that the position of each paired X and Y in their respective distributions is the same: the individual who scores highest on X is highest on Y, the individual who scores at the mean of the X distribution also scores at the mean of Y, and so on. This in turn indicates that for each pair, $z_X = z_Y$, so that $z_X z_Y$ can be expressed as z^2. When there is a perfect positive correlation, the formula for r therefore can be rewritten as $\Sigma z^2/N$. This expression is also the formula for the variance of a set of z scores which, we remember, is equal to 1.00. We have thus demonstrated that when the correlation is perfect positive, $r = 1.00$. As positive correlations decrease in magnitude, r becomes smaller and smaller, reaching 0 when there is no relationship. Parallel reasoning leads to the demonstration that a perfect negative correlation takes the value of -1.00. The value of r, then, ranges from $+1.00$ for a perfect positive correlation through zero for no correlation to -1.00 for a perfect negative correlation. This restriction of the range of possible coefficient values is extremely fortunate, because *it permits a direct comparison of* r *values obtained from widely different sets of data without a correction for the size of the original X and Y values.* In this respect r is similar to z.

The Computational Formula for *r*

Despite the ease with which our basic formula for r can be remembered, an equation that permits raw scores (X and Y) to be used in place of z scores is more convenient for computing r. Of the several computational formulas available, a very useful version is shown below:

$$r = \frac{\Sigma XY - (\Sigma X)(\Sigma Y)/N}{\sqrt{\Sigma X^2 - (\Sigma X)^2/N}\ \sqrt{\Sigma Y^2 - (\Sigma Y)^2/N}} \tag{10.2}$$

All the components in the formula are familiar except for the expression ΣXY. This value is found by multiplying each X by the Y value paired with it and summing these XY products.

Table 10.2 shows how to use the computational formula to find r. The table shows the scores of 10 students in a statistics class on their first and final examinations. The r between these two distributions is .363. We may conclude that there was a moderate tendency for students who did well in comparison to their classmates on the first exam to continue to do well on the final, and for students who initially did not do well to continue their poor performance on the final.

What *r* Means

The Pearson product-moment correlation coefficient for a particular set of data measures a specific type of relationship: the *linear correlation* between two variables. By this, we mean that r measures the degree to which a *straight line* relating X and Y can summarize the trend in a scatter plot. Figure 10.4 presents two scatter plots, part (a) exhibiting a linear correlation and part (b) a nonlinear (or curvilinear) relationship between X and Y.

What would happen if we computed r, a measure of linear correlation, for data that have a curvilinear relation? The answer is that we would be measuring how well those data approximate a linear relationship. When the curvilinearity is small, a straight line may have some usefulness for summarizing the relationship between X and Y. When there is marked

Table 10.2 Demonstration of the Use of the Computational Formula for *r*

Student	First exam X	X^2	Final exam Y	Y^2	XY
1	31	961	31	961	961
2	23	529	29	841	667
3	41	1681	34	1156	1394
4	32	1024	35	1225	1120
5	29	841	25	625	725
6	33	1089	35	1225	1155
7	28	784	33	1089	924
8	31	961	42	1764	1302
9	31	961	31	961	961
10	33	1089	34	1156	1122
	$\sum X = 312$	$\sum X^2 = 9920$	$\sum Y = 329$	$\sum Y^2 = 11003$	$\sum XY = 10331$

$$r = \frac{\sum XY - (\sum X)(\sum Y)/N}{\sqrt{\sum X^2 - (\sum X)^2/N}\ \sqrt{\sum Y^2 - (\sum Y)^2/N}}$$

$$= \frac{10331 - (312)(329)/10}{\sqrt{9920 - (312)^2/10}\ \sqrt{11003 - (329)^2/10}}$$

$$= \frac{10331 - 10264.8}{\sqrt{185.6}\ \sqrt{178.9}} = \frac{66.2}{182.22}$$

$$= .363$$

departure from a straight line, however, *r* may be low or even drop to approximately zero. For example, the data of Figure 10.4(b) are best described by the curved line of that figure. The relationship between the variables is actually quite high, but it is so strongly curvilinear that a straight line does not fit the data at all well and Pearson *r* would be small.

Before computing a Pearson *r*, it is therefore wise to inspect the scatter plot to determine the nature of the relationship. When the data show a pronounced curvilinearity, methods for determining the amount of the curvilinear relationship should be applied. These methods, which may be found in more advanced statistical texts, will not be discussed here.

Testing the Significance of *r*

In computing a correlation, our interest typically is in the relationship between the variables in the population as a whole rather than in the particular sample of individuals we happen to measure. We therefore set up a null hypothesis about the population *r* and use our sample *r* to evaluate this hypothesis. The null hypothesis that is usually tested is that the population correlation is zero.

Testing the null hypothesis that the population *r* is zero is quite simple. At any given α

(a) An example of a linear relationship between X and Y

(b) An example of a curvilinear relationship between X and Y

Figure 10.4 Scatter plots of two hypothetical sets of data showing different kinds of relationships between X and Y.

level, the value of r required for significance turns out to be the same for all samples with the same df. The df is given by $N - 2$, one less than you might have expected; N, remember, is the number of *pairs* of scores. Table D in Appendix III lists the critical values of r for the 5% and 1% levels. Whenever our obtained r is equal to or greater *in absolute size* than the tabled value, we can conclude it is significant at the α level we have specified. That is, we reject the hypothesis that the population r is zero and conclude that there is some degree of relationship between the variables.

As an illustration, suppose that 152 10-year-old children were given a test of verbal ability and a test of motor coordination and r was calculated to be .17. Table D shows that for $df = 150$, the critical values of r are .159 and .208 at the 5% and 1% significance levels. We reject at $\alpha = .05$ the null hypothesis that the population r is zero and conclude instead that children who are high in verbal ability tend to be somewhat more coordinated than those of lesser verbal ability.

Two assumptions are required for testing the null hypothesis about r. First, the sample of pairs must have been obtained by random sampling from the population concerned. Second, the population of X and Y scores must have a distribution that we will characterize by saying that X and Y must each be normally distributed, and that the relationship between X and Y must be linear. This is by no means a complete statement of the second assumption, but it suggests what to consider before testing the null hypothesis about the population r. If the sample is randomly drawn, if X and Y are each normally distributed, and if the correlation between X and Y is linear, one may reasonably decide to perform this significance test.

USE OF *r* IN PREDICTION

We select at random from a college directory the names of 40 male students. How tall is each of them? If forced to guess, our most sensible estimate is that each of their heights is the same as the mean height of all male students which, let us say, is 68 inches. Men's heights are variable, so it is highly unlikely that all 40 men would be 68 inches; some would be taller and some would be shorter. But our guess of the mean will result, overall, in smaller errors of overestimation or underestimation than any other value. Now suppose we had an additional bit of information about each of these men: the number of pairs of shoes they own. As far as is known, the number of shoes a college student owns has nothing to do with his height, so we would still guess that each of the men is 68 inches tall.

Suppose instead that we had information about each of their weights. We are told that Sam Smith, for example, weighs 120 pounds. Commonsense observation suggests that height is related to weight—that is, that there is some degree of correlation between these two variables. We also know that 120 pounds is well below average for male students. We would therefore adjust our guess downward, predicting that Sam is of less than average height. Similarly, if Tom Jones weighs 220 pounds, we would adjust our prediction about his height upward from the mean.

These examples serve as an informal introduction to the use of the correlation coefficient, *r*, in predicting the value of an unknown variable from the value of a known variable. In practice, correlations are often used for this purpose. For example, a college registrar may determine the correlation between college grades (Y) and scores made by high school seniors on a measure of academic aptitude (X). With this correlation, the registrar can predict college grades from aptitude scores, using these predictions to determine which applicants for admission would be most likely to succeed in college and which would be most likely to fail. With this information, the registrar is able to admit only those students with a reasonable chance of success. This is exactly what is done in many colleges. Or an analyst may use an economic indicator, such as number of new housing starts last month, to forecast the state of the economy at some future point, based on knowledge of the correlation of the indicator and later economic conditions.

To predict scores on one variable from scores on another (Y from X or X from Y), we first obtain pairs of scores in which one X and one Y appear in each pair. Let us suppose we want to predict Y, given X. We then determine the best Y value to predict for each X value if the actual Y value were not known to us. The predicted Y's can be compared with the obtained Y values to indicate the success of the predictions. The ultimate usefulness of this technique will be in predicting unknown Y values when only X values are available.

Now that we know our goals in the prediction of one variable from another, we can turn our attention to the method of making such predictions. We will work into this method gradually by first discussing its general logic.

Logic of the Regression Line

In Figure 10.5, we show a scatter plot that represents the relationship between college students' scores on a measure of achievement motivation and their grade point average (GPA). Inspection of the scatter plot suggests that achievement scores (X) and GPA's (Y) are moderately

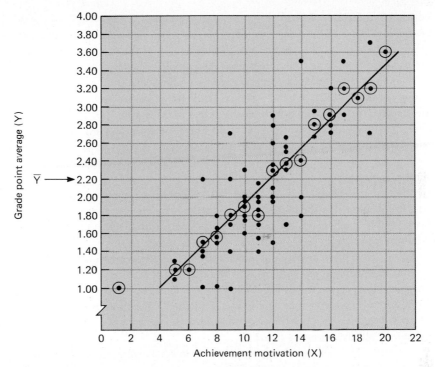

Figure 10.5 Scatter plot relating achievement motivation score (X) to grade point average (Y). Open circles indicate mean Y score for individuals with each X score.

correlated. Also shown in the figure is the mean GPA for the total sample ($\overline{Y}$) and the mean GPA for each set of students who have the same achievement score (X score). These latter means are shown in each column. Note that as the X score increases, the mean Y score in the columns also increases. This is exactly what we would expect, given the positive correlation between achievement score and GPA. We have also drawn a straight line through the scatter plot that comes closest to the data points in the columns. This straight line is called a prediction or *regression* line. Note that the column means also fall quite close to this regression line.

We could use the column means to predict Y scores. For example, in Figure 10.5, the mean GPA of all those who earn a score of 9 on the achievement (X) measure is approximately 1.80; we might predict that anyone whose X = 9 will have Y = 1.80. However, it is reasonable to assume that if we had obtained achievement scores and GPAs for the entire population of students, the column means—the mean GPA for each subgroup of students with the same achievement score—would have fallen exactly on a straight line, and that the deviations of our obtained values of the mean from this line are largely due to sampling error. Thus, points on the regression line can essentially be regarded as a set of means and used for prediction instead of the calculated column means.

To illustrate, suppose we know only that a particular student had a score of 17 on the achievement measure. What would we predict her GPA to be? Locating the score 17 on the baseline of Figure 10.5, we go up to the regression line and then over to the Y axis. Our prediction is a GPA of 3.00. We can see that everyone who scores 17 on the achievement measure does not earn this GPA; some have better grades and some have worse. But using the regression line, which gives us the best single estimate of the GPA of all students whose X score is 17, gives more accurate predictions than would predicting the overall $\overline{Y}$ of 2.20.

Figure 10.5 represents a positive correlation of moderate value. An example of a perfect negative correlation ($r = -1.00$) is shown at the left of Figure 10.6. As we learned earlier, a perfect correlation is one in which *all* the points in the scatter plot fall along a straight line. Unlike the situation in Figure 10.5, in which the correlation was less than 1.00, everyone in Figure 10.6 who earned a given X score earned the same Y score. If we were given an individual's X score and wanted to predict the individual's Y score, we could therefore do so with complete accuracy.

Finally, the plot at the right of Figure 10.6 represents an example of a correlation that is close to zero. Note that the regression line—the line that comes closest to the column values—is horizontal to the baseline and takes the same value of the overall $\overline{Y}$. Therefore, whatever a person's X score, we always predict Y as equal to $\overline{Y}$.

These examples illustrate the basic logic of using the regression line to predict Y when only X is known. They also illustrate how the accuracy of prediction varies with the magnitude of the correlation between X and Y. When $r = 0$, there is no increase in accuracy of predicting Y from X over and above that obtained by predicting $\overline{Y}$ for all individuals. As r departs from zero, *in either direction*, predictions become increasingly accurate. When r reaches ± 1.00, prediction is perfect; no errors occur.

We have so far discussed only the situation in which we are given X and want to predict Y, or as it is more technically described, as determining the regression of Y from X. Using the

Figure 10.6 Scatter plots and regression lines for predicting Y from X in which $r = -1.00$ and $r = 0$.

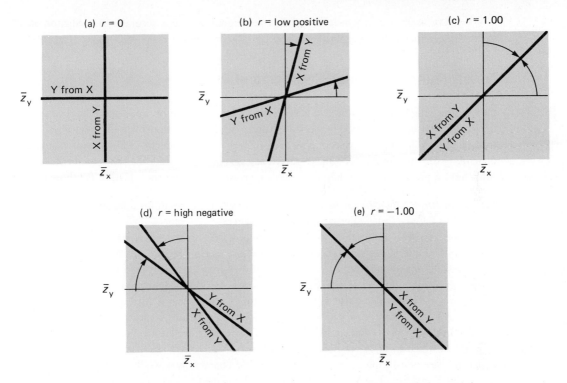

Figure 10.7 Regression lines of X on Y and Y on X for illustrative values of *r*.

same general logic, we can also determine the regression line of X from Y, thus allowing us to predict X from a given Y. The regression line of X from Y is basically the straight line that best fits the data points in the *rows* of the scatter plot.

Relationship of the Two Regression Lines.   The statements above imply that there are *two* regression lines, one allowing prediction of Y from X and the other of X from Y. The relationships between the two regression lines for different magnitudes of *r* are illustrated in Figure 10.7. You will note that both regression lines always pass through the point representing the mean of the X and Y variables ($\overline{X}$ and $\overline{Y}$). Panel A shows the regression lines for *r* = 0. The two lines are at right angles to each other, the regression line of Y from X being parallel to the baseline and taking the value of the overall mean of the Y scores and the regression line of X from Y being parallel to the Y axis and taking the value of the overall mean of the X scores. In short, when *r* = 0, knowing X does not improve our prediction of Y; conversely, knowing Y does not improve our prediction of X. As the correlation increases from zero to a positive value, the regression lines pivot around the point of intersection and approach each other, as shown in panel B. When *r* = +1.00, the two regression lines are identical, going from lower left to upper right, as shown in panel C. As the correlation goes from zero to a negative value, the regression lines pivot in the opposite direction and become identical when

$r = -1.00$, as shown in panels D and E. We remind you that accuracy of prediction also improves as r increases in magnitude and becomes perfect when $r = \pm 1.00$.

Determining the Linear Regression Line

Determining regression lines by eye is not a satisfactory procedure, since many lines could be drawn that would seem to be acceptable. Similarly, determination of predicted values of X from Y or of Y from X by inspecting regression lines in a graph might yield different estimates, depending on the observer. To make sure that everyone will make the same predictions, we must have a procedure for finding the "best" regression lines and the equation for those lines.

Equation for a Straight Line. Before presenting the equation for a linear regression line, we need to know a little about straight lines in general.

We start with an example. A race car driver is driving at a steady pace of 100 miles per hour (mph) and then begins to accelerate evenly at a rate per second of 10 mph. Acceleration continues, let us say, until he reaches a speed of 200 mph. Let Y refer to the speed of the car at any given moment and X refer to time in seconds during the interval in which the car is accelerating. When we plot speed (Y) against time (X), the result is a straight line, as shown at the left in Figure 10.8. How can we describe this line? The first important characteristic of a straight line is its *slope constant*, which tells us how fast the line climbs or declines. In our example in which speed (Y) is plotted against time (X) in seconds, the slope constant is 10 (that is, an increase of 10 mph per second). The second characteristic we need to know is what is called the *Y intercept*. The Y intercept is simply the value of Y when X = 0. In our example, the initial speed of the car was 100 mph. At the start of the acceleration period, the Y intercept is therefore 100. In Figure 10.8 the Y intercept is called *b* and the slope constant is called *a*.

Knowing the slope constant and the Y intercept, we can write an equation that describes any specific straight line and allows us to plot a figure showing its values, such as Figure 10.8. The general form of this linear equation is:

$$Y = aX + b$$

$$\text{where} \quad a = \text{value of the slope constant}$$

$$b = \text{value of the Y intercept}$$

When X = 0, the equation reduces to Y = *b*, which is just as it should, since *b* is the value of the Y intercept when X = 0. If *b* = 0 (for example, if our race car driver made a dead start), then the equation reduces to Y = *a*X. This shows that when *a* is positive, Y increases *a* times as fast as X. Similarly, when *a* is negative (for example, if our driver were decelerating at a steady rate from his initial speed), there is a corresponding rate of decline. So *a* does act like the slope constant that it is. We can illustrate how to use the equation for a specific straight line by our race car example. Since *a* = 10 and *b* = 100, we have:

$$Y = 10X + 100$$

Figure 10.8 Speed of race car related to time illustrating three straight lines with different slope constants (a) and Y intercepts (b).

With this formula, we can predict Y (speed in mph) for any X (time). For example, with X = 3.5 seconds:

$$Y = 10(3.5) + 100 = 35 + 100$$

$$= 135 \text{ mph}$$

As an illustration of the use of the linear equation when *a* is negative (when the line is going from high to low rather than from low to high), suppose that after reaching and maintaining for a while a speed of 200 mph, our driver begins to decelerate each second at the rate of 5 mph. This is shown graphically at the right of Figure 10.8. The equation for this period of deceleration is:

$$Y = -5(X) + 200$$

Setting X = 0 when deceleration begins, after 6 seconds (X = 6) his speed will be:

$$Y = -(5)(6) + 200 = 170 \text{ mph}$$

Finally, we will call your attention to the line that is generated when *a* = 0: it is flat—horizontal to the baseline. This is illustrated in the middle panel of Figure 10.8, in which the driver is maintaining a constant speed of 200 mph so that *b* = 200 and *a* = 0.

The Equation of a Regression Line.   We now have the background information that permits us to introduce the equation of a regression line. The particular method statisticians have adopted for finding the best-fitting regression line for predicting Y from X (or X from Y) is known as the *least-squares method*. This method attempts to specify the line that keeps at a minimum the squares of the deviations of all the points in the scatter diagram from the line (and hence keeps the sum of these squares at a minimum). The equation for the straight line yielded by this least-squares method is known as the *regression equation*.

We remind you first of the general equation for a straight line:

$$Y = aX + b$$

Statisticians have shown that *a*, or the slope constant, in the regression line of Y on X is given by:

$$a = r\left(\frac{s_Y}{s_X}\right) \tag{10.3}$$

where s_X and s_Y are the corrected estimates of the population σ values derived from the samples of X scores and Y scores, respectively, and *r* is the Pearson correlation between the pairs of X and Y scores.

The Y intercept, *b*, is given by the formula:

$$b = \overline{Y} - a\overline{X}$$

Substituting the right side of Formula 10.3 for a, we have

$$b = \overline{Y} - r\left(\frac{s_Y}{s_X}\right)\overline{X} \tag{10.4}$$

Substituting the quantities on the right of the equal sign in Formulas 10.3 and 10.4 into the equation for a straight line, we thus have:

$$Y_{pred} = r\left(\frac{s_Y}{s_X}\right)(X) + \overline{Y} - r\left(\frac{s_Y}{s_X}\right)(\overline{X}) \tag{10.5}$$

where Y_{pred} is the predicted value of Y, given the value of X.

To restate what Formula 10.5 represents, it is the equation for the regression line of Y from X which permits us to predict the value of Y for any given X value, providing we know the values of r, s_X, s_Y, $\overline{X}$, and $\overline{Y}$.

Application of the same statistical logic yields a parallel equation for the regression line of X from Y, which allows us to predict X for any given value of Y. Thus:

$$X_{pred} = r\left(\frac{s_X}{s_Y}\right)(Y) + \overline{X} - r\left(\frac{s_X}{s_Y}\right)(\overline{Y}) \tag{10.6}$$

Note carefully that the expression s_X/s_Y in Formula 10.6 is the *inverse* of the corresponding expression in Formula 10.5, which is s_Y/s_X.

The use of these equations may be illustrated by the results of a study in which 20 eighth-graders were given, several days apart, two parallel forms of a mathematics achievement test. The scores on each test (X and Y) are listed for each student in Table 10.3, along with the values of the statistics that enter into the regression equations. You will note that $r = .80$, indicating that students' scores on the parallel X and Y tests were highly similar. Also listed in the table are the predicted Y score for each X score and the predicted X scores for each Y score. We will now demonstrate how these predicted scores were determined.

We can develop the regression equation for predicting scores on test Y from scores on test X by entering the values shown in Table 10.3 into Formula 10.5:

$$Y_{pred} = .80\left(\frac{5.10}{5.47}\right)(X) + 16.90 - .80\left(\frac{5.10}{5.47}\right)(16.85)$$

After the appropriate multiplications and divisions have been performed, this equation reads:

$$Y_{pred} = .75X + 16.90 - 12.56$$

Finally, subtraction of 12.56 from 16.90 leads us to the final form for this regression equation:

$$Y_{pred} = .75X + 4.34$$

Table 10.3 An Application of the Regression Equations for X from Y and Y from X in Predicting Scores on Two Forms X and Y of an Aptitude Test

Student	X (actual)	X_{pred}	Y (actual)	Y_{pred}
1	12	11.81	11	13.34
2	20	17.83	18	19.34
3	16	15.25	15	16.34
4	6	10.95	10	8.84
5	19	16.97	17	18.59
6	15	13.53	13	15.59
7	29	21.27	22	26.09
8	10	8.37	7	11.84
9	19	18.69	19	18.59
10	17	22.13	23	17.09
11	13	16.11	16	14.09
12	18	20.41	21	17.84
13	16	16.97	17	16.34
14	11	12.67	12	12.59
15	22	26.43	28	20.84
16	15	16.97	17	15.59
17	27	22.99	24	24.59
18	17	17.83	18	17.09
19	14	14.39	14	14.84
20	21	16.11	16	20.09

$$\overline{X} = 16.85 \qquad r = .80 \qquad \overline{Y} = 16.90$$

$$s_X = 5.47 \qquad\qquad\qquad s_Y = 5.10$$

This last equation was used to determine the predicted Y scores shown in Table 10.3. (In practice, of course, we would predict Y from X only if Y were unknown.) Comparison of the predicted Y scores with the actual Y scores indicates that the regression equation for these data leads to rather successful predictions, as we would expect from the substantial correlation between X and Y. For example, when $X = 12$, $Y_{pred} = 13.34$ and the actual Y is 11. When $X = 20$, $Y_{pred} = 19.34$ and the actual Y is 18.

We can similarly develop the regression equation for predicting X scores from Y scores by substituting the values from Table 10.3 into Formula 10.6:

$$X_{pred} = .80\left(\frac{5.47}{5.10}\right)(Y) + 16.85 - .80\left(\frac{5.47}{5.10}\right)(16.90)$$

$$= .86Y + 16.85 - 14.50$$

$$= .86Y + 2.35$$

Application of the last equation yielded the predicted X scores shown in Table 10.3. Inspection of the scores in X_{pred} and actual X columns also indicates that overall, the regression equation is quite successful in predicting X scores.

However, not all predictions of X from Y or Y from X in Table 10.3 are equally successful. You can observe from inspecting the table that in some instances predicted scores are markedly discrepant from actual scores, despite the high correlation between the two sets of scores. This observation brings us to the topic of errors of prediction.

Errors of Prediction

As we have noted, when r is ± 1.00, use of the regression equation to predict X from Y or Y from X will yield perfectly accurate predictions, since all the data points in the scatter plot fall on the single regression line. Another way of stating this fact is to say that variations in X completely explain variations in Y and, conversely, that variations in Y completely explain variations in X. On the other hand, when $r = 0$, knowing X does not improve the accuracy of our predictions of Y (and vice versa); variations in one variable explain *none* of the variations in the other.

As these statements imply, the amount of variability in one factor that can be accounted for or explained by variability in the other increases as r goes from 0 to ± 1.00. A statistic called the *coefficient of determination* allows us to state the amount of explained variability. More precisely, the coefficient of determination tells us the proportion of the total variability among one set of scores that can be explained by variability among the other set of scores. The coefficient of determination, which is the same for X from Y as for Y from X, is equal to the square of the correlation that has been computed between X and Y. Thus:

$$\text{Coefficient of determination} = \frac{\text{explained variation}}{\text{total variation}} = r^2 \qquad (10.7)$$

Conversely, the proportion of *unexplained* variability among a set of measures is given by $1 - r^2$. This is called the *coefficient of nondetermination*. Thus:

$$\text{Coefficient of nondetermination} = \frac{\text{unexplained variation}}{\text{total variation}} = 1 - r^2 \qquad (10.8)$$

When $r = 0$, $r^2 = 0$; this is as it should be, since variation in X explains none of the variation in Y, and vice versa, when there is no correlation between X and Y. Similarly, when $r = \pm 1.00$, $r^2 = 1.00$, which indicates that the variability among scores is completely explained. Taking a few representative values between these extremes, when $r = \pm.30$, $r^2 = .09$; only 9 percent of the variability among one set of measures can be accounted for by variations among the other. When $r = \pm.50$, $r^2 = .25$ and when $r = \pm.80$, $r^2 = .64$.

As these examples illustrate, the proportion of explained variability increases as r increases but lags behind the value of r until r reaches ± 1.00.

Standard Error of Estimate. In earlier chapters we have learned that when a group of individuals is measured, the resulting scores are seldom all identical, and that the mean is a single number useful in characterizing the whole distribution of numbers. The standard deviation adds information about the variability in the distribution, representing as it does a kind of average of the amount by which scores deviate from the mean.

The points on a regression line, we have said, are comparable to means. If we were to predict Y from X using the regression line and found, for example, that for X = 103, Y_{pred} = 66, we would essentially be saying that for all individuals having an X score of 103, 66 is the most representative Y score. Assuming that r is not ± 1.00, we know that all individuals earning an X score of 103—or any other X score—do not earn exactly the same Y score. For any given X score, there is some degree of variability in the distribution of Y scores. The same statements can be made, of course, about the distribution of X scores for any given Y.

It would be informative to have a measure of variability of Y scores around the predicted Y scores (or of X scores around the predicted X scores) that is comparable to the standard deviation. Such a measure would be useful when we predict one score from another, since it gives us an idea of the range of values within which the unknown score might reasonably be expected to fall.

The *standard error of estimate* (s_{est}) is such a measure of variability and represents the standard deviation of the scores in a distribution around the regression line at any specific value of the predictor score.

When predictions are made from X to Y, the standard error of estimate of Y is given by the formula below:

$$s_{est\,Y} = s_Y\sqrt{1 - r^2} \tag{10.9}$$

where s_Y is the s for the distribution of Y scores.

When predictions are made from Y to X, the standard error of estimate of X is given by the parallel formula:

$$s_{est\,X} = s_X\sqrt{1 - r^2} \tag{10.10}$$

where s_X is the s for the distribution of X scores.

To illustrate the application of the standard error of estimate, suppose that in a certain college in which the same final examination is given each year in the introductory psychology course and in the elementary statistics course, the following data are obtained for students who have taken both courses:

Intro. Psych. (X)	Elem. Stat. (Y)
$\overline{X} = 108$	$\overline{Y} = 68$
$s_X = 9$	$s_Y = 8$
$r = .35$	

The correlation indicates that those who did well on the final exam in one course also tended to do well on the other final. One year the statistics instructor decides at the beginning of the semester to predict the final exam scores for all her students, using the appropriate regression equation. These predictions cannot be expected to be completely accurate, of course. In fact, the coefficient of determination, r^2, shows that introductory psychology scores account for only 12.25 percent of the variability in statistics scores.

The standard error of estimate of Y applied to these data turns out to be:

$$s_{est\,Y} = s_Y\sqrt{1 - r^2} = 8\sqrt{1 - (.35)^2}$$

$$= 8\sqrt{.8775} = 8(.9367)$$

$$= 7.49$$

The estimated standard deviation of all the statistics exam (Y) scores for any single X score is thus 7.49 score units.

What should the standard error of estimate be when $r = 0$? In the case of predicting Y from X, we expect that except for sampling error, the mean Y for any given X is equal to $\overline{Y}$ and that the variability of Y scores around the mean Y should be the same for individuals with any given X as for the group as a whole. Thus the standard deviation of Y scores for any given X should be the same as the standard deviation for the Y distribution as a whole (s_Y). This in turn implies that $s_{est\,Y} = s_Y$. Inspection of Formula 10.9 shows that this is indeed the case:

$$s_{est\,Y} = s_Y\sqrt{1 - 0^2} = s_Y$$

In parallel fashion, when $r = 0$, $s_{est\,X}$ is equal to s_X, the standard deviation of the total distribution of X scores.

On the other hand, when $r = \pm1.00$, there is *no* variability among the Y scores for any X (and vice versa); that is, for any given X or Y score, all scores on the other variable are the same. This implies that each standard error of estimate should be 0. Inspection of Formulas 10.9 and 10.10 shows that this is so:

$$s_{est\,X} = s_X\sqrt{1 - (\pm1)^2} = 0$$

and

$$s_{est\,Y} = s_Y\sqrt{1 - (\pm1)^2} = 0$$

THE RANK-ORDER CORRELATION COEFFICIENT (r_S)

Occasionally sets of data either are reported by their rank orders only, or it seems desirable to assign ranks to them and work with the ranks rather than the raw scores. Thus, a collection of rocks might be ranked in order from hardest to softest; or we might convert the performance of baseball teams, first reported as percentages of games won, to ranks by giving the team with the highest percentage rank number 1, the next team rank number 2, and so on. In these situations the r between the ranks themselves could be determined by means of our computational formula. However, a new formula will give exactly the same results with even less computational work. This formula, called the formula for the *rank-order correlation coefficient*, symbolized by r_S, is shown below. The symbol for the rank-order coefficient, you will note, differs from the one we used for the product-moment coefficient (r) by the addition of the subscript S. The letter S has been chosen for this purpose in honor of Charles Spearman, who popularized the method.

$$r_S = 1 - \frac{6 \sum d^2}{N(N^2 - 1)} \tag{10.11}$$

where N is the number of pairs of ranks and d is the difference between a pair of *ranks* (never the difference between a pair of *scores*). You should notice that the 1 and the 6 in the formula are always used when r_S is to be found. They are constant regardless of the values of N or of the differences (d's).

We may illustrate the application of this formula for the rank-order correlation coefficient by showing the computations required to find the correlation between two movie critics' rankings of 10 movies that were released last year. Table 10.4 presents these computations. The ranks of one critic are listed as X and those of the other as Y. The difference, d, for each movie is equal to X − Y. The value of r_S proves to be .636. This coefficient indicates a substantial agreement between the two critics.

Table 10.4 Computation of r_S for the Rankings of 10 Movies by Two Movie Critics

Movie	(Critic 1) X	(Critic 2) Y	d = X − Y	d²
A	1	6	−5	25
B	2	2	0	0
C	3	3	0	0
D	4	4	0	0
E	5	7	−2	4
F	6	1	5	25
G	7	5	2	4
H	8	9	−1	1
I	9	8	1	1
J	10	10	0	0
				$\sum d^2 = 60$

$$r_S = 1 - \frac{6 \sum d^2}{N(N^2 - 1)}$$

$$= 1 - \frac{6(60)}{10(99)} = 1 - \frac{360}{990} = .636$$

The Case of Tied Ranks

The rules for calculation of r_S must include what to do if there are ties for some ranks. What if, for example, we were correlating the final standings of the teams in the Big Ten Football Conference in the past two seasons and found that Indiana and Northwestern tied for sixth last year? We need to know how to treat their ranks before finding the correlation. A simple method is to assign each of the two tied teams the rank of 6.5, the average of the sixth and seventh ranks, since Indiana and Northwestern together must account for the ranks 6 and 7— the ranks *between* 5 and 8. Then r_S is computed as before.

We illustrate the assignment of values for the case of tied ranks by the following example, in which we are converting the IQ scores of 10 persons, A through J, into ranks.

| | \multicolumn{10}{c}{Person} |
	A	B	C	D	E	F	G	H	I	J
IQ	130	128	128	122	115	110	100	100	100	95
Rank	1	2.5	2.5	4	5	6	8	8	8	10

First, notice that B and C tied for second place in their IQ's. Since B and C together account for the second and third persons in order of rank, 2 and 3 were averaged, giving 2.5 for B and 2.5 for C. Then D was assigned the fourth rank, since three persons were superior to him. Finally, G, H, and I were all assigned rank 8, because they were all tied and together represent the three ranks of 7, 8, and 9, which have an average of 8; and J, the last person, received a rank of 10 because nine persons were superior to him. (See footnote, page 316 for another approach to tied ranks.)

Interpreting the Rank-Order Correlation Coefficient

When r_S is found for data originally measured in ranks, it has the same value that r would have (except where ties have occurred) and may therefore be interpreted as a measure of the amount of linear correlation between ranks. If the original data were score values that were then converted to ranks, the rank-order correlation, r_S, would *not* be equal to the r between the original scores. However, r_S and r will have similar values so that it is possible to infer the *approximate* size of the r between the original variables from the size of r_S.

Testing the Significance of r_S

When no ties in ranks have occurred, it is possible to test the hypothesis that in the population, Spearman r is 0. Table E in Appendix III presents the critical values of r_S at the 5% and 1% significance levels. As in the case of r, the required values for significance depend upon the number of pairs, N. In Table E, we use N directly and do not have to find *df*. To illustrate the use of the table, suppose we have calculated an r_S of .514 between two sets of ranks obtained from a sample of twelve individuals. Can we conclude that r_S in the population from which the sample was drawn is greater than zero? When we refer to Table E, we see that with N = 12, an r_S of .591 is required for significance at the 5% level. Since our obtained r_S is below this value, we accept the hypothesis of no relationship between the two variables at the 5% level. Notice that in this case an r_S that seems quite large (.514) is not significantly different from zero at the 5% level because it is based upon a relatively small N.

For complicated reasons, there is no adequate way to test a null hypothesis about r_S for data sets with tied ranks. However, if our obtained r_S is substantially higher than the values listed in Table E for the .05 and .01 alpha levels, it is quite safe to conclude that in the population, r_S is not zero.

Step-by-Step Procedures

Pearson Correlation Coefficient (r)

Twenty men were given a personality inventory assessing their tendency to become angry and aggressive and a questionnaire that measured their tolerance of rape and other sexually coercive behaviors. The data are shown below.

Person	Aggress (X)	Coercion (Y)	Person	Aggress (X)	Coercion (Y)
1	6	9	11	17	18
2	12	10	12	12	11
3	3	14	13	18	21
4	13	23	14	8	13
5	11	17	15	21	19
6	5	15	16	11	19
7	14	21	17	14	12
8	9	13	18	12	14
9	16	23	19	19	20
10	12	16	20	10	15

Determine the Correlation Coefficient between the Two Measures:

Formula 10.2 is used in preference to the definitional formula involving z scores because it is more convenient to calculate r directly from raw scores. This formula is reproduced below.

$$r = \frac{\sum XY - (\sum X)(\sum Y)/N}{\sqrt{\sum X^2 - (\sum X)^2/N} \sqrt{\sum Y^2 - (\sum Y)^2/N}}$$

The first step is to determine each of the components of the formula: $\sum X$, $\sum X^2$, $\sum Y$, $\sum Y^2$, $\sum XY$, and N, where N is the number of pairs. You are already familiar with sums and sums of squares. The quantity $\Sigma\, XY$ is obtained by first multiplying each X by its Y (in our example, $6 \times 9 = 54$; $12 \times 10 = 120$; $3 \times 14 = 42$; and so forth) and then summing these products. These quantities turn out to be:

$$\Sigma\, X = 243 \qquad \Sigma\, Y = 323 \qquad \Sigma\, XY = 4142$$

$$\Sigma\, X^2 = 3365 \qquad \Sigma\, Y^2 = 5557 \qquad N = 20$$

so that:

$$r = \frac{4142 - (243)(323)/20}{\sqrt{3365 - (243)^2/20}\ \sqrt{5557 - (323)^2/20}}$$

$$= \frac{4142 - 3924.45}{\sqrt{3365 - 2952.20}\ \sqrt{5557 - 5216.45}} = \frac{217.55}{\sqrt{412.80}\ \sqrt{340.55}}$$

$$= \frac{217.55}{374.94} = .58$$

Use of calculator

Most third-level calculators allow you to enter each pair of X and Y values and then to press a set of keys that will immediately give you the value of r. Other keys will give you the components entering into the computation of r ($\Sigma\, X$, $\Sigma\, X^2$, $\Sigma\, Y$, $\Sigma\, Y^2$, $\Sigma\, XY$, and N), as well as s_X and s_Y. These values may be useful for other purposes. In the case of practice problems, they also allow you to check your calculations against those given in the Answers when the value of r you found does not agree with the answer in the text. With second-level calculators, check the instruction booklet to determine how many components can be found simultaneously (e.g., $\Sigma\, X$ and $\Sigma\, X^2$).

Determine the Significance of r:

We test the H_0 that the population r is 0. This H_0 can be tested by looking in Table D to find the critical values of r at $\alpha = .05$ and $.01$ for $df = N - 2$. We find in Table D that for $df = 20 - 2 = 18$, $r_{.05} = .444$ and $r_{.01} = .561$

Our calculated r was $.58$. We therefore reject the hypothesis that the population r is 0 and conclude that our r is significantly different from zero at $\alpha = .01$. Angry, aggressive men tend to be more tolerant of sexually coercive behaviors than do less aggressive men.

Determine the Equation for the Regression Line for Predicting Y from X:

By Formula 10.5:

$$Y_{pred} = r\left(\frac{s_Y}{s_X}\right)X + \overline{Y} - r\left(\frac{s_Y}{s_X}\right)\overline{X}$$

1. The first step is to compute $\overline{X}$, $\overline{Y}$, s_X, and s_Y. The sums and sums of squares needed to calculate these statistics were determined in the course of computing r. Thus:

$$\overline{X} = \frac{243}{20} = 12.15 \qquad\qquad \overline{Y} = \frac{323}{20} = 16.15$$

$$s_X = \sqrt{\frac{3365 - (243)^2/20}{20}} \qquad\qquad s_Y = \sqrt{\frac{5557 - (323)^2/20}{20}}$$

$$= \sqrt{\frac{412.55}{20}} = \sqrt{20.63} \qquad\qquad = \sqrt{\frac{340.55}{20}} = \sqrt{17.028}$$

$$= 4.54 \qquad\qquad\qquad\qquad\quad = 4.13$$

2. Enter the values of r, s_X, s_Y, $\overline{X}$, and $\overline{Y}$ into the formula.

$$Y_{pred} = .58\left(\frac{4.13}{4.54}\right)(X) + 16.15 - .58\left(\frac{4.13}{4.54}\right)(12.15)$$

$$= .58(.91)(X) + 16.15 - .58(.91)(12.15)$$

$$= .53(X) + 16.15 - 6.41$$

$$= .53(X) + 9.74$$

The equation for the regression line for predicting X from Y is determined by a parallel set of procedures, using Formula 10.6. We therefore will not illustrate how this equation is found.

Using the Regression Equation for Y on X, Predict Y for a Given Value of X:

The regression equation was determined above. Predict Y (coercion score) from an X (aggression) score of 18.

$$Y_{pred} = .53(18) + 9.74 = 19.28$$

Determine the Proportion of the Variability in Y That Can Be Explained by Variability in X (and Vice Versa) and the Percent of Unexplained Variability:

These quantities are identified as the coefficient of determination and the coefficient of nondetermination, respectively.

$$\text{Coefficient of determination} = r^2$$

$$r^2 = (.58)^2 = .34$$

$$\text{Coefficient of nondetermination} = 1 - r^2$$

$$1 - r^2 = 1 - .34 = .66$$

These figures indicate that 34 percent of the variability in coercion scores is accounted for by the variability in aggression scores. Sixty-six percent of the variability remains unexplained.

Determine the Standard Error of Estimate for Y:

By Formula 10.9:

$$s_{\text{est Y}} = s_Y\sqrt{1 - r^2}$$

$$= 4.13\sqrt{1 - .58^2} = 4.13(.81)$$

$$= 3.35$$

With $r = .58$, the standard deviation of the distribution of Y scores for any given X is 3.35. The standard deviation, we recall, is a kind of average, the "average" amount by which scores deviate from the mean of a distribution. The standard error of estimate, $s_{\text{est Y}}$, indicates the "average" amount of error we expect in making these estimates of Y from a given X.

Similar procedures are used to calculate the standard error of X, $s_{\text{est X}}$, the "average" error in predicting X from a given Y.

Spearman Rank-Order Correlation Coefficient (r_S)

The Spearman correlation coefficient (r_S) can be applied to rank-order data or to magnitude data that are converted to ranks. We will use as our illustration magnitude data that we have decided to convert to ranks.

In this example, 10 eighth-grade students are given a test of mechanical aptitude (MA) and a speed test in arithmetic (speed), with the results shown at the left below.

Student	X Mech. Apt.	Y Speed	X Rank (MA)	Y Rank (Sp)	d	d^2
1	56	25	2	8	−6	36
2	41	34	9	2	7	49
3	61	32	1	3	−2	4
4	49	29	5	4	1	1
5	52	24	3	9	−6	36
6	44	28	7	5	2	4
7	42	23	8	10	−2	4
8	51	35	4	1	3	9
9	45	27	6	6	0	0
10	39	26	10	7	3	9
						$\Sigma d^2 = 152$

Compute r_S:

1. Our first step is to convert the scores into ranks. This has been done above with the highest score in each distribution being assigned the rank of 1.

2. The next step is to find the difference (d) and the squared difference (d^2) between each pair of ranks and then the sum of the d^2's.

3. The equation for r_S (Formula 10.11) is:

$$r_S = 1 - \frac{6 \sum d^2}{N(N^2 - 1)}$$

where N = number of pairs.

In our example:

$$r_S = 1 - \frac{6(152)}{10(100 - 1)} = 1 - \frac{912}{990}$$

$$= 1 - .92 = .08$$

Determine the Significance of r_S:

As there were no ties, we can test the H_0 that the population $r_S = 0$. We test this H_0 by entering Table E with N pairs to find the critical values of r_S and then comparing our obtained r_S with these values.

For N = 10, $r_S = .648$ at $\alpha = .05$ and $r_S = .794$ at $\alpha = .01$. Our calculated value of r_S is only .08. Our r_S is not significant. We retain the hypothesis that $r_S = 0$ in the population. ■

DEFINITIONS OF TERMS AND SYMBOLS

Scatter plot. A graph in which points are plotted, each point representing the values of a pair of X and Y scores.

Linear correlation. The line that best describes the points in a scatter plot of X and Y scores is a straight line.

Nonlinear correlation. The line that best describes the points in a scatter plot of X and Y scores is a curved line.

Pearson product-moment correlation coefficient (r). Pearson r, which is defined as the mean of the z score cross-products of paired X and Y scores ($\sum z_X z_Y / N$), indicates the magnitude and direction of the linear relationship between the two variables. The value of r ranges from $+1.00$ to -1.00.

Perfect correlation. In a perfect linear correlation, all the points in the scatter plot lie along a straight line. When the correlation is perfect positive, $r = +1.00$; when it is perfect negative, $r = -1.00$.

Regression or prediction line. The regression line used to predict Y from X is the straight line that comes closest vertically to the columns of Y scores in a scatter plot, and the regression line used to predict X from Y is the straight line that comes closest horizontally to the rows of X scores. When $r = \pm 1.00$, the two regression lines are identical, but as r departs from ± 1.00, they diverge. When $r = 0$, they are at right angles to each other, the line for Y from X being parallel to the X axis (baseline of the scatter plot) and taking the value of $\overline{Y}$, and the line for X from Y being parallel to the Y axis and taking the value of $\overline{X}$.

Coefficient of determination (r^2). The proportion of the total variability in one set of scores (X or Y) that is explained by variations in the other set of scores.

Coefficient of nondetermination ($1 - r^2$). The proportion of the total variability in one set of scores that is unexplained by variations in the other.

Standard errors of estimate ($s_{est\ X}$ and $s_{est\ Y}$). The standard deviation of the scores in a distribution of X scores around the regression line of X from Y ($s_{est\ X}$) or in a distribution of Y scores around the regression line of Y from X ($s_{est\ Y}$).

Spearman correlation coefficient (r_S). The correlation between pairs of ranks. The value of r_S ranges from $+1.00$ to -1.00.

PROBLEMS

1. For each of the following examples, state whether or not you would expect a relationship (correlation) between the two variables and, if yes, whether you expect the relationship to be linear or nonlinear (curvilinear). In the case of an expected linear relationship, state whether the Pearson correlation (r) would be positive or negative.

   (a) Lung capacity and number of cigarettes smoked per day.

   (b) Weight and state of general health in adult women.

   (c) Years of education and annual income in 40-year-old men.

   (d) Intelligence and neuroticism.

2. Ten college students were given a set of four seemingly simple puzzles to solve and for each, allowed 3 minutes in which to find a solution. Unknown to the students, the puzzles were actually unsolvable. They were then given a group of anagrams, and the number they correctly unscrambled in 2 minutes was determined. Scores were also available for each subject on a personality measure of depression, the investigator reasoning that after a failure experience, depressed individuals might do less well than nondepressed individuals. The two sets of raw scores are shown below, along with the sum and sum of squares for each distribution. Shown at the right are the z score equivalents and the z score cross-products.

	Raw Scores		z Scores		
Subject	X (No. correct)	Y (Depression)	z_X	z_Y	$z_X z_Y$
1	5	14	0	$-.26$	0
2	3	11	$-.71$	-1.03	.73
3	9	22	1.41	1.79	2.52
4	1	12	-1.41	$-.77$	1.09
5	4	16	$-.35$	.26	$-.09$
6	2	10	-1.06	-1.28	1.36
7	6	20	.35	1.28	.45
8	10	19	1.77	1.03	1.82
9	3	12	$-.71$	$-.77$	.55
10	7	14	.71	$-.26$	$-.18$
	$\sum X = 50$	$\sum Y = 150$			
	$\sum X^2 = 330$	$\sum Y^2 = 2402$			

(a) From inspection of the pairs of z scores, what direction and approximate magnitude (high, medium, low) do you expect Pearson r to have?

(b) Make a scatter plot of the data, using z scores. Then draw a straight line that seems to come closest to all the points. Does the correlation appear to be linear?

(c) Find r, using Formula 10.2 involving raw scores.

(d) Test H_0: $r = 0$.

3. Eight swimmers participated in two heats of a race, finishing in the orders shown below. Compute r_S for these data. Is the correlation significant?

Individual	Heat 1	Heat 2
A	6	8
B	1	2
C	5	5
D	8	7
E	2	1
F	4	6
G	7	3
H	3	4

4. A school psychologist has noticed that children who are self-confident seem to have more playmates than children who are more timid and unsure of themselves. To determine whether formal evidence will confirm this observation, she asks 60 fourth-graders to write down the names of children with whom they play after school. She also has observers watch the children in several settings and obtains an overall rating of each child's self-confidence. The mean and s of each distribution of measures and the correlation between the two sets of measures are shown below.

Self-confidence	Playmates
$\overline{X} = 16.8$	$\overline{Y} = 5.2$
$s_X = 2.0$	$s_Y = 1.4$
$N = 60$	$r = .50$

(a) A teacher who learned of the results of the study suggested that instituting special play groups in which timid children would have opportunities to make friends would be an excellent way to raise their self-confidence. Comment on this proposal.

(b) Find the regression equation for predicting Y from X—that is, number of playmates from self-confidence ratings.

(c) For three of the children, their X scores were 14, 17, and 19. For each of these three X scores, use the regression equation determined in (b) to predict their Y scores.

(d) The actual Y scores for these three children were, respectively, 2, 4, and 7. How well do the predictions obtained in (c) compare to the scores these three children actually obtained?

(e) How much of the variability in one set of scores is explained by variations in the other set of scores?

5. Shown below are the scores of 20 male college professors on a measure of satisfaction with their work (X) and a measure of satisfaction with their life in general (Y). Also shown are the means, s values, and r.

Work (X)	Life (Y)	Work (X)	Life (Y)	Work (X)	Life (Y)	Work (X)	Life (Y)
44	57	49	57	49	61	43	55
53	64	54	62	39	48	57	68
47	60	40	53	60	69	47	56
50	59	52	66	46	58	51	62
36	49	48	55	48	61	45	55

$\overline{X} = 47.90$ 　　　 $s_X = 5.90$ 　　　 $\overline{Y} = 58.75$ 　　　 $s_Y = 5.64$

$N = 20$ 　　　 $r = .94$

(a) Find the regression equation for predicting work satisfaction (X) from life satisfaction (Y).

(b) Predict work satisfaction (X) scores from the Y scores of 50 and 70.

(c) Graph the 20 pairs of X and Y scores in a scatter plot. Then plot the regression line determined in (a). [*Note:* This can be done by first plotting the point representing Y = 50 and the X_{pred} calculated in (b) for this Y value and then plotting the point for Y = 70 and its X_{pred}. The straight line obtained by connecting these two points is the regression line.]

(d) Compute $s_{est\,X}$. What does this statistic represent? Relate it to what you have plotted in the graph.

11

Sampling Distributions:

Matched Pairs

- TYPES OF MATCHED PAIRS
- ADVANTAGE OF MATCHED PAIRS
- THE *t* TEST WITH MATCHED SAMPLES

Chapter 10 was devoted to the subject of *correlation*, the degree to which paired measures tend to covary so that as scores on one measure change, scores on the other measure also tend to change. In this chapter we return to the topic of two-group experiments introduced in Chapter 9, that is, studies in which the behavior of two groups of subjects tested under different conditions is compared. In that chapter we considered experiments in which we tested two random or randomized samples and we discussed the t test for independent groups as a method of testing the null hypothesis that the two independent samples came from populations with the same mean (H_0: $\mu_1 - \mu_2 = 0$).

In this chapter we consider a third sampling technique, *matched pairs*, and the statistical methods that are used in experiments using matched pairs to test the H_0 that the difference between μ's is 0. As we will see, the correlation between the pairs of measures enters into these methods.

TYPES OF MATCHED PAIRS

Although most research requires that different individuals be used, there are circumstances in which the same individuals can take part in each experimental condition. For example, in a study of speed of recognition of words, a series of randomly ordered five-letter words, half of them highly familiar and half of them less familiar, might be exposed very briefly to determine whether familiarity influences speed of recognition. Each subject is required to guess what each word is, the independent variable being the number of correct guesses of the two types of words. The result is a *pair of scores* for each individual: number correct for familiar words, and number correct for unfamiliar words.

Whenever possible, it is advantageous to use the same individuals in both conditions. In the first place, the actual mechanics of obtaining the individuals and testing them in the experiment are usually simpler because only a single group of individuals is employed. More important, there is no problem in obtaining comparable groups. The individuals serving in the two conditions are ideally matched; individuals are better matches for themselves than anyone else.

Matched pairs can also consist of different individuals who are similar in characteristics that can be assumed to influence the dependent variable to be measured in the experiment. For example, identical twins or pairs of brothers or sisters could be employed. It is also possible to select an individual from an available pool and then to find another individual in the pool who is biologically unrelated but who is a "twin" on one or more characteristics that might affect the particular behavior to be observed. Age, sex, physical or mental abilities, interests, and occupation can be mentioned as possible bases for matching. After pairs of individuals who are matched in some way have been selected, one member of each pair is chosen at random and assigned to one of the experimental conditions. The other member of each pair is then automatically assigned to the other condition. As in the case in which the same individuals are tested under both conditions, the end result is a set of pairs of scores, each pair representing the performance of an individual in one condition and the performance of the individual's "twin" in the other condition.

We have previously described random samples as being independent. That is, except for the restriction that the same individual cannot serve in both groups, the composition of one random sample does not in any way affect the composition of the second sample. In contrast, matched samples are not independent. Once one member of each pair has been assigned to one experimental group, composition of the second group is fixed.

ADVANTAGE OF MATCHED PAIRS

A major advantage in using matched pairs is that the method has the potential of increasing the power of the t test to detect the falsity of the null hypothesis that $\mu_1 - \mu_2 = 0$—that is, the hypothesis that conditions have no differential effect on the dependent variable. To explain this statement, we return to the topic of the power of a test, discussed in the last chapter, and the formula for t when sample N's are equal:

$$t = \frac{\overline{X}_1 - \overline{X}_2}{s_{\overline{X}_1 - \overline{X}_2}} = \frac{\overline{X}_1 - \overline{X}_2}{\sqrt{\dfrac{s_1^2}{N_1} + \dfrac{s_2^2}{N_2}}}$$

With $(\overline{X}_1 - \overline{X}_2)$ and sample N's held constant, the value of t is inversely related to the values of s_1^2 and s_2^2, our estimates of the population σ^2 values. As these measures of variability become smaller, $s_{\overline{X}_1 - \overline{X}_2}$ becomes smaller.* In turn, as the standard error of the difference becomes smaller, t becomes larger and H_0 is more often rejected.

Each s^2 reflects, of course, the amount of variability among the individuals within each group. Where does this variability in subjects' performance come from? In part it comes from fluctuations in external conditions: The room temperature and lighting may not always be exactly the same, the experimenter's behavior may vary slightly from one occasion to another, and so forth. In part it comes from temporary variations in the subjects themselves. A particular individual may not be feeling well, may be preoccupied with some personal matter, or may suffer some momentary lapse of attention to the experimental task. Collectively, these kinds of variability are identified as an error source of variability.

Although experimenters attempt to minimize these random fluctuations in subjects and conditions within practical limits, perfect control is impossible, and some variability among subjects' behavior due to these sources is therefore inevitable.

Another source of variability comes from differences among subjects that are relatively stable over time. Individuals vary in their ability to perform the experimental task and in the case of human subjects, in such characteristics as cooperativeness, their desire to impress the experimenter, their interest in psychology experiments, and their general motivation to perform well. In many experiments, much of the variability among subjects within experimental groups

---

*Although the formula $s_{\overline{X}_1 - \overline{X}_2} = \sqrt{s_1^2/N_1 + s_2^2/N_2}$ makes clear the contribution of within-group variability (s) to the standard error of the difference between $\overline{X}$'s, it may not be intuitively obvious why the variability of the sampling distribution of the differences between $\overline{X}$'s is related to s. If there were *no* variability between individuals in each population, that is, if $\sigma = 0$, then all scores in a sample would take the same value as $\overline{X}$ and all $\overline{X}$'s the same value as μ. Thus the difference between $\overline{X}$'s of a series of pairs of random samples would always be the same, so that $s_{\overline{X}_1 - \overline{X}_2} = 0$, and each $\overline{X}_1 - \overline{X}_2$ would be equal to $\mu_1 - \mu_2$. As σ's increase in value, the distribution of $\overline{X}$'s from each population becomes more variable due to sampling error, and the differences between pairs of sample $\overline{X}$'s also become more variable for the same reason.

is due to stable individual differences of this sort. When experiments employ independent groups, there is no way to determine how much these stable, preexisting individual differences contribute to the variability among subjects and when we compute t they remain part of the estimated error variance. However, when matched pairs are employed, there is a way to determine their contribution and to reduce the error variance by taking it into account.

To explain this statement, we start with the observation that the existence of these individual differences implies is that if individuals were tested on similar tasks on two occasions, their performance would likely be *positively correlated*. That is, the person who performed best on the first occasion is also likely to perform well on the second occasion, the person who performed worst on the first occasion is also likely to exhibit a poor performance on the second occasion, and so forth. A positive correlation is also expected when the same individual or a pair of previously matched individuals is observed under two experimental conditions. That is, even if conditions have an effect, so that the two $\overline{X}$'s differ, the *relative position* of each member of pairs of scores may be similar; that is, within a pair, an individual's standing in the distribution of scores for the first condition may be similar to the individual's (or his "twin's") standing in the distribution of scores for the second condition.

In discussing the concept of correlation in Chapter 10, we noted that the correlation coefficient provides an indication of the amount of *explained* variability in distributions of two measures; the greater the correlation, the greater the amount of *explained*, as opposed to *unexplained*, variability. By finding the correlation between pairs of scores in an experiment employing matched pairs of individuals or the same individuals in both conditions, we have a device for accounting for some of the variability within groups. As will be explained in the next section, this correlation can be used to reduce the error variance, which can be regarded as a measure of unexplained variability in a sampling distribution of differences between $\overline{X}$'s. This, in turn, leads to a reduction in $s_{\overline{X}_1 - \overline{X}_2}$, the square root of our estimate of the error. With a sufficient reduction in $s_{\overline{X}_1 - \overline{X}_2}$, the power of the t test increases.

THE t TEST WITH MATCHED SAMPLES

When matched pairs are used, there will be, as usual, two distributions of scores at the conclusion of the research. Just as with random or randomized groups, the distributions represent performance under the two experimental conditions, and the difference between the $\overline{X}$'s is evaluated by the t test. The formula for t, $(\overline{X}_1 - \overline{X}_2)/s_{\overline{X}_1 - \overline{X}_2}$, remains the same, but the equation for $s_{\overline{X}_1 - \overline{X}_2}$ is expanded to take the correlation between the pairs of scores into account. This formula is:

$$s_{\overline{X}_1 - \overline{X}_2} = \sqrt{s_{\overline{X}_1}^2 + s_{\overline{X}_2}^2 - 2r_{12}s_{\overline{X}_1}\, s_{\overline{X}_2}} \qquad (11.1)$$

where $s_{\overline{X}_1}$ = standard error of the mean of one group
$\quad s_{\overline{X}_2}$ = standard error of the mean of the other group
$\quad r_{12}$ (read r sub one two) = the Pearson product-moment correlation between the scores of two groups—that is, between the two distributions of measures being tested for the significance of the difference

Note that the initial part of the formula, up to the minus sign, is the same as the formula for random samples with equal N's and consists of the square root of the sum of the two $s_{\overline{X}}^2$'s. For matched samples, the term $(2 r_{12} s_{\overline{X}_1 - \overline{X}_2})$ is subtracted from this sum.

Let us consider the correlation coefficient r_{12} in that term. *It is the correlation between the two distributions, the $\overline{X}$'s of which are to be tested for significance.* Recall that to compute a Pearson r between two distributions, we must be able to pair a score from one distribution with a score from the other. In any experiment using matched groups, each pair of scores comes from the already paired subjects. Thus, all the terms under the radical sign in the $s_{\overline{X}_1 - \overline{X}_2}$ formula, the standard errors and the correlation, are obtained from the two distributions of scores resulting from the experiment. Either of these distributions may be identified by the subscript 1 and the other by the subscript 2.

What happens to the $s_{\overline{X}_1 - \overline{X}_2}$ for matched groups as r_{12} takes various values? When r_{12} is zero, the last term under the radical (everything after the minus sign) becomes zero, and we have the $s_{\overline{X}_1 - \overline{X}_2}$ formula for independent groups. If there is no correlation between the groups, they are, in that respect, the same as independent random groups. If r_{12} is some positive value, the $s_{\overline{X}_1 - \overline{X}_2}$ will be *smaller* than when r_{12} is zero, and the higher the r_{12} the greater the reduction in the $s_{\overline{X}_1 - \overline{X}_2}$. Since a reduction in $s_{\overline{X}_1 - \overline{X}_2}$ leads to an increased t value with a given difference between two $\overline{X}$'s, we can see that this difference in $\overline{X}$'s is more likely to result in a significant t when divided by the $s_{\overline{X}_1 - \overline{X}_2}$ obtained from matched samples than from independent samples. We also can see why there would be little point in using matched samples in an experiment unless the members of a pair originally were fairly similar. Unless the r_{12} is at least some medium to high value, there will be little reduction in $s_{\overline{X}_1 - \overline{X}_2}$.

Having computed the $s_{\overline{X}_1 - \overline{X}_2}$ for matched groups, we proceed to test the null hypothesis that the μ values are equal by obtaining t by the usual formula:

$$t = \frac{\overline{X}_1 - \overline{X}_2}{s_{\overline{X}_1 - \overline{X}_2}} \tag{11.2}$$

In assessing the t value, the df that we use is $N - 1$, the number of *pairs* of measures minus one. Notice that df is less than if independent groups had been used, in which case df would have been $N_1 + N_2 - 2$. This means that for correlated samples a larger t will be required for significance at a given α level than if a t for independent samples had been calculated instead. When r is large enough (in a positive direction), the reduction in $s_{\overline{X}_1 - \overline{X}_2}$ that it brings about more than compensates for this problem, making it easier to find a significant difference with matched pairs when the null hypothesis is false.

Computing $s_{\overline{X}_1 - \overline{X}_2}$ for matched pairs requires a good deal of calculation. Fortunately, there are two shorter methods for testing the null hypothesis about the difference between μ values for matched pairs, both of which lead to the same conclusion about the null hypothesis as the method just described. The first is the *direct-difference method* for computing t.

Direct-Difference Method for Computing t

We start by describing an experiment in which the same subjects were used in both conditions of the study. The investigator was concerned with the influence that children's physical attractiveness has on adults' judgment of their behavior. She gave 20 adults a series of descriptions of minor offenses, each supposedly committed by a real child. The subjects were asked to indicate on an objective rating scale how severe the punishment for each misbehavior ought to have been. A photograph of the purported miscreant accompanied each description, half of the photographs picturing children who had previously been judged to be physically attractive and the other half picturing children judged to be relatively unattractive. All 20 subjects therefore served in both conditions of the experiment. The raw data are presented in Table 11.1. The table shows the average severity of punishment rating made by each subject for the attractive and unattractive children, high scores indicating more severe punishment.

To perform the *t* test for matched groups by the direct-difference method, we first obtain for each subject the *difference* between the pair of scores. This has been done in Table 11.1 in the column labeled *Difference*. In obtaining the difference score, it does not matter which raw score is subtracted from which as long as it is done in the same way for every subject. In Table 11.1 the attractive children's severity score is subtracted from the unattractive children's severity score; thus the difference score is negative whenever the attractive child's score is larger. The difference scores, for which we shall use the symbol D, can be considered and treated in the same way as a distribution of raw scores.

Once the distribution of direct differences, each difference having its correct algebraic sign, has been obtained, *all* further computations are based on it. First, we compute the algebraic mean of the differences ($\overline{D}$). This is done by summing all the positive values, summing all the negative values, adding the sum of the negative values to the sum of the positive values to get ΣD, and then dividing ΣD by N to get $\overline{D}$. In any matched-groups experiment N is always the number of *pairs* of raw scores, or the number of direct differences; thus, in this experiment N is 20.

The algebraic mean of the differences ($\overline{D}$) is *always* the same as the difference between the $\overline{X}$'s of the two raw-score distributions. Accordingly, in Table 11.1 $\overline{D}$ is 4.65 and identical with the difference between the two raw-score $\overline{X}$'s (31.55 and 26.90). The $\overline{D}$ is therefore the *numerator* in the *t* ratio; it is not necessary to compute the $\overline{X}$'s of the raw-score distributions, except as a check on accuracy of computation.

The $s_{\overline{X}_1 - \overline{X}_2}$ that is needed is obtained by computing *the standard error of the mean difference* ($s_{\overline{D}}$). Except for the fact that we are using difference scores, we obtain the $s_{\overline{D}}$ in the same way as any standard error of the mean.

First, we compute s^2 for the distribution of difference scores, which we symbolize as $s_D{}^2$. The most convenient way to compute $s_D{}^2$ is to use the raw score formula (see Formula 5.8 in Chapter 5). Rewriting this formula to indicate that we are now concerned with a distribution of difference scores and letting D stand for difference, we thus have:

$$s_D{}^2 = \frac{\Sigma D^2 - (\Sigma D)^2/N}{N - 1} \tag{11.3}$$

Then we compute $s_{\overline{D}}$, the standard error of the mean difference, by the formula:

$$s_{\overline{D}} = \sqrt{\frac{s_D{}^2}{N}} \tag{11.4}$$

The standard error of the mean difference ($s_{\overline{D}}$) is identical with the standard error of the difference between means that would be obtained by use of the long formula involving the correlation.

Table 11.1 Severity of Punishment Ratings of Physically Attractive and Unattractive Children

Subject	Unattractive Offender	Attractive Offender	Difference (U − A)	(Difference)^2
1	15	17	−2	4
2	49	36	13	169
3	21	21	0	0
4	17	14	3	9
5	21	15	6	36
6	25	25	0	0
7	20	22	−2	4
8	56	38	18	324
9	16	19	−3	9
10	31	31	0	0
11	28	33	−5	25
12	44	39	5	25
13	35	29	6	36
14	48	41	7	49
15	32	31	1	1
16	37	27	10	100
17	45	21	24	576
18	29	27	2	4
19	28	32	−4	16
20	34	20	14	196

$$\sum D(+) = 109 \qquad \sum D^2 = 1583$$
$$\sum D(-) = -16$$
$$\sum D = 93$$

$$\overline{X}_U - \overline{X}_A = 31.55 - 26.90 = 4.65 \qquad \overline{D} = \frac{\sum D}{N} = \frac{93}{20} = 4.65$$

$$s_D^2 = \frac{\sum D^2 - (\sum D)^2/N}{N-1} \qquad s_{\overline{D}} = \sqrt{\frac{s_D^2}{N}}$$

$$= \frac{1583 - (93)^2/20}{20 - 1} \qquad = \sqrt{\frac{60.56}{20}} = \sqrt{3.03}$$

$$= \frac{1150.55}{19} = 60.56 \qquad = 1.74$$

$H_0: \mu_A - \mu_U = 0$

$H_1: \mu_A - \mu_U \neq 0$

$$t = \frac{\overline{D}}{s_{\overline{D}}} = \frac{4.65}{1.74} = 2.67$$

with $df = N - 1 = 19$, $t_{.05} = 2.09$, and $t_{.01} = 2.86$

Since $\overline{D}$ is equal to $(\overline{X}_1 - \overline{X}_2)$ and $s_{\overline{D}}$ is equal to $s_{\overline{X}_1 - \overline{X}_2}$, it follows from Formula 11.2 that:

$$t = \frac{\overline{D}}{s_{\overline{D}}}$$ (11.5)

Notice that we are testing the usual null hypothesis that the two μ's are equal in value.

For the data in Table 11.1, $s_{\overline{D}} = 1.74$. Our t ratio is therefore $4.65/1.74$, or 2.67. In any experiment using matched groups the number of degrees of freedom (df) for evaluating the t is $N - 1$, where again N is the number of pairs of measures. In our example there are twenty pairs of measures, so df is 19. With 19 df our t of 2.67 is significant at the 5% level. We conclude (with no great pleasure) that children who are physically attractive are judged less severely for their misbehavior than their less attractive peers.

The direct-difference method automatically takes into account the correlation that exists between the raw-score distributions (r_{12}), regardless of the size or algebraic sign of the correlation. Therefore, as we have said, the t value obtained by this method will be identical with the t value obtained by use of the long formula for the $s_{\overline{X}_1 - \overline{X}_2}$. Use of a third-level computer makes it relatively easy to compute $s_{\overline{X}_1 - \overline{X}_2}$ by the long formula but even so, we would probably save time using the direct difference method unless we also wanted to know r_{12}.

Sandler's *A* Statistic

An even simpler method of testing the hypothesis that $\mu_1 - \mu_2 = 0$ for matched pairs is provided by Sandler's *A* statistic, named after its discoverer, Joseph Sandler. The *A* statistic is based on the same difference or D scores and squares of difference scores as are obtained in the direct-difference method just described. The formula for *A* is as follows:

$$A = \frac{\sum D^2}{(\sum D)^2}$$ (11.6)

To interpret the *A* statistic, we must refer to Table H in Appendix III. We use Table H to find the critical value of *A* for $df = N - 1$ associated with our chosen α level. In assessing our computed *A*, we reverse the procedure used in assessing t. That is, if our computed *A* is equal to *or less than* the tabled value at the given α level, H_0 is *rejected* at that level.

An exact equivalence can be shown between the critical value of t at any given probability level and the critical value of *A* at that level. The conclusion that is reached about H_0: $\mu_1 - \mu_2 = 0$ is therefore the same for t and *A*.

The data from our previous example can be used to illustrate the application of the *A* statistic. Filling in the values of $\sum D$ and $\sum D^2$ from Table 11.1, we find:

$$A = \frac{\sum D^2}{\left(\sum D\right)^2} = \frac{1583}{(93)^2} = .183$$

Reference to Table H shows that with $df = 19$, the critical values of *A* for a two-tailed test are 0.267 at $\alpha = .05$ and 0.166 for $\alpha = .01$. Our calculated *A* of 0.183 is less than the value of A at $\alpha = .05$ but is greater than the value of A at $\alpha = .01$. Since the *smaller* the A the more significant it is, we are able to reject H_0 at $\alpha = .05$ but not at $\alpha = .01$. This conclusion is the same as the one we reached earlier for the direct difference t.

A Decision Tree for Selecting an Appropriate Statistical Test

In this and earlier chapters we have discussed a number of statistical techniques that allow us to use sample data to test a null hypothesis (H_0) about a population parameter or to establish a confidence interval for its value. These techniques, some of which involve categorical data and others of which involve numerical data, include a z test to evaluate an H_0 about the population proportion in situations in which there are two mutually exclusive categories; a t test using data from a single sample to evaluate an H_0 about the population mean (μ); a confidence interval for μ; a t test based on data from two independent samples from different populations to evaluate the H_0 that the population means are equal; a t test of the same H_0 based on matched pairs; and for the correlation between pairs of measures, tests of the H_0 that the population value for Pearson r and for Spearman r (r_S) equals zero. In later chapters we discuss still further statistical techniques applied to other kinds of data.

One of the purposes of this text, we remind you, is to acquaint you with some of the basic techniques of data analysis used in psychology and related behavioral sciences so that you can comprehend research reports employing these techniques. An equally important purpose is to teach you about some statistical methods that you will find useful to employ in your own research. One of the critical decisions that investigators must make is how to analyze their data, that is, they must select the appropriate kinds of statistical tests to answer their research questions. Understanding how to choose appropriate techniques is nearly as important to a research worker as understanding the techniques themselves.

To help you learn how to select appropriate techniques, we have developed what is called a *decision tree*. This decision tree, which is presented in Chapter 16, outlines a series of questions that you should ask about the characteristics of your research problem. Your answer (decision) to each question leads to the next decision point until you eventually determine the appropriate test or tests to select from among those you have studied. We suggest that you do not wait to read Chapter 16, but consult it now to increase your understanding of the techniques we have already discussed.

Step-by-Step Procedures

The computation of the direct difference t and Sandler's A is illustrated by the following experiment. An experimental psychologist wondered whether the training students received in his graduate program improved their ability to think logically. He therefore gave a test of logical thinking to eight students who had just entered the program, and then four years later he gave the same test to these students again. The number of errors made by each student are shown below. Did errors decrease on the second testing?

Student	Year 1	Year 4	D	D^2
1	10	5	5	25
2	15	2	13	169
3	6	7	−1	1
4	11	4	7	49
5	7	0	7	49
6	13	10	3	9
7	8	2	6	36
8	12	4	8	64
			$\sum D = 48$	$\sum D^2 = 402$

Direct Difference Method

Set Up H_0:

$$H_0: \mu_D = 0$$

$$H_1: \mu_D \neq 0$$

where $\mu_D = \mu_1 - \mu_2$.

Compute Direct Difference t:

1. Find the difference (D) between each pair of scores, always in the same order. In our illustrative experiment, we have subtracted the year 4 score from the year 1 score. Then find the square of each difference score (D^2) and $\sum D$ and $\sum D^2$.

Use of Calculator

With a second-level calculator you can enter each difference score and then with a special key, determine $\sum D$ and $\sum D^2$. (See below for use of a third-level calculator.)

2. Find the mean D.

$$\overline{D} = \frac{\sum D}{N}$$

$$= \frac{48}{8} = 6$$

3. Find s_D^2 by Formula 11.3.

$$s_D^2 = \frac{\sum D^2 - (\sum D)^2/N}{N - 1}$$

$$= \frac{402 - (48)^2/8}{8 - 1} = \frac{402 - 2304/8}{7}$$

$$= \frac{402 - 288}{7}$$

$$= 16.29$$

Use of Calculator

With a third-level calculator, you can enter the D scores and then with special sets of keys determine $\overline{D}$ and $s_D{}^2$ or s_D. Instead of first finding and then entering D scores, you may be able instead to enter each pair of original scores in the form (X_1 minus X_2) or (X_2 minus X_1) and then with special keys proceed to find $\overline{D}$ and s_D. (Check the instruction manual that came with your calculator.)

4. Find $s_{\overline{D}}$ by Formula 11.4.

$$s_{\overline{D}} = \sqrt{\frac{s_D{}^2}{N}}$$

$$= \sqrt{\frac{16.29}{8}} = \sqrt{2.04} = 1.43$$

5. Find t by Formula 11.5.

$$t = \frac{\overline{D}}{s_{\overline{D}}}$$

$$= \frac{6}{1.43} = 4.20.$$

6. Evaluate t, using $df = N - 1$ and a two-tailed test. N is number of pairs. For $df = 8 - 1 = 7$:

$$t_{.05} = 2.36 \quad \text{and} \quad t_{.01} = 3.50 \text{ (Table C)}$$

The obtained t of 4.20 exceeds the critical value of t at $\alpha = .01$. The H_0 is rejected. It is concluded that the errors in logical thinking significantly decreased over the four years.

Sandler's *A*

Needed for Sandler's A are ΣD and ΣD^2. These sums have already been obtained above.

Compute Sandler's A by Formula 11.6:

$$A = \frac{\Sigma D^2}{(\Sigma D)^2}$$

$$= \frac{402}{(48)^2} = \frac{402}{2304}$$

$$= .174$$

Evaluate A, Using df = N − 1:

The critical values of A are found in Table H. For $df = 7$ and a two-tailed test, $A_{.05} = .278$ and $A_{.01} = .196$. H_0 is rejected if the calculated A is *less than* these critical values. Our calculated A is .174; H_0 can be rejected at the .01 significance level. As it should be, this is the same conclusion that we reached by the direct difference method in the section above. ■

DEFINITIONS OF TERMS AND SYMBOLS

Matched pairs. A method of obtaining comparable groups in a two-group experiment. The same individual is tested twice, once under each experimental condition, or a series of pairs of individuals who are similar in one or more characteristics is selected, one member of each pair being assigned at random to one experimental condition and the second member then automatically assigned to the second condition. The result in both cases is a set of pairs of scores.

Direct-difference method. A method for computing t to test $H_0: \mu_1 - \mu_2 = 0$ that is used with matched pairs and is based on an analysis of the difference (D) between each pair of scores $(X_1 - X_2)$.

Mean difference ($\overline{D}$). The mean of the sample of difference (D) scores, obtained by summing the D's and dividing by N, the number of paired scores.

Estimated standard error of mean difference ($s_{\overline{D}}$). The estimated value of the standard deviation of the sampling distribution of mean difference scores ($\overline{D}$) that would otherwise be obtained from an infinite number of samples consisting of matched pairs. The estimated standard error, $s_{\overline{D}}$, is determined from the data of a single sample of D scores by the formula $s_D/\sqrt{N}$.

Degrees of freedom (df) for matched pairs. Degrees of freedom (df) used in evaluating t for matched pairs is $N - 1$, where N is the number of pairs.

Sandler's A statistic. A simple method of testing the hypothesis that $\mu_1 - \mu_2 = 0$ based on the difference (D) scores from a sample of matched pairs. The A statistic, defined as $\Sigma D^2/(\Sigma D)^2$, is interpreted by means of a special A table (shown in Table H). At any given α level, there is an exact equivalence between the critical value of A and the critical value of t, leading to the same conclusion about H_0.

PROBLEMS

1. In an experiment designed to test whether schizophrenics are more likely to exhibit a deficit in information processing than nonschizophrenics, 15 hospitalized schizophrenics are first selected. Then each of these patients is matched with a nonpsyiatric patient with a medical problem on the basis of age, education, and socioeconomic background. Shown below are the $\overline{X}$ and standard error of the mean ($s_{\overline{X}}$) for each group, derived from their performance on an information-processing task. Also shown is the correlation between the scores for the matched pairs of subjects.

	Schizophrenic	Medical
$\overline{X}$	84.2	91.1
$s_{\overline{X}}$	2.3	2.6

$$N = 15 \quad r = .45$$

(a) What does the r indicate?

(b) Calculate t, using the *independent groups* method for determining $s_{\bar{X}_1 - \bar{X}_2}$ (see Chapter 9). What do you conclude about the performance of the two groups of patients, using $\alpha = .05$?

(c) Recalculate t, using Formula 11.1 to determine $s_{\bar{X}_1 - \bar{X}_2}$. Do you come to a different conclusion from the one in (b)? Why?

2. In a study of taste aversion, 10 laboratory rats were fed twice a day, their diet alternating between a sugar-flavored and a chocolate-flavored mash. As determined by amount eaten, the rats found the two mixtures equally palatable. After several weeks on these diets, the rats were injected with a chemical immediately after consuming the chocolate-flavored mash. The chemical was one that had the effect of making the animals temporarily ill. The amount of each type of food each animal ate during the next feeding cycle is shown below.

Subject	Chocolate	Sugar
1	10	9
2	4	7
3	14	18
4	5	5
5	11	19
6	9	14
7	16	22
8	11	16
9	12	9
10	7	6

(a) Calculate t by the direct difference method. Using $\alpha = .05$, what do you conclude about the effect of the chemically induced illness on the palatability of the chocolate-flavored mash?

(b) Compare the two groups by means of Sandler's A statistic. What do you conclude? [Your conclusion should be the same as in (a), above.]

12

One-Way Analysis of Variance

- THE PURPOSE OF ANALYSIS OF VARIANCE
- THE PRINCIPLES OF ONE-WAY ANALYSIS OF VARIANCE
- THE CONCEPT OF SUMS OF SQUARES
- THE CONCEPT OF VARIANCE OR MEAN SQUARE
- THE F RATIO
- EFFECT SIZE
- A MULTIPLE-COMPARISON TEST FOLLOWING ANALYSIS OF VARIANCE

In previous chapters we have explained techniques for analyzing data from two different experimental conditions in order to test hypotheses about the effects of those conditions. We saw how to test the significance of differences between $\overline{X}$'s for two independent groups treated differently and also how to test the significance of differences between $\overline{X}$'s for the same group or matched pairs of subjects tested under two different conditions. As yet, however, we have not considered the statistical analysis of findings from experiments in which the effects of three or more conditions are compared. This chapter will describe a technique called analysis of variance, one of the most widely used methods for making such analyses.

THE PURPOSE OF ANALYSIS OF VARIANCE

First of all, we ask why an experiment should ever include more than two conditions. Two answers may be given: (a) We may be interested in studying more than two conditions at a time, and (b) the data obtained with two conditions may give quite a different answer to our experimental problem than would comparable data from three or more conditions. Referring to our first point, suppose that an investigator is interested in the relative effectiveness of various kinds of psychological treatments for depression. We can see that there might be three, four, or even more kinds of psychotherapeutic techniques whose efficacy the investigator would like to compare rather than only two. However (and this is our second point), if only two treatment methods were studied and no significant differences were found between their means, it would be tempting to conclude that all psychotherapeutic methods are equally effective, when in fact some other method that could have been included in an experiment with more than two conditions might have had an appreciably different outcome.

Let us consider another experiment in which more than two experimental conditions would be desirable. We wish to determine how alcohol consumption during pregnancy affects infants' neurological development. For ethical reasons we could not do an experiment involving human beings to investigate this question, but we are able to do such a study with laboratory rats. We could lace the water of one group of pregnant rats with a specified amount of alcohol each day and compare their offspring on a measure reflecting neurological functioning with the offspring of female rats given no alcohol during pregnancy. This would tell us whether or not the dosage of alcohol we chose had any effect, but it would not tell us about the magnitude of the effects of lesser or greater amounts of alcohol. Here, too, we need more than two groups to obtain a picture of the relationship between our experimental variable and the outcome measure being observed.

Once we conduct an experiment involving more than two groups or conditions, we face the necessity of testing the significance of the differences among the $\overline{X}$'s obtained with the several conditions. Our first thought would surely be to compute t ratios to assess for each pair of groups the null hypothesis that the populations from which the groups were drawn had the same μ. We would thus test the significance of the difference between $\overline{X}$'s for all possible pairs of conditions. However, the use of separate t tests for analyzing the results of an experiment based upon more than two groups would lead to results that could not easily be interpreted. If we obtain one significant t value out of six, what does this mean? Had we performed a single t test, we would have had a .05 probability of obtaining a t significant at the 5% level by random sampling alone, but with six t tests our chances of having at least one of them significant because of random sampling is much larger. To carry this argument to its extreme, if a million t tests were involved in an experiment, a single significant t value would certainly be no indication that the conditions being varied had an effect.

We would not be handicapped by the fact that increasing the number of t ratios to be computed for an experiment increases the probability that a significant t will be found by chance if we could state how this probability changes with the number of t values to be computed. Unfortunately, this cannot readily be done, and so our use of t leads us to results we cannot evaluate easily.* Consequently, a single test for the significance of the differences among all the $\overline{X}$'s of the experiment seems necessary as a means of permitting a more correct determination of the significance of differences obtained in the experiment. This chapter will introduce you to one such test, *analysis of variance*. This technique, which is often identified by the acronym ANOVA, is appropriate for use with two or more groups. However, it is most frequently employed with three or more groups, since the t test is available for two-group experiments.

In this chapter we describe the principles of analysis of variance (ANOVA) as they apply to experiments employing two or more conditions, each representing the manipulation of a single type of independent variable; for example, different kinds of diet or amounts of time between memorization and a test of recall. Since only one basic variable is being studied, this method is identified as *one-way analysis of variance*. (In the next chapter, *two-way analysis of variance*, suitable for analyzing data of experiments in which two types of independent variables are manipulated, is discussed.)

In conducting a one-way ANOVA, we first set up a null hypothesis (H_0) about the μ's of the populations from which our samples were drawn, namely that they are all the same. This implies that any differences between the $\overline{X}$'s we obtain are due to sampling error. The alternative hypothesis (H_1) is that not all of the μ's are identical; at least one μ differs from the others. For example, in an experiment employing four groups or conditions, our hypotheses are:

$$H_0: \mu_1 = \mu_2 = \mu_3 = \mu_4$$

$$H_1: \mu\text{'s are not all equal}$$

We will first present the principles of one-way ANOVA and then demonstrate how to apply the method to the data of investigations employing two or more conditions.

---

*There is a conservative procedure for evaluating the significance of several t tests performed at once. This procedure, called Dunn's test, consists of changing the usual .05 (or .01) significance level to a more stringent level that depends upon the number of t tests being performed. See G. Keppel, *Design and Analysis*, 2nd ed. (Englewood Cliffs, N.J.: Prentice Hall, 1983), pp. 147–49.

THE PRINCIPLES OF ONE-WAY ANALYSIS OF VARIANCE

In this section we will describe the one-way ANOVA technique in very general terms. In Chapter 9, in which we discussed samples drawn independently from two populations, we pointed to the fact that the total variability in a set of scores (that is, the two samples combined) can be divided into two categories or sources. These sources are the variability of individuals *within each group* and the variability *between the different groups*. This is true not merely of a pair of samples from two populations but of any number of samples drawn from different populations. To repeat, the total variability from a set of scores from *two or more* groups can be divided into the variability within groups and the variability between groups. The analysis of variance (ANOVA) technique rests on this basic fact.

To visualize these two types of variability, we will use an illustration in which we have only two groups or conditions. The logic, however, applies to any number.

Imagine, then, that we have two groups of equal size, each of which is tested under a different condition. Suppose that the two distributions of scores have the same shape and the same *s*. However, they have very different $\overline{X}$'s and the distributions as a whole show little overlap. This gives us the situation graphed at the top of Figure 12.1.

We can also combine the subjects from the two groups into one large group of subjects. The resulting distribution has been plotted at the bottom of Figure 12.1. Also shown is the mean of the total group, which we designate as $\overline{X}_{tot}$. You can see that the variability within the total group is much larger than the variability within each of the two groups, the scores in the total group ranging from the smallest score in group 1 to the largest score in group 2.

The total variability, we have said, can be broken down into two categories or sources. The first is the deviation of each of the scores from the $\overline{X}$ of their own group, called the *variability within groups*. The second is the deviation of each of the group $\overline{X}$'s from $\overline{X}_{tot}$, called the *variability between groups*. Consider, for example, the raw score marked X_2 in Figure 12.1. (The subscript indicates that the score belongs to group 2.) The deviation of this score from $\overline{X}_{tot}$, $(X_2 - \overline{X}_{tot})$, can be broken down into two quantities, $(X_2 - \overline{X}_2)$ and $(\overline{X}_2 - \overline{X}_{tot})$, as shown in Figure 12.1. Because every score's deviation from $\overline{X}_{tot}$ can be divided algebraically into these two parts, it is possible to express the total variability observed in an experiment as the sum of these two types of variability—the sum of the variability between groups and the sum of the variability within groups.

In Figure 12.2 we have shown the idealized results of two hypothetical experiments, each of which involved four groups of subjects. For each experiment, the $\overline{X}$'s of the groups are shown on the baseline. The $\overline{X}_{tot}$ for the total group of subjects is also shown on the baseline.

The $\overline{X}$'s of the four groups in experiment 1, shown at the top of Figure 12.2, vary widely, so that many of the deviations of the $\overline{X}$'s from $\overline{X}_{tot}$ are quite large. This implies that the variability between groups contributed strongly to the total variability among the total set of scores. A different situation is shown in experiment 2 at the bottom of Figure 12.2. The four groups are equal in size to those in the first experiment and the variability within each of the groups is also the same. However, unlike the first experiment, the four distributions obtained in the second experiment overlap and the four $\overline{X}$'s are relatively similar. Thus, the variability

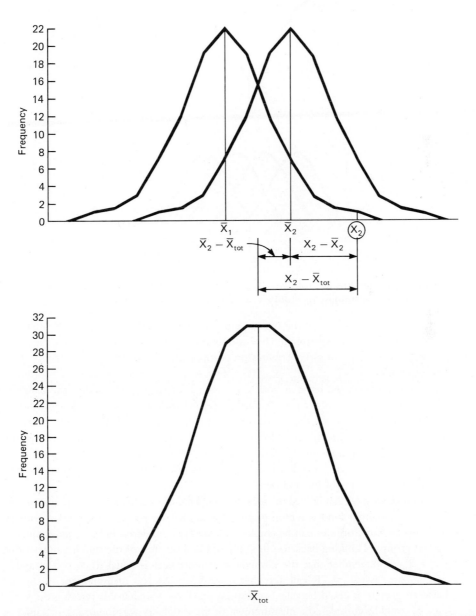

Figure 12.1 Two-group experiments illustrating variability within groups and variability between groups (top curves) and total variability (bottom curve).

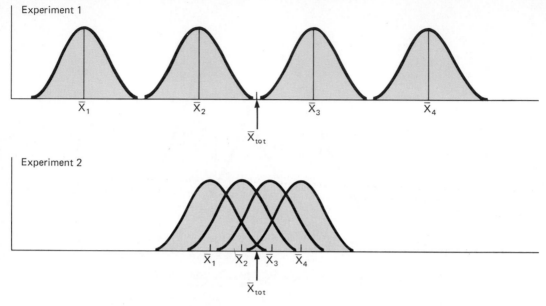

Figure 12.2 Illustration of two hypothetical four-group experiments with the same within-groups variability and different between-groups variability.

within groups is the same in the two experiments but in experiment 2, the variability between groups is less than in experiment 1. This outcome implies that in the second experiment, the variability between groups contributes proportionately less to the total variability than in the first experiment.

The question we have in both experiments, of course, is whether the conditions had different effects. Put another way, we are concerned with whether the differences between $\overline{X}$'s reflect differences between the μ's of the populations from which the samples were drawn or are merely due to sampling error. Intuitively, we strongly suspect that there are genuine differences among the groups in the first experiment, that is, they come from populations with different μ's. However, it is hard to tell what to conclude about the groups in the second experiment. How might we find out?

Once we have assimilated the idea that one kind of variability in an experiment is between groups and another kind is within groups, we can let our previous experience with statistical tests suggest how this idea can be employed in analyzing differences in $\overline{X}$ values obtained from several groups. Thinking back to our study of t and our test of the null hypothesis that $\mu_1 - \mu_2 = 0$, we remember that the numerator of the t ratio is equal to $\overline{X}_1 - \overline{X}_2$ and that the denominator is $s_{\overline{X}_1 - \overline{X}_2}$. Recall also that since $\overline{X}_1 - \overline{X}_2$ is a measurement of the difference between groups, it could be called an expression of the variability between groups. Similarly, $s_{\overline{X}_1 - \overline{X}_2}$ could be considered a measurement of the variability within groups, making t the ratio of variability between groups to variability within groups. In that case we could say that a significant t occurs only when the ratio of between-groups variability to within-groups variability is as large as the significant t values presented in Table C.

Applying the same reasoning to experiments involving more than two groups, we first assume the null hypothesis that the μ values of the groups are all the same ($\mu_1 = \mu_2 = \mu_3 = \cdots = \mu_k$), so that the overall difference is zero. We then determine the variability between groups and the variability within groups. In both cases, the measure of variability we use is the *variance* or s^2. The sample variance, we remind you, is defined as $\Sigma x^2/df$, the sum of the squared deviations of a set of scores from their mean divided by the *degrees of freedom* associated with the set of scores. We then obtain a ratio of these variances, one reflecting between-groups variability and the other reflecting within-groups variability. Provided that this ratio is sufficiently large, we call the differences among $\overline{X}$'s significant. This ratio is identified by the letter F. The analysis of variance technique is simply a method that provides an objective criterion for deciding whether the variability between groups is large enough in comparison with the variability within groups to justify the inference that the means of the populations from which the different groups were drawn are not all the same.

The relationship between the t and the F ratio is more formal than the parallel we have just described. In fact, when only two groups are being compared, F has the value of t^2 and when one is significant (or nonsignificant) at a given α level, so is the other.

THE CONCEPT OF SUMS OF SQUARES

Basic Ideas

The cornerstone in the analysis of variance technique is the *sum of squares*, an old concept masquerading under a new name. *The sum of squares is simply Σx^2, the sum of squared deviations from the mean.* You will recall that Σx^2 is the numerator of the formula for the variance, s^2, as we discussed in Chapter 5 (see, for example, Formula 5.4).

When the value of x is large [that is, when a score (X) is far from $\overline{X}$] x^2 is also large. Thus a large Σx^2 (sum of squares) occurs when the scores tend to be widely dispersed about $\overline{X}$. But this is also what we mean by great variability. Consequently, a large value for the sum of the squares indicates a large amount of variability; small sums of squares values indicate small amounts of variability.

Types of Sums of Squares Values

We have already stated that the total variability in an experiment may be divided into two parts: the variability of subjects within groups, and the variability between different groups. Now we wish to find ways of computing sums of squares that will correspond to the total variability and to its two parts. These three sums of squares, which we shall call, respectively, total sum of squares (SS_{tot}), within-groups sum of squares (SS_{wg}), and between-groups sum of squares (SS_{bg}), will be discussed presently. First, however, we must list some new symbols that will be used in the remainder of this chapter:

$\overline{X}_{tot}$ = the mean of all scores in the experiment (also called the grand mean or the overall mean)

$\overline{X}_{g}$ = a general expression for the mean of the scores in any group (g)

N_{tot} = the total number of scores in the experiment

N_{g} = a general expression for the number of scores in any group

k = the number of groups

$\sum_{tot} X$ = the sum of all the scores in the experiment

$\sum_{tot} X^2$ = the sum of all the squared scores in the experiment

We also need to distinguish between the scores of the different groups. A score from group 1 is indicated by X_1, a score from group 2 by X_2, a score from group 3 by X_3, and so forth. This numerical subscript is similarly used to identify the mean and N of each group. For example, $\overline{X}_4$ is the mean of group 4 and N_4 is the number of cases in that group.

The Definition of SS_{tot}. The total sum of squares (SS_{tot}) is just what our previous statement would suggest: *the sum of the squared deviations of every score from the grand mean* ($\overline{X}_{tot}$) *of all the scores in the experiment.* This definition may also be expressed in an equation:

$$SS_{tot} = \sum (X - \overline{X}_{tot})^2 \qquad (12.1)$$

Because SS_{tot} is to represent all the variability recorded in an experiment, we must find $(X - \overline{X}_{tot})^2$ for each X in the entire experiment and then sum all of these $(X - \overline{X}_{tot})^2$ quantities. Accordingly, the number of squared deviations to be added will be equal to the total number of subjects in the experiment (N_{tot}). To repeat, we subtract $\overline{X}_{tot}$ from each person's score (X), square this deviation, and then sum these squared deviations.

The Definition of SS_{wg}. The sum of squares within groups is most easily understood as a combination of sums of squares within separate groups. For example, we define the sum of squares within group 1 (SS_{wg1}) by the following equation:

$$SS_{wg1} = \sum (X_1 - \overline{X}_1)^2$$

Note that X_1 is a score in group 1, and that we must find $(X_1 - \overline{X}_1)^2$ for every X_1 in group 1. The sum of these squared deviations is an expression of the variability within group 1. You can see that it serves the same purpose for group 1 that SS_{tot} does for the entire experiment.

We define the sum of squares within group 2 (SS_{wg2}) by writing the preceding equation in terms of X_2 and $\overline{X}_2$ rather than X_1 and $\overline{X}_1$. A similar change is made for group 3 and for any other group in the experiment. Once the sum of squares within each of the groups is known, we add them, because we want only one SS_{wg} expression. Accordingly, we define SS_{wg}

for the entire experiment as the sum of the SS_{wg} values for the separate groups. Writing this definition in terms of the quantities that make up the individual SS_{wg} values, we have for the case of three groups:

$$SS_{wg} = SS_{wg1} + SS_{wg2} + SS_{wg3}$$

With a different number of groups (k), the number of terms on the right-hand side of the equation would equal the new value of k. For example, with five groups (when $k = 5$), SS_{wg} would be defined as:

$$SS_{wg} = SS_{wg1} + SS_{wg2} + SS_{wg3} + SS_{wg4} + SS_{wg5}$$

A general expression for SS_{wg} can be written as:

$$SS_{wg} = SS_{wg1} + SS_{wg2} + \cdots + SS_{wgk} \tag{12.2}$$

or

$$SS_{wg} = \Sigma (X_1 - \overline{X}_1)^2 + \Sigma (X_2 - \overline{X}_2)^2 + \cdots + \Sigma (X_k - \overline{X}_k)^2$$

where the subscript k indicates the last in a set of k groups. Notice that SS_{wg} is like SS_{tot} in consisting of squared deviations from a mean. But instead of using deviations from a single mean, $\overline{X}_{tot}$, we now employ several different means for the different groups: $\overline{X}_1, \overline{X}_2, \ldots, \overline{X}_k$.

The Definition of SS_{bg}. From the above we would expect that SS_{bg} would be based upon the squared deviation of each $\overline{X}_g$ from $\overline{X}_{tot}$, just as other SS's are based upon deviations of scores from $\overline{X}$'s. This is exactly what is done. First we find $(\overline{X}_g - \overline{X}_{tot})^2$ for each group. Then we weight each $(\overline{X}_g - \overline{X}_{tot})^2$ quantity with the number of cases in its group (N_g) and add the weighted quantities $N_g(\overline{X}_g - \overline{X}_{tot})^2$ to find SS_{bg}. In general, then, we can say the following:

$$SS_{bg} = \Sigma [N_g(\overline{X}_g - \overline{X}_{tot})^2] \tag{12.3}$$

Taking a specific number of groups ($k = 3$), we can write this equation in a new form:

$$SS_{bg} = N_1(\overline{X}_1 - \overline{X}_{tot})^2 + N_2(\overline{X}_2 - \overline{X}_{tot})^2 + N_3(\overline{X}_3 - \overline{X}_{tot})^2$$

since N_g is N_1 for the first group, N_2 for the second group, and N_3 for the third group and $\overline{X}_g$ has comparable values. Notice that SS_{bg} uses squared deviations of the group means, $\overline{X}_g$, from $\overline{X}_{tot}$ rather than the squared deviations of raw scores (X's) from $\overline{X}_{tot}$ or $\overline{X}_g$ used in SS_{tot} and SS_{wg}.

Relationships between SS_{tot} and Its Components

We have seen that SS_{tot} can be divided into two components or sources, SS_{wg} and SS_{bg}. We now consider the relative contributions of these two components to SS_{tot}.

In Table 12.1 we have summarized the results of a hypothetical experiment involving three methods of teaching reading to retarded children. Included in the table are the values we

Table 12.1 Summary of Hypothetical Results of Three Methods of Teaching Reading in which the Three Methods Produced Equal $\overline{X}$'s

Method 1	Method 2	Method 3
$N = 10$	$N = 10$	$N = 10$
$\sum X_1 = 165; \overline{X}_1 = 16.5$	$\sum X_2 = 165; \overline{X}_2 = 16.5$	$\sum X_3 = 165; \overline{X}_3 = 16.5$

$$\sum_{tot} X = 165 + 165 + 165 = 495$$

$$\overline{X}_{tot} = \frac{495}{30} = 16.5$$

$$SS_{tot} = \sum (X - \overline{X}_{tot})^2 = 159.5$$

$$SS_{wg} = \sum (X_1 - \overline{X}_1)^2 + \sum (X_2 - \overline{X}_2)^2 + \sum (X_3 - \overline{X}_3)^2$$

$$= 30.5 + 74.5 + 54.5 = 159.5$$

$$SS_{bg} = N_1(\overline{X}_1 - \overline{X}_{tot})^2 + N_2(\overline{X}_2 - \overline{X}_{tot})^2 + N_3(\overline{X}_3 - \overline{X}_{tot})^2$$

$$= 10(16.5 - 16.5)^2 + 10(16.5 - 16.5)^2 + 10(16.5 - 16.5)^2 = 0$$

$$SS_{tot} = SS_{wg} + SS_{bg}$$

$$159.5 = 159.5 + 0$$

have calculated for SS_{tot}, SS_{wg}, and SS_{bg}. The data are unusual in that the three $\overline{X}_g$'s have exactly the same value, 16.5. It follows that $\overline{X}_{tot}$ also equals 16.5. The deviation between $\overline{X}_{tot}$ and each $\overline{X}_g$ ($\overline{X}_g - \overline{X}_{tot}$) is therefore 0. This means that SS_{bg} is also 0, as you can see by examining Formula 12.3. As there is no variability among $\overline{X}_g$'s, this is as it should be.

You will notice in Table 12.1 that SS_{tot} and SS_{wg} have the same value. We have illustrated this in Figure 12.3 in the form of a balance. You can see why the two quantities on either side of the fulcrum balance each other when you recall that $SS_{tot} = SS_{wg} + SS_{bg}$. Since SS_{bg} is 0, SS_{wg} must equal SS_{tot}. You can also see from inspecting Formula 12.2 that $SS_{tot} = SS_{wg}$ when $SS_{bg} = 0$. That is, when each $\overline{X}_g$ is equal to $\overline{X}_{tot}$, we may substitute $(X_g - \overline{X}_{tot})$ for each $(X_g - \overline{X}_g)$ in the formula for SS_{wg}; the formula for SS_{wg} thus becomes the same as for SS_{tot}.

In the example in Table 12.1, all the variability in the total group of 30 subjects comes from variability within each of the groups. A very different situation is shown in Table 12.2. To make the point we want to demonstrate clear, we have set up the data so that $\overline{X}_{tot}$ is the same as in Table 12.1 and also so that SS_{wg1}, SS_{wg2}, and SS_{wg3} are the same as for the parallel groups in Table 12.1. Therefore, the SS_{wg} we have calculated for the data is the same (159.5) as we calculated for the data summarized in Table 12.1. However, in Table 12.2, the $\overline{X}$'s of the three groups are different, so that they do not all take the same value as $\overline{X}_{tot}$. This means that SS_{bg} is no longer 0. The fact that the $\overline{X}_g$'s differ also means that the variability among the

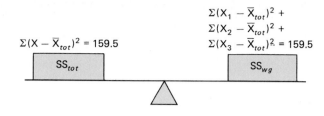

$$\Sigma(X - \bar{X}_{tot})^2 = 159.5$$

$$\begin{array}{c}\Sigma(X_1 - \bar{X}_{tot})^2\ + \\ \Sigma(X_2 - \bar{X}_{tot})^2\ + \\ \Sigma(X_3 - \bar{X}_{tot})^2 = 159.5\end{array}$$

SS_{tot} SS_{wg}

Figure 12.3 Data from Table 12.1 showing that SS_{tot} is equal to SS_{wg} when $\bar{X}$'s are equal.

total group is greater, which is reflected in a larger SS_{tot}. SS_{tot} is now larger than SS_{wg}, as we have illustrated in Figure 12.4. How much larger? Because $SS_{tot} = SS_{wg} + SS_{bg}$, it must be increased by an amount equal to the value calculated for SS_{bg}. Inspection of Table 12.2 shows that this indeed is so. To achieve balance in our graphic illustration of the relationship between SS_{tot} and its components, we must add SS_{bg} to SS_{wg}, as shown in Figure 12.4.

Even when the various conditions in an experiment have identical effects on performance, it is extremely unlikely that the means of the experimental groups will be exactly alike because of chance factors. When the size of SS_{bg} is small and contributes relatively little to SS_{tot}, we therefore suspect that our experimental variables have no differential effects. That is, we suspect that the populations from which our experimental groups were drawn have the same mean. On the other hand, when SS_{bg} is relatively large, we suspect that the conditions do have differential effects. The question, of course, is how large the differences among $\bar{X}$'s

---

Table 12.2 Summary of Hypothetical Results of Three Methods of Teaching Reading in which $\bar{X}$'s Differ

Method 1	*Method 2*	*Method 3*
N = 10	*N = 10*	*N = 10*
$\Sigma X_1 = 145; \bar{X}_1 = 14.5$	$\Sigma X_2 = 165; \bar{X}_2 = 16.5$	$\Sigma X_3 = 185; \bar{X}_3 = 18.5$

$$\Sigma_{tot} X = 145 + 165 + 185 = 495$$

$$\bar{X}_{tot} = \frac{495}{30} = 16.5$$

$$SS_{tot} = 239.50$$

$$SS_{wg} = 30.5 + 74.5 + 54.5 = 159.5$$

$$SS_{bg} = 10(14.5 - 16.5)^2 + 10(16.5 - 16.5)^2 + 10(18.5 - 16.5)^2 = 80$$

$$SS_{tot} = SS_{wg} + SS_{bg}$$

$$239.50 = 159.5 + 80$$

Figure 12.4 Data from Table 12.2 showing that SS_{tot} is greater than SS_{wg} when all $\overline{X}$'s are not equal.

must be, relative to the variability within groups, before we can reasonably reject the null hypothesis that the conditions had the same effects and differences among $\overline{X}$'s were due solely to chance. To answer this question, we must find the sample variances, that is, SS_{bg}/df_{bg} and SS_{wg}/df_{wg}. Before we proceed to this next step, however, we will discuss the computational formulas that should be used to calculate the several sums of squares.

Computational Formulas for Finding Sums of Squares

Application of the basic formulas we have just discussed for finding sums of squares is a long, laborious process that involves determining the deviation of each score from the overall or grand mean, the deviation of each score from its own mean, squaring each of these sets of deviations, and so on. We can simplify our work in calculating SS values by using special computational formulas that lead to precisely the same answers as do the basic formulas but are more convenient because they involve only raw scores. Although these new equations can be derived algebraically from the basic definitions, we will present them without proof. Following this presentation, we will demonstrate their application to a set of data.

First, SS_{tot} is found by the computational formula:

$$SS_{tot} = \left(\sum_{tot} X^2\right) - \frac{\left(\sum_{tot} X\right)^2}{N_{tot}} \tag{12.4}$$

The formula states that SS_{tot} is computed by first squaring each X and adding all the X^2 values together, giving us $\sum_{tot} X^2$. Next the sum of all the X values is found; this *sum* is squared and then divided by the total N, giving us $(\sum_{tot} X)^2/N$. Finally, this latter result is subtracted from $\sum_{tot} X^2$ to give SS_{tot}.

Next, SS_{bg} is found by the formula:

$$SS_{bg} = \sum_{g} \left[\frac{(\sum X_g)^2}{N_g}\right] - \frac{\left(\sum_{tot} X\right)^2}{N_{tot}} \tag{12.5}$$

Thus, we determine SS_{bg} by first finding for each group its $\sum X$, squaring it, and dividing the result by the corresponding N. The resulting quantities from all the groups are added together, as indicated by the symbol Σ, and the quantity obtained by dividing $(\underset{tot}{\Sigma} X)^2$ by N_{tot} subtracted from this sum. (You will note that the latter quantity was also used in determining SS_{tot} so it needs to be calculated only once.) The computational formula for SS_{bg} could also be written for k groups as follows:

$$SS_{bg} = \left[\frac{(\Sigma X_1)^2}{N_1} + \frac{(\Sigma X_2)^2}{N_2} + \cdots + \frac{(\Sigma X_k)^2}{N_k} \right] - \frac{\left(\underset{tot}{\Sigma} X\right)^2}{N_{tot}}$$

Finally, since we know that SS_{tot} is composed of SS_{bg} and SS_{wg}, we can find SS_{wg} by subtraction:

$$SS_{wg} = SS_{tot} - SS_{bg} \tag{12.6}$$

We could also compute SS_{wg} directly, instead of by subtraction, by calculating SS_{wg} for each group separately and then adding these values together to obtain the overall SS_{wg}. These operations are expressed by the following formula:

$$SS_{wg} = \underset{g}{\Sigma} \left[(\Sigma X_g^2) - \frac{(\Sigma X_g)^2}{N_g} \right] \tag{12.7}$$

With the computational formulas for SS_{tot}, SS_{bg}, and SS_{wg} before us, we can illustrate their use with a specific set of scores.

Table 12.3 presents a summary of the results of a hypothetical experiment in which college students were asked to read aloud either a statement said to be written by another student in favor of a proposal to raise tuition (group 1), a favorable statement said to be written by the university president (group 2) or a statement on an irrelevant topic (group 3). The students then answered an attitude questionnaire assessing their reactions to a change in tuition. (High scores indicate positive reaction.) The first step, shown in the table, is to find ΣX and ΣX^2 for each group and then to sum each of these quantities across groups to obtain $\underset{tot}{\Sigma} X$ and $\underset{tot}{\Sigma} X^2$. We then compute SS_{tot}, SS_{bg}, and SS_{wg} using our raw-score computational formulas. You will notice that we have obtained the value of SS_{wg} twice, first by subtracting SS_{bg} from SS_{tot} and then by computing it directly. The fact that the two procedures yield the same value for SS_{bg} not only suggests that our calculations were accurate, but also demonstrates our earlier statement that $SS_{bg} + SS_{wg}$ always equals SS_{tot}.

One more fact about the computation of SS values is important to us. If we look carefully at the basic formulas for SS values, we see that no SS can ever have a negative value. This is not obvious from the computational formulas, but must also be true for them. Consequently, a negative SS value is always a sign that a mistake in arithmetic has been made and that recalculations are necessary.

Table 12.3 Application of the Computational Formulas for SS_{tot}, SS_{bg}, and SS_{wg} to the Data from the Hypothetical Attitude Experiment

X_1	X_1^2	X_2	X_2^2	X_3	X_3^2
68	4624	78	6084	94	8836
63	3969	69	4761	82	6724
58	3364	58	3364	73	5329
51	2601	57	3249	67	4489
41	1681	53	2809	66	4356
40	1600	52	2704	62	3844
34	1156	48	2304	60	3600
27	729	46	2116	54	2916
20	400	42	1764	50	2500
18	324	27	729	32	1024
420	20448	530	29884	640	43618

$$\sum_{tot} X = \sum X_1 + \sum X_2 + \sum X_3 = 420 + 530 + 640 = 1590$$

$$\sum_{tot} X^2 = \sum X_1^2 + \sum X_2^2 + \sum X_3^2 = 20448 + 29884 + 43618 = 93950$$

$$N_{tot} = N_1 + N_2 + N_3 = 10 + 10 + 10 = 30 \quad \overline{X}_1 = 42 \quad \overline{X}_2 = 53 \quad \overline{X}_3 = 64$$

$$SS_{tot} = \left(\sum_{tot} X^2\right) - \frac{\left(\sum_{tot} X\right)^2}{N_{tot}}$$

$$= 93950 - \frac{(1590)^2}{30}$$

$$= 93950 - 84270$$

$$= 9680$$

$$SS_{bg} = \sum_g \left[\frac{(\sum X_g)^2}{N_g}\right] - \frac{\left(\sum_{tot} X\right)^2}{N_{tot}}$$

$$= \frac{(\sum X_1)^2}{N_1} + \frac{(\sum X_2)^2}{N_2} + \frac{(\sum X_3)^2}{N_3} - \frac{\left(\sum_{tot} X\right)^2}{N_{tot}}$$

$$= \frac{(420)^2}{10} + \frac{(530)^2}{10} + \frac{(640)^2}{10} - \frac{(1590)^2}{30}$$

$$= \frac{176400}{10} + \frac{280900}{10} + \frac{409600}{10} - 84270$$

$$= \frac{866900}{10} - 84270$$

$$= 2420$$

$$SS_{wg} = \sum_g \left[(\sum X_g^2) - \frac{(\sum X_g)^2}{N_g}\right]$$

$$= 20448 - \frac{(420)^2}{10} +$$

$$29884 - \frac{(530)^2}{10} +$$

$$43618 - \frac{(640)^2}{10}$$

$$= 2808 + 1794 + 2658$$

$$= 7260$$

OR

$$SS_{wg} = SS_{tot} - SS_{bg}$$

$$= 9680 - 2420$$

$$= 7260$$

THE CONCEPT OF VARIANCE OR MEAN SQUARE

The use of sums of squares as measurements of variability has only one disadvantage: The size of SS depends very much on the number of measurements on which it is based. Other things being equal, a sample of 100 measurements from a given population will yield about twice as large an SS as a sample of 50 from that population, because there will be twice as many squared deviations involved in the former. For this reason, a large SS may result either from a large variability of the characteristic being measured or from a large N in the sample. Consequently, SS is an unsatisfactory measurement of variability. We can overcome this disadvantage by finding the mean SS. The mean SS, we recall from Chapter 5, is the sample *variance*, s^2. In the present context we will call this quantity the *mean square* rather than the variance, because the label, mean square (MS), has come to be used by statisticians in place of variance in discussing the analysis of variance technique.

Recall also from Chapter 5 that the formula for s^2, the unbiased estimate of the population variance (or mean square) obtained from the data of a single sample, is $\Sigma x^2/(N - 1)$, where $N - 1$ is the number of degrees of freedom associated with the sample. Since we have agreed in this chapter to call the sum of the squared deviations (Σx^2) a sum of squares or SS, we can now present a general expression for the unbiased estimate of the population variance or mean square: $MS = SS/df$.

As we said when we discussed the principles of analysis of variance, we want to judge whether our group $\overline{X}$'s differ significantly by comparing a measure of variability between groups, which you can now surmise to be a mean square between groups, with a measure of variability within groups, which will be the mean square within groups. We then discover how large a value of the ratio of these two variabilities is required to indicate that the group $\overline{X}$'s differ more than would be expected if the null hypothesis of equal μ's were true. With this in mind, it appears that what we want now is to find one MS (mean square) value to represent variability between groups and another MS value to represent variability within groups. Once these values (MS_{bg} and MS_{wg}, respectively) are known for any experiment, the size of their ratio can be used as the basis for drawing statistical conclusions about the data being analyzed.

Degrees of Freedom (*df*)

Before we are able to find MS_{bg} and MS_{wg}, we must find the degrees of freedom (*df*) associated with SS_{bg} and SS_{wg}. We do this by first considering the total *df*, that is, the *df* associated with the combined groups of subjects. This *df* is given by:

$$df_{tot} = N_{tot} - 1$$

In the same way that SS_{tot} can be divided into two components, SS_{bg} and SS_{wg}, df_{tot} can be divided into two components, df_{bg} and df_{wg}. To find df_{bg}, we subtract 1 from k, the number of groups:

$$df_{bg} = k - 1$$

Finally, df_{bg} is given by:

$$df_{wg} = N_{tot} - k$$

where k, you recall, is the number of groups. You may understand df_{bg} better if you recognize that df within a single group is one less than the number of scores in the group, that is, $N_g - 1$. This makes the df within all k groups equal to $(\Sigma N_g) - k$ or $N_{tot} - k$, since 1 df is lost in each of the k groups.

Finding MS Values

To find each MS value, we simply divide the appropriate SS by its df. Thus MS_{bg} is based upon SS_{bg} and df_{bg}, the number of degrees of freedom between groups:

$$MS_{bg} = \frac{SS_{bg}}{df_{bg}} \tag{12.8}$$

where $df_{bg} = k - 1$.

The second MS value, MS_{wg}, is the ratio of SS_{wg} to df_{wg}:

$$MS_{wg} = \frac{SS_{wg}}{df_{wg}} \tag{12.9}$$

where $df_{wg} = N_{tot} - k$.

We do not compute a MS based on SS_{tot}, as it is not useful for our purposes. Our interest is in the ratio of MS_{bg} to MS_{wg}.

We now illustrate the determination of MS_{bg} and MS_{wg} with a computational example. By referring to Table 12.3, we find that $SS_{bg} = 2420$ and $SS_{wg} = 7260$ in our hypothetical attitude experiment. Since $N_{tot} = 30$ and $k = 3$ for this experiment, $df_{bg} = 3 - 1 = 2$ and $df_{wg} = 30 - 3 = 27$. Notice that $df_{bg} + df_{wg} = 2 + 27 = 29$, which is one less than N_{tot}. From this example it can be seen that total degrees of freedom, df_{tot}, is given by $df_{tot} = df_{bg} + df_{wg} = N_{tot} - 1$.

First we find MS_{bg}:

$$MS_{bg} = \frac{2420}{2} = 1210$$

Then we compute MS_{wg}:

$$MS_{wg} = \frac{7260}{27} = 268.9$$

In our discussion of the t ratio in Chapter 9, we described the difference between sample means as a potential *systematic* source of variability; i.e., if μ's differ, the $\overline{X}$'s of a pair of samples are likely to show a similar difference. Similarly, in one-way ANOVA, MS_{bg} represents the potential systematic source of variability. In Chapter 9 we also described the standard error of the difference between means, which reflects the variability between groups, as the *error* source of variability. In one-way ANOVA, the comparable error term is MS_{wg}.

Thus, our systematic term, MS_{bg} will not be greatly larger than MS_{wg} in an experiment unless the group $\overline{X}$'s differ appreciably. We have just found an MS_{bg} of 1210, compared with an MS_{wg} of 268.9, our error term. This leads us to suspect that the variability between group $\overline{X}$ values is too great to be attributed to random differences between samples from populations with identical means. To make a more precise comparison of these MS values, we now form what is called the F ratio and evaluate it.

THE F RATIO

Before we present the F ratio, we remind you what the one-way ANOVA is intended to accomplish. We have two or more groups (samples) that differ in some way (for example, the experimental condition in which they were tested) and want to compare their $\overline{X}$'s. Our basic aim is to test the null hypothesis that the samples come from populations with the same μ and that any difference among our obtained $\overline{X}$'s is due to chance. If the variability among the $\overline{X}$'s of the groups is large in comparison to the variability within the groups, we are likely to reject the null hypothesis; if it is small, we are likely to retain the null hypothesis. In the ANOVA technique our index of variability is the variance or mean square (MS) and the F ratio is simply a numerical expression of the relative size of MS_{bg} and MS_{wg}.

The F ratio is thus defined by the following equation:

$$F = \frac{MS_{bg}}{MS_{wg}} \tag{12.10}$$

When an F ratio has been found in an experiment, a decision regarding the significance of the differences in group $\overline{X}$'s is made by comparing that ratio with the F values to be expected if the null hypothesis that the population μ values are equal were true. The information necessary for this comparison is presented in Table F in Appendix III. (Note the happy accident that the values of F appear in Table F.) Table F shows the F values required at the 5% and 1% levels of significance. That is, this table presents the F values that are so large that they would be exceeded only 5% or 1% of the time by random sampling if the null hypothesis were true. If MS_{bg} is enough greater than MS_{wg}, so that the resulting F ratio exceeds the tabled F at the 5% (or 1%) level, then we realize it would be very unlikely that such an F would occur unless the null hypothesis were false. Therefore, we would reject the null hypothesis that the population μ values are equal and say that our obtained F is significant at the 5% (or 1%) level.

One step in this procedure remains to be explored: We must know where to look in Table F for the significant values of the F ratio with which to compare the F obtained in a particular experiment. This step is much like the procedure for finding a significant *t* value in Table C. There we had to look for a *t* associated with a *df* value. Now we must find an F associated with two *df* values, because the degree of significance of any obtained F depends upon two factors—the number of groups and the number of subjects within the groups. Accordingly, we employ the values of df_{bg} and df_{wg} in using Table F.

Knowing that $df_{bg} = 2$ and $df_{wg} = 27$ in our attitude experiment, we can find a cell in Table F that is appropriate for that experiment. Since the df for the MS in the numerator of the F ratio is df_{bg} and the df for the MS in the denominator is df_{wg}, we see from the table that we must go to the *column* labeled $df = 2$ and proceed down to the *row* labeled $df = 27$. There we find two F values, one for the 5% level of significance and the other for the 1% level. The F ratio at the 5% level of significance is 3.35 and at the 1% level, 5.49. An F obtained in an experiment with three groups, each of 10 subjects, must be compared with these values to determine whether or not it is significant.

To illustrate the use of the F ratio, we again employ our data from the attitude experiment. Since $MS_{bg} = 1210$ and $MS_{wg} = 268.9$, we find F with the following equation:

$$F = \frac{1210}{268.9} = 4.50$$

This F ratio of 4.50 is significant at the 5% level because it is greater than 3.35, the F value tabled at the 5% level for 2 and 27 df. However, it is not significant at the 1% level because it is less than 5.49, the value required for significance at that level. Thus, in this situation we would reject the null hypothesis if we were using a 5% level of significance but accept it if we were using a 1% level. We may notice that, if df_{wg} had been between 30 and 40 rather than at 27 as it was, Table F would not have indicated the exact F values required for significance at the 5% and 1% levels. In that case we would have used the tabled values for 2 and 30 df, because they are higher than those for 2 and 40 df, thereby behaving with extra caution when we conclude that an F is significant at the 5% or 1% level.

Finally, the results of our ANOVA can be summarized in a table, as shown in Table 12.4. The format in Table 12.4 is the one conventionally used to present the results of ANOVA.

Computational Procedures

We now can list in sequence all the steps required to perform a one-way ANOVA.

Basic data

1. Find for each separate group ΣX, ΣX^2, and N.
2. By summing the appropriate figures for each of the groups, find $\Sigma_{tot} X$, $\Sigma_{tot} X^2$, and N_{tot}.

Table 12.4 Summary of the Analysis of Variance of the Attitude Experiment (from data in Table 12.3)

Source of variation	SS	df	MS	F	p
Between groups	2420	2	1210	4.50	< .05
Within group	7260	27	268.9		
Total	9680	29			

Calculational steps

Find the SS's by the formulas:

3. $SS_{tot} = \left(\sum_{tot} X^2\right) - \dfrac{\left(\sum_{tot} X\right)^2}{N_{tot}}$

4. $SS_{bg} = \sum_{g} \left[\dfrac{(\sum X_g)^2}{N_g}\right] - \dfrac{\left(\sum_{tot} X\right)^2}{N_{tot}}$

5. $SS_{wg} = SS_{tot} - SS_{bg}$

   OR

   $SS_{wg} = \sum_{g} \left[(\sum X_g^2) - \dfrac{(\sum X_g)^2}{N_g}\right]$

Find df's by the formulas:

6. $df_{bg} = k - 1$
7. $df_{wg} = N_{tot} - k$

Find MS's by the formulas:

8. $MS_{bg} = \dfrac{SS_{bg}}{df_{bg}}$

9. $MS_{wg} = \dfrac{SS_{wg}}{df_{wg}}$

Find and determine the significance of F:

10. $F = \dfrac{MS_{bg}}{MS_{wg}}$

11. Entering Table F with the df_{bg} and df_{wg} found in steps 6 and 7, find the F's required for significance at the 5% and the 1% levels.

12. If the obtained F exceeds the required F at the 5% level (or the 1% level) reject the null hypothesis at that level; otherwise, accept it.

13. Summarize the results of the ANOVA in a table like Table 12.4.

In the Step by Step Procedures section, we illustrate the application of these procedures to the results of an experiment.

Assumptions Underlying the Analysis of Variance

Like every other statistical test we have studied, the analysis of variance involves certain assumptions that had to be made in order to derive the table of significant values for the test. Table F is known to present the F values required for significance at the 5% and 1% levels when the null hypothesis is assumed to be true and three assumptions are satisfied: (a) each of the k populations from which the groups in the experiment were drawn is normally distributed; (b) the σ^2 values for the k populations are equal; (c) the subjects of the experiment have been randomly and independently drawn from their respective populations.

If we know that these assumptions have been met, we can accept conclusions based upon the use of Table F at their face value. If these assumptions are not satisfied, the mathematical demonstrations that the values presented in Table F are the exact values required at the 5% and 1% levels can no longer be made. However, the practical usefulness of the analysis of variance procedure may be nearly as great when one or two of these assumptions are fulfilled as when all are satisfied.* If one of these assumptions appears not to be met, the experimenter may prefer to perform the analysis of variance and interpret it conservatively—for example, require that F values reach the tabled values for a higher level for significance such as 1% when the experimenter would otherwise have required only a 5% level for concluding that F is significant.†

To decide whether the assumptions of normality and equal σ^2's have been met is not easy. Since the groups involved in this type of experiment are usually small, there are seldom enough scores to indicate the shape of the distribution for each population. If the sample distribution is very far from normal, we may suspect that the distribution of the population is not normal. Similarly, very great differences among the s^2's for the different groups suggest that the population σ^2's may be unequal. Statistical tests of normality and equality of σ^2's could be presented here; we omit them because of the space they would require and the impracticability of applying a test of normality except when N is large.

EFFECT SIZE

In Chapter 9 we discussed the concept of effect size. That is, after we have determined the significance of the difference between a pair of $\overline{X}$'s, we may be interested in the strength of the influence that variations in our experimental conditions (the independent variable) have on our response measure (the dependent variable). We found that $\hat{\omega}^2$ could be used as an estimate of effect size. More precisely, $\hat{\omega}^2$ provides an estimate of the proportion of the variability in the dependent variable accounted for by the independent variable.

---

*The ability of a statistical test to yield approximately correct results when certain assumptions are not met is known as its robustness. See H. Scheffé, *The Analysis of Variance* (New York: Wiley, 1959), chapter 10.

†If there is a great discrepancy between the assumptions of analysis of variance and the characteristics of the obtained data, it may be advisable to use a so-called nonparametric test such as the Kruskal-Wallis test, presented in Chapter 15. Nonparametric tests require no assumptions to be made about population parameters.

There is also a formula for $\hat{\omega}^2$ that can be applied to the data from a one-way ANOVA. This formula is as follows:

$$\hat{\omega}^2 = \frac{SS_{bg} - (k - 1)MS_{wg}}{SS_{tot} + MS_{wg}} \tag{12.11}$$

The value of $\hat{\omega}^2$ can be interpreted according to the standards we outlined in Chapter 9. Values of .15 to .20 or greater, indicating that 15 to 20 percent or more of the variability in the dependent variable can be explained by the independent variable, are typically regarded as indicating a relatively strong effect size. Values of .01 or .02 or less are typically regarded as indicating a weak effect size.

A MULTIPLE-COMPARISON TEST FOLLOWING ANALYSIS OF VARIANCE

When we have performed a one-way ANOVA and found a significant F between the groups, we are able to reject the hypothesis that all the groups were drawn from populations with the same mean. But when more than two groups are being compared, a significant F does not imply that each sample $\overline{X}$ necessarily differs significantly from every other sample $\overline{X}$; quite often we are interested in pinpointing more precisely where the differences lie. Our experimental interests, for example, may lead us to inquire about the significance of the differences between specific pairs of means. Or in other instances we may observe that the data pattern themselves in interesting ways. We may find, for example, that the means appear to fall into subsets or clusters, and we may want to determine whether the clusters differ significantly from each other, or we may find that one of the means is markedly different from all the rest. What is required, then, is some technique that will allow us to follow up the analysis of variance with further statistical comparisons.

Although *t* might seem an appropriate test for this purpose, several statistical difficulties prohibit its use, as we noted earlier. But a number of other tests for making multiple comparisons following analysis of variance have been suggested by statisticians. Here we present one such multiple-comparison test, a method devised by Tukey,* which we will call the *honestly significant difference* test or *hsd*.

The Tukey *hsd* usually is performed only if the F obtained in the analysis of variance is significant, but it is theoretically permissible to perform whatever the significance of F. The test has the advantage of allowing us to compare any pair of means, or any pair of subsets of means, that we wish to select and of placing no limits on the number of comparisons that may be made with any set of data. We will illustrate its use only for the simple case in which we

---

*J. W. Tukey, The problem of multiple comparisons (mimeographed, Princeton, N.J., 1953). The computational procedures are adapted from R. P. Runyon and A. Haber, *Fundamentals of Behavioral Statistics*, 2nd ed. (Reading, Mass.: Addison-Wesley, 1971).

wish to compare individual pairs of means and in which the N's in each group are equal. Procedures are available that permit comparisons of subsets of means (e.g., $\overline{X}$'s of groups 1 and 2 vs. $\overline{X}$'s of groups 3, 4, and 5) and of groups of unequal size, but they are more complex.

The test involves computing a quantity that we will identify as *hsd*. The difference between any pair of means is significant at a given α level if it equals or exceeds the absolute value of *hsd* we have computed.

The formula for *hsd* is as follows:

$$hsd = q_\alpha \sqrt{\frac{MS_{wg}}{N_g}} \qquad (12.12)$$

In this equation, MS_{wg} is the within-groups mean square calculated in the analysis of variance, and N_g is the number of cases in each group. The value of q_α, also called the Studentized range statistic, is found from the appropriate entry in Table G in Appendix III. We enter Table G at the specified α level for the *df* associated with MS_{wg} and k, the total number of groups in the experiment. Suppose, for example, that we wished to compare one or more pairs of means, using $\alpha = .05$, from a 4-group experiment in which there were 5 subjects per group. Looking at Table G for $k = 4$ and $df_{wg} = 20 - 4 = 16$, we find that $q_{.05} = 4.05$.

We will illustrate the application of the test by using the data from the hypothetical attitude experiment reported in Table 12.3 that involved three groups of 10 cases each. The results of the ANOVA are summarized in Table 12.4. We repeat below the data from Tables 12.3 and 12.4 that we need to determine *hsd*.

$$\overline{X}_1 = 42 \qquad \overline{X}_2 = 53 \qquad \overline{X}_3 = 64$$

$$MS_{wg} = 268.9 \qquad df_{wg} = 27 \qquad k = 3$$

where $k =$ the total number of groups and $df_{wg} = N_{tot} - k$.

The first step, assuming we wish to compare all possible pairs of means, is to find the *absolute difference* between each pair of $\overline{X}$'s (for example, the absolute difference between $\overline{X}_1$ and $\overline{X}_2$ is $53 - 42 = 11$). In Table 12.5 we show these differences for our experiment.

The next step is to compute *hsd*. Suppose that we set $\alpha = .05$. In order to find $q_{.05}$ we consult Table G to find the value associated with this alpha level for $df_{wg} = 27$ and $k = 3$. Unfortunately, by looking down the *df* column at the left, we discover that just as in the case of the F table, Table G is incomplete and has no entry for $df = 27$. Again, we choose to be conservative and use the next lowest *df*, which turns out to be 24. Going across this row to the $k = 3$ column, we find that the tabled value for q at $\alpha = .05$ is 3.53. We now enter this value, along with the values of MS_{wg} and N_g, into the *hsd* equation:

$$hsd = q_{.05} \sqrt{\frac{MS_{wg}}{N_g}} = 3.53 \sqrt{\frac{268.9}{10}} = 3.53(5.19) = 18.32$$

We have now computed the critical value that the difference between a pair of means must equal or exceed in order to be significant at the 5% level. By inspecting Table 12.5 we

Table 12.5 Absolute Differences Between Pairs of Means in Hypothetical Attitude Experiment

	$\overline{X}_1$	$\overline{X}_2$
$\overline{X}_2$	11	—
$\overline{X}_3$	22	11

see that the difference between $\overline{X}_1$ and $\overline{X}_3$ is the only one that exceeds 18.32. The mean differences for the remaining pairs are not significant.

We said above that the Tukey test places no limits on the number of comparisons that may be made with any set of data. By this we mean that the probability of finding a significant difference by chance at a given α level does not increase with each additional comparison, as it does in the case of t. When all population means are equal and a series of Tukey multiple-comparison tests such as the three *hsd* tests just reported are made at a given α level (let us say, .05), the probability is .05 that a Type I error will occur *anywhere* in the set of comparisons that are to be performed. Since the 5% significance level applies to the *total* experiment, and not just to individual comparisons, we can perform as many comparisons as we choose and remain confident that we are not increasing our chances of a Type I error.

Step-by-Step Procedures

One-Way ANOVA

We will illustrate the steps in conducting a one-way ANOVA by applying the technique to the results of a hypothetical experiment in which the effects of a drug designed to improve the memory of patients with Alzheimer's disease was tested. Group 1, the control group, received a pill with an inactive substance, whereas groups 2, 3, and 4 received pills with three levels of dosage of the drug. There were five patients in each group. Table 12.6 presents the scores for the four groups of patients together with the X^2 value for each X. (Scores represent number of errors.)

Basic Data

1. Find for each separate group ΣX, ΣX^2, and N.
2. By summing the appropriate figures for each of the groups, find ΣX, ΣX^2, and N_{tot}. These values are shown in Table 12.6.

Table 12.6 Preliminary Steps in the Analysis of Variance of Effectiveness of Drug Dosage on Number of Errors on a Memory Task Made by Alzheimer Patients

Group 1: Control		Group 2: Low		Group 3: Medium		Group 4: High	
X_1	X_1^2	X_2	X_2^2	X_3	X_3^2	X_4	X_4^2
16	256						
8	64	24	576	8	64	28	784
28	784	24	576	36	1296	8	64
24	576	16	256	16	256	20	400
48	2304	12	144	20	400	8	64
8	64	32	1024	24	576	8	64
$\sum X_1 = 132$	$\sum X_1^2 = 4048$	$\sum X_2 = 108$	$\sum X_2^2 = 2576$	$\sum X_3 = 104$	$\sum X_3^2 = 2592$	$\sum X_4 = 72$	$\sum X_4^2 = 1376$

$$\sum_{tot} X = \sum X_1 + \sum X_2 + \sum X_3 + \sum X_4 = 132 + 108 + 104 + 72 = 416$$

$$\sum_{tot} X^2 = \sum X_1^2 + \sum X_2^2 + \sum X_3^2 + \sum X_4^2 = 4048 + 2576 + 2592 + 1376 = 10592$$

$$N_{tot} = N_1 + N_2 + N_3 + N_4 = 6 + 5 + 5 + 5 = 21$$

Calculational Steps

The SS's are first calculated as follows:

3. $SS_{tot} = \left(\sum_{tot} X^2 \right) - \dfrac{\left(\sum_{tot} X \right)^2}{N_{tot}}$

$= 10592 - \dfrac{(416)^2}{21} = 10592 - 8240.76$

$= 2351.24$

4. $SS_{bg} = \sum_{g} \left[\dfrac{(\sum X_g)^2}{N_g} \right] - \dfrac{\left(\sum_{tot} X \right)^2}{N_{tot}}$

$= \left[\dfrac{(132)^2}{6} + \dfrac{(108)^2}{5} + \dfrac{(104)^2}{5} + \dfrac{(72)^2}{5} \right] - \dfrac{(416)^2}{21}$

$= 8436.80 - 8240.76$

$= 196.04$

5. $SS_{wg} = SS_{tot} - SS_{bg}$

$= 2351.24 - 196.04$

$= 2155.20$

   OR

$SS_{wg} = \sum_{g} \left[(\sum X_g^2) - \dfrac{(\sum X_g)^2}{N_g} \right]$

$= \left(4048 - \dfrac{132^2}{6} \right) + \left(2576 - \dfrac{108^2}{5} \right) + \left(2592 - \dfrac{104^2}{5} \right) + \left(1376 - \dfrac{72^2}{5} \right)$

$= 1144 + 243.2 + 428.8 + 339.2$

$= 2155.20$

Then df's and MS's are found as follows:

6. $df_{bg} = k - 1 = 4 - 1 = 3$

7. $df_{wg} = N_{tot} - k = 21 - 4 = 17$

8. $MS_{bg} = \dfrac{SS_{bg}}{df_{bg}} = \dfrac{196.04}{3}$

$= 65.35$

9. $MS_{wg} = \dfrac{SS_{wg}}{df_{wg}} = \dfrac{2155.20}{17}$

$= 126.78$

Table 12.7 Summary of the Analysis of Variance of the Experiment on Effects of Drug Dosage on Memory

Source of variation	SS	df	MS	F	p
Between groups	196.04	3	65.35	.52	>.05
Within groups	2155.20	17	126.78		
Total	2351.24	20			

Finally, the F is obtained and its significance determined:

10. $F = \dfrac{MS_{bg}}{MS_{wg}} = \dfrac{65.35}{126.78} = .52$

11. Looking in Table F for the case where $df_{bg} = 3$ and $df_{wg} = 17$, we find that F must be 3.20 or greater to be significant at the 5% level, and 5.18 or greater to be significant at the 1% level.

12. Our F of .52 is not significant, since it is much less than the F of 3.20 required for significance at the 5% level. In fact, as Table F shows, no F below 1 is significant regardless of the df values. Therefore, we cannot reject the null hypothesis that the groups come from populations with the same μ.

13. Summarize the results of the ANOVA, listing the SS's, df's, MS's, F, and the p value of F. This has been done in Table 12.7.

Tukey *Honestly Significant Difference (hsd)* test

We will illustrate the computation of the *hsd* test by applying it to the results of the following experiment. Individuals who sought help because they became extremely tense and upset in stress situations were assigned to one of three therapeutic treatments: systematic relaxation (SR), biofeedback (B), or tranquillizing drug (D). There were 20 individuals per group. Twenty additional individuals were assigned to a wait-list control condition (C), in which no treatment was given during the duration of the experiment. Thus there were four groups, each of 20 persons. After four weeks, a measure of stress tolerance was obtained from each participant. (High scores indicate greater tolerance.) An ANOVA, conducted to compare the efficacy of the methods, yielded a significant F.

We illustrate below the application of the Tukey *hsd* test to the results so that the locus of these significant effects can be determined. The *hsd* formula is:

$$hsd = q_\alpha \sqrt{\dfrac{MS_{wg}}{N_g}}$$

Determine the X̄'s of the Groups, and from the ANOVA MS$_{wg}$, df$_{wg}$, k (Number of Groups), and N$_g$ (Number per Group):

Assume that we have determined these values to be as follows:

$$\overline{X}_{SR} = 44.3 \quad \overline{X}_B = 52.4 \quad \overline{X}_D = 43.9 \quad \overline{X}_C = 34.8$$

$$MS_{wg} = 65.6 \quad df_{wg} = N_{tot} - k = 76 \quad k = 4 \quad N_g = 20$$

Determine q_α:

The value of q_α at $\alpha = .05$ or $.01$ is determined from Table G.

The Table is Entered with df_{wg} and k.

We enter Table G with $df_{wg} = 76$ and $k = 4$. As our df_{wg} is not tabled, we find the values of q_α associated with the closest df_{wg} below 76, which is 60. For $df_{wg} = 60$ and $k = 4$,

$$q_{.05} = 3.74 \quad \text{and} \quad q_{.01} = 4.59$$

Enter the Values at a Given α Level into the *hsd* Formula:

For $\alpha = .05$:

$$hsd = q_{.05} \sqrt{\frac{MS_{wg}}{N_g}}$$

$$= 3.74 \sqrt{\frac{65.6}{20}} = 3.74(1.81)$$

$$= 6.77$$

If we decide to use $\alpha = .01$, then:

$$hsd = 4.59 \sqrt{\frac{65.6}{20}} = 4.59(1.81)$$

$$= 8.31$$

Differences between $\overline{X}$'s that equal or exceed these *hsd* values are significant at the given α level.

Find the Absolute Difference between Pairs of $\overline{X}$'s:

Find the differences and display them in a table such as the one below. Note that for ease of interpretation, we have ordered the groups from high to low in terms of the magnitude of their $\overline{X}$'s: C, D, SB, B. We have not included a row for the differences for the $\overline{X}$ first in order (C) or a column for the differences for the $\overline{X}$ last in order (B) because their inclusion would have resulted in duplicate entries.

	$\overline{X}_C$	$\overline{X}_D$	$\overline{X}_{SR}$
$\overline{X}_D$	9.1**		
$\overline{X}_{SR}$	9.5**	.4	
$\overline{X}_B$	17.5**	8.5*	8.1*

*$p < .05$ **$p < .01$.

Compare the Differences between $\overline{X}$'s with the Value of hsd at a Given α Level to Determine Which Pairs Differ Significantly:

In our example, at $\alpha = .05$, the difference between $\overline{X}_{SR}$ and $\overline{X}_D$ is less than $hsd = 6.77$. They therefore do not differ significantly. However, there is a significant difference between all other pairs.

At $\alpha = .01$, $hsd = 8.31$. The difference between the control group and each of the treatment groups is significant, but all other comparisons are nonsignificant. The significant differences at each α level are indicated in the table by a single ($p < .05$) or double ($p < .01$) asterisk.

Computation of $\hat{\omega}^2$

To illustrate the computation of $\hat{\omega}^2$ we will use the data from the attitude experiment described earlier in which students read a statement favorable to a raise in tuition written by a student, a favorable statement written by the university president or a statement on an irrelevant topic. As shown in Table 12.4, the ANOVA produced a significant F of 4.50. The items of information we need are found in Tables 12.3 and 12.4 and are repeated below.

$$SS_{bg} = 2420 \qquad MS_{wg} = 268.9$$

$$SS_{tot} = 9680 \qquad k = 3$$

$$\hat{\omega}^2 = \frac{SS_{bg} - (k - 1)MS_{wg}}{SS_{tot} + MS_{wg}} = \frac{2420 - (3 - 1)268.9}{9680 + 268.9}$$

$$= \frac{1882.2}{9448.1} = .19$$

Our calculated value of $\hat{\omega}^2$ tells us that approximately 20% of the variability in attitude scores was explained by the type of statement that students read before answering the attitude questionnaire. The effect size is relatively high in magnitude. ■

DEFINITIONS OF TERMS AND SYMBOLS

One-way analysis of variance (ANOVA). A statistical technique for testing the null hypothesis that two or more samples come from populations with the same μ's.

Total variability. In a study involving two or more groups, the variability of the scores from the overall mean of the total set of scores ($\overline{X}_{tot}$).

Variability within groups. The variability of scores from the mean of the particular group to which the scores belong.

Variability between groups. The variability of the group $\overline{X}$'s from the overall mean ($\overline{X}_{tot}$).

Total sum of squares (SS_{tot}). The sum of the squared deviations of the scores from the overall mean ($\overline{X}_{tot}$). The total sum of squares can be broken down into two components: the sum of squares within groups and the sum of squares between groups.

Sum of squares within groups (SS_{wg}). The sum of the squared deviations of the individual scores from the mean of the group to which they belong.

Sum of squares between groups (SS_{bg}). The sum of the squared deviations of the group $\overline{X}$'s from $\overline{X}_{tot}$.

Mean square (MS). A mean square (MS) is an unbiased estimate of the population variance, obtained by dividing a sum of squares by its corresponding degrees of freedom.

Mean square within groups (MS_{wg}). The within-groups MS or variance is obtained by dividing SS_{wg} by df_{wg} where df_{wg} equals the total number of scores minus the number of groups ($N_{tot} - k$).

Mean square between groups (MS_{bg}). The between-groups MS or variance is obtained by dividing SS_{bg} by df_{bg} where df_{bg} equals number of groups minus one ($k - 1$).

F ratio. The F ratio in a one-way analysis of variance is defined as MS_{bg}/MS_{wg}. The value of F is compared with the critical value of F for df_{bg} and df_{wg} at $\alpha = .05$ or $.01$ to evaluate the null hypothesis that population means are equal.

Assumptions of analysis of variance. The analysis of variance for independent groups asssumes that (a) each of the populations from which the groups were drawn is normally distributed, (b) the variances (σ^2 values) of the populations are equal, and (c) the members of each group have been randomly and independently selected from their respective populations. If any of these assumptions is seriously violated, the analysis of variance technique should not be applied.

Tukey honestly significant difference (hsd) test. The *hsd* test is an example of a multiple-comparison test used following analysis of variance to determine the significance of the difference between pairs of $\overline{X}$'s or pairs of subsets of $\overline{X}$'s. The value of the *hsd* statistic at a given α level gives the minimal difference between pairs of $\overline{X}$'s that is significant at that α level.

PROBLEMS

In all problems requiring computation of an analysis of variance (ANOVA) show all your computational steps and place the results in a summary table. For ease of computation, round off SS's to the nearest whole number, MS's to the first decimal place, and F's to the second decimal place.

1. In a study on the effects of object orientation on identification of shape, three groups of five subjects each were shown a series of pairs of common objects in a special viewing apparatus. In each pair, one of the objects was shown in a normal, upright position. For one group of subjects (group 1), the second member of each pair was tilted 45 degrees from upright. For group 2, it was tilted 90 degrees, and for the group 3 it was upside down (180 degrees from upright). For each pair, subjects pressed a button as soon as they determined whether the tilted figure was on the right or left, the time being recorded from exposure of the stimulus pair to the button press. The

total reaction time (in seconds) over the series of pairs was determined for each subject. The sums and sums of squares for each group are shown below.

$$\Sigma X_1 = 80 \qquad \Sigma X_2 = 64 \qquad \Sigma X_3 = 51 \qquad N_g = 5$$

$$\Sigma X_1^2 = 1300 \qquad \Sigma X_2^2 = 852 \qquad \Sigma X_3^2 = 535$$

(a) Determine the $\overline{X}$ for each group and then graph the $\overline{X}$'s.

(b) State the null hypothesis to be tested by means of a one-way analysis of variance. Be specific, describing H_0 for this specific experiment.

(c) Conduct the appropriate ANOVA.

(d) After considering the outcome of the ANOVA and the $\overline{X}$'s graphed in (a), describe your conclusions about the effect of object orientation.

2. Compute $\hat{\omega}^2$ for the data in problem 1. Come to a conclusion about effect size in this experiment. (Check your calculations in problem 1 with the answer on page 381.)

3. An educational psychologist teaches a large introductory course in which students also participate in smaller discussion sections. He decides to experiment with different ways to conduct the discussion sections and assigns the 120 students at random to four equal sections, each taught by a different method. At the end of the course, the students' final examination scores are analyzed. The results of the ANOVA are summarized below. Also shown are the means for each of the four groups of 30.

Source	df	MS	F
Between groups	3	94.73	3.47*
Within groups	116	27.30	
Total	119		

*$p < .05$.

$$\overline{X}_1 = 81.5 \qquad \overline{X}_2 = 80.3 \qquad \overline{X}_3 = 88.3 \qquad \overline{X}_4 = 85.9$$

Perform a follow-up analysis of the means of the individual method groups with $\alpha = .05$. What do you conclude?

4. Three experiments were conducted, each involving three or more groups. For each experiment, the mean, median, and range of scores are shown below for each of the experimental groups. From the information given, does it appear that one or more assumptions underlying analysis of variance is violated? If your answer is yes, specify the assumption(s).

(a)

Group	$\overline{X}$	Mdn	Range
1	62	67	53–72
2	72	74	60–83
3	81	89	73–92

(b)

Group	$\overline{X}$	Mdn	Range
1	104	106	85–126
2	98	97	79–116
3	108	109	88–127
4	115	113	95–134

(c)

Group	$\overline{X}$	Mdn	Range
1	25	23	18–29
2	28	29	17–39
3	31	31	15–45

13

Two-Way Analysis of Variance

- MAIN EFFECTS AND INTERACTION IN ANALYSIS OF VARIANCE
- COMPUTATIONAL STEPS IN TWO-WAY ANALYSIS OF VARIANCE FOR EQUAL N's

All the types of experiments we have considered so far have involved two or more groups differing with respect to some single independent variable. In a good many experiments, however, the investigator studies simultaneously the effects of more than one independent variable. For example, in a study of the effects of hormones on animal development, we might have four groups of male animals who are 1, 7, 14, or 21 days old and divide each of these groups into three subgroups, injected with hormone dosages of 0, 2, or 6 units. This general arrangement, in which we study the effects of two or more variables, is known as a *factorial design*. In this chapter we will be considering the analysis of variance appropriate for data from experiments employing a double classification or *two-way* factorial design—that is, experiments in which two variables are simultaneously manipulated.

We have seen that experiments investigating a single variable need not compare only two groups but may involve any number. Similarly, there is no limit to the number of groups representing each variable in a two-way factorial study. In our animal experiment, for example, we suggested studying four age groups and three dosage levels, a design calling for 4×3, or 12, independent groups. We could extend our study to include more conditions within each variable, such as 1, 2, 7, 14, 21, and 28 days of age and dosages of 0, 2, 6, or 10 units, thus calling for 6×4, or 24, groups. As we increase the number of specific conditions within each type of variable, the total number of groups that needs to be tested to form a complete factorial design increases quite drastically, requiring considerable time and effort to conduct the experiment. However, the logic of the two-way design and the statistical methods we use to analyze the experimental results remain the same, whatever the number of experimental conditions within each of the variables.

There are two reasons why investigators employ factorial designs in which the effects of two or more independent variables are studied. The first is quite obvious. In most situations, behavior is influenced by many factors, and investigators may be interested in the possible effects of more than one variable. It is often more efficient to investigate several variables in a single experiment than one at a time in different experiments. The second reason is not so apparent. Variables combine or *interact* in various ways to determine a dependent variable and it is very important to determine the nature of this interaction.

Before amplifying these remarks, we should introduce some terminology. We will refer to the two kinds of conditions being investigated as *variables*, using the letters A and B as identifying labels. The specific experimental conditions employed in investigating each of the variables we will identify by the numerals 1, 2, 3, and so on to the *m*th condition for the A variable or to the *n*th condition for the B variable.

Many of the variables investigators wish to study involve some kind of quantifiable dimension such as time, distance, or amount, so that the specific conditions being investigated can be rank-ordered in magnitude from least to most, and the numerals 1, 2, 3, and so forth used to reflect this order. Often, however, the variables we study involve two or more discrete categories or types of conditions. We may, for example, be interested in comparing several different kinds of teaching methods, persons of different nationalities, men versus women, and so on. In these instances, the groups or conditions obviously cannot be rank-ordered along some dimension, so our use of identifying numerical labels is purely nominative, the assignment of number to group being completely arbitrary.

MAIN EFFECTS
AND INTERACTION IN ANALYSIS
OF VARIANCE

Application of the analysis of variance technique to the data from a two-way factorial experiment allows us to make three kinds of statements about our results: (1) the effects on our dependent measure of the different conditions of variable A, independent of variations in B conditions (*main effects of A*), (2) the effects of the different conditions of variable B, independent of variations in A conditions (*main effects of B*), and (3) the joint effects or *interaction* of variables A and B. Rather than proceeding directly to the statistical steps that will allow us to make these comparisons, we first will explain what each of them involves.

Table 13.1 presents the results of three hypothetical experiments employing 2×2, 2×3, and 3×3 factorial designs, respectively, with equal N's per group in each experiment. The numbers entered in the cells are the means obtained for each of the specific groups. For each table we have also reported the mean of all the cases represented in each column and in each row. For example, in the 3×3 experiment whose results are reported in Table 13.1, we added together the scores of all individuals tested under the first A condition (A1), whatever their B condition, and divided the sum by 15, the total number of A1 subjects. This yielded a mean of 30.0, as shown at the right of the A1 row. (Since the N's in each cell of the table are equal, we could also get the row mean by averaging the three A1 cell means.) The means of all the A2 groups and of all the A3 groups, shown at the right of the second and third rows, were obtained in a similar fashion, as were the column means, shown at the bottom of the table. These column values, of course, are the means of all 15 of the cases tested under the B1, B2, and B3 conditions, respectively, whatever their A condition.

Main Effects

Determination of the main effects of variable A and variable B by means of a two-way analysis of variance (ANOVA) involves testing a particular null hypothesis about the row $\overline{X}$'s and about the column $\overline{X}$'s. Each of these hypotheses states that the means of the populations from which the samples were drawn are all equal. Thus, in the case of the A variable, H_0 states that each A group, averaged over all B groups, is drawn from a population with the same mean ($\mu_{A1} = \mu_{A2} = \cdots = \mu_{Am}$) and that therefore any differences among the $\overline{X}$'s of the A groups (row $\overline{X}$'s) are due to chance factors.

For example, in the third experiment reported at the bottom of Table 13.1, observe that the mean of all the subjects in the A1 condition (ignoring their B condition) was 30.0. Similarly, the subjects in the A2 condition had a mean of 33.3 and the subjects in the A3 condition had a mean of 37.0. Our H_0 is that the three A groups came from populations with the same μ's. This hypothesis implies that the variations in the A condition have no differential effects on our dependent measure, with the obtained differences among $\overline{X}$'s (row $\overline{X}$'s) being due to chance factors. Similarly, H_0 for variable B states that each B group, averaged over all A groups, is drawn from a population with the same mean ($\mu_{B1} = \mu_{B2} = \cdots = \mu_{Bn}$) and that any differences among the $\overline{X}$'s of the B groups (column $\overline{X}$'s) are therefore due to chance.

Table 13.1 Two-Way Tables Showing Means for Hypothetical 2 × 2, 2 × 3, and 3 × 3 Factorial Experiments, with Equal N's per Group

I. 2 × 2, N per group = 20

		Variable B		$\overline{X}_{row}$	N_{row}
		1	2	$\overline{X}_{row}$	N_{row}
Variable A	1	20	27	23.5	40
	2	26	18	22.0	40
$\overline{X}_{col}$		23.0	22.5		
N_{col}		40	40		

II. 2 × 3, N per group = 10

		Variable B			$\overline{X}_{row}$	N_{row}
		1	2	3	$\overline{X}_{row}$	N_{row}
Variable A	1	3	7	8	6	30
	2	5	9	10	8	30
$\overline{X}_{col}$		4	8	9		
N_{col}		20	20	20		

III. 3 × 3, N per group = 5

		Variable B			$\overline{X}_{row}$	N_{row}
		1	2	3	$\overline{X}_{row}$	N_{row}
	1	29	30	31	30.0	15
Variable A	2	30	34	36	33.3	15
	3	31	38	42	37.0	15
$\overline{X}_{col}$		30.0	34.0	36.3		
N_{col}		15	15	15		

A method of testing these null hypotheses may occur to you immediately. In comparing the means of the A groups (row $\overline{X}$'s), why not ignore the B variable and consider all those tested under the same A condition (all those in the same row) as forming a single group? Then we could perform a one-way analysis of variance of the A groups, following the procedures outlined in Chapter 12. Another one-way ANOVA could then be performed in the same way on the column data, allowing us to test the null hypothesis about the means of the B groups. In conducting this type of analysis, you will recall, we find an F ratio that compares the relative size of two measures of variability: the variability between the means of the groups and the variability within each of the groups, the latter being due to uncontrolled, unidentified factors such as original differences in ability among our subjects, and identified as the error term. If the between-groups measure is sufficiently larger than the within-groups measure, we reject the null hypothesis.

However, if we were to perform these one-way analyses of variance on the data from a two-way experiment, we would run into a major problem. Our measure of within-groups variability for the A (row) variable would reflect differences among the subjects in each row that are due not only to uncontrolled, unidentified factors, but also to any systematic effect of variations in B (column) conditions. In like manner, our within-groups measure for the column data would reflect any differences among subjects due to the effects of variations in A conditions (rows). These systematic effects would inflate each of the measures of within-group variability and hence decrease the size of the F ratio. To avoid this complication, we modify our approach by computing a *single* within-groups measure based on each of our separate experimental groups—that is, within each *cell* of our two-way table. We then obtain our F ratios for the main effects of variables A and B by dividing each of our measures of between-groups variability (one between column $\overline{X}$'s, the other between row $\overline{X}$'s) by this single error term or measure of within-groups (within-cells) variability.

Interaction Between Variables

We have said that the reason we conduct a factorial study is not simply to investigate the main effects of more than one variable. One of the major advantages of the factorial experiment is that it allows us to study the *joint effects* of the two variables, how the variables combine or *interact* to influence our response measure.

The ways in which variables can combine are numerous. One simple type of combination is an *additive* one—a combination of the form A + B. The data from the hypothetical 2 × 3 experiment reported in Table 13.1 illustrate this type of combination. We can most easily explain an additive relationship by referring to the graphic presentation of these data in Figure 13.1. We have shown the three B conditions along the baseline and have plotted the means of the three A1 groups and the three A2 groups in separate curves. As you can see by inspection,

Figure 13.1 Graph of $\overline{X}$'s from 2 × 3 experiment of Table 13.1 illustrating additive combination of effects.

the curves for the A1 and A2 groups are *parallel*. This fact indicates that the magnitude of the effect of the A variable is the *same* for each condition of B. An alternate way of describing this type of relationship is to state that the difference in $\overline{X}$'s between A1 and A2 groups tested under the same B condition is the same for each of the B conditions. In this example, as you can easily see from the values reported in Table 13.1, the difference in $\overline{X}$'s (A2 − A1) at each level of B is 2 ($5 − 3 = 2$, $9 − 7 = 2$, $10 − 8 = 2$). We could have graphed the data the other way around, representing the two A conditions along the baseline and plotting the means of the B1, B2, and B3 groups in separate curves. As you may determine for yourself by graphing the data in this manner, the three curves would again turn out to be parallel. You can also see that this would be so by examining the means of groups shown in Table 13.1. The difference between the $\overline{X}$'s of any given pair of B groups (1 versus 2, 2 versus 3, or 1 versus 3) is the same whatever the A condition under which the pair was tested. For B1 versus B2, for example, the difference at both levels of A is 4, while for B_2 versus B_3, a new but constant difference of 1 occurs at both levels of A, and so on.

The data from the 2 × 2 and 3 × 3 experiments reported in Table 13.1 are examples of two kinds of *nonadditive* combination, as can again be conveniently demonstrated by presenting their results graphically. Looking first at the data of the 3 × 3 experiment plotted in Figure 13.2, you will observe that the curves for the three A groups are not parallel; rather, they diverge. That is, the magnitude of the differences between the A groups becomes larger as one goes from B1 to B2 and from B2 to B3. Had the curves for the three B groups been plotted instead, these curves would also have been shown to diverge with changes in the A condition. This kind of interaction is often called an amplifier effect. That is, higher levels of A amplify or make larger the effects of B, and vice versa.

An example of a very complex type of nonadditive interaction is found in the data of the 2 × 2 experiment reported in Table 13.1. Scores are affected by both A and B conditions but, as you can see from the plot of the data in Figure 13.3, the *direction of* the effect of variation in the A condition is different for each B condition (and vice versa). Strange as it may seem at first glance, this type of crossover interaction, as it is called, occurs fairly frequently in psychological data. For example, individuals who are given a long list of very simple arithmetic problems to solve with instructions that emphasize the importance of speed may produce not only more answers in a given period of time, but more *correct* answers than individuals given

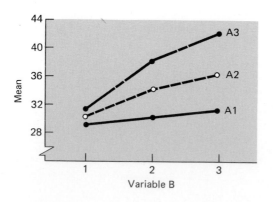

Figure 13.2 Graph of $\overline{X}$'s from 3 × 3 experiment of Table 13.1 illustrating an amplifier effect.

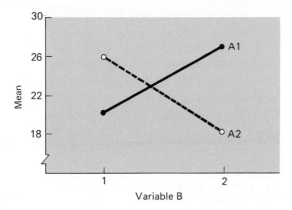

Figure 13.3 Graph of $\overline{X}$'s from 2 × 2 experiment of Table 13.1 illustrating a crossover interaction.

the same problems with instructions that emphasize the importance of accuracy more than speed. The same sets of instructions, however, may produce the *opposite* results with respect to correct responses when a list of complicated problems is used; individuals given speed instructions might make all sorts of errors in their attempt to hurry and therefore arrive at a smaller number of correct solutions than the group trying to be accurate. Thus, speed instructions may lead to either better or worse performance than accuracy instructions, depending on the type of problems employed; the direction of the effects of variations in A is dependent on the particular B condition under which subjects were tested.

One by-product of this type of complex interaction should be mentioned. Since the direction of the influence of one variable is dependent on the other variable, comparisons of the overall means of the various A groups, ignoring B conditions, or of the overall means of the B groups, ignoring A conditions, may reveal that neither variable has any significant main effect. You can see, for example, that in the 2 × 2 experiment shown in Table 13.1 the two column means are very similar in value, as are the two row means. We would not conclude, however, that neither variable has any kind of effect but rather, assuming that the relevant statistical term is significant, that the *direction* of the effects of one variable is dependent on the specific condition employed with respect to the second variable.

A major purpose in conducting a two-way factorial study, as we have said, is to determine how the two variables combine. The two-way ANOVA technique is of assistance in this process since it allows us to test a hypothesis about the nature of the interaction between the variables. The specific hypothesis being tested is that the variables combine in an *additive* fashion—that the magnitude of the effects of one variable is constant over all conditions of the second variable. Expressing this in another way, we test the hypothesis that the curves resulting from a plot of the $\overline{X}$'s of the groups are *parallel*. If the F ratio found for the interaction between variables A and B is nonsignificant at a given α level, we *accept* the hypothesis that the variables combine additively. If, on the other hand, the F for the interaction between variables is significant, we *reject* this hypothesis and conclude that the variables combine nonadditively. Versatile as the analysis of variance technique is, however, it cannot tell us in this latter instance precisely what kind of nonadditive relationship has occurred. This we must determine by inspection of our data. Plotting the $\overline{X}$'s, as we have in Figures 13.1 to 13.3, helps us to determine the form and meaning of the interaction.

In summary, then, a two-way analysis of variance yields F ratios that allow us to test the null hypothesis that μ's are equal concerning differences between the means of the A groups and between the means of the B groups—the *main effects* of each of the two variables—and a hypothesis concerning the *interaction* between the two variables: that they combine in an additive manner. We turn now to the computational steps involved in conducting such an analysis. We will present formulas only for the case in which all groups have the same N.*

COMPUTATIONAL STEPS IN TWO-WAY ANALYSIS OF VARIANCE FOR EQUAL N's

In describing the procedures employed in performing a two-way analysis of variance, we will omit the basic formulas defining the various sums of squares and present only the computational formulas, illustrating their application with the data from the hypothetical experiment shown in Table 13.2. In the experiment, six groups of male students in a business administration program were presented with one of six versions of a description of a 28-year-old midlevel manager that contained both personal and job relevant information. The students were told that next year, salary increases for persons at this level would be 5 to 15 percent, with an average of 10 percent, and asked to recommend a raise for the person whose description they had read. All descriptions were alike except that in three, the manager was a man and in the other three, the manager was a woman. Within each sex, one version described the person as single; in the other two versions, the person was described as married but childless or as married with two children. The experiment thus formed a 2×3 factorial design with five subjects in each of the six groups. The score obtained for each subject was the percent raise he recommended.

In Table 13.2 we have also reported the ΣX and ΣX^2 for each of the six groups in our hypothetical experiment, since these are the basic data entering into our calculations. We will find it convenient to have the ΣX values in each of the groups set up in a two-way table so that we can determine the sums for each column and row, as well as ΣX. This type of two-way table is also shown in Table 13.2.

Computational Steps in Finding SS's

You will remember that in performing a one-way analysis of variance on the data from a collection of k groups, we first find the total sum of squares, the SS for all the subjects in the experiment. We then proceed to break down SS_{tot} into two components: SS_{bg} and SS_{wg}. Our first step in analyzing the results of a two-way factorial experiment is to treat the data as a single collection of k groups and find SS_{tot}, SS_{bg}, and SS_{wg} using exactly the same procedures as

---

*The calculational procedures for a two-way ANOVA for unequal N's are lengthy and it is more convenient to do this and other complex analyses on a computer. Several well-known statistical packages for the computer are listed in Appendix I.

Table 13.2 Data from the Hypothetical Study of Salary Recommendations

Man (A1)						Woman (A2)					
Single		Married		Married-Ch		Single		Married		Married-Ch	
X	X²	X	X²	X	X²	X	X²	X	X²	X	X²
10	100	10	100	12	144	12	144	7	49	12	144
11	121	14	196	15	225	10	100	11	121	15	225
9	81	13	144	13	169	8	64	9	81	14	196
8	64	13	169	14	196	7	49	8	64	13	169
12	144	9	81	13	169	11	121	5	25	12	144
Sum 50	510	57	690	67	903	48	478	40	340	66	878

$$N_g = 5 \quad N_{tot} = 30$$

Summary of $\Sum X$ and $\Sum X^2$ values

		Status (Variable B)			
		1(S)	2(M)	3(M-C)	Sum
Sex	1 (Man)	50	57	67	174
(Variable A)	2 (Woman)	48	40	66	154
	Sum	98	97	133	328

$$\Sum X^2 = 510 + 690 + 903 + 478 + 340 + 878 = 3799$$

we employed in the the last chapter. Illustrating these procedures* with the data from our 2 × 3 experiment in Table 13.2 (where $k = mn = 6$), we thus have:

$$SS_{tot} = \left(\sum_{tot} X^2\right) - \frac{\left(\sum_{tot} X\right)^2}{N_{tot}} \tag{13.1}$$

$$= 3799 - \frac{(328)^2}{30} = 3799 - 3586.13$$

$$= 212.87$$

$$SS_{bg} = \sum_{g} \left[\frac{\sum (X_g)^2}{N_g}\right] - \frac{\left(\sum_{tot} X\right)^2}{N_{tot}} \tag{13.2}$$

Since the N's in each group are the same, Formula 13.2 can be rewritten for our 2 × 3 experiment as:

$$SS_{bg} = \left[\frac{(\sum X_{A1B1})^2 + (\sum X_{A1B2})^2 + (\sum X_{A1B3})^2 + \cdots + (\sum X_{A2B3})^2}{N_g}\right] - \frac{\left(\sum_{tot} X\right)^2}{N_{tot}} \tag{13.3}$$

*Note that Formulas 13.1 to 13.4 parallel Formulas 12.4 to 12.7.

where N_g = the number of subjects in each cell. Notice that the final term, $(\sum X)^2_{tot}/N_{tot}$, is the same as in Formula 13.1. Thus:

$$SS_{bg} = \left[\frac{(50)^2 + (57)^2 + (67)^2 + (48)^2 + (40)^2 + (66)^2}{5} \right] - 3586.13$$

$$= \frac{18498}{5} - 3586.13 = 113.47$$

We now proceed to find SS_{wg}:

$$SS_{wg} = SS_{tot} - SS_{bg} \tag{13.4}$$
$$= 212.87 - 113.47 = 99.40$$

We remind you that we could also have computed SS_{wg} directly rather than by subtraction, using the formula:

$$SS_{wg} = \sum_g \left[(\sum X_g^2) - \frac{(\sum X_g)^2}{N_g} \right] \tag{13.5}$$

The SS_{wg} we have just determined is based on the variability within each of our six experimental groups—within each *cell* of our two-way table. As we discussed earlier, we will use this SS_{wg} to obtain a measure of within-groups variability against which to assess the main effects of both variable A and variable B. This same measure is also used in determining the F for the interaction of the variables.

The SS_{bg} that we have computed, however, is not of direct interest to us, since it is based on the variability among the means of all our independent groups, considered as a single collection of *k* groups. This variability among the *k* means comes from three sources: (a) differences in the $\overline{X}$'s of the A groups (row means); (b) differences in the $\overline{X}$'s of the B groups (column means); and (c) the interaction between variables A and B—that is, any departure from an additive combination of the two variables.

Since it is these sources of variability that concern us, we now proceed to break down SS_{bg} and find the SS's for its three components: SS_A, SS_B, and the interaction, $SS_{A \times B}$.

Sum of Squares for Variable A (SS_A). The sum of squares for variable A, assuming an equal N in each A condition, is determined by the formula:

$$SS_A = \frac{(\sum X_{A1})^2 + (\sum X_{A2})^2 + \cdots + (\sum X_{Am})^2}{N_A} - \left[\frac{\left(\sum_{tot} X \right)^2}{N_{tot}} \right] \tag{13.6}$$

where N_A = number in each A condition.

This formula indicates that we first find the sum of all the individuals tested under the A1 condition (the $\sum X$ of the A1 row) and square this sum. We then find the same quantity for each of the other A groups, on to the last or mth A group. We then add these quantities together and divide the sum by N_A, the number of cases in each of the A conditions. Then we subtract the value $(\Sigma X)^2_{tot} / N_{tot}$. Be sure to note that the latter quantity appears in the formula for SS_{tot} and SS_{bg} so that its value has already been determined.

In our illustrative experiment, there were two A conditions (sex of manager), each based on a total of 15 cases, 5 each from the B1, B2, and B3 conditions. Thus:

$$SS_A = \left[\frac{(\Sigma X_{A1})^2 + (\Sigma X_{A2})^2}{N_A} \right] - \frac{\left(\underset{tot}{\Sigma X} \right)^2}{N_{tot}}$$

$$= \left[\frac{(174)^2 + (154)^2}{15} \right] - 3586.13$$

$$= 3599.47 - 3586.13 = 13.14$$

Sum of Squares for Variable B (SS_B). The SS_B is determined in a parallel manner:

$$SS_B = \left[\frac{(\Sigma X_{B1})^2 + (\Sigma X_{B2})^2 + \cdots + (\Sigma X_{Bn})^2}{N_B} \right] - \frac{\left(\underset{tot}{\Sigma X} \right)^2}{N_{tot}} \tag{13.7}$$

where N_B = number of each B condition.

For the three B (status) groups of our experiment, we thus have:

$$SS_B = \left[\frac{(98)^2 + (97)^2 + (133)^2}{10} \right] - 3586.13$$

$$= 3670.20 - 3586.13 = 84.07$$

Sum of Squares for Interaction ($SS_{A \times B}$). You will recall that SS_{bg} can be divided into three components, representing the SSs for variable A, variable B, and the A × B interaction. Since we have already computed SS_{bg}, SS_A, and SS_B, we can obtain the SS for interaction by subtraction:

$$SS_{A \times B} = SS_{bg} - SS_A - SS_B \tag{13.8}$$

For our experiment:

$$SS_{A \times B} = (113.47) - (13.14) - (84.07) = 16.26$$

Although SS for interaction is typically obtained by subtraction, it may be computed directly by the following basic formula:

$$SS_{A \times B} = N_g \left[\sum_g (\overline{X}_{AB} - \overline{X}_A - \overline{X}_B + \overline{X}_{tot})^2 \right] \tag{13.9}$$

where N_g = number of cases per group, $\overline{X}_{AB}$ = the mean of a particular group, $\overline{X}_A$ = the mean of all the cases tested under the same A condition as this group (row $\overline{X}$), $\overline{X}_B$ = the mean of all cases tested under the same B condition as this group (column $\overline{X}$), and $\overline{X}_{tot}$ = the mean of all the cases. We will leave the application of this formula to the data of Table 13.2 as an exercise for those curious enough to find out that it does indeed yield the same value as we obtained by subtraction. Remember that the hypothesis being tested concerning the A × B interaction is that the two variables combine additively. If the variables combined in perfect additive fashion, we would expect no variability due to interaction and hence that $SS_{A \times B}$ would be equal to zero. This implies in turn that the term $(\overline{X}_{AB} - \overline{X}_A - \overline{X}_B + \overline{X}_{tot})^2$ in our formula for $SS_{A \times B}$ would be zero for each AB group. We may demonstrate this by applying the formula to the data from the 2 × 3 experiment of Table 13.1, which, as we saw earlier, were an example of a perfect additive relationship between variables. The grand mean for all of them is 7. Applying our formula to these data gives us:

$$SS_{A \times B} = N_g \left[\sum_g (\overline{X}_{AB} - \overline{X}_A - \overline{X}_B + \overline{X}_{tot})^2 \right]$$

$$= 10[(3 - 6 - 4 + 7)^2 + (7 - 6 - 8 + 7)^2 + (8 - 6 - 9 + 7)^2$$
$$+ (5 - 8 - 4 + 7)^2 + (9 - 8 - 8 + 7)^2 + (10 - 8 - 9 + 7)^2]$$

$$= 10(0)$$

$$= 0$$

Computation of MS's and *df*'s

Having determined the SS within groups and the SS's between A groups, between B groups, and the A × B interaction, the three components making up SS_{bg}, we now can find the variance or mean square (MS) for each of these sources of variability. Just as we stated in the last chapter, these MS's are found by dividing each SS by its *df*. Thus:

$$MS_A = \frac{SS_A}{df_A} \tag{13.10}$$

where $df_A = m - 1$ (the number of A groups minus one).

$$MS_B = \frac{SS_B}{df_B}$$

where $df_B = n - 1$ (the number of B groups minus one).

$$MS_{A \times B} = \frac{SS_{A \times B}}{df_{A \times B}}$$

where $df_{A \times B} = (m - 1)(n - 1)$ or $(df_A)(df_B)$.

$$MS_{wg} = \frac{SS_{wg}}{df_{wg}}$$

where $df_{wg} = N_{tot} - (m)(n)$ [the total number of cases minus the total number of groups—that is, A groups $\times$ B groups].

We should also note that the df for SS_{tot} is equal to $N_{tot} - 1$. Since SS_{tot} is composed of SS_{wg}, SS_A, SS_B, and $SS_{A \times B}$, the dfs for these four components, when summed, equal the total df or $N_{tot} - 1$.

Applying these formulas to the data of our illustrative experiment shown in Table 13.2, we find the following df's:

$$df_A = m - 1 = 2 - 1 = 1$$
$$df_B = n - 1 = 3 - 1 = 2$$
$$df_{A \times B} = (m - 1)(n - 1) = (1)(2) = 2$$
$$df_{wg} = N_{tot} - (m)(n) = 30 - (2)(3) = 24$$

The df_{tot} in our experiment is equal to $30 - 1$ or 29, and you will observe that the four df's obtained above do indeed add up to this number.

The MS's are thus:

$$MS_A = \frac{SS_A}{df_A} = \frac{13.14}{1} = 13.14$$

$$MS_B = \frac{SS_B}{df_B} = \frac{84.07}{2} = 42.03$$

$$MS_{A \times B} = \frac{SS_{A \times B}}{df_{A \times B}} = \frac{16.26}{2} = 8.13$$

$$MS_{wg} = \frac{SS_{wg}}{df_{wg}} = \frac{99.40}{24} = 4.14$$

Computation of F Ratios

Finally we compute F ratios by dividing the MS's for A, B, and the A $\times$ B interaction by MS_{wg}. To illustrate:

$$F_A = \frac{MS_A}{MS_{wg}} \qquad (13.11)$$

$$= \frac{13.14}{4.14} = 3.17$$

$$F_B = \frac{MS_B}{MS_{wg}}$$

$$= \frac{42.03}{4.14} = 10.15$$

$$F_{A \times B} = \frac{MS_{A \times B}}{MS_{wg}}$$

$$= \frac{8.13}{4.14} = 1.96$$

The results of our calculations of the various values of SS, *df*, MS, and F are summarized in Table 13.3. Now all that remains is to evaluate each F ratio by comparing it with the value of F at the 5% or the 1% level of significance associated with the appropriate *df*'s, as listed in Table F (see pages 358–60). Looking at this table, we find that with 1 and 24 *df*, the *df*'s associated with the F for variable A, a value of 4.26 is required at $\alpha = 0.5$. Since our obtained F is 3.17, we conclude that the A (sex) groups did not significantly differ at the 5% level and that the observed differences in the means for men and women in our experiment were due to chance. We cannot reject the H_0 that the population means for salary recommendations are the same for the male and female managers. For 2 and 24 *df*, $F_{.05} = 3.40$ and $F_{.01} = 5.61$. Since we obtained an F of 10.15 for variable B (status), we reject H_0 at the 1% level. Inspection of the data in Table 13.2 suggests that this significant F came about because salary recommendations were higher for married individuals with children than for the other two groups. Finally, the $F_{A \times B}$ of 1.96 fell short of $F_{.05} = 3.40$, leading us to conclude that there was not a significant departure from an additive relationship between variables A and B. The *p* of each F, in terms of whether it reaches or fails to reach the 5% or 1% level, is shown in the final column of Table 13.3.

Graphing the Data

An important final step is to calculate the means of the six groups from the data in Table 13.2 and to graph them as shown in Figure 13.4. In fact, we might graph the $\overline{X}$'s first, before computing the ANOVA, to give us an idea of what it might reveal. The graph allows us to see clearly that on average, the married man and woman with children were recommended for the highest raise. Inspection of the graph also suggests the presence of an interaction, the married woman without children being recommended for a lesser raise than the single woman and the married man without children being recommended for a greater raise than the single man. However, the nonsignificant F suggests that this observed departure from additivity may have come about because of chance effects.

It is possible that there is actually an interaction in the population of the sort we found and our F was not significant because of the small N's in each group. N, you recall, is related to the power of a test to detect a false H_0. With a larger N, we might have obtained significance. We cannot know this, however, without repeating the experiment with a larger N and have no choice but to retain H_0. This observation serves as a reminder that we must be

Table 13.3 Summary of the Two-Way ANOVA of Effects on Salary Recommendations of Sex and Family Status

Source	SS	df	MS	F	p
Sex (A)	13.14	1	13.14	3.17	> .05
Status (B)	84.07	2	42.03	10.15	< .01
Interaction (A×B)	16.26	2	8.13	1.96	> .05
Within groups	99.40	24	4.14		
Total	212.87	29			

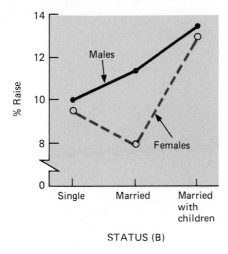

Figure 13.4 Mean salary recommendations for male and female managers who are either single, married without children, or married with children.

especially cautious in interpreting nonsignificant results. This is one reason why the statement that we "fail to reject H_0" is preferable to the statement that we "accept H_0" when we obtain nonsignificant results.

Follow-Up Tests

Tukey hsd.   If one or more of the F values are significant, we may want to make further comparisons to determine precisely which groups or conditions contributed to the significant differences. This may be done by comparing $\overline{X}$'s by the Tukey *hsd* discussed in Chapter 12. The only new idea to note is that in a two-way ANOVA, the number of experimental groups, k, in Table G is equal to m times n (i.e., number of A groups × number of B groups) for any *hsd* test comparing two groups.

To illustrate the use of the technique, we compute *hsd* for the Status groups in our experimental example. The F for this variable was significant at the 1% level. By Formula 12.1:

$$hsd = q_\alpha \sqrt{\frac{MS_{wg}}{N_g}}$$

In our example, $M_{wg} = 4.14$ with $df = 24$. We find in Table G that for $df = 24$ and $k = 2 \times 3 = 6$, $q_{.01} = 5.37$. Thus:

$$hsd = 5.37 \sqrt{\frac{4.14}{10}} = 5.37 \sqrt{.41}$$

$$= 3.44$$

The $\overline{X}$'s for the three Status groups, we determine from the data in Table 13.2, are 9.8, 9.7, and 13.3% for Single, Married, and Married with Children, respectively. The difference between $\overline{X}$'s of the Married with Children group and each of the other two groups is significant at $\alpha = .01$. That is, $13.3 - 9.8 = 3.5$ and $13.3 - 9.7 = 3.6$, with both differences being greater than $hsd = 3.44$. However, the difference between the $\overline{X}$'s of the other two groups is not significant.

Estimated Effect Size.   A formula is available to estimate omega squared for the effect associated with each F in a two-way ANOVA, that is, for A, B, and A $\times$ B. The formula is:

$$\hat{\omega}_E^2 = \frac{SS_E - (df_E)(MS_{wg})}{SS_{tot} + MS_{wg}} \tag{13.12}$$

where E = the particular effect, A, B, or A $\times$ B we are assessing. The values of SS_E, SS_{tot}, MS_E, and MS_{wg} are those found in the two-way ANOVA.

For example, in our illustration, the $\hat{\omega}^2$ for the Status (B) variable is determined as follows:

$$\hat{\omega}^2 = \frac{SS_B - (df_B)(MS_{wg})}{SS_{tot} + MS_{wg}}$$

$$= \frac{84.07 - (2)(4.14)}{212.87 + 4.14}$$

$$= \frac{75.79}{217.01} = .35$$

We estimate that 35% of the variability is accounted for by the status variable, a strong effect.*

Step-by-Step Procedures

We will now summarize the steps taken in computing a two-way ANOVA, starting first with a description of the basic data that will enter into our calculations. Formulas specially suitable for computation are then given.

Basic Data

1. Find the ΣX of each group and enter them in a two-way table such as is illustrated in the lower portion of Table 13.2. By adding the appropriate sums, find the ΣX for each column, each row, and for the total experiment.

2. Find the ΣX^2 for each group and by adding these values, for the total experiment.

---

*Several statisticians have advised that $\hat{\omega}^2$ be computed without regard to the significance of F. Computation of $\hat{\omega}^2$ for the B variable and the A $\times$ B interaction for our data yielded values of .05 and .04, respectively. These values are relatively small, which is not surprising in light of the nonsignificant F's.

Calculate SS's by the Formulas:

3. $SS_{tot} = \left(\sum_{tot} X^2\right) - \dfrac{\left(\sum_{tot} X\right)^2}{N_{tot}}$

4. $SS_{bg} = \sum_{g} \left[\dfrac{(\sum X_g)^2}{N_g}\right] - \dfrac{\left(\sum_{tot} X\right)^2}{N_{tot}}$

5. $SS_{wg} = SS_{tot} - SS_{bg}$

   Check: $SS_{wg} = \sum_{g} \left[(\sum X_g^2) - \dfrac{(\sum X_g)^2}{N_g}\right]$

6. $SS_A = \dfrac{(\sum X_{A1})^2 + (\sum X_{A2})^2 + \cdots + (\sum X_{Am})^2}{N_A} - \dfrac{\left(\sum_{tot} X\right)}{N_{tot}}$

7. $SS_B = \dfrac{(\sum X_{B1})^2 + (\sum X_{B2})^2 + \cdots + (\sum X_{Bn})^2}{N_B} - \dfrac{\left(\sum_{tot} X\right)^2}{N_{tot}}$

8. $SS_{A \times B} = SS_{bg} - SS_A - SS_B$

   Check: $SS_{A \times B} = N_g \left[\sum_{g} (\overline{X}_{AB} - \overline{X}_A - \overline{X}_B + \overline{X}_{tot})^2\right]$

Determine df 's by the Formulas:

9. $df_A = m - 1$
10. $df_B = n - 1$
11. $df_{A \times B} = (m - 1)(n - 1)$
12. $df_{wg} = N_{tot} - (m)(n)$

Calculate MS's by Dividing Each SS by Its df

13. $MS_A = \dfrac{SS_A}{df_A}$

14. $MS_B = \dfrac{SS_B}{df_B}$

15. $MS_{A \times B} = \dfrac{SS_{A \times B}}{df_{A \times B}}$

16. $MS_{wg} = \dfrac{SS_{wg}}{df_{wg}}$

Calculate F Ratios by Dividing the MS's for A, B, and A × B by MS$_{wg}$:

17. $F_A = \dfrac{MS_A}{MS_{wg}}$

18. $F_B = \dfrac{MS_B}{MS_{wg}}$

19. $F_{A \times B} = \dfrac{MS_{A \times B}}{MS_{wg}}$

Determine the Significance of F's:

20. For each of the F ratios found in steps 17–19 find the values required for significance at the 5% and 1% level by entering Table F with the *df*'s associated with the numerator and the denominator of each of these F's.

21. If a given F exceeds the required F at either the 5% or 1% level, reject the null hypothesis at that level; if it falls short, do not reject the null hypothesis.

Summarize the Results:

22. Prepare a summary table, similar to the one in Table 13.3, that contains the values of the SS, *df*, MS, and F for the main effects of variables A and B and for the A × B interaction.

We may also find it useful to plot the $\overline{X}$'s of the groups in a graph such as the one in Figure 13.4.

Example of Two-Way ANOVA

We now illustrate these steps with the data from an investigation on achievement motives with a 2 × 2 design. A large group of college students was given an inventory which included a measure of their enjoyment of working hard to master difficult tasks (Mastery) and a measure of Competitiveness, the desire to compete with other people. Four groups of 10 students each were chosen. Two groups had very high scores and the other two had very low scores on Mastery. Within each of these groups, one had high scores and the other had low scores on Competitiveness. Each student's grade point average (GPA), based on a 4-point scale, was obtained. Of interest was the relationship between GPA and the two individual difference measures, Mastery and Competitiveness.

Basic Data

For convenience, GPA's were rounded to one decimal place and multiplied by 10 to produce whole numbers of 40 or less. We will *not* show the raw scores but only the Σ X's for each group and ΣX^2 for the total group. The ΣX's are shown in the following table and the ΣX^2_{tot} is shown below the table.

		Mastery (A)		
		High (1)	**Low (2)**	**Sum**
Competitiveness (B)	**High (1)**	295	267	562
	Low (2)	370	246	616
	Sum	665	513	1178

$$\underset{tot}{\Sigma} X^2 = 36266 \qquad N_g = 10 \qquad N_{tot} = 40$$

Calculate SS's:

$$SS_{tot} = \left(\underset{tot}{\Sigma} X^2\right) - \frac{\left(\underset{tot}{\Sigma} X\right)^2}{N_{tot}}$$

$$= 36266 - \frac{(1178)^2}{40} = 36266 - 34692.1$$

$$= 1573.9$$

$$SS_{bg} = \Sigma \left[\frac{(\Sigma X_g)^2}{N_g}\right] - \frac{\left(\underset{tot}{\Sigma} X\right)^2}{N_{tot}}$$

$$= \left[\frac{(295)^2 + (267)^2 + (370)^2 + (246)^2}{10}\right] - 34692.1$$

$$= 35573 - 34692.1$$

$$= 880.9$$

$$SS_{wg} = SS_{tot} - SS_{bg}$$

$$= 1573.9 - 880.1 = 693.0$$

$$SS_A = \left[\frac{(\Sigma X_{A1})^2 + (\Sigma X_{A2})^2}{N_A}\right] - \frac{\left(\underset{tot}{\Sigma} X\right)^2}{N_{tot}}$$

$$= \left[\frac{(665)^2 + (513)^2}{20}\right] - 34692.1$$

$$= 35269.7 - 34692.1 = 577.6$$

$$SS_B = \left[\frac{(\Sigma X_{B1})^2 + (\Sigma X_{B2})^2}{N_B} \right] - \frac{\left(\Sigma_{tot} X\right)^2}{N_{tot}}$$

$$= \left[\frac{(562)^2 + (616)^2}{20} \right] - 34692.1 = 34765 - 34692.1$$

$$= 72.9$$

$$SS_{A \times B} = SS_{bg} - SS_A - SS_B$$

$$= 880.9 - 577.6 - 72.9 = 230.4$$

Determine df's:

$$df_A = m - 1 = 2 - 1 = 1 \qquad df_{A \times B} = df_A \times df_B = 1$$

$$df_B = n - 1 = 2 - 1 = 1 \qquad df_{wg} = N_{tot} - (m)(n) = 40 - 4 = 36$$

Determine MS's:

$$MS_A = \frac{SS_A}{df_A} = 577.6$$

$$MS_B = \frac{SS_B}{df_B} = 72.9$$

$$MS_{A \times B} = \frac{SS_{A \times B}}{df_{A \times B}} = 230.4$$

$$MS_{wg} = \frac{SS_{wg}}{df_{wg}} = 19.2$$

Calculate F's:

$$F_A = \frac{MS_A}{MS_{wg}} = \frac{577.6}{19.2} = 30.08$$

$$F_B = \frac{MS_B}{MS_{wg}} = \frac{72.9}{19.2} = 3.80$$

$$F_{A \times B} = \frac{MS_{A \times B}}{MS_{wg}} = \frac{229.6}{19.2} = 12.00$$

Determine the Significance of F's:

For 1 and 30 *df* (the Table F entry most appropriate for 1 and 36 *df*), $F_{.05} = 4.17$ and $F_{.01} = 7.56$. We conclude at $\alpha = .01$ that both variable A (Mastery) and the A × B interaction were significant. Variable B (Competitiveness) was not significant.

Table 13.4 Summary of Two-Way ANOVA of Relationship between GPA and Mastery and Competitiveness

Source	SS	df	MS	F	p
Mastery (A)	577.6	1	577.6	29.93	< .01
Competitiveness (B)	72.9	1	72.9	3.78	> .05
A × B	230.4	1	230.4	12.00	< .01
Within	693.0	36	19.2		
Total	1573.9	39			

Summarize the Results

The results are summarized in Table 13.4. We have also found the $\overline{X}$'s of the four groups and plotted them in Figure 13.5. The graph makes it easier to see that at both levels of Competitiveness, students high in Mastery had higher GPA's than those of students low in Mastery. There was a crossover interaction, such that in comparison to those low in Competitiveness, students high in Competitiveness had a slightly higher GPA when they were also low in Mastery but they had a much lower GPA when they were also high in Mastery. Thus, the magnitude and direction of the effect of Competitiveness on GPA depended on the level of Mastery.

Calculation of $\hat{\omega}^2$:

We will illustrate the calculation of $\hat{\omega}^2$ with data from the Mastery variable in the achievement motive study whose results we just analyzed. (We remind you once more, however, that in practice we should find $\hat{\omega}^2$ for all effects we assessed in the ANOVA.)

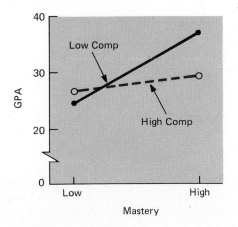

Figure 13.5 Mean GPA for students high and low in Mastery scores and high and low in Competitiveness scores.

1. The formula for $\hat{\omega}^2$ is:

$$\hat{\omega}^2 = \frac{SS_E - (df_E)(MS_{wg})}{SS_{tot} + MS_{wg}}$$

where E = effect being assessed, in this case Mastery.

2. Enter values from ANOVA in the formula. The values in our examples are found in Table 13.4.

$$\hat{\omega}^2 = \frac{577.6 - (1)(19.2)}{1573.9 + 19.2} = \frac{558.4}{1593.1}$$

$$= .35$$

We estimate that Mastery accounted for a substantial amount of the variability in GPA's, 35 percent.

This concludes our discussion of the analysis of variance technique—one of the most useful tools of statistics. Still further extensions allow us to analyze the data from factorial designs involving three or more separate variables. Modifications also have been developed that are appropriate, for example, for analyzing matched groups, such as might be involved in experiments in which a number of measures are obtained from the same subjects rather than from independent groups. Accordingly, the one-way and two-way analysis of variance techniques that we have discussed are the first steps toward the statistical analysis of many experimental problems more complicated than those discussed in this book. ■

DEFINITIONS OF TERMS AND SYMBOLS

Two-way factorial design. An experimental design in which two variables, A and B, are manipulated and in which all possible combinations of A conditions and B conditions are represented. For example, with three A conditions and four B conditions, the factorial design calls for 3 × 4 = 12 groups.

Two-way ANOVA. Application of the analysis of variance technique to the data from a two-way factorial design.

Main effects. In a two-way design, the effects of variations in A conditions, independent of variations in B conditions, and the effects of variation in B conditions, independent of variations in A conditions.

H_0 for main effects. The null hypothesis for variable A is that the population μ's from which the A groups are drawn are all equal. Similarly, the null hypothesis for variable B is that the population μ's from which the B groups are drawn are all equal.

A × B interaction. The manner in which variables A and B combine or interact to determine the dependent variable.

H_0 for A × B interaction. The null hypothesis is that the combination of A and B is additive. An additive combination is reflected graphically in a set of parallel curves when the means of the A conditions for each B condition (or the means of the B conditions for each A condition) are plotted.

PROBLEMS

1. A series of experiments employing a two-way factorial design is described below. For each experiment, do the following: I. Plot the $\overline{X}$'s in a single graph, like those in Figures 13.1–13.3. II. Present the $\overline{X}$'s in a two-way table, such as the one in Table 13.1, then find and enter in the table the row and column means. (Assume equal N's in each group.) III. After inspecting your graph and table, state which F's would probably be significant if a two-way ANOVA were performed and what you would conclude about the main effects and the interaction between the variables. Be specific in describing your conclusions. (Your conclusions cannot be definite because no information about variability within groups is given.)

   (a) A company introduced an experimental "flextime" program in one of its plants in which employees were expected to work 40 hours per week but had the option of working more than 8 hours on some days and less on others. Members of two departments, one consisting of assembly line workers and the other of office workers, took part in the program. Members of two other departments of assembly and office workers served as a control group, continuing to work 8 hours per day. After the program had been in operation for six months, a measure of morale and job satisfaction was given to all four groups. The means are as follows, high values indicating high satisfaction.

Exp. − Assembly = 35	Control − Assembly = 25
Exp. − Office = 37	Control − Office = 32

   (b) An agriculturist performed an experiment to compare the yield of three different types of hybrid corn (H) in two different soil conditions. In conducting his study, he divided each of two plots, differing in type of soil, into 15 rectangular strips of equal size and planted the three types of seeds in alternating strips. The mean yields (in bushels) were as follows:

Plot 1 − H_1 = 61	Plot 1 − H_2 = 71	Plot 1 − H_3 = 66
Plot 2 − H_1 = 72	Plot 2 − H_2 = 81	Plot 2 − H_3 = 75

   (c) In a study of the effects of success and failure, a psychologist gave subjects a timed digit-substitution task and afterward told subjects assigned to the success condition that they had performed very well in comparison to others and subjects in the failure condition that they had not performed well. Then all subjects were given a second example of the task and the time to completion was recorded. Subjects had previously been classified as high or low in self-esteem and self-confidence, and half in each self-esteem group had been assigned to the success and failure conditions. The mean time to completion (in seconds) for the groups on the second task were as follows:

Success − High self-esteem = 63	Failure − High self-esteem = 57
Success − Low self-esteem = 58	Failure − Low self-esteem = 64

2. One hundred twenty male students, 40 majoring in business administration, 40 majoring in education, and 40 majoring in psychology, were shown one of two videotapes of a man being interviewed. (Actually, the interview was staged.) Twenty in each of the three groups viewed a tape in which the man portrayed himself as being very competent in a number of areas and as hardworking and ambitious to be highly successful vocationally. The other 20 in each group viewed a tape in which the man portrayed himself as competent in the same ways but was more relaxed

about his work and had only moderate vocational ambitions. After watching the tape, the subjects rated the man on a 7-point scale to indicate how personally likable they found him. A rating of 7 indicated "very likable" and a rating of 1 indicated "not at all likable." Shown below are the sums and sums of squares for the several groups (N per group = 20).

Tape		Business	Major Education	Psychology
Ambitious	ΣX	117	67	81
	ΣX^2	703	299	387
Unambitious	ΣX	60	95	78
	ΣX^2	212	499	358

(a) Find the $\overline{X}$'s of the groups and graph them.

(b) Specify the null hypotheses that are to be tested.

(c) Conduct the appropriate ANOVA. To shorten your labors, round off SS's and MS's to one decimal place and F's to two decimal places. Summarize the results in a table patterned after Table 13.3.

(d) Describe the outcome of the experiment.

(e) Perform a series of three Tukey *hsd* tests to determine whether the ratings of the two tapes differ significantly within each group of majors.

(f) Estimate effect size by $\hat{\omega}^2$ for the two main effects and the interaction.

14

Chi Square

- CHI SQUARE APPLIED TO A SINGLE SAMPLE
- RESTRICTIONS ON THE USE OF χ^2
- TESTING SIGNIFICANCE OF DIFFERENCE IN PROPORTIONS BY χ^2

Most of the statistical procedures we have discussed in previous chapters have involved numerical data—that is, characteristics that may vary in amount. We therefore assign each individual in the group we are measuring a number reflecting how much of the characteristic that individual exhibits. Techniques are also available for analyzing *categorical data*. Categorical data, you recall, involve the assignment of each member of a group of individuals to one of two or more discrete categories. The group of individuals is described by reporting the number or proportion of the group falling into each category.

For example, we might ask each of 200 people whether they favor a constitutional amendment permitting classroom prayers in public schools. Assuming that everyone had an opinion, we would in this case have only two categories of responses, Yes or No. We would not measure for each individual the "amount" of his or her response, but rather classify the response as belonging to one of the two categories, and for the group as a whole, record the number of people (the frequency) within each category. Note that all the persons included in each category have the same "score"; there is no variability in the response as classified *within* a category.

Our purpose in questioning this sample of 200 people might be to determine whether in the population as a whole, there is a majority sentiment for or against the constitutional amendment. We might therefore wish to test the hypothesis that in the population the split is 50:50, and to determine whether it is reasonable to reject this hypothesis. In Chapter 8, we discussed a method for testing a hypothesis of this sort. That method, which involves converting the difference between a sample proportion and a hypothetical population proportion into a z score, is applicable to the binomial case in which there are only *two* mutually exclusive categories.

In this chapter we discuss an alternative technique for analyzing categorical data of this kind. The statistic we compute is called *chi square*, symbolized as χ^2. One of the desirable features of χ^2 is that it permits hypotheses to be tested about the distribution of individuals among any number of mutually exclusive categories rather than being restricted to the two-category case. Chi square can also be used for another purpose that will be explained later in this chapter.

CHI SQUARE APPLIED TO A SINGLE SAMPLE

When members of a sample have been assigned to categories and the frequency of cases in each category has been determined, the question we typically want to answer is whether the frequencies observed in our sample of N individuals deviate significantly from some *theoretical* or *expected frequencies* based on N and the population frequencies. We have some hypothesis about the proportion in the population that falls into each category and therefore what frequencies should theoretically be expected in our sample of N individuals. In some cases, we may hypothesize equal frequencies in each category, so we want to determine whether the observed frequencies deviate significantly from what would be expected from a hypothesis of equal likelihood. In other cases, we may adopt some other hypothesis.

Having classified a sample of individuals, we have the problem of evaluating the deviations of the *observed* frequencies from theoretically *expected* frequencies if our hypothesis about the population proportions were true. Should our hypothesis about population frequencies be accepted and the deviations attributed to sampling error? Or is it more reasonable to conclude, at a certain probability level, that our hypothesis is false and a nonchance factor was operating? Chi square is used for this purpose. The formula for χ^2 is:

$$\chi^2 = \Sigma \left[\frac{(O - E)^2}{E} \right]$$

where O = observed frequency

(14.1)

E = the corresponding expected frequency

According to this formula, we first get the deviation of each observed frequency from its corresponding expected frequency and then square the deviations. Next, each squared deviation is divided by the appropriate expected frequency. The remaining step is to sum these quotients; the sum is the value of χ^2.

Let us see how this works with our example of 200 people questioned about prayers in the public schools. We will test the hypothesis that opinion neither favors nor opposes the constitutional amendment, that in the population from which our sample was drawn opinion is equally divided. The expected frequency is, therefore, 100 in each category. Table 14.1, which shows the computation, indicates that for a 50:50 hypothesis with these data, $\chi^2 = 5.12$. How is this value to be interpreted? The interpretation of a value of χ^2 is basically the same as for t. We assume a certain null hypothesis—for the data in Table 14.1 the hypothesis that there is no difference in the population between the two categories of response. Then we ask: If the hypothesis is true, how often would values of χ^2 as large as or larger than our obtained value arise by random sampling error? If we find that values of χ^2 as large as or larger than the value obtained would occur by sampling error only 5 percent or 1 percent of the time, we reject the hypothesis at the 5% or 1% level of significance.

Table 14.1 A 50:50 Hypothesis Tested by χ^2

	Favor	Do Not Favor	Total
Observed (O)	84	116	200
Expected (E)	100	100	200
O − E	−16	+16	
(O − E)^2	256	256	
$\dfrac{(O - E)^2}{E}$	2.56	2.56	

$$\chi^2 = \Sigma \left[\frac{(O - E)^2}{E} \right] = 2.56 + 2.56 = 5.12 \quad df = 1$$

In order to evaluate obtained values of χ^2 we need to know the distribution of χ^2. Table I in Appendix III shows for each df value from 1 to 30 the value of χ^2 that would occur by sampling error at both the .05 and .01 levels of probability. Thus, for 1 df (first row in Table I) a value of χ^2 as large as 6.64 occurs 1 percent of the time by sampling error alone. Similarly, with 6 df, an obtained χ^2 would have to be at least 12.59 to be called significant at the 5% level. Note that, unlike F or t, values of χ^2 necessary for significance at a given level *increase* with increasing df.

Degrees of Freedom. The df for a particular χ^2 does *not* depend upon the number of individuals in the sample. For χ^2, the df is determined by the number of *deviations* between observed and expected frequencies that are *independent;* that is, are free to vary. For example, what is the df for Table 14.1? First, we have to note a condition that must always be true for any χ^2: *The sum of the expected frequencies must equal the sum of the observed frequencies.* In Table 14.1 this is true; both observed and expected frequencies sum to 200. Now if, in Table 14.1, we write down 100 as the expected frequency for one category, the expected frequency for the other category (and, therefore, the deviation) is *not* free to vary; it must also be 100, in order that the expected frequencies sum to the same total as the observed frequencies. Therefore, there is 1 df for the data in Table 14.1, because only one deviation is free to vary.

What if the number of categories were four instead of two? The number of expected frequencies that are free to vary and still have the sum of the expected frequencies equal the sum of the observed frequencies is three. Generalizing from these examples, it can be seen that degrees of freedom are equal to the number of categories minus one:

$$df = \text{number of categories} - 1 \qquad (14.2)$$

Returning to Table 14.1, in which $df = 1$, we can now use Table I to evaluate the calculated χ^2. Table I shows that for 1 df, $\chi^2 = 3.84$ at the 5% level and 6.64 at the 1% level. Our obtained value of 5.12 exceeds the value at the 5% but not at the 1% level, so we may reject our null hypothesis at the 5% level of significance. We conclude that opinion is quite probably not evenly split in the population from which our sample was drawn.

We have noted that chi square is not restricted to testing the hypothesis of equally distributed frequencies or to the two-category situation, but may be used to test any *a priori* hypothesis about any number of categories. By an *a priori* hypothesis we mean one the investigator has formulated before the research is done. For example, the ads for Zippy cola brag that in blind tasting tests of Zippy and two competing brands, 50 percent of adults prefer Zippy, whereas only 30 percent prefer Brand X, and 20 percent prefer Brand Y. A consumer organization decides to investigate this claim and conducts a test with 150 people. The results show that 54 prefer Zippy, 51 prefer Brand X, and 45 prefer Brand Y. If the advertising claim is true, the expected frequencies are 75, 45, 30, respectively, that is, 50 percent of 150 people, 30 percent of 150, and 20 percent of 150. After these three pairs of observed and expected frequencies have been determined, χ^2 can be computed, as in Table 14.1. With three categories, $df = 2$.

RESTRICTIONS
ON THE USE OF χ^2

Before taking up the use of χ^2 in more complex cases, we shall note some of the conditions that must be met before data may appropriately be analyzed by χ^2. Like any statistical method, the use of χ^2 is subject to certain limitations; if these are kept in mind, many incorrect applications will be avoided.*

First, χ^2 can be used only with frequency data. It is not correct, for example, to test by χ^2 the deviation between the obtained mean score on some trait for a group, and some expected or predicted mean. These are numerical data, and one of the reasons why χ^2 cannot be used with such data is that the value of χ^2 varies with the size of the unit of measurement. Thus, weight may be measured either in pounds or in kilograms. But the value of χ^2 between observed and expected weights will be different, even for the same subjects, if the score is recorded in pounds than if it is recorded in kilograms. Who is to say which value of χ^2 is "correct"?

Second, the individual events or observations must be independent of each other. The data for the example on prayers in school may be used as an illustration. There is no reason to think that the answer of any one of the subjects in the sample is dependent upon or correlated with the answer of any other subject; the individual responses are independent. But it would be incorrect, for example, to ask each of 50 people to make guesses as to what card will be drawn from a deck on each of five successive draws and then to claim the total frequency was 250 events. In such a case we would not have 250 independent responses; successive responses by the same individual are very probably related.

Third, no theoretical frequency should be smaller than 5. The distribution of χ^2, part of which is given in Table I, may take different values from those shown in the table if any expected frequency is less than 5. The discrepancy is not large, however, when χ^2 is computed from contingency tables with a fairly large number of cells (more than 4, at a minimum) and only a few theoretical frequencies are less than 5. In this latter instance, it is permissible to relax the stringent rule that *no* theoretical frequency may be less than 5 and to go ahead and compute χ^2.

Fourth, there must be some basis for the way the data are categorized. Preferably, the categories should have some logical basis, or be based on previous acceptable research, and should be set up before the data are collected. Suppose, for example, we asked a large random sample of people what magazine they would take if they could subscribe to only one. We find that 31 magazines were named, ranging from a few mentioned very frequently to several preferred by one person each. We now categorize the data into several "types" of magazines in order to apply χ^2. Such an application would be questionable, because we have not demonstrated that the types (categories) we set up are any more defensible than any others that might be used. And it would be even worse to continue reclassifying the data until we got categories that would give a significant χ^2. Our categories must be set up beforehand, and it must be demon-

---

*D. Lewis and C. J. Burke, The use and misuse of the chi-square test, *Psychological Bulletin*, 1949, *46*, 433–87.

strated that the categories are reliable. Reliability would be demonstrated if there were a high degree of agreement among a group of qualified judges as to what magazines should be assigned to what categories.

Finally, recall we said above that *the sum of expected and the sum of observed frequencies must be the same*. The requirement is related to another: *If we are recording whether or not an event occurs, we must include in our data, and use in computing χ^2, both the frequency of occurrence and the frequency of nonoccurrence*. For example, suppose we roll a die 120 times and note the frequency with which a one-spot turns up. The expected frequency is 20, since a die has six sides. It would not be correct to test by χ^2 only whether the observed frequency of occurrence of the one-spot deviated significantly from the expected frequency. The χ^2 must be based *both* on the deviation of observed frequency of occurrence from expected frequency of occurrence, and the deviation of observed frequency of nonoccurrence from expected frequency of nonoccurrence. If we ignore the frequency of nonoccurrence, the *sums* of observed and expected frequencies will not be the same, except by chance. The value of χ^2 must be based on the deviation of observed from expected frequency for both the category of occurrence and the category of nonoccurrence.

TESTING SIGNIFICANCE OF DIFFERENCE IN PROPORTIONS BY χ^2

Chi square probably has its greatest usefulness in testing for significance of differences between groups. Although there may be any number of groups and any number of categories, most often in research we have two groups and two categories of response; the data are expressed in a 2 × 2 table. Our initial illustrations of χ^2 as it is used to test for significance of difference therefore will be based on a 2 × 2 table, although the method is the same for any number of groups and categories.

Test of Homogeneity between Groups

Suppose we want to determine whether there is any relation between the amount of education a person has had and method of keeping up with the news. We ask a random sample of 125 college graduates and a random sample of 125 high school graduates whether they keep up with the news mostly by reading a newspaper or mostly by watching television. Table 14.2 shows the data that might have been obtained, arranged in a 2 × 2 table.

Table 14.2 shows that 52 of the 125 college graduates in the sample said they got news mostly by watching television; the other 73 relied mostly on the newspaper. Among the 125 high school graduates, 81 said television, 44 the newspaper. We want to know whether these frequencies indicate a significant difference between the two groups.

When χ^2 is used to test for the significance of a difference between two or more groups, it is often said to be a test of *independence*. Perhaps this can best be explained by pointing out that the observed frequencies in Table 14.2 are classified two ways. One way is television

Table 14.2 Chi-Square Test of Homogeneity between Educational Groups

	Television	Newspapers	Total
High school graduates	81 (66.5)	44 (58.5)	125
College graduates	52 (66.5)	73 (58.5)	125
Total	133	117	250

O	E	O – E	(O – E)²	$\dfrac{(O - E)^2}{E}$
81	66.5	14.5	210.5	3.17
52	66.5	– 14.5	210.5	3.17
44	58.5	– 14.5	210.5	3.60
73	58.5	14.5	210.5	3.60

$$\chi^2 = 13.54$$

With $df = 1$, $\chi^2_{.01} = 6.64$

versus newspaper; the other way is by educational level. Our problem, stated above in terms of significance of difference, can therefore be restated as the question: Are the two ways of classifying the observed frequencies independent of each other? If they *are* independent, then preference for television or newspaper does *not* depend on educational level and we could combine the educational groups, categorizing merely on the basis of television versus newspaper. This is the same as saying the groups do *not* differ significantly. On the other hand, if the classifications are *not* independent—that is, if they are correlated—then when we categorize the data one way, we must categorize the other way too. In our example this would mean that the educational groups *differ significantly* in their preference for television or newspaper.

Let us now see how we use χ^2 to test for significance of difference, using our example in Table 14.2. We start by assuming the null hypothesis that our two groups were drawn from the same population with respect to method of keeping up with the news. Note that we are not concerned, for either group, with whether television is preferred over the newspaper. If we were, we could use χ^2, as explained earlier, to test an *a priori* hypothesis in each group separately.

Our next step is to determine the expected frequency for each of the four cells of the table. Since we have no *a priori* hypothesis, we reason as follows: if our null hypothesis is correct—if the true (expected) frequencies are the same for both samples—then combining the two samples should give us a better estimate of the true frequencies than we could get from either sample alone. Thus we add, within each column, the observed frequencies for the samples to get the marginal column totals of 133 and 117. We use these values as the best estimates of the division in the single assumed population between television preference and newspaper preference. Since our total sample is 250 cases, the expected percent frequency in the population for television preference is 133/250 or 53.2 percent. In other words, our best estimate of what we would obtain if we measured the whole population is 53.2 percent getting news mostly by television. In similar fashion, 117/250 or 46.8 percent of the total frequency, is the expected percent frequency for the newspaper category.

All we have to do now, to get the expected raw frequencies for each sample, is divide the sample N on the basis of these expected percent frequencies. There are 125 college graduates; since we expect 53.2 percent of them to fall in the television category, we have 53.2 percent of 125, or 66.5, as the expected frequency for the upper left-hand cell of the table. This value is shown in parentheses in that cell in Table 14.2. Similarly, 53.2 percent of the 125 high school graduates gives us 66.5 as the expected frequency in the television category for those subjects. The expected frequencies for the newspaper cells are determined by taking 46.8 percent of 125.

Now that we have stated the logic for the method of determining the expected frequencies, we can state a simple rule that may be more easily remembered: Simply multiply the marginal total for any column by the marginal total for any row and divide the product by the total N. The result is the expected frequency for the cell common to the row and column whose totals were multiplied together. Thus, in our example, $(133)(125)/250 = 66.5$, $(117)(125)/250 = 58.5$, and so forth.

Returning to our problem, now that we have the expected frequencies, we compute χ^2 in the usual manner: Each deviation of an observed frequency from its expected frequency is squared and divided by the expected frequency, and the quotients summed. We find that $\chi^2 = 13.54$ for this example. Now, what are the *df*? We will state a general rule for determining the *df* for any table that has at least two rows and two columns, and in which the marginal totals are used in determining the expected frequencies:

$$df = (\text{number of columns} - 1)(\text{number of rows} - 1) \qquad (14.3)$$

The rule applies to tables of any number of rows and columns, as long as there are at least two of each. Thus in a 2 × 2 table, the *df* = (2 − 1)(2 − 1), or 1.

With 1 *df*, our χ^2 value of 13.54 is larger than the value given in Table I for the 1% level. We shall therefore reject the hypothesis at the 1% level of significance that the two groups were drawn from the same population with respect to method of getting the news. We could say the same thing by stating that we reject the hypothesis of independence; the frequencies in the television versus newspaper categories are probably *not* independent of educational level, high school graduates relying more on TV than college graduates.

The example we have used illustrates a chi-square test of *homogeneity* between preexisting groups. That is, we selected two groups that already differed in a specified way—in our example, educational level. We then classified each individual with respect to a second categorical variable. Our concern was whether the two groups were alike (*homogeneous*) with respect to the second categorical variable, in this instance, the proportion of each group obtaining the news by each method.

Another type of test of homogeneity using χ^2 involves experimental rather than preexisting groups. For example, we might identify a pool of adolescents who are suffering from acne and assign them at random to one of two treatment conditions. At the end of three weeks of treatment, each adolescent is rated as improved or not improved. Our interest is in the significance of the difference between the two experimental groups, whether the treatment groups were homogeneous with respect to the proportion rated as improved after three weeks of treatment. In applying χ^2 to such data we follow the procedures shown in Table 14.2.

Contingency Test Using χ^2

Suppose that we survey a sample of 150 graduating seniors in a liberal arts college. Among the items of information we gather are the students' sex and whether they will be going on for more schooling (graduate school, professional school, etc.) in the year following graduation. We are interested in whether there is any relationship between students' sex and their postgraduate plans, that is, whether the proportion of men and women going on is the same or different. Note that unlike our previous discussion, in which we had two preexisting or experimentally established groups and gather data on a second categorical variable, we start with a *single* sample and gather information from each individual in the sample about two categorical variables. The results can be displayed in a *contingency table* such as the 2 × 2 table shown in Table 14.3 in which the 150 students were classified according to sex and educational plans.

Note also that in asking whether the proportion going on to advanced training is the same in each sex, we are not interested in whether in the population of seniors from which the sample was drawn there is a difference in the proportion of men and women or a difference in the proportion of students who are and are not going on. Rather, we are concerned with whether there is any *contingency* or dependency between the two ways of classifying each student, sex and postgraduate plans.

Chi square can also be used as a test of contingency. This is illustrated in Table 14.3, in which we have analyzed data from our hypothetical sample of seniors. For $df = 1$, our calculated χ^2 is significant at the 5% level. Inspection of Table 14.3 indicates that a higher proportion of men $(48/77 = 62\%)$ than women $(31/73 = 42\%)$ plan to go on for more schooling.

Table 14.3 Test of Contingency between Seniors' Sex and Postgraduate Plans Using χ^2 Test of Independence

	More school	*None*	*Total*
Males	48 (40.55)	29 (36.45)	77
Females	31 (38.45)	42 (34.55)	73
Total	79	71	150

O	*E*	*O − E*	*(O − E)²*	$\dfrac{(O-E)^2}{E}$
48	40.55	7.45	55.50	1.37
31	38.45	−7.45	55.50	1.44
29	36.45	−7.45	55.50	1.52
42	34.55	7.45	55.50	1.61
				$\chi^2 = 5.94$

With $df = 1$, $\chi^2_{.05} = 3.84$

Alternative Method of Computing a 2 × 2 Chi Square

Before we leave this example we may note that χ^2 can be computed for a 2 × 2 table without computation of expected frequencies. Let us schematize a 2 × 2 table as follows, where the letters in the cells indicate the *observed* frequencies:

A	B	A + B
C	D	C + D

A + C   B + D   N

With this schema, χ^2 can be computed directly as follows:

$$\chi^2 = \frac{N(AD - BC)^2}{(A + B)(C + D)(A + C)(B + D)} \tag{14.4}$$

Thus for the data in Table 14.3:

$$\chi^2 = \frac{250[(81)(73) - (44)(52)]^2}{(81 + 44)(52 + 73)(81 + 52)(44 + 73)} = 13.54$$

A Sidelight on Chi Square.   The critical values of χ^2's used to assess hypotheses about expected frequencies have been derived from theoretical distributions that involve continuous rather than discrete values of χ^2. Calculated values of χ^2, on the other hand, vary in discrete fashion. This fact may create a problem in interpreting χ^2, particularly when *df* and expected frequencies are small. Statisticians have therefore historically advised introducing what is called a correction for continuity into the calculational steps for computing χ^2 when *df* and expected frequencies are small. This correction results in reducing the value of χ^2 in comparison to the value obtained with the formulas presented above. Recently there has been controversy among statisticians about the suitability of using this correction with the kinds of data usually obtained in psychology.* In light of its currently controversial status, it seems inappropriate to present the correction for continuity here, beyond this brief mention of its existence.

Significance of Differences among Several Groups

The method of applying χ^2 to test for significance of differences among several groups is identical with the method illustrated in the previous section with two groups. As an example, consider the data in Table 14.4. The data represent the number of bachelor's degrees awarded

---

*See W. J. Conover, Some reasons for not using the Yates continuity correction on 2 × 2 contingency tables (with comments and rejoinder), *Journal of the American Statistical Association*, 1974, *69*, 374–82; and G. Camilli and K. D. Hopkins, Applicability of chi square to 2 × 2 contingency tables with small expected frequencies, *Psychological Bulletin*, 1978, *85*, 163–67. The continuity correction is defended in the comments on Conover's article and in other articles, such as N. Mantel and B. J. Hankey, The odds ratios of a 2 × 2 contingency table, *American Statistician*, 1975, *29*, 143–45.

Table 14.4 Testing Overall Significance
of Difference among Several Groups by χ^2

Degree	1955	1965	1975	Total
Social sciences	46	67	195	308
Humanities	51	53	88	192
Natural sciences	85	100	154	339
Education	118	163	280	561
Total	300	383	717	1400

O	E	O − E	(O − E)²	$\frac{(O-E)^2}{E}$
46	66.00	−20.00	400.00	6.06
51	41.14	9.86	97.22	2.36
85	72.64	12.36	152.77	2.10
118	120.21	−2.21	4.88	.04
67	84.26	−17.26	297.91	3.54
53	52.53	.47	.22	.00
100	92.74	7.26	52.71	.57
163	153.47	9.53	90.82	.59
195	157.74	37.26	1388.31	8.80
88	98.33	−10.33	106.71	1.09
154	173.62	−19.62	384.94	2.22
280	287.31	−7.31	53.44	.19

$$\chi^2 = 27.56$$

by a university in 1955, 1965, and 1975 in four different fields: social sciences, natural sciences, humanities, and education.

Let us apply χ^2 to the data in Table 14.4. We will be testing for any overall significance of differences among the groups. The procedure is the same as that previously illustrated with a 2 × 2 table. We obtain the theoretical frequency for each cell by multiplying the total for the row containing the cell by the total for the column containing the cell and dividing by the total N, which here is 1400. For example, for the cell in the row for social sciences and the column for the year 1955 we have 308(300)/1400 = 66.00. In Table 14.4 the theoretical frequencies are shown in the E column. Then χ^2 is computed in the usual way: In each cell subtract the theoretical frequency from the observed frequency to get the deviation (O − E), square the deviation, and divide by the theoretical frequency of the cell; the sum of the quotients is the value of χ^2. For the data in Table 14.4, χ^2 = 27.56. Since this is a 3 × 4 table, there are 6 *df*: (3 − 1)(4 − 1). Looking at Table I, we see that for 6 *df* a χ^2 of 16.81 is required for significance at the 1% level. Our obtained χ^2 is far greater than this value. We therefore reject the hypothesis that the proportion of degrees awarded was constant in the three years for which data were collected. Inspection of Table 14.4 suggests that social sciences and education were gaining in popularity while the natural sciences and, even more, the humanities were losing.

Chi Square with More than 30 df.   Occasionally, we may have so many groups and categories that there are more than 30 *df*. This would be the case in a 6 × 8 table (35 *df*), a 9 × 9 table (64 *df*), and so on. Table I does not go beyond 30 *df*. To evaluate a χ^2 based on more than 30 *df*, we convert the χ^2 value to an x/σ or z-score value and look up the probability in the normal curve table (Table B). The following expression is used to convert a χ^2 based on more than 30 *df* to an x/σ value:

$$\frac{x}{\sigma} = \sqrt{2\chi^2} - \sqrt{2n - 1} \qquad (14.5)$$

where n = the number of *df* for the χ^2 value.

Let us conclude by reemphasizing the importance of the restrictions on the use of χ^2. These restrictions are not mere hairsplitting, since the use of χ^2 when it is inappropriate may lead us to erroneous conclusions about our data. The same statement can be made about any statistical test; we must be sure before applying a statistical test to any set of data that the assumptions underlying its use are not violated.

In Chapter 15 we consider several additional statistical techniques that may be appropriate when the assumptions of some of the tests we have discussed so far cannot be met.

Step-by-Step Procedures

We have considered two major types of situations. The first is one in which individuals are classified by means of a single set of two or more mutually exclusive categories. In this case we can use χ^2 to test an *a priori* hypothesis about the proportion of individuals in the population that fall into each category.

The second situation is one in which individuals are classified by means of two sets of categories. For example, we might have category set A1 and A2 and category set B1, B2, and B3, an arrangement that results in 2 × 3 = 6 cells. In this type of situation, χ^2 can also be used to test an *a priori* hypothesis about the proportion that fall into each cell. However, investigators rarely have specific hypotheses of this nature that they wish to test. More often, a χ^2 test of independence is conducted to test the hypothesis that classification by one set of categories is unrelated to classification by the other set.

Test of an *a priori* Hypothesis

A food company puts on a special promotional campaign advertising that one of every five boxes (20 percent) of its new product has a watch in it and two of every five boxes (40 percent) have a coupon for a free box. (No box has both a watch and a coupon.) A consumer organization investigates the accuracy of the advertising by buying 60 boxes and opening them to see how many boxes contain a watch or a coupon. They found 10 watches and 27 coupons.

Set up H_0:

There is one set of 3 categories: Watch, Coupon, and No Prize. The H_0 is that the population proportions are .20, .40, and .40, respectively, in these categories.

Determine Expected Frequencies under H_0:

The expected frequencies are .20(60) = 12 for Watch, .40(60) = 24 for Coupon, and .40(60) = 24 for No Prize. The expected frequencies, along with the observed frequencies, are shown in Table 14.5.

Calculate χ^2 by Formula 14.1:

This has been done in Table 14.5 by finding for each of the three categories (O − E), (O − E)^2, and (O − E)^2/E. The latter values are summed to yield χ^2 = .75.

Assess χ^2 using df = no. categories − 1:

With df = 3 − 1 = 2, the critical value of χ^2 at α = .05 is 5.99 (Table I). Our calculated χ^2 is far less than this value. We retain H_0 and conclude that the advertising is probably accurate.

Test of Independence

In a midsized city, 80 single homeless men were interviewed. One of the questions determined whether the man usually, infrequently, or never slept at night in shelters provided by the Salvation Army or other agencies. The interviewer also made a judgment about whether the man (1) had an alcohol or drug problem or (2) was mentally ill (but showed no evidence of substance abuse). Note that all 80 cases have to be accounted for. The men were not diagnosed

---

Table 14.5 Test of an *A Priori* Hypothesis about Proportion in Each of Three Prize Categories

	Watch	*Coupon*	*No Prize*	*Total*
Observed (O)	10	27	23	60
Expected (E)	12	24	24	60
O − E	−2	3	−1	
(O − E)^2	4	9	1	
(O − E)^2/E	.333	.375	.042	

$$\chi^2 = \Sigma \left[\frac{(O - E)^2}{E} \right] = .750$$

as being either mentally ill or a substance abuser were therefore assigned to a third category, Neither. The results are shown below in the form of a 3 × 3 contingency table.

| | | Shelter Usage | | |
Diagnosis	Never	Infrequently	Usually	Total
Substance abuse	12	10	7	29
Mentally ill	3	6	17	26
Neither	8	13	4	25
Total	23	29	28	80

The investigator had no hypothesis about the proportion of homeless men who fall in each diagnostic category or the proportion who fall in each category of shelter usage. The question, rather, was whether diagnostic category is related to shelter usage. This calls for computation of a χ^2 test of independence.

Determine the Expected Frequency (E) for Each Cell:

The expected frequency for each cell is determined by multiplying the total for the row in which the cell is located (R) by the total for the column in which the cell is located (C) and dividing the product by the total N: $(R \times C)/N$. For example, for the Substance Abuse–Never cell, at the upper left of the table, $E = (29 \times 23)/80 = 8.34$. These expected frequencies are shown in Table 14.6 along with the observed frequencies for each cell.

Determine Each $(O - E)$, $(O - E)^2$, and $(O - E)^2/E$:

The sum of the $(O - E)^2/E$ quantities is χ^2. These computations, shown in Table 14.6, yield $\chi^2 = 17.77$.

Table 14.6 Observed and Expected Frequencies for the 3 × 3 Contingency Table of Homeless Men[a]

	O	E	O − E	(O − E)²	$\dfrac{(O - E)^2}{E}$
SA–Ne	12	8.34	3.66	13.40	1.61
MI–Ne	3	7.48	−4.48	20.07	2.68
N–Ne	8	7.19	.81	.66	.09
SA–I	10	10.51	−.51	.26	.02
MI–I	6	9.42	−3.42	11.70	1.24
N–I	13	9.06	3.94	15.52	1.71
SA–U	7	10.15	−3.15	9.92	.98
MI–U	17	9.10	7.90	62.41	6.86
N–U	4	8.75	−4.75	22.56	2.58
					$\chi^2 = 17.77$

[a]The observed frequencies are from the table above. SA, substance abuse; MI, mentally ill; N, neither; Ne, never; I, infrequently; U, usually.

Assess χ^2:

The *df* is found by multiplying (no. of rows − 1) by (no. of columns − 1). In our example, *df* = (3 − 1)(3 − 1) = 4.

For *df* = 4, $\chi^2_{.01}$ = 13.28. Our computed χ^2 of 17.77 is greater than the critical value at α = .01. We reject the H_0 that diagnostic category and shelter use are unrelated. Inspection of the data in the 3 × 3 contingency table shows that the mentally ill men are the most likely of the three groups to use shelters and substance abusers are the the least likely to use shelters. (This may be shown more clearly by setting up a conditional probability table, as outlined in Chapter 6, in which the probability of using a shelter, given mental status, is determined. For example, for substance abusers, 12/29 = .41, 10/29 = .34, and 7/29 = .24 for Never, Infrequently, and Usually, respectively.) ■

DEFINITIONS OF TERMS AND SYMBOLS

Frequency data. Data showing the number of cases (frequency) in each category in a set of two or more mutually exclusive categories.

Observed frequency (O). Actual number of cases in a sample observed to fall in a certain category.

Expected frequency (E). Theoretically expected number of cases in a certain category, according to some null hypothesis about population proportions that is to be tested.

Chi square (χ^2). A statistic used to test a null hypothesis, usually based on the comparison of observed and expected frequencies. Observed values of chi square are compared to critical values at a given α level that presume the null hypothesis is true.

A priori **hypothesis.** A hypothesis about expected frequencies, based on a related hypothesis about population proportions, that is set up by the investigator beforehand. This hypothesis is the H_0 to be tested by χ^2.

Test of independence. The use of χ^2 to test the hypothesis that individuals' classification according to one property is unrelated to their classification according to another property. For example, a test of the hypothesis that voters' sex (male or female) is unrelated to whether or not they voted Republican or Democrat in the last election.

Test of homogeneity. Groups differing in some characteristics may be preselected or individuals may be assigned at random to different experimental conditions; individuals are then classified on a dependent variable that is categorical in nature. Chi square applied to such data is a test of homogeneity among the groups, i.e., the H_0 is that the groups are alike in the proportion assigned to each category of the dependent variable.

Contingency test. When members of a single group of individuals are each classified according to two or more sets of categories, χ^2 can be used as a test of contingency. The H_0 is that there is no relationship (contingency) between the different ways of categorization.

PROBLEMS

In all problems requiring that you compute χ^2, specify the α level you will use to evaluate the hypothesis you are testing, give the df, and state whether or not χ^2 is significant at the given α level.

1. A psychology professor, interested in various kinds of "response bias," asked students in one of his classes to act as subjects in an investigation of bias. He flipped a fair coin and then asked the students to write down their guess about whether the coin had come up a head or a tail. Of the 200 students, 118 guessed heads and 82 guessed tails.

   (a) In order to determine whether or not students exhibit a guessing bias, what statistical hypothesis should be tested using these data?

   (b) Test the hypothesis specified in (a) by computing χ^2. What do you conclude?

2. In the investigation of response bias described in problem 1, the students were also asked to guess the suit of a card the professor drew at random from a bridge deck of 52 cards. Of the 200 students, 43 guessed a club, 51 guessed a spade, 54 a heart, and 52 a diamond.

   (a) Compute χ^2 to determine whether or not there is a response bias.

   (b) What do you conclude?

3. Random samples of 20 physicians and 20 lawyers were asked whether, if they had to do it all over again, they would enter the same or a different occupation. The observed frequencies of their responses are shown below. Do members of the two professions differ?

	Same	Different
Physicians	14	6
Lawyers	12	8

   (a) What kind of a χ^2 test is called for?

   (b) Compute χ^2 by Formula 14.1.

   (c) Recompute χ^2 using Formula 14.4 involving only observed frequencies.

4. A group of adult women were questioned about whether they had a paid job outside the home and whether they planned to vote in the next election. Chi square applied to these data would constitute what kind of test?

5. Three-year-old and 6-year-old children were repeatedly presented with a row of three circles differing in size. (On each trial, the same three circles were presented, but they appeared in different order.) On each occasion, the child was asked to pick one and was given a colored sticker whenever he or she chose the circle of intermediate size. Presentations continued until the child chose the intermediate circle five times in succession. After reaching this criterion, the child was presented with three triangles, also differing in size, and again asked to choose one. The experimenter was interested in determining whether the child's age was related to the degree to which he or she generalized from training to pick the intermediate-size circle to choice of intermediate-size triangle on the test trial.

   Shown below are the numbers of children in each age group who selected each size of triangle. Also shown, in parentheses, are the expected frequencies.

	Small	Medium	Large
Three-year-olds	11(7.97)	13(18.06)	10(7.97)
Six-year-olds	4(7.03)	21(15.94)	5(7.03)

(a) Compute χ^2.

(b) What do you conclude about the effects of age on choice of triangle on the test trial following training on the circles?

6. A random sample of high school seniors planning to go to college has been surveyed in each of five geographical regions. One of the questions asks the students to select the subject matter in which they think they will major. Ten categories are listed (modern languages, natural science, education, social science, and so forth). The numbers of students who selected each category in each region are determined and placed in a 5 × 10 table. A χ^2 is performed to determine whether or not the proportion of seniors choosing each category of college major is related to the part of the country in which they live. The χ^2 is 55.05. Using $\alpha = .05$, determine whether this χ^2 is significant.

15

Nonparametric Tests

- NONPARAMETRIC VERSUS PARAMETRIC TESTS
- SOME NONPARAMETRIC TESTS
- RELATIVE EFFICIENCY OF PARAMETRIC AND NONPARAMETRIC TESTS

When we have measured two or more samples, we may determine the significance of the difference between or among their $\overline{X}$'s by means of a t test or of the F in an analysis of variance. These statistical techniques are examples of what are called *parametric* tests, since they require that we estimate from the sample data the value of at least one population parameter, such as its standard deviation. One of the assumptions we make in applying these parametric techniques to sample data is that the variable we have measured is normally distributed in the populations from which the samples were obtained.

In this chapter we consider several of the *nonparametric* techniques statisticians have devised, techniques whose theory makes no use of parameter values. A second attribute of these nonparametric methods is that they are based on less restricting assumptions than those underlying parametric ones concerning the shape of the distribution of the characteristic being measured. Thus an alternative label for these methods is *distribution-free*.

NONPARAMETRIC VERSUS
PARAMETRIC TESTS

Quite obviously, nonparametric techniques become valuable when the samples we have measured suggest that the assumptions underlying an otherwise appropriate parametric test cannot be met. Nonparametric tests, however, can be applied not only to magnitude data, but also to other types such as sets of ranks or classified frequencies. For example, we might ask a factory foreman to rank 20 men working under his supervision, from the best to the poorest worker, and then compare the ranks received by 10 of the men who had been given a training course before being assigned to the job with the ranks of the 10 men who had been given no special training. It is unnecessary to give an illustration of classified frequencies, since we have just dealt with such data in Chapter 14 on χ^2. We should mention, however, that χ^2 is itself an example of a nonparametric technique and that several of the tests we will be discussing in this chapter involve converting our raw data into classified frequencies and then computing a χ^2.

When we have magnitude data for which it is permissible to apply a parametric test, we may find it more time-consuming and computationally involved to compute the t, analysis of variance, or whatever, than a parallel nonparametric test. However, whenever possible we continue to use parametric tests in preference to nonparametric ones, for the following reason: If we apply both to the same data, we usually find that a nonparametric test is less powerful in terms of rejecting the null hypothesis. Other things being equal, a larger sample difference is needed between groups to reject the null hypothesis at a given significance level for a nonparametric than for a parametric test. Since, as research workers, we are particularly concerned with minimizing the probability that we will accept our null hypothesis when it is false, we use the more powerful parametric tests whenever we can.

Nonparametric techniques, then, are reserved for situations in which the nature of our data makes the use of a parametric test inappropriate. The latter occurs either because we are not dealing with magnitude data or because our magnitude data suggest that the assumptions underlying the use of parametric tests are not met and that important errors may result from their use.

SOME NONPARAMETRIC TESTS

Median Test with Two Independent Samples

The first nonparametric procedure we will consider, the *median test*, is appropriate when we wish to compare two independent, random samples. With this technique we test the null hypothesis that the two samples were drawn from populations with the same *median*.

In conducting the test, we first combine the two samples and find the median of the total, combined group. Then we count the number of cases in each sample that fall below and those that fall at or above the overall median.

To illustrate these initial steps, let us assume we have two independent samples with the following scores:

Sample 1 (N = 20)

6	10	3	4	8	2	9	2	7	4
5	3	6	1	9	11	4	8	9	3

Sample 2 (N = 22)

3	15	11	9	14	15	11	4	10	12	15
14	11	12	6	13	6	12	7	14	8	15

When all 42 cases are pooled, the median for the total group is found to be 8.5. When we count the number of cases in each sample that are at or *above* the median and the number of cases that are below the median, we find:

	At or above median	Below median	Total
Sample 1	5	15	20
Sample 2	16	6	22
Total	21	21	42

Now if the samples came from populations with the same median, we would expect that except for sampling error, half of the cases in each sample would fall at or above the median of the total group and half below it. To determine whether there is a significant departure from a $50:50$ split within each of our samples, we now perform a χ^2 test with $df = 1$, following the procedures for testing an *a priori* hypothesis outlined in Chapter 14.

In Table 15.1 we have computed the χ^2 value for the data presented above. Since we were testing a $50:50$ hypothesis, we obtained the expected frequencies for the cases above and below the median in each sample simply by dividing the sample N by 2. The χ^2 we found, 9.54, is greater than the value of 6.64 required for significance at the 1% level with 1 *df*. We therefore reject the null hypothesis and conclude that the samples came from populations with different medians.

Table 15.1 Median Test: χ^2 Testing the 50:50 Hypothesis for Two Groups

	At or Above Median	*Below Median*	*Total*
Sample 1	5(10)	15(10)	20
Sample 2	16(11)	6(11)	22
	21	21	

O	*E*	*O – E*	*(O – E)^2*	$\dfrac{(O - E)^2}{E}$
5	10	−5	25	2.50
16	11	5	25	2.27
15	10	5	25	2.50
6	11	−5	25	2.27
				$\chi^2 = 9.54$

Median Test with More than Two Independent Samples

The median test we have just described may actually be used to compare any number of independent samples, not merely two. To review our method, the k samples are first combined and the median for the total group of cases determined. We then set up a $2 \times k$ table, entering the number of cases in each of the k samples that fall at or above and below the overall median. Using these data, we then compute a χ^2 testing the hypothesis that there is a 50:50 split in each of the samples. In interpreting this χ^2 we use $df = (2 - 1)(k - 1)$, which, of course, reduces to $k - 1$, or one less than the number of samples. If our computed χ^2 exceeds the tabled χ^2 value for $df = k - 1$ at the 5% or 1% level, we reject the null hypothesis that the samples all came from populations with the same median.

You will note that in conducting a median test, scores taking the same value as the median are classified with the scores falling *above* the median. In situations in which some scores actually do fall exactly at the median, chi square tends to be more significant, even if there is no real effect. In this instance, the median test may be improved upon by obtaining the observed frequencies, as we have just described, but computing a χ^2 test of independence using the methods outlined later in Chapter 14. More specifically, the method shown in Table 14.2 should be used in the case of two samples, and the method used in Table 14.3 should be used in the case of more than two samples.

A Rank Test for Two Independent Samples (Mann-Whitney U)

The U test, devised by Mann and Whitney and also, independently, by Wilcoxon, is a technique based on score ranks that is appropriate for comparing two independent groups. Our first step is to combine the two samples and rank the total set of scores, assigning the rank of

1 to the largest score, 2 to the second largest, and so on. (The same final result would be obtained if scores were instead ranked from *smallest* to largest.) If tied scores occur, we handle them in the usual way: Each is assigned the average of the ranks the tied scores jointly occupy; for example, if two scores are tied for fourth place, each is assigned a rank of 4.5, the average of 4 and 5.*

Having assigned a rank to each score, we find the sum of the ranks for each sample, identifying these sums by R_1 and R_2. Next we calculate a statistic designated as U, one for each sample. (Actually, we need only one of these U values but can use the other as a check on the accuracy of our calculations.) For sample 1, this statistic is determined by the following formula:

$$U_1 = N_1N_2 + \frac{N_1(N_1 + 1)}{2} - R_1 \qquad (15.1)$$

where R_1 is the sum of the ranks assigned to the first sample.

Assuming the null hypothesis, which states, in effect, that the samples come from the same population with respect to the measured characteristic, the sampling distribution of U has a mean (expected U or U_E) equal to the value given by the formula:

$$U_E = \frac{N_1N_2}{2} \qquad (15.2)$$

and a standard deviation whose value is given by the formula:

$$\sigma_U = \sqrt{\frac{N_1N_2(N_1 + N_2 + 1)}{12}} \qquad (15.3)$$

We now convert our obtained U into a z score:

$$z = \frac{x}{\sigma} = \frac{U_1 - U_E}{\sigma_U} \qquad (15.4)$$

The U for the second sample could be obtained by a parallel formula, with R_1 being replaced by R_2 and, in the second term of the formula, the N_1 values by N_2 values. We could then find z by subtracting U_E from U_2 instead of U_1 in the numerator of the formula, since the two resulting differences are opposite in sign but of the same absolute value; that is, U_1 and U_2 deviate equally from U_E but in the opposite direction. The scores of the sample whose U is less than U_E are, of course, lower than those of the other sample and vice versa.

---

*No problem results from this method of assigning ranks to tied scores when they all occur in a single sample, since the sum of ranks is unaffected. When ties occur across groups, the sum for each group *is* affected, being determined by the particular rank given to each tied score. This, in turn, affects U_1 (or U_2) and z. One statistician, J. V. Bradley, *Distribution-free Statistical Tests* (Englewood Cliffs, N.J.: Prentice-Hall, 1968), has recommended that this problem be resolved by considering all possible rankings of tied values and computing and reporting the z's based on the U's of all the various combinations. This recommendation seems reasonable in instances in which the conclusion one reaches about the significance of the findings is likely to be affected.

If the N of each of our samples is 8 or more, the sampling distribution of U is normal or approximately so, and we may use the normal curve table to assess the null hypothesis. Thus, if we are testing a bidirectional H_1 and the z we have calculated is greater in absolute value than 1.96 (or 2.58), we reject the null hypothesis at the 5% (or 1%) level and conclude that the samples differed significantly. If z is less than this value, we accept the null hypothesis. When the N of one or both of the samples is less than 8, the sampling distribution of U is not normal and we must use a special table, which is not included in this book, to interpret z.

In Table 15.2 we have performed a Mann-Whitney U test on the hypothetical data from two independent samples. The z has been calculated twice, first using U_1 and then U_2 to demonstrate that z will be the same except for sign. Since the sample N's are greater than 8, we use the normal curve to assess our calculated z of 1.34 and see that it falls far short of 1.96, the value needed for significance at the 5% level. We therefore accept the null hypothesis and conclude that the two samples could have come from the same population.

In both our discussion and illustration of the Mann-Whitney U test, we have assumed that the raw scores were measurement data of some kind and that we first had to convert them into ranks in order to perform the test. Sometimes, however, the raw scores *are* the ranks we need, as in the example given earlier in which the work efficiency of 20 men had been ranked, and we wished to compare the efficiency of those in the total group who had been given a special training course with the efficiency of those who had not. Except for omitting the initial step of converting raw scores to ranks, we would compute the Mann-Whitney U in the usual manner with data of this type. The same remarks hold true for the other rank tests we will discuss.

A Rank Test for Two or More Independent Groups (Kruskal-Wallis One-Way Analysis of Variance by Ranks)

The Kruskal-Wallis one-way analysis of variance by ranks is an extension of the Mann-Whitney U test that allows us to compare any number of independent groups rather than only two. We first pool all the *k* groups, arrange the total group of scores in order, and assign the *smallest* score a rank of 1, the next smallest a rank of 2, and so on, handling ties in the usual manner. (It is essential in this test that the *smallest* score be given a rank of 1, and so on down to the *largest* score.) Having ranked the total group, we then find the sum of the ranks (R_i) for each of the *k* samples.

If each of the samples came from the same population, then each of these sums of ranks (each R_i) should be equal except for sampling error. We test this null hypothesis by computing a statistic H by the following formula:

$$H = \frac{12}{N(N + 1)} \sum \left(\frac{R_i^2}{n_i} \right) - 3(N + 1) \tag{15.5}$$

where N = total number of cases in the *k* groups

n_i = number of cases in a given sample

R_i = sum of the ranks in a given sample

Table 15.2 Illustration of the Calculation of the Mann-Whitney U Test[a]

Sample 1 (N = 11)		Sample 2 (N = 10)	
X	*Rank*	*X*	*Rank*
35	1	34	2
33	3	31	5
32	4	26	9
30	6	25	11
27	7	23	13
26	9	22	14
26	9	21	15
24	12	18	19
20	16.5	17	20
20	16.5	16	21
19	18		$R_2 = 129$
	$R_1 = 102.0$		

$$U_1 = N_1 N_2 + \frac{N_1(N_1 + 1)}{2} - R_1$$

$$= (11)(10) + \frac{11(11 + 1)}{2} - 102$$

$$= 110 + \frac{132}{2} - 102$$

$$= 176 - 102 = 74$$

$$U_2 = N_1 N_2 + \frac{N_2(N_2 + 1)}{2} - R_2$$

$$= (11)(10) + \frac{10(10 + 1)}{2} - 129$$

$$= 110 + \frac{110}{2} - 129$$

$$= 165 - 129 = 36$$

$$U_E = \frac{N_1 N_2}{2} = \frac{(11)(10)}{2} = 55$$

$$\sigma_U = \sqrt{\frac{N_1 N_2(N_1 + N_2 + 1)}{12}}$$

$$= \sqrt{\frac{(11)(10)(11 + 10 + 1)}{12}}$$

$$= \sqrt{201.67} = 14.20$$

$$z = \frac{U_1 - E_E}{\sigma_U} \qquad \textbf{OR} \qquad z = \frac{U_2 - U_E}{\sigma_U}$$

$$= \frac{74 - 55}{14.20} = \frac{19}{14.20} \qquad\qquad = \frac{36 - 55}{14.20} = \frac{-19}{14.20}$$

$$= 1.34 \qquad\qquad\qquad = -1.34$$

[a]Each listed rank is the overall rank of the associated X in the total group of 21 cases.

The expression $\Sigma(R_i^2/n_i)$, then, indicates that, for each group, we are to square the sum of ranks (R_i), divide this R_i^2 by the number of cases in the group, and finally to sum these quantities for the k groups. An illustration of these procedures involving four groups is shown in Table 15.3.

When each of the samples has five or more cases, the statistic H takes the chi-square distribution with df equal to $k - 1$, the number of groups minus one. In our example where $k = 4$, therefore, we enter Table I with $4 - 1$ or 3 df and find that a χ^2 of 11.34 is required for significance at the 1% level. The H of 22.93 we obtained in Table 15.3 is greater than this value, so we are able to reject the hypothesis that all of our samples came from the same population.

A Rank Test for Two Matched Samples (Wilcoxon Signed-Ranks)

The nonparametric techniques we have discussed so far are used to compare two or more *independently* selected groups. The test we take up now was designed to allow us to compare distributions consisting of matched pairs: the same individual tested under two conditions, or pairs of different individuals matched on some basis of similarity before being tested. The

---

Table 15.3 Illustration of the Calculation of the Kruskal-Wallis One-Way Analysis of Variance for Ranks[a]

Group I (n = 6)		Group II (n = 8)		Group III (n = 7)		Group IV (n = 7)	
X	Rank	X	Rank	X	Rank	X	Rank
99	28	85	18.5	75	9	91	23
98	27	82	16	70	6	89	22
96	26	81	14	68	5	86	20
95	25	81	14	67	4	85	18.5
93	24	78	11	65	3	84	17
88	21	76	10	62	2	81	14
	$R_1 = 151$	73	8	59	1	79	12
		72	7		$R_3 = 30$		$R_4 = 126.5$
			$R_2 = 98.5$				

$$H = \frac{12}{N(N + 1)} \Sigma \left(\frac{R_i^2}{n_i}\right) - 3(N + 1)$$

$$= \left[\frac{12}{28(28 + 1)}\right]\left[\frac{151^2}{6} + \frac{98.5^2}{8} + \frac{30^2}{7} + \frac{126.5^2}{7}\right] - 3(28 + 1)$$

$$= (.0148)(7427.56) - 87 = 22.93$$

[a]Each listed rank is the overall rank of the associated X in the total group of 28 cases.

procedure, devised by Wilcoxon, is identified as a matched-pairs signed-ranks test or, more simply, as the Wilcoxon signed-ranks test.

To illustrate, assume we have tested each member of a group under two different experimental conditions. Our first step is to find the difference (D) between the pair of scores (I and II) for each subject. We now discard from further consideration any pair of scores for which the D is 0. We then rank the remaining D's in order of *absolute* magnitude, assigning the rank of 1 to the *smallest* absolute D, 2 to the next *smallest*, and so on. As always, ties are handled by assigning to each tied D the average of the ranks the ties jointly occupy. Next we give to each of these absolute ranks the sign of the associated D score, giving us a set of *signed ranks*.

These procedures are illustrated in Table 15.4, in which, for convenience, we ordered the 10 subjects in terms of the absolute magnitude of their D scores, shown in the fourth column. Since the first subject received the same score in both conditions, so that D = 0, no rank was assigned to the D for this individual. For the nine remaining D's the *smallest* absolute D was given a rank of 1, and so on, down to rank 9 for the largest absolute D. Finally, in the last column we have given each of the absolute ranks the same sign, + or −, as its D.

Our next step is to sum the positive signed ranks and then to sum the negative signed ranks. If the two distributions of scores come from the same population—that is, if the null hypothesis that our two experimental conditions have no differential effects is correct—we would expect that the positive and negative sums would have the same absolute value except for sampling error.

For small samples a special table has been set up that allows us to test the null hypothesis directly from the sums of our signed ranks. This table is reproduced in Table J of Appendix III for N's up to 25, where N is the *total number of signed ranks* (N_{S-R}). Since some of our D's may be 0 and thus discarded, N_{S-R} may be less than the total number of original pairs of scores. The table is used as follows. The *smaller* (in absolute value) of the two sums of signed

Table 15.4 Illustration of the Calculation of the Wilcoxon Signed-Ranks Test[a]

Subject	Score I	Score II	D	Rank of |D|	Signed Rank
1	39	39	0	—	—
2	47	48	−1	1	−1
3	29	27	2	2.5	2.5
4	33	35	−2	2.5	−2.5
5	36	33	3	4	4
6	48	43	5	5	5
7	38	31	7	6.5	6.5
8	43	36	7	6.5	6.5
9	32	23	9	8	8
10	52	40	12	9	9

$\Sigma + = 41.5$

$N_{S-R} = 9$　　T = 3.5　　　　　　　　$\Sigma - = -3.5$

[a]The raw data are from 10 subjects tested under two experimental conditions.

ranks is designated as T. We then look up in Table J the *maximum* value T may take and still be significant at the 5% or 1% level (two-tailed test) for our N_{S-R}. (Unlike t or F, the smaller the T the more significant it is.) In our example in Table 15.4 the number of signed ranks is 9 and T is 3.5. Looking at Table J, we find that for $N_{S-R} = 9$, a T of 6 *or less* is required for significance at the 5% level and a T of 2 *or less* at the 1% level. Since our obtained T of 3.5 is less than 6 but not less than 2, we reject the null hypothesis at the 5% level.

For larger samples the sampling distribution of T is approximately normal with a mean (expected T or T_E) given by the formula:

$$T_E = \frac{N(N + 1)}{4} \tag{15.6}$$

and a standard deviation given by the formula:

$$\sigma_T = \sqrt{\frac{N(N + 1)(2N + 1)}{24}} \tag{15.7}$$

where N = the number of *signed ranks*. We can then determine the z for our calculated T:

$$z = \frac{T - T_E}{\sigma_T} \tag{15.8}$$

We assess the null hypothesis by comparing our calculated z with the values of 1.96 and 2.58 required for significance in a normal distribution at the 5% and 1% levels, respectively.

A Rank Test for Two or More Matched Groups (Friedman Two-Way Analysis of Variance by Ranks)

On occasion we might want to test the same subjects not merely twice but three or more times. We might, for example, give each of a group of students three passages to memorize that contain political opinions with which they agree strongly, disagree strongly, or have no reactions, in order to determine whether this content factor affects their memorization. Or we might train a group of animals to run to a 10-unit food reward, then give 20 trials with a 5-unit reward to see if there is any systematic decline in running speeds to the reduced reward over the 20 trials. If the underlying assumptions are met, the data obtained by repeated measurement of the same subject may be analyzed by extensions of the analysis of variance techniques discussed in earlier chapters—extensions that will not be presented in this text.

If the assumptions for the analysis of variance are not fulfilled by our data, a nonparametric test that may be applied to data involving two or more measures from each subject is the Friedman two-way analysis of variance for ranks. In this analysis one variable is considered to be subjects and the other variable is measures.

In applying the Friedman rank test we first set up a table such as the one at the upper left of Table 15.5, in which each of the rows contains the k scores earned by each of the N subjects. In our example each subject was measured three times. As shown at the upper right of Table 15.5 we now rank, from 1 to k, the scores in each *row*—the scores of each *subject*. We have chosen in our example to go from largest to smallest in ranking the scores of each subject but could have done it the opposite way if we wished.

The next step is to find the sums of the ranks for each of the k measures—that is, for each of the *columns*. If our experimental conditions had no differential effects, any difference in the rank of the scores for a given subject is due to chance factors, and across subjects, any given rank is therefore as likely to be found with one measure as another. This implies, of course, that if the null hypothesis is true, each of the column sums of ranks would be equal except for sampling error.

We test the null hypothesis by computing a χ^2 based on the column sums. This χ^2 is given by the formula:

$$\chi_R{}^2 = \frac{12}{Nk(k+1)} \left(\sum R_i{}^2 \right) - 3N(k+1) \tag{15.9}$$

where k = number of measures
N = number of subjects
R_i = a column sum of ranks

The resulting $\chi_R{}^2$ approximates the chi-square distribution with $df = k - 1$. In Table 15.5 we calculated $\chi_R{}^2$ to be 2.00 and df to be 2. This value is far less than the χ^2 of 5.99 found in Table I to be associated with the 5% level for 2 df. We therefore accept the null hypothesis and conclude that there was no significant difference among the three measures.

Table 15.5 Illustration of the Calculation of $\chi_R{}^2$ in the Friedman Two-Way Analysis of Variance by Ranks[a]

| | Raw Scores | | | | Scores Ranked by Rows | | |
| | Measure | | | | Measure | | |
Subject	I	II	III	Subject	I	II	III
1	12	14	11	1	2	1	3
2	13	19	16	2	3	1	2
3	15	18	19	3	3	2	1
4	17	22	20	4	3	1	2
5	17	15	22	5	2	3	1
6	19	21	24	6	3	2	1
7	21	19	18	7	1	2	3
					17	12	13

$$\chi_R{}^2 = \frac{12}{Nk(k+1)} \left(\sum R_i{}^2 \right) - 3N(k+1)$$

$$= \left[\frac{12}{(7)(3)(3+1)} \right] [17^2 + 12^2 + 13^2] - 3(7)(3+1)$$

$$= 86 - 84 = 2 \qquad df = k - 1 = 2$$

[a]The raw data are from seven subjects tested under three experimental conditions.

RELATIVE EFFICIENCY
OF PARAMETRIC
AND NONPARAMETRIC TESTS

We stress once more that a nonparametric test may not be as powerful as the corresponding parametric test such as t or F. One measure of the relative usefulness of these types of tests is the *relative efficiency* of two tests. Relative efficiency is defined as the *ratio of the sample sizes required by each test to obtain the same power value*. For example, suppose that for a given $\mu_1 - \mu_2$ value a t test had a power of .70 when N = 10 and a certain nonparametric test had the same power with an N of 12. According to our definition, the relative efficiency of the nonparametric test (compared to the t test) is $\frac{10}{12}$ or .833. This example illustrates the greater efficiency of the parametric test, the usual finding when sample N's are moderate or large in size. However, if very small samples are used (total N's of about 6), many nonparametric tests have relative efficiencies nearly equal to 1, compared to the corresponding parametric tests.

The relative efficiencies just mentioned were computed under the assumption that the data came from populations and samples satisfying the assumptions of the parametric test involved. Such data are precisely those for which parametric tests such as the t and the F test were developed. So nonparametric tests often work quite well even in cases where parametric tests are preferable. But once assumptions such as normality, which are required by the t and F tests, are known to be false, we know that t or F may lead to inappropriate conclusions about significance levels. In that case a nonparametric test will probably be preferable, even if it has low relative efficiency, because we can then be sure about our significance level.

Unfortunately, relative efficiency is not a constant that can be determined for any pair of tests. Rather, its value changes as the size of the sample or samples for one test changes. Relative efficiency also changes as other factors change, such as the α level desired and the value of the population difference (such as the value of $\mu_1 - \mu_2$) to be detected. Although we may want to know the relative efficiency for small-sample situations, it is more convenient to find a related measure, called the *asymptotic relative efficiency* (or ARE), which is constant in value despite variations in such factors as we have mentioned.

What is asymptotic relative efficiency? *Asymptotic* means the final level reached or almost reached at the end or *asymptote* of a process, such as the level of proficiency reached on a motor task so well practiced that no further improvement is noticeable. Similarly, *asymptotic relative efficiency* is attained after N becomes large enough that relative efficiency does not change appreciably with further increases in the N for each group. The asymptotic relative efficiencies for the five nonparametric tests described in this chapter are given in Table 15.6.

The tabled values help us decide what nonparametric test to use in a given situation. If we have two independent groups of scores with no tied ranks between groups, for example, we would prefer the Mann-Whitney U test to the median test because of the latter's inefficiency, particularly with larger N's. Similarly, the Kruskal-Wallis test, which can be used with more than two groups, is more efficient than the median test and should be used in preference to the latter. However, if there are several cases of tied ranks across groups, complications from these ties may make the median test preferable to the Kruskal-Wallis or Mann-Whitney, even though its ARE is lower.

Table 15.6 Asymptotic Relative Efficiencies (ARE's) of Five Nonparametric Tests Compared to the Corresponding Parametric Tests

Test	ARE
Median test (two or more independent samples)	.637
Mann-Whitney U test (two independent samples)	.955
Kruskal-Wallis H test (two or more independent samples)	.955
Wilcoxon signed-ranks test	.955
Friedman rank test[a]	.637 for $k = 2$
	.716 for $k = 3$
	. . .
	.910 for $k = 20$
	. . .
	.955 for $k = \infty$

[a]Where k = number of treatments given to each of N subjects.

Nonparametric, distribution-free tests are a relatively recent development in statistics, and new techniques of this type continue to be devised to handle different kinds of statistical problems presented by empirical data. Although parametric tests continue to be preferable if the assumptions underlying their use can be met, nonparametric tests, a selected group of which we have presented in this chapter, are often of invaluable assistance to the research worker.

DEFINITIONS OF TERMS AND SYMBOLS

Nonparametric or distribution-free test. A statistical test that does not require estimation of population parameters and makes few assumptions about the shape of the distribution from which the data to be analyzed come.

Median test. A technique for testing the null hypothesis that two or more independent random samples come from populations with the same median. The test involves classifying members of each sample as falling above or below the overall median for the total group and then performing a chi-square test to determine whether all groups have equivalent proportions of scores at or above the median.

Mann-Whitney U test. A substitute for the t test with two independent groups, useful for situations in which normal distributions cannot be assumed. All scores in the two groups are ranked together, and separate sums of ranks are obtained for each group. Then either sum may be used with other information to calculate first a U and then a z to be compared to entries in Table B to determine the significance of the difference between the two groups. For small samples, a special table must be used in place of Table B.

Kruskal-Wallis one-way analysis of variance by ranks. The generalization of the Mann-Whitney U test for the case of two or more independent groups.

Wilcoxon signed-ranks test. A distribution-free analog of the *t* test for matched pairs, for use when the parent populations are not normal. A statistic called T, based on a ranking of the differences between pairs of scores, is calculated and its value is compared to entries in Table J in order to determine the significance of the difference between the two conditions being compared.

Friedman two-way analysis of variance by ranks. A chi-square test using ranks to compare the effects of treatments in two or more matched groups.

Relative efficiency. A method of comparing the power of two tests to detect a false null hypothesis. Relative efficiency is equal to the ratio of the sample sizes required by each test to obtain the same power value with the N for a nonparametric test being evaluated going in the denominator.

Asymptotic relative efficiency (ARE). Relative efficiency when N is very large for each group.

PROBLEMS

1. Randomly selected groups of male professional football players, college professors, and business executives were given a test of their enjoyment of interpersonal competition. The results are shown below, with high scores indicating high competitiveness.

Football players	College professors	Businessmen
35	31	35
35	28	34
35	26	31
34	22	27
34	21	26
34	20	24
33	19	23
32	19	21
30	18	21
28	18	19

   (a) If the groups were compared by means of a one-way analysis of variance, what assumptions underlying this parametric test appear to be violated?

   (b) Compare the groups by a median test, using $\alpha = .05$. What do you conclude about the competitiveness of the three groups?

2. Twenty students participated in an experiment in which they studied a prose passage for 3 minutes and then were asked to recall its content. The passage was an essay on the merits of the capitalistic economic system. The students had previously responded in their class to a political attitudes questionnaire and on the basis of the class median, were divided into those who were below the median (liberal) or above the median (conservative) in their attitudes. The recall data for the two groups are reported below. Perform a Mann-Whitney U test on these data, using $\alpha = .05$. What do you conclude about the effects on recall of material that agrees or disagrees with one's attitudes?

   Conservative: 25, 23, 21, 21, 20, 19, 14, 11
   Liberal: 24, 22, 18, 17, 16, 15, 15, 14, 13, 12, 11, 10

3. Laboratory rats prefer a sucrose solution to plain water and will run down a straight alley faster when they anticipate a sucrose reward. In a study of taste threshold, one group of thirsty rats was given 50 trials in a straight alley to a water reward, a second group was tested with a very weak sucrose solution, and a third with a slightly stronger solution. The running times in the last block of 10 trials are shown below. Analyze the data by the Kruskal-Wallis test. What do you conclude about the capacity of the animals to detect the sucrose?

Water: 30, 29, 26, 21, 18
Lower sucrose: 31, 28, 27, 22, 20
Higher sucrose: 33, 33, 30, 25, 19

4. In a word recognition study, subjects were shown a list of words for $\frac{1}{100}$ second each and asked to guess what the word was. Before each of these test words, they were shown another word for 1 second. For half of the list, the word shown first was associated with the test word (such as "table" followed by "chair") and for the other half, the first word had no discernible association with the test word ("green" followed by "horse"). The number of correct guesses made by each subject for test words preceded by associated and nonassociated words is shown below. Perform a Wilcoxon signed-ranks test of these data, using $\alpha = .05$. What do you conclude about the effects of the experimental conditions?

Subject	Associated	Nonassociated
1	19	17
2	18	19
3	18	13
4	17	11
5	16	12
6	15	15
7	15	12
8	12	10
9	10	8
10	9	10

5. A child psychologist has devised a behavior modification program to be applied by parents whose young children frequently throw temper tantrums. He asks parents to record the number of tantrums exhibited by their children for a period of one week during which they are being trained how to treat their children, for another week one month later, and a final week six months later. The following results are obtained from five children. Compare the distribution by means of the Friedman two-way analysis of variance by rank. What do you conclude about the effect of the training program?

Child	Week I	Week II	Week III
1	18	8	2
2	17	6	0
3	13	14	3
4	11	3	4
5	10	11	5

16

Determination of the Appropriate Statistical Test

- SUMMARY OF STATISTICS OF INFERENCE
- DECISION TREE

We have stressed throughout this text that in scientific research, investigators are seldom interested in the properties of the particular groups of individuals they have observed. Rather, their aim is to make reasonable guesses about the properties of populations, based on the data collected from samples of individuals drawn in an unbiased manner from the populations under scrutiny. For this reason, the major portion of this textbook has been devoted to the *statistics of inference*, that is, statistical techniques that allow us to come to conclusions about population characteristics at specified probability levels.

One of our goals in introducing students to some of the statistics of inference that are frequently used in psychology and other behavioral sciences is to make them more sophisticated consumers of research in these disciplines—that is, to enable them to read and comprehend research reports in which data are analyzed by means of these techniques. Another major goal is to give students some basic statistical tools that will help them analyze and interpret the data from studies they themselves conduct. Formulation of a research question is only the first step in doing an empirical study. Investigators must determine how the study is to be conducted and must decide what statistical techniques to use in analyzing the data that will answer the research question.

In this chapter we first present a summary of the kinds of research questions and designs we have discussed and the appropriate statistical tests and techniques to use with them. Then we will introduce you to a "decision tree," shown in Figure 16.1, that outlines a series of decisions about a specific research study that will lead you to an appropriate statistical technique to use. We should note, however, that only a limited number of fairly basic statistical tests have been presented in this text and that they are applicable only to relatively simple research designs. Our summary and decision tree are correspondingly limited.

SUMMARY OF STATISTICS
OF INFERENCE

We have discussed two basic types of data that are collected and analyzed in research studies. The first type is *numerical data*. These usually involve the assignment of a number to the individual case that reflects the amount or *magnitude* of a property the individual exhibits. Sometimes the property being observed varies in amount but individuals in a group are only assigned numbers indicating their relative position or *rank order* in the group. The second type is *categorical data*, which involve a set of discrete, mutually exclusive categories into which each individual case can be classified. Because different statistical techniques are applied to the two types of data, the inferential tests we have discussed are classified by the type of data involved.*

---

*We call your attention to the fact that type of data refers to the data being *collected and analyzed*. Students sometimes get confused when confronted with an experiment involving two or more conditions (e.g., learning Russian or Italian words) in which some numerical property (e.g., speed of acquisition) is measured for subjects in each group. As conditions are categorical, they ask, why aren't such experiments classified as involving categorical as opposed to numerical data? The answer is that the data that are being collected and analyzed are not conditions (the independent variable) but measures of the numerical property being observed during the experiment (the dependent variable).

Numerical Data

I. *Parametric techniques*

Most of the statistical tests applied to numerical data that we have discussed are identified as *parametric* techniques. That is, in order to be used appropriately, certain properties (parameters) of the population, such as σ, must be estimated. Further, certain assumptions must be met—for example, that the property under consideration is normally distributed in the population and, in the case of more than one population, that the σ's are equal. Techniques that make assumptions about population parameters are therefore called parametric statistics.

A. Single distribution (sample) of measures

When a study involves a distribution of measures from a single sample, we have discussed only questions about the μ of the population from which the sample was drawn.

1. H_0 about μ

A hypothesis about the exact value of μ is either stated directly or implied in the research question. The H_0 is evaluated by means of a *t*-test, using Formula 8.4: $t = (\overline{X} - \mu)/s_{\overline{X}}$ where $df = N - 1$.

2. Confidence interval (CI) about μ

The question is about the range of values within which it can be asserted, at a particular confidence level, that μ falls. Use Formulas 8.6 and 8.7 to test the 99% CI and 95% CI, respectively, for $df = N - 1$.

B. Two distributions (samples) of measures

1. Independent distributions

Members of one sample are chosen in a way that does not influence choice of members of the second sample.

Only a technique for testing a hypothesis about a difference between μ's has been discussed. The hypothesis that is almost always tested is:

$$H_0: \mu_1 - \mu_2 = 0$$

This H_0 implies that the two conditions or types of groups (independent variable) have no differential effects on the dependent variable, so that the population means are equal.

(a) Independent groups *t*

The H_0 is tested by an independent groups *t*. By Formula 9.5:

$$t = \frac{(\overline{X}_1 - \overline{X}_2)}{s_{\overline{X}_1 - \overline{X}_2}}$$

with $df = N_1 + N_2 - 2$. When N's are equal, use Formula 9.3 to calculate the standard error of the difference and when N's are unequal, use Formula 9.6 or 9.7.

(b) Estimated effect size

An estimate of effect size is obtained by $\hat{\omega}^2$. This statistic, calculated by Formula 9.10, is an estimate of the proportion of the total variability that is accounted for by the effect of conditions or groups.

2. Matched pairs of measures

The same individual is tested once under one condition and once under another condition, or pairs of individuals who are very similar on relevant variables are identified beforehand and assigned at random to the two conditions. Distributions of paired measures are the result. Two different kinds of questions can be asked.

(a) Difference between μ's

Of interest is whether the two distributions differ in their means. The H_0 that is tested is:

$$H_0: \mu_1 - \mu_2 = 0$$

This H_0 may be tested by a direct difference t (Formula 11.5) where $df =$ no. of pairs $- 1$, or even more conveniently, by Sandler's A (Formula 11.6).

(b) Relationship (correlation) between the pairs of measures

The question is whether the pairs of measures (X and Y) tend to be associated or to covary. Two types of correlation coefficients are available.

(1) Pearson r

Pearson r is computed when the numbers represent magnitude data, that is, numbers indicating the amount of the characteristic the individual exhibits. A raw-score formula for computing r is shown in Formula 10.2.

The H_0 that is tested is that the population $r = 0$. The critical values of r at $\alpha = .05$ and $.01$ that are used to evaluate this H_0 can be found in a special table (Table D) using $df = N - 2$.

(2) Spearman $r(r_S)$

Spearman r is computed when the initial distributions represent rank-order data or for some reason it is appropriate to translate magnitude data into ranks, e.g., the assumptions underlying Pearson r cannot be met. The formula for r_S is shown in Formula 10.11. The H_0 that $r_S = 0$ is evaluated by finding the critical values at $\alpha = .05$ and $.01$ in Table E, using $df = N - 2$. It is appropriate to test this H_0 only when the data do not contain tied ranks.

C. Two or more distributions

1. Single independent variable

When two or more groups or conditions differ with respect to only a single independent variable, the question is about the μ's of the populations from which the samples were selected.

(a) One-way analysis of variance (ANOVA)

The H_0 that is tested is:

$$H_0: \mu_1 = \mu_2 = \cdots = \mu_k$$

The H_0 that all μ's are equal is tested by conducting a one-way ANOVA using Formulas 12.4 to 12.10.

(b) *hsd* test

When more than two groups or conditions are involved, the Tukey *hsd* test can be conducted following the computation of F in one-way ANOVA to determine the significance of the differences between specific pairs of sample means. Use Formula 12.12.

(c) Estimated effect size

An estimate of effect size is provided by $\hat{\omega}^2$, calculated by Formula 12.11.

2. Two independent variables

When groups or conditions differ according to two variables (A and B), forming a two-way factorial design, three H_0's are tested:

$$H_0: \mu_{A1} = \mu_{A2} = \cdots = \mu_{Am}$$
(main effects of A)

$$H_0: \mu_{B1} = \mu_{B2} = \cdots = \mu_{Bn}$$
(main effects of B)

$$H_0: \text{A and B combine additively}$$
(A $\times$ B interaction)

These H_0 are tested by means of a two-way ANOVA, using Formulas 13.1 to 13.10.

II. *Nonparametric techniques*

When the assumptions underlying parametric techniques are seriously violated, their use in testing null hypotheses may lead to erroneous conclusions. In these instances, nonparametric techniques are more appropriate.

Listed below are four parametric techniques and for each, parallel nonparametric techniques that can be used in their place.

Parametric Technique	Parallel Nonparametric Technique
A. *t*-test for comparing $\overline{X}$'s of independent groups	1. Median test with two independent samples (Formula 14.1) 2. Mann-Whitney U for two independent samples (Formulas 15.1 to 15.4)
B. *t*-test for comparing $\overline{X}$'s of matched samples	Wilcoxon signed-ranks test for two matched samples (Formulas 15.6 to 15.8)
C. One-way ANOVA for independent samples	Kruskal-Wallis ANOVA by ranks test for more than two samples (Formula 15.5)
D. ANOVA for matched groups*	Friedman two-way ANOVA by ranks (Formula 15.9)

III. *Categorical data*

A. One set of categories

1. Two categories

Test H_0 about a population proportion (p_t). The hypothesis is either stated or implied in the problem. Either of two tests may be used:

(a) z test, using Formulas 8.8 and 8.9

(b) χ^2 test

The χ^2 is computed by Formulas 14.1 in which expected frequencies are those expected under H_0.

---

*This parametric test is not presented in the text.

332 ■ Chapter 16

2. More than two categories

Test H_0 about proportion of the population falling into each category as stated or implied in the problem. Compute χ^2 by Formula 14.1 in which expected frequencies are those expected under H_0.

B. Two sets of categories

Two types of hypotheses can be tested.

1. H_0 about population proportions

Compute χ^2 by Formula 14.1, in which expected frequencies are those expected under H_0.

2. H_0 that the proportions in the two sets of categories do not differ.

This H_0 states that classification by one set of categories has no relation to the likelihood of being assigned to a particular category among the second set.

This H_0 is tested by a χ^2 test of independence, using Formula 14.1. The observed total frequencies in the columns and rows are used to determine the expected frequencies in the cells.

DECISION TREE

In Figure 16.1 we have presented a decision tree that should be useful when you are presented with a research question and have to decide on an appropriate analytic technique to answer the question being posed in the study. The decision tree indicates a series of decisions you must make in order to pick the appropriate test. The first decision you must always make is whether the data that are to be analyzed are numerical or categorical in nature. (If this distinction is not absolutely clear to you, be sure to go back and review pages 9–11.)

Before you apply a parametric technique to a set of numerical data, you should also examine the data to determine whether the assumptions underlying the use of the technique are met. If the assumptions are seriously violated, a nonparametric technique should be substituted. These substitute nonparametric techniques are not included in the decision tree in Figure 16.1 on pages 334–35. You should instead consult the summary on page 331 for parallel parametric and nonparametric tests. We should also mention that our decision tree, like the summary we have just presented, is limited to the types of research designs and statistical techniques discussed in this text.

Step-by-Step Procedures

We will illustrate the use of the decision tree by presenting a number of hypothetical investigations and showing the series of decisions that lead to identification of the appropriate statistical test.

Problem 1

Research Question

A group of mothers who abused their children and another group who did not participated in a study in which they were shown a series of slides of 6-month-old babies. For each slide the mother was asked to identify what emotion the baby was experiencing. The number of correct choices made by each mother was recorded. The investigators suspected that mothers who abuse their children are less accurate.

Decisions

Examination of the decision tree in Figure 16.1 shows that the first decision is always whether the data are numerical or categorical. In this study, the answer is *numerical*, each mother having a score indicating *how many* correct responses she made. Thus:

> *Decision 1:* numerical

Having made this decision, we go to the "IF NUMERICAL" box. This box leads to a second decision: the number of distributions (samples) of data to be analyzed. In our study, there are *two distributions*, one for abusive mothers and one for nonabusive mothers. Thus:

> *Decision 2:* two distributions

The "IF TWO" box leads to a third decision: independently selected samples or matched pairs. The women who were selected from one population of mothers had no influence on which women were selected from the other population, so the two groups and their distributions of scores are *independent*. Thus:

> *Decision 3:* independent distributions

The "IF INDEPENDENT" box points to *independent groups t*. Thus:

Statistical Test: independent groups *t*

We compute this *t* to test H_0: $\mu_1 - \mu_2 = 0$, the hypothesis that the populations of abusive and nonabusive mothers are equally accurate (have the same μ's) in judging babies' emotions. (Note that the investigator's *experimental* hypothesis was that abusive mothers are less accurate.)

In the examples below, we will go through the steps in arriving at the appropriate statistical test in a more abbreviated fashion. By following the arrows from the boxes from the decision and the IF statements in Figure 16.1, you should be able to locate the statistical test that will answer the experimental question.

Problem 2

Research Question

Ten years ago, residents of a midwestern city were given a survey which included the question: "Do you think most politicians are honest?" Recently, the same survey was given in the same city. Determine whether opinions about politicians' honesty have changed.

334

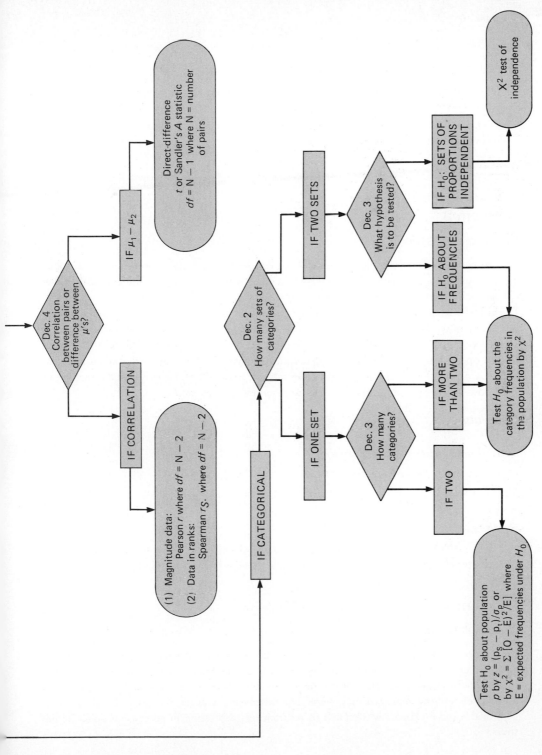

Figure 16.1 Decision tree used to determine appropriate statistic test.*

*Not listed are nonparametric tests used to replace parametric tests when their assumptions are not met. Consult the summary on page 331 for parallel parametric and nonparametric tests.

Decisions

1. Categorical data: the answers were yes or no

2. Two sets of categories: respondents were classified by answer to question (yes or no) and by date of survey.

3. H_0 is that the two methods of classification are unrelated, that the proportion of yes and no answers hasn't changed between 10 years ago and now.

Statistical Test: χ^2 test of independence (significant differences in proportions)

Problem 3

Research Question

In a study of ingroup and outgroup stereotypes, college students were given information about one of four (fictional) male students. Two of the four men were said to be students at the same college as the participants and the other two men were said to attend another, rival college. Within each college condition (same–different), one of the men was described as possessing predominantly desirable characteristics and the other man was described as possessing predominantly undesirable characteristics. To summarize, each subject was presented with a description of one of four male students, the descriptions varying in the college the student attended (same or different) and his characteristics (desirable or undesirable). Subjects rated on a 7-point scale how likable they found the man whose description they read.

Decisions

1. Numerical data: degree of likability.

2. More than two distributions; there are four groups.

3. Two variables, same vs. different college and desirable vs. undesirable characteristics.

Statistical Test: Two-way ANOVA

The ANOVA tests 3 hypotheses: μ's for same or different college are equal, μ's for type of characteristics are equal, and the two variables are additive in their effects.

Problem 4

Research Question

High school students who had recently experienced negative life events of a serious nature (for example, death of a close friend or relative) were questioned about the number of people that they confided in or could count on for help when they were under stress and were also given a test assessing how depressed they were. The investigator was interested in whether amount of available social support was related to resistance to depression in adolescents suffering life stress.

Decisions

1. Numerical data: degree of depression and amount of social support.

2. Two distributions.

3. Matched pairs; for each student, a score on depression and on social support.

4. Correlation; the question concerns the relationship between the two measures.

Statistical Test: Pearson r since magnitude data were collected

Problem 5

Research Question

Children played a game in which the points they earned were worth money. Each played under one of three conditions: play alone, play competitively with another child, or play cooperatively with another child. The game was rigged so that (unknown to the children), each was given the same amount of money following the game. Each child was then privately asked to give some of it to a charity that "helped poor children." The investigator believed that the amount the children were willing to give would be influenced by the condition under which they played the game.

Decisions

1. Numerical data: amount of money given to charity.

2. Three distributions, one for each of the three experimental conditions.

3. Single independent variable, type of playing condition.

Statistical Test: One-way ANOVA testing H_0: μ's for each condition are equal

Problem 6

Research Question

An experimenter gave each subject in a group of 200 a pair of words and asked each subject to guess which one was "correct." There were 20 different word pairs, each given to 10 subjects. The investigator wanted to select pairs of words for which there was no initial guessing preference for use in a later study. A separate statistical analysis had to be conducted for each word pair.

Decisions

1. Categorical; number of subjects choosing word A or B in the given pair.

2. One set of categories.

3. Two categories, choice of word A or B.

Statistical Test: Test H_0 for population proportion (p_t) by either z or χ^2: The H_0 in this problem is $p_t = .50$; that is, there is no preference for one word over the other.

PROBLEMS

Each problem describes a study. Using Figure 16.1, decide what statistical test to use to test the research question. Also specify in concrete terms the H_0 that is to be tested.

1. A study of 100 married couples with children was conducted in which a number of kinds of information was collected.

   (a) One measure was a rating by each spouse of overall satisfaction with the marriage on a 7-point scale. Was level of satisfaction of one spouse related to level of satisfaction of the other?

   (b) Were husbands as a group equally satisfied as their wives?

2. In the early 1970's, a professor gave his introductory sociology class a list of 15 then illegal or socially disapproved acts (e.g., abortion, armed robbery, rape, drunk driving) and asked them to rank them in order of seriousness. He arrived at a final set of ranks, 1–15, by obtaining the group totals for each offense and ranking these. This year he gave his current introductory class the same list to see if students' views had changed.

3. In an investigation of neural mechanisms in learning and memory, an experimenter had one group of animals (rats) learn to traverse a maze to obtain food. Then the animals were operated on, during which a brain lesion in a specific region was made. Another group received a sham operation after learning the maze; that is, all the same procedures were performed but no lesion was made. A week following the operation, each rat was retested in the maze and errors were recorded.

4. Children were randomly assigned to one of three conditions. In each, the children worked on two sets of problems. In the first condition, the children were praised for doing well on the first set; in the second condition, they were praised and given a prize for having done so well; in the third condition, they were given no feedback. All children were then given the second set of problems and encouraged to do their best. Number of correct solutions on the second set of problems was determined.

5. In Problem 6 in the Step by Step Procedure section on page 337, an experiment was described in which the investigator wanted to identify pairs of words for which there was no initial preference. He also wanted to identify trios of equally preferred words. Each subject was given a set of 3 words and asked to guess which word was "correct." There were 20 different word sets, 10 subjects per word. A test is conducted for each set of words.

6. In a study of perceptions of injustice, subjects were promised up to $10 for taking part in the experiment. Three subjects were tested at a time, each subject working on a proofreading task in the same room as the other two subjects. After 30 minutes, the subjects were stopped and told to go to one of three adjacent cubicles, A, B, and C, one subject per cubicle, and to wait for further instructions. The experimenter went to each cubicle, giving the subjects in cubicle A, B, and C $10, $7, and $4, respectively, as their reward. All subjects were informed about the three reward levels. Half of the subjects in each reward condition were told that the money they received had been determined by how well they had done in comparison to the other two people with whom they had worked. The other half were told (in fact, truthfully) that the amount of reward they received was determined by the cubicle they happened to pick. Subjects then filled out a rating scale asking how fair they thought the reward procedure was.

7. In a study of career aspirations among psychology graduate students, one question asks whether the student's career or family will be more important. A comparison is made of the answers of male students specializing in clinical psychology versus the answers of male students specializing in biopsychology.

Appendix I
The Use of Computers
in Statistical Analyses

Computers vary in size, they are manufactured by many different companies, and each model has its own peculiarities. All computers, however, have certain features in common: ways of transmitting information to the computer (*input*), so-called "hardware" that permits the computer to store and to manipulate data according to the user's instructions, and ways of transmitting information from the computer to the user (*output*).

In this appendix we first discuss various methods used to input and output data. Then we describe three major types of computers: *mainframe computers*, *minicomputers*, and *microcomputers*, more often called *personal computers* or PC's. Finally, we discuss several sets of statistical programs (or statistical packages, as they are called) that are widely used by behavioral scientists to organize and analyze data.

A good deal of detailed knowledge is required to use computers, much of it peculiar to specific programs or to specific models of computers. Our purpose here is only to give a general overview of the use of computers for data analysis. We will, however, give specific suggestions from time to time about useful sources of information and instruction.

TRANSMISSION OF INFORMATION

Data Input

When investigators use a computer to analyze their research results the information they submit to the computer includes statistical programs in addition to their actual data. Computer programs are sets of instructions telling the computer what to do. In this section we discuss the input of data, leaving the topic of computer programs until the final section.

Originally, mainframe computers received their input from special paper cards. Investigators used a keypunch designed for the purpose to enter their raw data onto cards by punching

339

holes in each card that represented numbers or letters. The information was transferred from the cards to the computer by means of a card reader.

Currently, magnetic messages stored on Mylar plastic tapes or on disks are in much greater use. There are two types of disks: hard disks and floppy disks. Hard disks, which are used on all types of computers, are typically made of metal coated with a magnetic film and hold an enormous amount of information. Floppy disks, which are used only with personal computers and minicomputers, are smaller and, as the name implies, they are more flexible than hard disks. They also hold far less information. Although the latter feature limits their usefulness, floppy disks have their advantages. Most data sets in psychology fit easily onto a floppy disk, and as the disks are relatively inexpensive, it is possible to store different sets of data on different disks. Floppy disks can also be easily inserted into and removed from the computer, which makes them simple to store and makes it possible for them to be used in any compatible computer. When investigators share computer facilities with others, the portability of floppy disks that belong to individual investigators is an attractive feature.

It is sometimes possible in research studies to record the initial data on printed forms that can be read by an optical scanning device that enters the data on a magnetic tape or a disk. You may have taken objectively scored examinations or taken part in research studies in which you were given objectively scored questionnaires and required to record your choices to the questions on a printed answer sheet. Although you may not have recognized the fact, these answer sheets were probably devised to be machine scored, with the results to be recorded magnetically for use with a computer. Recording the raw data on machine-scorable sheets is a very efficient way of transforming data into a form that can be transmitted to a computer.

On many occasions, however, it is necessary or more convenient to record data as they occur in other more ordinary ways. For example, an investigator may write down on regular paper what research subjects do or how much of some property they exhibit. Data originally recorded in this way are typically transmitted to the computer by typing them on a computer keyboard. Except for the addition of several special keys, computer keyboards resemble those of standard typewriters. (The keyboard is also used to give the computer directions about what data analyses to perform.) The computer may be instructed to "save" the data conveyed in this way by transferring them to a tape or hard disk where they will be preserved.

Data Output

A video display unit, similar to a TV screen, is linked to the computer, along with the keyboard. The outcome of data analyses can be displayed temporarily on the display screen. The instructions to the computer that are typed on the keyboard are also displayed on the screen.

The computer is also linked to a printer, which is able to provide a *hard copy* or *printout* of the data given to the computer and the results of the data analyses the computer was instructed to conduct. There are many kinds of printers. For example, printers attached to personal computers vary from relatively inexpensive dot matrix printers to expensive laser printers which print copy that is similar in quality to the kind of print produced by typesetting machines and seen in magazines and books such as this one.

TYPES OF COMPUTERS

The three types of computers, mentioned earlier, vary in size. The largest are mainframe computers and the smallest are microcomputers (or personal computers). In between are minicomputers.

Mainframe Computers

Mainframe computers are not only large in size but also have a large working memory; that is, they can copy a great deal of information from the hard disk or tape where it is stored and make it available for analysis. Further, these computers are able to process large amounts of data rapidly and to accept programs that call for a variety of exceedingly complex data analyses.

In universities and other organizations, mainframe computers are usually located in special computer centers. Users have access to the computer through one of a number of *computer terminals*, which may be located at some distance from the computer center and communicate with the computer through telephone lines. Terminals include a keyboard and a display screen. Printers are also linked to the computer but not necessarily at the same location as the input terminal. The investigator may therefore have to go elsewhere (typically, the computer center) to pick up the printout of the results of the data analyses.

Because of the large amount of information they can handle and their high speed, mainframe computers can serve a number of users, each stationed at a different terminal, at the same time. Computers do this by responding successively to the input from the various terminals. This arrangement is called *time sharing*. The computer is so fast that unless there are a number of users asking that very lengthy procedures be performed, no user is conscious of any delay.

Minicomputers

Minicomputers are smaller than mainframe computers. They are variable in size, the larger of them having many of the same virtues as mainframe computers, including time-sharing capacity. Smaller organizations and even individual laboratories (which may use them to conduct experiments as well as to record and analyze data) are often able to afford smaller minicomputers and find that they serve their needs very adequately.

At some universities, large minicomputers as well as mainframe computers are housed in a central computing facility. The mainframe computer is usually reserved for extremely extensive data sets requiring lengthy and complex analyses. The analyses of smaller collections of data, such as those found in almost all psychological research, are done on the minicomputer.

As most data analysis is currently done on mainframe computers or personal computers, we will not refer further to minicomputers.

Microcomputers

Microcomputers, as we have said, are more usually called personal computers (PC's) or sometimes desktop computers. The latter term is literally correct, as personal computers, along with a keyboard and display screen, are small enough to keep on the top of a desk. The desk can also accommodate a printer, used as an output device. The unit is self-contained and serves only one user at a time.

Personal computers differ in price and capacity. The most versatile are those designed for business use, such as the IBM PC and IBM-compatible PC's currently manufactured by a number of companies. Although these personal computers are more expensive than many others, they are affordable by individual investigators for their own use or by educational institutions for the use of students and faculty.

Information to be transmitted to a personal computer is usually stored on a floppy disk. As we stated earlier, floppy disks can hold far less information than can be held on hard disks. Recently, hard disks costing several hundred dollars have become available for personal computers, a price that is considerably less than it was in the recent past. When large data sets are to be subjected to complex analytic procedures, it may be necessary to use a hard disk.

A device called a *modem* can be installed on a personal computer to connect it to a mainframe computer at a computer center by the use of telephone lines. (Many investigators have personal computers equipped with modems in their offices or in their homes, far from the computer center.) Data entered on the personal computer can be transferred or "uploaded" to the mainframe and the investigator may use the personal computer as a terminal to run statistical programs on the mainframe. The results can be "downloaded" from the mainframe to the personal computer and printed out on the personal computer's printer.

USEFUL STATISTICAL PACKAGES AND HOW TO LEARN ABOUT THEM

The development of high-speed computers revolutionized research in a number of ways. In psychology, for example, investigators were encouraged to undertake large-scale research involving the collection of multiple measures from large groups of individuals which would have taken many hundreds of hours to analyze without the assistance of a computer. The availability of computers also stimulated statisticians to develop new, sophisticated analytic techniques that have increased the capacity of research workers to test complicated hypotheses and theoretical models.

Use of the computer requires that programs be written that transmit investigators' data to the computer and tell the computer what kinds of operations to perform. A vast number of programs have been written for a variety of techniques to meet the needs of many groups, including research workers in various scientific disciplines. Programs relevant to the activities of a specific group of users are often gathered together and sold as a single unit or *statistical package*.

In this section we call your attention to several of the most widely used statistical packages in psychology and other behavioral sciences and offer some suggestions about how to go about learning to use them. These packages include programs for developing frequency distributions and stem and leaf displays; for plotting histograms, scatter plots, and other types of graphic representations; for finding descriptive statistics such as the mean and standard deviation; and for calculating many statistics of inference that go well beyond those covered in this textbook. Packages are available that include both parametric techniques (such as t, ANOVA, and r) and nonparametric techniques (such as χ^2 and the tests discussed in Chapter 15). Statistical packages are bought or leased from the individual or company holding the copyright. Computer centers have libraries of statistical packages to which users have access. The prices of statistical packages designed for personal computers are becoming increasingly affordable by individual owners but are still expensive. If you plan to use a personal computer owned by your school or by one of your instructors, check to see what kinds of packages they have available.

Statistical Packages for Mainframe Computers

The largest and most sophisticated statistical packages were originally developed for use on mainframe computers. Three extensive packages that are currently popular among psychologists and other behavior scientists are the *Biomedical Computer Programs ®(BMDP)*, *Statistical Analysis System® (SAS)*, and *Statistical Package for the Social Sciences—Version X® (SPSS^x)*.* A fourth well-known statistical package for mainframe computers is MINITAB®.[†] MINITAB is less extensive than the three packages we mentioned above, but it has many attractive features, including being relatively easy to learn and having a clear instruction manual.

More and more students in the behavioral sciences learn to use computers and statistical packages such as BMDP, SAS, SPSS^x, and MINITAB as part of a course in statistics that is more advanced than this one or in a course devoted exclusively to the use of such packages. Many people, however, continue to learn to use these computer packages by reading their manuals, often in conjunction with advice from friends, instructors, or computer center consultants as they set up their statistical problems for running on a specific program. Because the procedures to be followed involve many small details and most such manuals are necessarily quite complicated, this learning process can be difficult.

If you want to start learning about any of the four mainframe statistical packages we have mentioned, it would be helpful to you to read relevant parts of a book by J. M. Lefkowitz, *Introduction to Statistical Computer Packages*,[‡] before you start to read the official manual for the package that you plan to use. One of the desirable features of the book is that the reader can learn the simplest statistical computer tasks first and then move on to more complicated procedures. One chapter covers the rules for writing statements to control the specific program the reader wants to use. Another part of the book shows how to print out data and label input

---

*W. F. Dixon (ed.), *BMDP Statistical Software* (Berkeley, Calif.: University of California Press, 1985); *SAS/ STAT User's Guide, Release 6.03 Edition:* (Cary, N.C.: SAS Institute, 1988); *SPSS^x User's Guide* (New York: McGraw-Hill, 1983).
[†]T. A. Ryan, B. L. Joiner, and B. F. Ryan, *Minitab Student Handbook* (Boston: Duxbury Press, 1982).
[‡]J. M. Lefkowitz, *Introduction to Statistical Computer Packages* (Boston: Duxbury Press, 1985).

and output materials for each kind of package. Readers do not need to read about any package except the one they choose to use in their data analyses.

Also available are books that are designed to teach people about a specific statistical package and how to use its programs. You should be able to obtain copies of such books from your school library.

Statistical Packages for Personal Computers

BMDP, SAS, and SPSS⁺ (the counterpart of SPSSˣ) are now available for use on IBM personal computer, XT, or AT microcomputers with special memory and processing capabilities.

A variety of other useful packages, generally less expensive and less comprehensive than these three, have been developed for IBM and IBM-compatible personal computers as well as for other types of computers. If any of these packages are available to you for the personal computer you plan to use, you will have to read the manual for that package and seek the help of someone who has already mastered the program.

You may already have a personal computer or be thinking of getting one and want to buy a statistical package for your own use. A good source of information about available options is J. B. Siegel's book, *Statistical Software for Microcomputers: A Guide to 40 programs.** The book emphasizes IBM microcomputer options as well as those for several other brands. For statistical programs appropriate to Apple Macintosh microcomputers (which are well known for their excellent graphics capacities), you might consult R. S. Lehman's article, "Macintosh statistical methods," in the journal *Behavior Research Methods, Instruments and Computers.*† However, new statistical packages and new versions of existing programs appear frequently. In addition to reading the sources we have suggested so you can get your bearings, we recommend that you consult recent issues of such publications as the journals *Behavior Research Methods, Instruments and Computers* and the *Journal of the American Statistical Association*, and popular magazines such as *Byte* and *Personal Computer World Magazine.*

Although prices for statistical packages for personal computers are coming down, none are cheap. (Prices listed by Lehman and by Siegel range approximately from $75 to $2000.) If you do not want to spend any money at all for a statistical package, you may be able to find a few packages in the public domain that anyone may copy without charge. For example, SYSTAT, a large, highly regarded package discussed by both Lehman and Siegel, has a smaller cousin in the public domain called MYSTAT.‡ This package works on certain IBM microcomputer configurations that you would find useful.

---

*J. B. Siegel, *Statistical Software for Microcomputers: A Guide to 40 Programs* (New York: North-Holland, 1985).
†R. S. Lehman, "Macintosh statistical packages," *Behavior Research Methods, Instruments and Computers*, 1986, *12*, 177–87.
‡For further information about MYSTAT, write to SYSTAT Inc., 603 Main St., Evanston, IL 60202.

Appendix II
List of Formulas

Formula	Page

(4.1) $\quad \bar{X} = \dfrac{\sum X}{N}$ 50

(4.2) $\quad \bar{X} = \dfrac{\sum (fX)}{N}$ 56

(4.3) $\quad \mu = \dfrac{\sum X}{N}$ where N is the total number of cases in the population   56

(5.1) $\quad$ Semi-interquartile range $= \dfrac{Q_3 - Q_1}{2}$ 69

(5.2) $\quad S^2 = \dfrac{\sum x^2}{N} = \dfrac{\sum (X - \bar{X})^2}{N}$ 72

(5.3) $\quad S = \sqrt{\dfrac{\sum x^2}{N}} = \sqrt{\dfrac{\sum (X - \bar{X})^2}{N}}$ 72

(5.4) $\quad s^2 = \dfrac{\sum x^2}{N - 1}$ 74

(5.5) $\quad s = \sqrt{\dfrac{\sum x^2}{N - 1}} = \sqrt{\dfrac{\sum (X - \bar{X})^2}{N - 1}}$ 74

(5.6) $\quad \sigma = \sqrt{\dfrac{\sum x^2}{N}} = \sqrt{\dfrac{\sum (X - \mu)^2}{N}}$ where N is the total number of cases in the population   75

(5.7) $\quad S = \sqrt{\dfrac{\sum X^2}{N} - \bar{X}^2}$ 76

345

Formula   Page

$$(5.8) \quad S = \sqrt{\frac{\sum X^2 - \left(\sum X\right)^2 / N}{N}}$$ 76

$$(5.9) \quad s = \sqrt{\frac{\sum X^2 - \left(\sum X\right)^2 / N}{N - 1}}$$ 78

$$(5.10) \quad S = \sqrt{\frac{\sum fX^2}{N} - \left(\frac{\sum fX}{N}\right)^2} = \sqrt{\frac{\sum fX^2 - \left(\sum fX\right)^2 / N}{N}}$$ 79

$$(5.11) \quad s = \sqrt{\frac{\sum fX^2 - \left(\sum fX\right)^2 / N}{N - 1}}$$ 80

$(5.12) \quad z = \dfrac{X - \overline{X}}{s} \quad$ (based on sample statistics)   83

$(5.13) \quad X = \overline{X} + z(s)$ 84

$(5.14) \quad \overline{z} = \dfrac{\sum z}{N} = 0$ 85

$(5.15) \quad s_z^2 = s_z = 1$ 85

$(5.16) \quad z = \dfrac{X - \mu}{\sigma} \quad$ (based on population values)   86

$(5.17) \quad U = (\sigma_U)(z_X) + \mu_U$ 87

$(5.18) \quad U = \dfrac{\sigma_U(X)}{\sigma_X} - \dfrac{(\sigma_U)(\mu_X)}{\sigma_X} + \mu_U$ 87

$(5.19) \quad s = S \sqrt{\dfrac{N}{N - 1}}$ 90

$(6.1) \quad p(A) = \dfrac{n_A}{N}$ 100

$(6.2) \quad p(A) = \dfrac{n_A}{n_A + n_{\overline{A}}}$ 101

$(6.3) \quad p(\overline{A}) = \dfrac{n_{\overline{A}}}{n_A + n_{\overline{A}}}$ 101

$(6.4) \quad p(A \text{ or } B \text{ or } C) = p(A) + p(B) + p(C) \quad$ (mutually exclusive events)   101

$(6.5) \quad p(A, B, C) = p(A) \times p(B) \times p(C) \quad$ (independent events)   102

Formula	Page
(6.6) $p(A, B, C) = p(A) \times p(B|A) \times p(C|A, B)$ (dependent or independent events)	104
(6.7) $p(A|B) = \dfrac{p(A, B)}{p(B)}$	105
(6.8) $p(B|A) = \dfrac{p(A, B)}{p(A)}$	106
(6.9) $P_N = N! = N(N - 1)(N - 2) \cdots (1)$	107
(6.10) $P_r^N = \dfrac{N!}{(N - r)!}$	108
(6.11) $C_r^N = \dfrac{N!}{r!(N - r)!}$	108
(7.1) $(p + q)^N = p^N + Np^{N-1}q + \dfrac{N(N - 1)}{1 \times 2} p^{N-2}q^2$ $+ \dfrac{N(N - 1)(N - 2)}{1 \times 2 \times 3} p^{N-3}q^3 + \cdots + q^N$	118
(7.2) $C_r^N p^r q^{N-r} = \dfrac{N!}{r!(N - r)!} p^r q^{N-r}$	119
(7.3) $\mu_b = Np$ (b is the binomial distribution)	121
(7.4) $\sigma_b^2 = Npq$	121
(7.5) $\sigma_b = \sqrt{Npq}$	121
(8.1) $\sigma_{\overline{X}} = \dfrac{\sigma}{\sqrt{N}}$	140
(8.2) $z = \dfrac{\overline{X} - \mu}{\sigma_{\overline{X}}} = \dfrac{x}{\sigma_{\overline{X}}}$	141
(8.3) $s_{\overline{X}} = \dfrac{s}{\sqrt{N}}$	142
(8.4) $t = \dfrac{\overline{X} - \mu}{s_{\overline{X}}}$	144
(8.5) $df = N - 1$ (use with Formula 8.4)	150
(8.6) 99% CI for μ: $\overline{X} \pm t_{(.01)}(s_{\overline{X}})$	153
(8.7) 95% CI for μ: $\overline{X} \pm t_{(.05)}(s_{\overline{X}})$	154
(8.8) $\sigma_{prop} = \sqrt{\dfrac{p_t q_t}{N}}$	156
(8.9) $z = \dfrac{p_s - p_t}{\sigma_{prop}}$	156

Formula	Page

(9.1) $\quad \sigma_{\overline{X}_1 - \overline{X}_2} = \sqrt{\sigma_{\overline{X}_1}^2 + \sigma_{\overline{X}_2}^2}$ — 169

(9.2) $\quad z = \dfrac{(\overline{X}_1 - \overline{X}_2) - (\mu_1 - \mu_2)}{\sigma_{\overline{X}_1 - \overline{X}_2}}$ — 170

(9.3) $\quad s_{\overline{X}_1 - \overline{X}_2} = \sqrt{s_{\overline{X}_1}^2 + s_{\overline{X}_2}^2} \quad$ (equal N's) — 170

(9.4) $\quad t = \dfrac{(\overline{X}_1 - \overline{X}_2) - (\mu_1 - \mu_2)}{s_{\overline{X}_1 - \overline{X}_2}}$ — 171

(9.5) $\quad t = \dfrac{\overline{X}_1 - \overline{X}_2}{s_{\overline{X}_1 - \overline{X}_2}}$ — 172

where H_0: $\mu_1 - \mu_2 = 0$ and $df = N_1 + N_2 - 2$

(9.6) $\quad s_{\overline{X}_1 - \overline{X}_2} = \sqrt{\dfrac{(N_1 - 1)s_1^2 + (N_2 - 1)s_2^2}{(N_1 + N_2 - 2)}\left(\dfrac{1}{N_1} + \dfrac{1}{N_2}\right)}$ — 176

(9.7) $\quad s_{\overline{X}_1 - \overline{X}_2} = \sqrt{\dfrac{\left(\sum X_1^2 + \sum X_2^2\right) - (N_1\overline{X}_1^2 + N_2\overline{X}_2^2)}{(N_1 + N_2 - 2)}\left(\dfrac{1}{N_1} + \dfrac{1}{N_2}\right)}$ — 176

(9.8) $\quad df = N_1 - 1 + N_2 - 1 = N_1 + N_2 - 2 \quad$ (use with Formula 9.5) — 177

(9.9) $\quad$ Power $= 1 - p(\text{Type II error}) = 1 - \beta$ — 181

(9.10) $\quad \hat{\omega}^2 = \dfrac{t^2 - 1}{t^2 + df + 1}$ — 185

(10.1) $\quad r = \dfrac{\sum z_X z_Y}{N} \quad$ where N = number of pairs, $df = N - 2$ — 200

and

$z_X = \dfrac{X - \overline{X}}{S_X} \quad$ and $\quad z_Y = \dfrac{Y - \overline{Y}}{S_Y}$

(10.2) $\quad r = \dfrac{\sum XY - \left(\sum X\right)\left(\sum Y\right)/N}{\sqrt{\sum X^2 - \left(\sum X\right)^2/N}\ \sqrt{\sum Y^2 - \left(\sum Y\right)^2/N}}$ — 203

(10.3) $\quad a = r\left(\dfrac{s_Y}{s_X}\right)$ — 212

(10.4) $\quad b = \overline{Y} - r\left(\dfrac{s_Y}{s_X}\right)\overline{X}$ — 213

(10.5) $\quad Y_{\text{pred}} = r\left(\dfrac{s_Y}{s_X}\right)X + \overline{Y} - r\left(\dfrac{s_Y}{s_X}\right)(\overline{X})$ — 213

(10.6) $\quad X_{\text{pred}} = r\left(\dfrac{s_X}{s_Y}\right)Y + \overline{X} - r\left(\dfrac{s_X}{s_Y}\right)(\overline{Y})$ — 213

Formula

(10.7) Coefficient of determination $= \dfrac{\text{explained variation}}{\text{total variation}} = r^2$

215

(10.8) Coefficient of nondetermination $= \dfrac{\text{unexplained variation}}{\text{total variation}} = 1 - r^2$

215

(10.9) $s_{\text{est}\,Y} = s_Y \sqrt{1 - r^2}$

216

(10.10) $s_{\text{est}\,X} = s_X \sqrt{1 - r^2}$

216

(10.11) $r_S = 1 - \dfrac{6 \sum d^2}{N(N^2 - 1)}$

218

(11.1) $s_{\overline{X}_1 - \overline{X}_2} = \sqrt{s_{\overline{X}_1}{}^2 + s_{\overline{X}_2}{}^2 - 2r_{12} s_{\overline{X}_1} s_{\overline{X}_2}}$ (matched pairs)

231

(11.2) $t = \dfrac{\overline{X}_1 - \overline{X}_2}{s_{\overline{X}_1 - \overline{X}_2}}$

232

(11.3) $s_D{}^2 = \dfrac{\sum D^2 - \left(\sum D \right)^2 \big/ N}{N - 1}$

233

(11.4) $s_{\overline{D}} = \sqrt{\dfrac{s_D{}^2}{N}}$

233

(11.5) $t = \dfrac{\overline{D}}{s_{\overline{D}}}$ where $df = N - 1$

235

(11.6) $A = \dfrac{\sum D^2}{\left(\sum D \right)^2}$

235

(12.1) $SS_{tot} = \sum (X - \overline{X}_{tot})^2$

248

(12.2) $SS_{wg} = SS_{wg1} + SS_{wg2} + \cdots + SS_{wgk}$

249

(12.3) $SS_{bg} = \sum [N_g (\overline{X}_g - \overline{X}_{tot})^2]$

249

(12.4) $SS_{tot} = \left(\sum_{tot} X^2 \right) - \dfrac{\left(\sum_{tot} X \right)^2}{N_{tot}}$

252

(12.5) $SS_{bg} = \sum_g \left[\dfrac{\left(\sum X_g \right)^2}{N_g} \right] - \dfrac{\left(\sum_{tot} X \right)^2}{N_{tot}}$

252

(12.6) $SS_{wg} = SS_{tot} - SS_{bg}$

253

(12.7) $SS_{wg} = \sum_g \left[\left(\sum X_g{}^2 \right) - \dfrac{\left(\sum X_g \right)^2}{N_g} \right]$

253

Formula	Page

$$(12.8) \quad \text{MS}_{bg} = \frac{\text{SS}_{bg}}{df_{bg}} \qquad \text{where } df_{bg} = k - 1 \text{ and } k = \text{number of groups}$$

256

$$(12.9) \quad \text{MS}_{wg} = \frac{\text{SS}_{wg}}{df_{wg}} \qquad \text{where } df_{wg} = \text{N}_{tot} - k$$

256

$$(12.10) \quad \text{F} = \frac{\text{MS}_{bg}}{\text{MS}_{wg}}$$

257

$$(12.11) \quad \hat{\omega}^2 = \frac{\text{SS}_{bg} - (k - 1)\text{MS}_{wg}}{\text{SS}_{tot} + \text{MS}_{wg}}$$

261

$$(12.12) \quad hsd = q_\alpha \sqrt{\frac{\text{MS}_{wg}}{\text{N}_g}}$$

262

$$(13.1) \quad \text{SS}_{tot} = \left(\sum_{tot} \text{X}^2 \right) - \frac{\left(\sum_{tot} \text{X} \right)^2}{\text{N}_{tot}}$$

279

$$(13.2) \quad \text{SS}_{bg} = \sum_g \left[\frac{\left(\sum \text{X}_g \right)^2}{\text{N}_g} \right] - \frac{\left(\sum_{tot} \text{X} \right)^2}{\text{N}_{tot}}$$

279

$$(13.3) \quad \text{SS}_{bg} = \frac{\left(\sum \text{X}_{A1B1} \right)^2 + \left(\sum \text{X}_{A1B2} \right)^2 + \left(\sum \text{X}_{A1B3} \right)^2 + \cdots + \left(\sum \text{X}_{A2B3} \right)^2}{\text{N}_g}$$

$$- \frac{\left(\sum_{tot} \text{X} \right)^2}{\text{N}_{tot}} \qquad \text{where N}_g = \text{the number of subjects in each cell.}$$

279

$$(13.4) \quad \text{SS}_{wg} = \text{SS}_{tot} - \text{SS}_{bg}$$

280

$$(13.5) \quad \text{SS}_{wg} = \sum_g \left[\left(\sum \text{X}_g^2 \right) - \frac{\left(\sum \text{X}_g \right)^2}{\text{N}_g} \right]$$

280

$$(13.6) \quad \text{SS}_A = \frac{\left(\sum \text{X}_{A1} \right)^2 + \left(\sum \text{X}_{A2} \right)^2 + \cdots + \left(\sum \text{X}_{Am} \right)^2}{\text{N}_A} - \left[\frac{\left(\sum_{tot} \text{X} \right)^2}{\text{N}_{tot}} \right]$$

$$\text{where N}_A = \text{number in each A condition}$$

280

Formula

Page

281

$$(13.7) \quad SS_B = \frac{\left(\sum X_{B1}\right)^2 + \left(\sum X_{B2}\right)^2 + \cdots + \left(\sum X_{Bn}\right)^2}{N_B} - \left[\frac{\left(\sum_{tot} X\right)^2}{N_{tot}}\right]$$

where N_B = number in each B condition

$$(13.8) \quad SS_{A \times B} = SS_{bg} - SS_A - SS_B \qquad\qquad\qquad 281$$

$$(13.9) \quad SS_{A \times B} = N_g \left[\sum_g (\overline{X}_{AB} - \overline{X}_A - \overline{X}_B + \overline{X}_{tot})^2\right] \qquad 281$$

$$(13.10) \quad MS_A = \frac{SS_A}{df_A} \qquad \text{where } df_A = m - 1; \ m = \text{no. of A groups} \qquad 282$$

$$MS_B = \frac{SS_B}{df_B} \qquad \text{where } df_B = n - 1; \ n = \text{no. of B groups}$$

$$MS_{A \times B} = \frac{SS_{A \times B}}{df_{A \times B}} \qquad \text{where } df_{A \times B} = (m - 1)(n - 1)$$

$$MS_{wg} = \frac{SS_{wg}}{df_{wg}} \qquad \text{where } df_{wg} = N_{tot} - (m)(n)$$

$$(13.11) \quad F_A = \frac{MS_A}{MS_{wg}}; \ F_B = \frac{MS_B}{MS_{wg}}; \ F_{A \times B} = \frac{MS_{A \times B}}{MS_{wg}} \qquad 283$$

$$(13.12) \quad \hat{\omega}_E^2 = \frac{SS_E - (df_E)(MS_{wg})}{SS_{tot} + MS_{wg}} \qquad\qquad 286$$

$$(14.1) \quad \chi^2 = \sum \left[\frac{(O - E)^2}{E}\right] \qquad\qquad 297$$

$(14.2) \quad df = \text{number of categories} - 1 \quad \text{(sample with one-way classification)} \qquad 298$

$(14.3) \quad df = (\text{col.} - 1)(\text{rows} - 1) \quad \text{(sample with two-way classification)} \qquad 302$

$$(14.4) \quad \chi^2 = \frac{N(AD - BC)^2}{(A + B)(C + D)(A + C)(B + D)} \quad \text{(sample with 2} \times \text{2 classification)} \qquad 304$$

$$(14.5) \quad \frac{x}{\sigma} = \sqrt{2\chi^2} - \sqrt{2n - 1} \qquad\qquad 306$$

$$(15.1) \quad U_1 = N_1 N_2 + \frac{N_1(N_1 + 1)}{2} - R_1 \quad \text{(Mann-Whitney U)} \qquad 316$$

$$(15.2) \quad U_E = \frac{N_1 N_2}{2} \qquad\qquad 316$$

$$(15.3) \quad \sigma_U = \sqrt{\frac{N_1 N_2 (N_1 + N_2 + 1)}{12}} \qquad\qquad 316$$

Formula	Page

$(15.4) \quad z = \dfrac{U_1 - U_E}{\sigma_U}$ 316

$(15.5) \quad H = \dfrac{12}{N(N + 1)} \Sigma \left(\dfrac{R_i^2}{n_i}\right) - 3(N + 1)$ 317

(Kruskal-Wallis one-way analysis of variance)

$(15.6) \quad T_E = \dfrac{N(N + 1)}{4}$ (Wilcoxon signed ranks) 321

$(15.7) \quad \sigma_T = \sqrt{\dfrac{N(N + 1)(2N + 1)}{24}}$ 321

$(15.8) \quad z = \dfrac{T - T_E}{\sigma_T}$ 321

$(15.9) \quad \chi_R^2 = \dfrac{12}{Nk(k + 1)} \left(\Sigma R_i^2\right) - 3N(k + 1)$ 322

(Friedman two-way analysis of variance)

Appendix III
Tables

CONTENTS

- TABLE A   RANDOM NUMBERS
- TABLE B   PERCENTAGE OF TOTAL AREA UNDER THE NORMAL CURVE
- TABLE C   CRITICAL VALUES OF t
- TABLE D   VALUES OF r AT THE 5% AND 1% LEVELS
- TABLE E   VALUES OF r_S AT THE 5% AND 1% LEVELS
- TABLE F   VALUES OF F AT THE 5% AND 1% LEVELS
- TABLE G   VALUES OF q_α (THE STUDENTIZED RANGE STATISTIC) AT THE 5% AND 1% LEVELS
- TABLE H   CRITICAL VALUES OF SANDLER'S A
- TABLE I   VALUES OF χ^2 AT THE 5% AND 1% LEVELS
- TABLE J   VALUES OF T AT THE 5% AND 1% LEVELS IN THE WILCOXON SIGNED-RANKS TEST

Table A Random Numbers

51645	98661	88422	26428	45198	97112	45964	90089	33098	97772
40550	53760	85879	20708	45861	56334	25416	50149	98693	55835
74535	68977	91426	42636	37570	46742	24752	95509	91849	57785
95421	88518	29311	11910	52808	78534	33741	42239	57559	61282
82073	36081	48877	06766	41307	17197	61531	53971	59280	42311
63183	66223	19937	66014	60160	47714	99520	59522	94782	40116
26780	26262	06010	86755	02820	27335	73665	49199	06690	99820
56432	62150	56003	61085	78492	46768	90508	71745	89590	42715
24380	65621	11298	07821	32725	54464	15733	72871	40300	23936
84752	94790	55405	21262	26036	09293	27952	69253	02076	08067
25691	31722	21715	01059	30389	64211	85558	24496	71369	97464
75959	66324	72381	43577	92298	10094	67799	49994	31886	66773
22564	64528	96588	75722	41460	88123	53507	93663	56136	99007
92388	60971	68037	35312	33843	23649	83106	87798	70699	01294
83497	98701	96442	60874	82103	41350	52770	50953	57656	94747
74469	91798	65091	22432	88248	71914	40804	43110	46960	94124
77841	37239	28922	77915	50378	54787	17897	04064	97463	68605
39642	31647	82528	75480	01718	39615	83303	27843	90364	38249
08456	44896	96370	01327	66730	74615	51954	21716	45985	15824
72338	98537	51112	71728	83864	72256	90992	93280	21458	62702
47770	38347	32186	08650	45220	36517	95131	83329	59349	76898
80836	30521	56718	81620	41500	52293	41362	77342	03121	11008
18352	95404	86417	06379	62319	21663	13592	56974	87497	53620
26778	64000	90764	38105	76210	30287	87823	65748	21821	61610
13716	62729	33795	87160	98516	76882	49223	25004	88223	64613
32985	26814	51833	57363	04067	84648	85505	41465	71769	99550
86675	38742	39639	67704	03454	22996	92696	35795	77185	45750
60438	60026	72498	71331	01121	72275	71667	38987	72864	02379
75188	55511	94496	01498	15935	45228	62286	91563	35899	92588
74107	65389	41614	16567	03801	58808	34609	37869	62248	12103
55904	45492	93459	97948	26999	63484	22844	26405	51929	89432
51722	49793	75248	49617	29035	04950	98602	47715	85247	73738
22701	43144	30281	94746	55393	51025	39757	51729	68780	71962
10119	94807	23987	99253	02173	63107	75148	10911	40047	94712
12717	94106	62367	71530	94688	68341	00996	64154	21125	04256
28516	45108	31054	51464	12364	19560	27992	23960	59285	01302
49961	51838	48316	20781	28576	18868	61128	74465	50206	60516
74018	61495	56744	30314	01001	41509	23222	29999	35083	13110
48999	29283	83865	22337	07139	95196	82131	13811	40242	20798
84394	31145	33299	87324	85165	94951	10944	93668	11797	18025

Source: The Rand Corporation, *A Million Random Digits with 100,000 Normal Deviates*, (Glencoe, Ill.: The Free Press, 1955), p. 243. By permission of the Rand Corporation.

Table B Percentage of Total Area under the Normal Curve between Mean Ordinate and Ordinate at Any Given Sigma Distance from the Mean

$\dfrac{x}{\sigma}$	.00	.01	.02	.03	.04	.05	.06	.07	.08	.09
0.0	00.00	00.40	00.80	01.20	01.60	01.99	02.39	02.79	03.19	03.59
0.1	03.98	04.38	04.78	05.17	05.57	05.96	06.36	06.75	07.14	07.53
0.2	07.93	08.32	08.71	09.10	09.48	09.87	10.26	10.64	11.03	11.41
0.3	11.79	12.17	12.55	12.93	13.31	13.68	14.06	14.43	14.80	15.17
0.4	15.54	15.91	16.28	16.64	17.00	17.36	17.72	18.08	18.44	18.79
0.5	19.15	19.50	19.85	20.19	20.54	20.88	21.23	21.57	21.90	22.24
0.6	22.57	22.91	23.24	23.57	23.89	24.22	24.54	24.86	25.17	25.49
0.7	25.80	26.11	26.42	26.73	27.04	27.34	27.64	27.94	28.23	28.52
0.8	28.81	29.10	29.39	29.67	29.95	30.23	30.51	30.78	31.06	31.33
0.9	31.59	31.86	32.12	32.38	32.64	32.90	33.15	33.40	33.65	33.89
1.0	34.13	34.38	34.61	34.85	35.08	35.31	35.54	35.77	35.99	36.21
1.1	36.43	36.65	36.86	37.08	37.29	37.49	37.70	37.90	38.10	38.30
1.2	38.49	38.69	38.88	39.07	39.25	39.44	39.62	39.80	39.97	40.15
1.3	40.32	40.49	40.66	40.82	40.99	41.15	41.31	41.47	41.62	41.77
1.4	41.92	42.07	42.22	42.36	42.51	42.65	42.79	42.92	43.06	43.19
1.5	43.32	43.45	43.57	43.70	43.83	43.94	44.06	44.18	44.29	44.41
1.6	44.52	44.63	44.74	44.84	44.95	45.05	45.15	45.25	45.35	45.45
1.7	45.54	45.64	45.73	45.82	45.91	45.99	46.08	46.16	46.25	46.33
1.8	46.41	46.49	46.56	46.64	46.71	46.78	46.86	46.93	46.99	47.06
1.9	47.13	47.19	47.26	47.32	47.38	47.44	47.50	47.56	47.61	47.67
2.0	47.72	47.78	47.83	47.88	47.93	47.98	48.03	48.08	48.12	48.17
2.1	48.21	48.26	48.30	48.34	48.38	48.42	48.46	48.50	48.54	48.57
2.2	48.61	48.64	48.68	48.71	48.75	48.78	48.81	48.84	48.87	48.90
2.3	48.93	48.96	48.98	49.01	49.04	49.06	49.09	49.11	49.13	49.16
2.4	49.18	49.20	49.22	49.25	49.27	49.29	49.31	49.32	49.34	49.36
2.5	49.38	49.40	49.41	49.43	49.45	49.46	49.48	49.49	49.51	49.52
2.6	49.53	49.55	49.56	49.57	49.59	49.60	49.61	49.62	49.63	49.64
2.7	49.65	49.66	49.67	49.68	49.69	49.70	49.71	49.72	49.73	49.74
2.8	49.74	49.75	49.76	49.77	49.77	49.78	49.79	49.79	49.80	49.81
2.9	49.81	49.82	49.82	49.83	49.84	49.84	49.85	49.85	49.86	49.86
3.0	49.87									
3.5	49.98									
4.0	49.997									
5.0	49.99997									

Source: Original data from *Tables for Statisticians and Biometricians*, edited by Karl Pearson, published by Cambridge University Press; used by permission of the publisher. The adaptation of these data is taken from E. F. Lindquist, *A First Course in Statistics*, rev. ed., with permission of the publisher, Houghton Mifflin Company.

Table C Critical Values of *t*

	Level of Significance for One-Tailed Test			
	5%	*2.5%*	*1%*	*.5%*
	Level of Significance for Two-Tailed Test			
df	*10%*	*5%*	*2%*	*1%*
1	6.3138	12.7062	31.8207	63.6574
2	2.9200	4.3027	6.9646	9.9248
3	2.3534	3.1824	4.5407	5.8409
4	2.1318	2.7764	3.7469	4.6041
5	2.0150	2.5706	3.3649	4.0322
6	1.9432	2.4469	3.1427	3.7074
7	1.8946	2.3646	2.9980	3.4995
8	1.8595	2.3060	2.8965	3.3554
9	1.8331	2.2622	2.8214	3.2498
10	1.8125	2.2281	2.7638	3.1693
11	1.7959	2.2010	2.7181	3.1058
12	1.7823	2.1788	2.6810	3.0545
13	1.7709	2.1604	2.6503	3.0123
14	1.7613	2.1448	2.6245	2.9768
15	1.7531	2.1315	2.6025	2.9467
16	1.7459	2.1199	2.5835	2.9208
17	1.7396	2.1098	2.5669	2.8982
18	1.7341	2.1009	2.5524	2.8784
19	1.7291	2.0930	2.5395	2.8609
20	1.7247	2.0860	2.5280	2.8453
21	1.7207	2.0796	2.5177	2.8314
22	1.7171	2.0739	2.5083	2.8188
23	1.7139	2.0687	2.4999	2.8073
24	1.7109	2.0639	2.4922	2.7969
25	1.7081	2.0595	2.4851	2.7874
26	1.7056	2.0555	2.4786	2.7787
27	1.7033	2.0518	2.4727	2.7707
28	1.7011	2.0484	2.4671	2.7633
29	1.6991	2.0452	2.4620	2.7564
30	1.6973	2.0423	2.4573	2.7500
35	1.6869	2.0301	2.4377	2.7238
40	1.6839	2.0211	2.4233	2.7045
45	1.6794	2.0141	2.4121	2.6896
50	1.6759	2.0086	2.4033	2.6778
60	1.6706	2.0003	2.3901	2.6603
70	1.6669	1.9944	2.3808	2.6479
80	1.6641	1.9901	2.3739	2.6387
90	1.6620	1.9867	2.3685	2.6316
100	1.6602	1.9840	2.3642	2.6259
110	1.6588	1.9818	2.3607	2.6213
120	1.6577	1.9799	2.3598	2.6174
∞	1.6449	1.9600	2.3263	2.5758

Source: Donald B. Owen, *Handbook of Statistical Tables,* © 1962. U.S. Department of Energy, Table 2.1. Published by Addison-Wesley Publishing Company, Inc., Reading, Massachusetts. Reprinted with permission of the publisher.

Table D Values of *r* at the 5% and 1% Levels of Significance (Two-Tailed Test)

Degrees of Freedom (df)	5%	1%	Degrees of Freedom (df)	5%	1%
1	.997	1.000	24	.388	.496
2	.950	.990	25	.381	.487
3	.878	.959	26	.374	.478
4	.811	.917	27	.367	.470
5	.754	.874	28	.361	.463
6	.707	.834	29	.355	.456
7	.666	.798	30	.349	.449
8	.632	.765	35	.325	.418
9	.602	.735	40	.304	.393
10	.576	.708	45	.288	.372
11	.553	.684	50	.273	.354
12	.532	.661	60	.250	.325
13	.514	.641	70	.232	.302
14	.497	.623	80	.217	.283
15	.482	.606	90	.205	.267
16	.468	.590	100	.195	.254
17	.456	.575	125	.174	.228
18	.444	.561	150	.159	.208
19	.433	.549	200	.138	.181
20	.423	.537	300	.113	.148
21	.413	.526	400	.098	.128
22	.404	.515	500	.088	.115
23	.396	.505	1000	.062	.081

Source: R. A. Fisher and F. Yates: *Statistical Tables for Biological, Agricultural and Medical Research*, published by Longman Group Ltd. London, 1978 (previously published by Oliver & Boyd Ltd. Edinburgh) and by permission of the authors and publishers. Part of this table is reprinted by permission from *Statistical Methods* by George W. Snedecor and William G. Cochran, 6th edition © 1967 by Iowa State University Press, Ames, Iowa.

Table E Values of r_S (Rank-Order Correlation Coefficient) at the 5% and 1% Levels of Significance (Two-Tailed Test)

N	5%	1%
5	1.000	—
6	.886	1.000
7	.786	.929
8	.738	.881
9	.683	.833
10	.648	.794
12	.591	.777
14	.544	.714
16	.506	.665
18	.475	.625
20	.450	.591
22	.428	.562
24	.409	.537
26	.392	.515
28	.377	.496
30	.364	.478

Source: Computed from E. G. Olds, "Distribution of the sum of squares of rank differences for small numbers of individuals," *Annals of Mathematical Statistics*, 1938, *9*, 133–48, and, "The 5% significance levels for sums of squares of rank differences and a correction," *Annals of Mathematical Statistics*, 1949, *20*, 117–18, by permission of the author and the Institute of Mathematical Statistics.

Table F Values of F at the 5% and 1% Significance Levels

(df Associated with the Denominator)		(df Associated with the Numerator)								
		1	2	3	4	5	6	7	8	9
1	5%	161	200	216	225	230	234	237	239	241
	1%	4052	5000	5403	5625	5764	5859	5928	5982	6022
2	5%	18.5	19.0	19.2	19.2	19.3	19.3	19.4	19.4	19.4
	1%	98.5	99.0	99.2	99.2	99.3	99.3	99.4	99.4	99.4
3	5%	10.1	9.55	9.28	9.12	9.01	8.94	8.89	8.85	8.81
	1%	34.1	30.8	29.5	28.7	28.2	27.9	27.7	27.5	27.3
4	5%	7.71	6.94	6.59	6.39	6.26	6.16	6.09	6.04	6.00
	1%	21.2	18.0	16.7	16.0	15.5	15.2	15.0	14.8	14.7
5	5%	6.61	5.79	5.41	5.19	5.05	4.95	4.88	4.82	4.77
	1%	16.3	13.3	12.1	11.4	11.0	10.7	10.5	10.3	10.2
6	5%	5.99	5.14	4.76	4.53	4.39	4.28	4.21	4.15	4.10
	1%	13.7	10.9	9.78	9.15	8.75	8.47	8.26	8.10	7.98
7	5%	5.59	4.74	4.35	4.12	3.97	3.87	3.79	3.73	3.68
	1%	12.2	9.55	8.45	7.85	7.46	7.19	6.99	6.84	6.72
8	5%	5.32	4.46	4.07	3.84	3.69	3.58	3.50	3.44	3.39
	1%	11.3	8.65	7.59	7.01	6.63	6.37	6.18	6.03	5.91
9	5%	5.12	4.26	3.86	3.63	3.48	3.37	3.29	3.23	3.18
	1%	10.6	8.02	6.99	6.42	6.06	5.80	5.61	5.47	5.35
10	5%	4.96	4.10	3.71	3.48	3.33	3.22	3.14	3.07	3.02
	1%	10.0	7.56	6.55	5.99	5.64	5.39	5.20	5.06	4.94
11	5%	4.84	3.98	3.59	3.36	3.20	3.09	3.01	2.95	2.90
	1%	9.65	7.21	6.22	5.67	5.32	5.07	4.89	4.74	4.63
12	5%	4.75	3.89	3.49	3.26	3.11	3.00	2.91	2.85	2.80
	1%	9.33	6.93	5.95	5.41	5.06	4.82	4.64	4.50	4.39
13	5%	4.67	3.81	3.41	3.18	3.03	2.92	2.83	2.77	2.71
	1%	9.07	6.70	5.74	5.21	4.86	4.62	4.44	4.30	4.19
14	5%	4.60	3.74	3.34	3.11	2.96	2.85	2.76	2.70	2.65
	1%	8.86	6.51	5.56	5.04	4.70	4.46	4.28	4.14	4.03
15	5%	4.54	3.68	3.29	3.06	2.90	2.79	2.71	2.64	2.59
	1%	8.68	6.36	5.42	4.89	4.56	4.32	4.14	4.00	3.89
16	5%	4.49	3.63	3.24	3.01	2.85	2.74	2.66	2.59	2.54
	1%	8.53	6.23	5.29	4.77	4.44	4.20	4.03	3.89	3.78
17	5%	4.45	3.59	3.20	2.96	2.81	2.70	2.61	2.55	2.49
	1%	8.40	6.11	5.18	4.67	4.34	4.10	3.93	3.79	3.68
18	5%	4.41	3.55	3.16	2.93	2.77	2.66	2.58	2.51	2.46
	1%	8.29	6.01	5.09	4.58	4.25	4.01	3.84	3.71	3.60
19	5%	4.38	3.52	3.13	2.90	2.74	2.63	2.54	2.48	2.42
	1%	8.18	5.93	5.01	4.50	4.17	3.94	3.77	3.63	3.52

Table F (*Continued*)

(df Associated with the Denominator)		1	2	3	4	5	6	7	8	9
20	5%	4.35	3.49	3.10	2.87	2.71	2.60	2.51	2.45	2.39
	1%	8.10	5.85	4.94	4.43	4.10	3.87	3.70	3.56	3.46
21	5%	4.32	3.47	3.07	2.84	2.68	2.57	2.49	2.42	2.37
	1%	8.02	5.78	4.87	4.37	4.04	3.81	3.64	3.51	3.40
22	5%	4.30	3.44	3.05	2.82	2.66	2.55	2.46	2.40	2.34
	1%	7.95	5.72	4.82	4.31	3.99	3.76	3.59	3.45	3.35
23	5%	4.28	3.42	3.03	2.80	2.64	2.53	2.44	2.37	2.32
	1%	7.88	5.66	4.76	4.26	3.94	3.71	3.54	3.41	3.30
24	5%	4.26	3.40	3.01	2.78	2.62	2.51	2.42	2.36	2.30
	1%	7.82	5.61	4.72	4.22	3.90	3.67	3.50	3.36	3.26
25	5%	4.24	3.39	2.99	2.76	2.60	2.49	2.40	2.34	2.28
	1%	7.77	5.57	4.68	4.18	3.86	3.63	3.46	3.32	3.22
26	5%	4.23	3.37	2.98	2.74	2.59	2.47	2.39	2.32	2.27
	1%	7.72	5.53	4.64	4.14	3.82	3.59	3.42	3.29	3.18
27	5%	4.21	3.35	2.96	2.73	2.57	2.46	2.37	2.31	2.25
	1%	7.68	5.49	4.60	4.11	3.78	3.56	3.39	3.26	3.15
28	5%	4.20	3.34	2.95	2.71	2.56	2.45	2.36	2.29	2.24
	1%	7.64	5.45	4.57	4.07	3.75	3.53	3.36	3.23	3.12
29	5%	4.18	3.33	2.93	2.70	2.55	2.43	2.35	2.28	2.22
	1%	7.60	5.42	4.54	4.04	3.73	3.50	3.33	3.20	3.09
30	5%	4.17	3.32	2.92	2.69	2.53	2.42	2.33	2.27	2.21
	1%	7.56	5.39	4.51	4.02	3.70	3.47	3.30	3.17	3.07
40	5%	4.08	3.23	2.84	2.61	2.45	2.34	2.25	2.18	2.12
	1%	7.31	5.18	4.31	3.83	3.51	3.29	3.12	2.99	2.89
60	5%	4.00	3.15	2.76	2.53	2.37	2.25	2.17	2.10	2.04
	1%	7.08	4.98	4.13	3.65	3.34	3.12	2.95	2.82	2.72
120	5%	3.92	3.07	2.68	2.45	2.29	2.18	2.09	2.02	1.96
	1%	6.85	4.79	3.95	3.48	3.17	2.96	2.79	2.66	2.56

(df Associated with the Numerator) spans columns 1–9.

Table G Values of q_α (The Studentized Range Statistic) at the 5% and 1% Levels of Significance

df_{wg}	α	2	3	4	5	6	7	8	9	10
						k = Number of Means				
1	.05	17.97	26.98	32.82	37.08	40.41	43.12	45.40	47.36	49.07
	.01	90.03	135.00	164.30	185.60	202.20	215.80	227.20	237.00	245.60
2	.05	6.08	8.33	9.80	10.88	11.74	12.44	13.03	13.54	13.99
	.01	14.04	19.02	22.29	24.72	26.63	28.20	29.53	30.68	31.69
3	.05	4.50	5.91	6.82	7.50	8.04	8.48	8.85	9.18	9.46
	.01	8.26	10.62	12.17	13.33	14.24	15.00	15.64	16.20	16.69
4	.05	3.93	5.04	5.76	6.29	6.71	7.05	7.35	7.60	7.83
	.01	6.51	8.12	9.17	9.96	10.58	11.10	11.55	11.93	12.27
5	.05	3.64	4.60	5.22	5.67	6.03	6.33	6.58	6.80	6.99
	.01	5.70	6.98	7.80	8.42	8.91	9.32	9.67	9.97	10.24
6	.05	3.46	4.34	4.90	5.30	5.63	5.90	6.12	6.32	6.49
	.01	5.24	6.33	7.03	7.56	7.97	8.32	8.61	8.87	9.10
7	.05	3.34	4.16	4.68	5.06	5.36	5.61	5.82	6.00	6.16
	.01	4.95	5.92	6.54	7.01	7.37	7.68	7.94	8.17	8.37
8	.05	3.26	4.04	4.53	4.89	5.17	5.40	5.60	5.77	5.92
	.01	4.75	5.64	6.20	6.62	6.96	7.24	7.47	7.68	7.86
9	.05	3.20	3.95	4.41	4.76	5.02	5.24	5.43	5.59	5.74
	.01	4.60	5.43	5.96	6.35	6.66	6.91	7.13	7.33	7.49
10	.05	3.15	3.88	4.33	4.65	4.91	5.12	5.30	5.46	5.60
	.01	4.48	5.27	5.77	6.14	6.43	6.67	6.87	7.05	7.21
11	.05	3.11	3.82	4.26	4.57	4.82	5.03	5.20	5.35	5.49
	.01	4.39	5.15	5.62	5.97	6.25	6.48	6.67	6.84	6.99
12	.05	3.08	3.77	4.20	4.51	4.75	4.95	5.12	5.27	5.39
	.01	4.32	5.05	5.50	5.84	6.10	6.32	6.51	6.67	6.81
13	.05	3.06	3.73	4.15	4.45	4.69	4.88	5.05	5.19	5.32
	.01	4.26	4.96	5.40	5.73	5.98	6.19	6.37	6.53	6.67
14	.05	3.03	3.70	4.11	4.41	4.64	4.83	4.99	5.13	5.25
	.01	4.21	4.89	5.32	5.63	5.88	6.08	6.26	6.41	6.54
15	.05	3.01	3.67	4.08	4.37	4.59	4.78	4.94	5.08	5.20
	.01	4.17	4.84	5.25	5.56	5.80	5.99	6.16	6.31	6.44
16	.05	3.00	3.65	4.05	4.33	4.56	4.74	4.90	5.03	5.15
	.01	4.13	4.79	5.19	5.49	5.72	5.92	6.08	6.22	6.35
17	.05	2.98	3.63	4.02	4.30	4.52	4.70	4.86	4.99	5.11
	.01	4.10	4.74	5.14	5.43	5.66	5.85	6.01	6.15	6.27
18	.05	2.97	3.61	4.00	4.28	4.49	4.67	4.82	4.96	5.07
	.01	4.07	4.70	5.09	5.38	5.60	5.79	5.94	6.08	6.20
19	.05	2.96	3.59	3.98	4.25	4.47	4.65	4.79	4.92	5.04
	.01	4.05	4.67	5.05	5.33	5.55	5.73	5.89	6.02	6.14

Table G (*Continued*)

df_{wg}	α	2	3	4	5	6	7	8	9	10
					k = **Number of Means**					
20	.05	2.95	3.58	3.96	4.23	4.45	4.62	4.77	4.90	5.01
	.01	4.02	4.64	5.02	5.29	5.51	5.69	5.84	5.97	6.09
24	.05	2.92	3.53	3.90	4.17	4.37	4.54	4.68	4.81	4.92
	.01	3.96	4.55	4.91	5.17	5.37	5.54	5.69	5.81	5.92
30	.05	2.89	3.49	3.85	4.10	4.30	4.46	4.60	4.72	4.82
	.01	3.89	4.45	4.80	5.05	5.24	5.40	5.54	5.65	5.76
40	.05	2.86	3.44	3.79	4.04	4.23	4.39	4.52	4.63	4.73
	.01	3.82	4.37	4.70	4.93	5.11	5.26	5.39	5.50	5.60
60	.05	2.83	3.40	3.74	3.98	4.16	4.31	4.44	4.55	4.65
	.01	3.76	4.28	4.59	4.82	4.99	5.13	5.25	5.36	5.45
120	.05	2.80	3.36	3.68	3.92	4.10	4.24	4.36	4.47	4.56
	.01	3.70	4.20	4.50	4.71	4.87	5.01	5.12	5.21	5.30
∞	.05	2.77	3.31	3.63	3.86	4.03	4.17	4.29	4.39	4.47
	.01	3.64	4.12	4.40	4.60	4.76	4.88	4.99	5.08	5.16

Source: Adapted from Table 29, E. S. Pearson and H. O. Hartley (eds.), *Biometrika Tables for Statisticians*, Vol. I, 3rd ed. (Cambridge: Published for the Biometrika Trustees at the University Press, 1966). By permission of the Biometrika Trustees.

Table H Critical Values of Sandler's *A* Statistic[a]

df = N − 1[b]	*Level of Significance for One-Tailed Test*				
	5%	2.5%	1%	.5%	.05%
	Level of Significance for Two-Tailed Test				
	10%	5%	2%	1%	.1%
1	.5125	.5031	.50049	.50012	.5000012
2	.412	.369	.347	.340	.334
3	.385	.324	.286	.272	.254
4	.376	.304	.257	.238	.211
5	.372	.293	.240	.218	.184
6	.370	.286	.230	.205	.167
7	.369	.281	.222	.196	.155
8	.368	.278	.217	.190	.146
9	.368	.276	.213	.185	.139
10	.368	.274	.210	.181	.134
11	.368	.273	.207	.178	.130
12	.368	.271	.205	.176	.126
13	.368	.270	.204	.174	.124
14	.368	.270	.202	.172	.121
15	.368	.269	.201	.170	.119
16	.368	.268	.200	.169	.117
17	.368	.268	.199	.168	.116
18	.368	.267	.198	.167	.114
19	.368	.267	.197	.166	.113
20	.368	.266	.197	.165	.112
21	.368	.266	.196	.165	.111
22	.368	.266	.196	.164	.110
23	.368	.266	.195	.163	.109
24	.368	.265	.195	.163	.108
25	.368	.265	.194	.162	.108
26	.368	.265	.194	.162	.107
27	.368	.265	.193	.161	.107
28	.368	.265	.193	.161	.106
29	.368	.264	.193	.161	.106
30	.368	.264	.193	.160	.105
40	.368	.263	.191	.158	.102
60	.369	.262	.189	.155	.099
120	.369	.261	.187	.153	.095
∞	.370	.260	.185	.151	.092

[a]*A* is significant at a given level if it is equal to or *less than* the value listed in the table. [b]*N* = number of pairs.

Source: J. Sandler, "A test of the significance of the difference between the means of correlated measures, based on a simplification of Student's *t*," *British Journal of Psychology*, 1955, *46*, 225–26. By permission of the author and the British Psychological Society.

Table I Values of Chi Square (χ^2) at the 5% and 1% Levels of Significance

Degrees of Freedom (df)	5%	1%
1	3.84	6.64
2	5.99	9.21
3	7.82	11.34
4	9.49	13.28
5	11.07	15.09
6	12.59	16.81
7	14.07	18.48
8	15.51	20.09
9	16.92	21.67
10	18.31	23.21
11	19.68	24.72
12	21.03	26.22
13	22.36	27.69
14	23.68	29.14
15	25.00	30.58
16	26.30	32.00
17	27.59	33.41
18	28.87	34.80
19	30.14	36.19
20	31.41	37.57
21	32.67	38.93
22	33.92	40.29
23	35.17	41.64
24	36.42	42.98
25	37.65	44.31
26	38.88	45.64
27	40.11	46.96
28	41.34	48.28
29	42.56	49.59
30	43.77	50.89

Source: R. A. Fisher and F. Yates, *Statistical Tables for Biological, Agricultural, and Medical Research*, published by Longman Group Ltd., London, 1978 (previously published by Oliver & Boyd Ltd. Edinburgh) and by permission of the authors and publishers.

Table J Values of T at the 5% and 1% Levels of Significance in the Wilcoxon Signed-Ranks Test

N_{S-R}	5%	1%
6	1	—
7	2	—
8	4	0
9	6	2
10	8	3
11	11	5
12	14	7
13	17	10
14	21	13
15	25	16
16	30	19
17	35	23
18	40	28
19	46	32
20	52	37
21	59	43
22	66	49
23	73	55
24	81	61
25	90	68

Source: Adapted from Table 2 of F. Wilcoxon and R. A. Wilcox, *Some Rapid Approximate Statistical Procedures* (Pearl River, N.Y.: Lederle Laboratories, 1964.) Reproduced with the permission of the American Cyanamid Company.

Appendix IV
Answers to Chapter Problems

Answers are given to all problems except those that call for the student to supply examples.

CHAPTER 1

1. **(a)** Population of all those who voted. Alternatively, a sample of all individuals who were eligible to vote in the election. **(b)** Sample of those with listings in the residential directory. **(c)** Sample from students enrolled in the course (assuming some students were absent). **(d)** Population.

2. **(a)** Random. **(b)** Matched. **(c)** Randomized.

3. Starting at the sixth entry in column 3 and continuing down the column and down column 4, the 10 students chosen are those assigned the numbers 19, 6, 11, 20, 7, 1, 8, 2, 4, and 3.

4. **(a)** Rank order. **(b)** Categorical. **(c)** Magnitude. **(d)** Magnitude.

5. **(a)** Discrete. **(b)** Continuous. **(c)** Discrete. **(d)** Continuous. **(e)** Continuous. **(f)** Discrete.

CHAPTER 2

1. The grouped frequency distribution shown below has $i = 3$. With $i = 2$, too many class intervals would result to reveal the pattern of the scores adequately. Although $i = 4$ would be acceptable, it would result in midpoints with fractional values rather than whole numbers. For this reason, $i = 3$ is preferable to $i = 4$.

Class Interval	f	Class Interval	f	Class Interval	f	Class Interval	f
63–65	1	51–53	5	39–41	7	27–29	0
60–62	0	48–50	4	36–38	3	24–26	1
57–59	2	45–47	6	33–35	5	21–23	2
54–56	3	42–44	9	30–32	2		$N = 50$

2. The distribution with $i = 3$ is preferable to the one with $i = 5$. The latter distribution is so compact that the group pattern is beginning to be obscured. Furthermore, comparison with the distribution in problem 1 will be easier if both use the same i.

$i = 3$ Class Interval	f	$i = 3$ Class Interval	f	$i = 5$ Class Interval	f
57–59	1	36–38	6	55–59	2
54–56	1	33–35	10	50–54	1
51–53	0	30–32	7	45–49	5
48–50	2	27–29	4	40–44	6
45–47	4	24–26	4	35–39	11
42–44	2	21–23	3	30–34	13
39–41	5	18–20	1	25–29	7
			$N = 50$	20–24	5
					$N = 50$

3. (a) $R = 65 - 21 = 44$. (b) Real limits of highest and lowest intervals: 62.5–65.5 and 20.5–23.5. (c) Midpoints: 64 and 22.

4. The i's shown below yield a desirable number of intervals for the given N. However, in items (2), (3), and (5), slightly different i's would also be acceptable. In grouped distributions, the number of intervals was obtained by dividing the range (R) by i and rounding upward to a whole number.

	i	Number of Intervals	Midpoint	Highest Class Real Limits	Apparent Limits
(1) Not useful to group because of small N					
(2)	5	13	73	70.5–75.5	71–75
(3)	10	19	278.5	273.5–283.5	274–283
(4)	1	10	—	24.5–25.5	—
(5)	.10	12	1.475	1.425–1.525	1.43–1.52
(6)	2	16	33.5	32.5–34.5	33–34

5. An appropriate stem and leaf display is shown below.

Stem	Leaf
6*	5
6	
5*	5 6 7 8
5	0 0 1 1 2 3 3 4
4*	5 5 6 6 7 7 8 9
4	0 0 1 1 1 2 2 2 3 3 3 3 4 4
3*	5 5 6 7 8 9 9
3	1 2 3 4 4
2*	5
2	1 3

CHAPTER 3

1. (a) A figure with the two polygons is shown below.
   (b) The distribution for the males competing with another male is slightly more skewed than the distribution of males competing with a female. For male partner, the skew is in a positive direction; for female partner, it is in a negative direction.

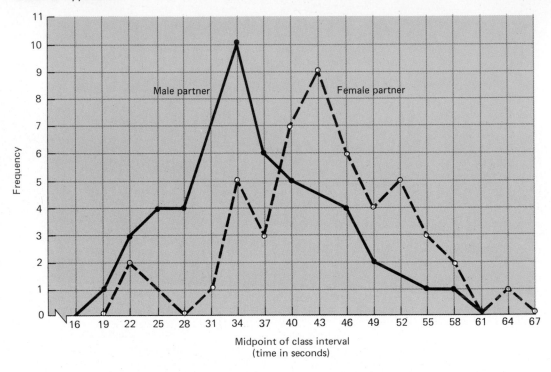

Frequency polygons for male students who believe they are competing with another male or a female on an anagram task.

(c) Male students competing with another male tend to complete the anagrams in a shorter time than males competing with a female.

(d) Histograms of the distributions are shown at the top of the following page.

2. (a) and (b) The cumulative frequencies, cumulative percentages, and the cumulative polygon based on these data are shown at the bottom of the following page.

Class Interval	*f*	*cum f*	*cum %*
36–40	6	50	100
31–35	9	44	88
26–30	12	35	70
21–25	13	23	46
16–20	6	10	20
11–15	0	4	8
6–10	3	4	8
1–5	1	1	2

N = 50

(c) Student A: 30.5; student B: 23; student C: 20.5. The procedures used to make these estimates are shown in the cumulative polygon above.

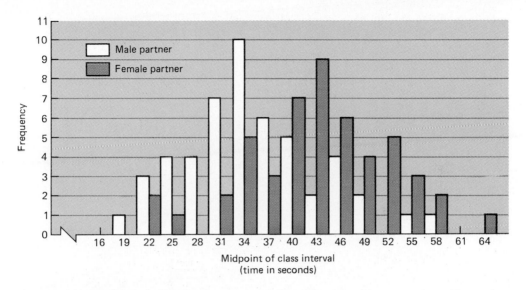

Problem 1(d): Histograms for male students who believe they are competing with another male or a female on an anagram task.

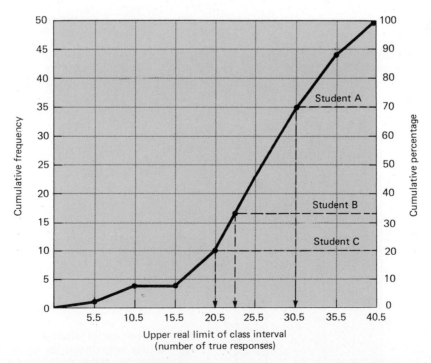

Problem 2(b): Cumulative polygon for response to true-false misconceptions test given to introductory psychology students.

3. (a) 53. (b) 65. (c) 68. (d) 43. (e) 75, 10.

4. (a)

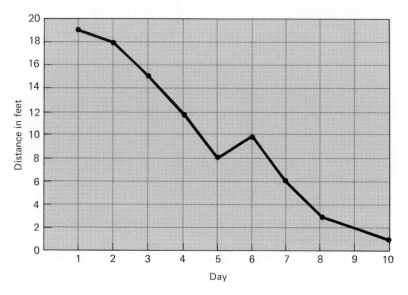

Distance from caged snake at which man stopped on each treatment day.

(b) Over the 10-day treatment period, the man quite regularly came closer and closer to the caged snake, stopping one foot away on the tenth day.

5.

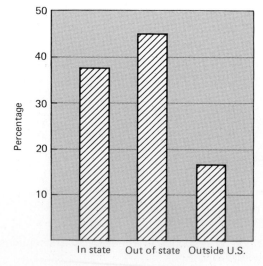

Percentage of students at the university who reside in state, out of state, or outside the United States.

6.

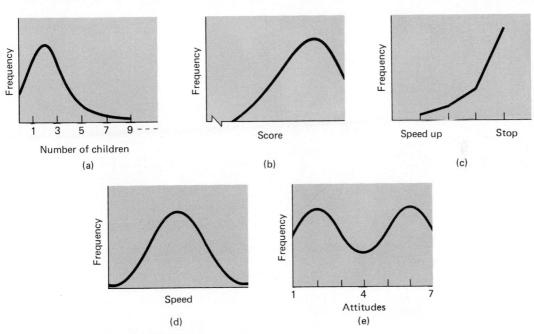

(a)

(b)

(c)

(d)

(e)

Labels: **(a)** Positively skewed.   **(b)** Negatively skewed.   **(c)** J curve.   **(d)** Symmetrical.
(e) It is possible that most people who came to the debate already had strong opinions, being either very much for or very much against legalized abortion. On this assumption (and the assumption that proponents and opponents were equally represented in the audience), the curve shown here is bimodal and symmetrical.

CHAPTER 4

1. **(a)** Sum of the X scores.   **(b)** Mean of the X scores; $\overline{X} = \Sigma\, X/N$.   **(c)** Sum of the Y scores.
(d) Mean of the Y scores.   **(e)** The square of the quantity $\Sigma\, X$.   **(f)** The sum of the squared X scores.   **(g)** The sum of the deviations of each X from $\overline{X}$; $\Sigma\, x = \Sigma(X - \overline{X})$. Except for rounding error in $\overline{X}$, $\Sigma\, x$ always equals 0.   **(h)** Multiply each X by the corresponding Y and sum the cross products.

Student	X	X^2	$x = X - \overline{X}$	Y	XY
A	4	16	− .5	5	20
B	1	1	− 3.5	2	2
C	7	49	2.5	6	42
D	4	16	− .5	3	12
E	9	81	4.5	8	72
F	2	4	− 2.5	2	4
G	6	36	1.5	5	30
H	3	9	− 1.5	1	3
	$\Sigma X = 36$	$\Sigma X^2 = 212$	$\Sigma x = 0.0$	$\Sigma Y = 32$	$\Sigma XY = 185$

$$\overline{X} = \frac{36}{8} = 4.5 \qquad\qquad \overline{Y} = \frac{32}{8} = 4.0$$

$$\left(\Sigma X\right)^2 = 36^2 = 1296$$

2. **(a)** Mode = 13, the midpoint of the class interval with the greatest frequency.   **(b)** Using Formula 4.2, $\overline{X} = \Sigma\,(fX)/N = 366/30 = 12.2$. $\Sigma\,(fX)$ is obtained by multiplying the midpoint (X) of each class interval by its corresponding frequency (f) and summing the resulting fX values.   **(c)** The median or 50th percentile is the 15th case from the bottom of the distribution (50% of the N of 30 = 15). The *15th* case is in the interval 12–14. The approximate median is the midpoint, 13.

3. Sample means are unbiased estimates of μ—that is, they systematically tend neither to underestimate or overestimate μ. When only one sample is available, the best single estimate of μ is therefore $\overline{X}$ which in this problem is 63.4.

4. **(a)** For N = 7, (N + 1)/2 = 4. When the seven numbers are rearranged in order, the value of the 4th (middle) case is 14.   **(b)** For N = 8, N/2 = 4 and (N + 2)/2 = 5. When the numbers are ordered, the midpoint between the 4th and 5th case is 18.   **(c)** For N = 6, N/2 = 3 and (N + 2)/2 = 4. The midpoint between the 3rd and 4th case is 165.5.

5. **(a)** Positively skewed   **(b)** Approximately symmetrical

(a)

(b)

(c) Negatively skewed

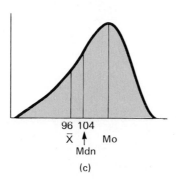

96 104
X̄ ↑ Mo
Mdn

(c)

CHAPTER 5

1. **(a)** Dist. 2.   **(b)** Dist. 1.   **(c)** Dist. 2.   **(d)** Dist. 1.

2. For distributions 1 and 2 respectively, the values of R are as follows: **(a)** 4, 7.   **(b)** 28, 14.
(c) 11, 28.   **(d)** 9, 9.

3. In (c), the two distributions are quite similar except for the lowest score (5) in dist. 1, which is very different from the rest. If this score were omitted, R for dist. 1 would drop from 28 to 7, a value that is closer to the R of 11 in dist. 2. Thus R is highly influenced by an extreme score, which may be quite deviant. In (d), the two R's are the same, even though the scores in dist. 2 are less variable, more of them clustering around the center of the distribution than in dist. 1. Being based on only the highest score and the lowest score in a distribution, R does not necessarily reflect the variability among the remainder of the scores.

4. Q_1 is the score value of the 10th case (25% of 40) and Q_3 is the score value of the 30th case (75% of 40). After the cumulative frequencies are found, it can be seen by inspection that $Q_1 = 55.5$ and $Q_3 = 58.5$. By Formula 5.1, the semi-interquartile range $= (58.5 - 55.5)/2 = 3/2 = 1.5$.

5. σ^2, S^2, and s^2 are symbols, respectively, for the variance of a population, the variance of a sample, and an unbiased estimate of the population σ^2 based on the data from a sample. σ, S, and s are symbols, respectively, for the standard deviation of a population, standard deviation of a sample, and an estimate of the population σ. A slight bias remains in s as an estimate of σ.

6. $S^2 = \dfrac{454}{10} - \left(\dfrac{60}{10}\right)^2 = 9.4$

$S = 3.06$

7. $S = \sqrt{\dfrac{454 - (60)^2/10}{10}} = \sqrt{9.4} = 3.06$

8. $s = \sqrt{\dfrac{94}{10 - 1}} = \sqrt{10.44} = 3.23$

X	f	fX	fX²
15	1	15	225
14	2	28	392
13	3	39	507
12	3	36	432
11	4	44	484
10	3	30	300
9	2	18	162
8	2	16	128
	$\sum f = 20$	$\sum fX = 226$	$\sum fX^2 = 2630$

$$s = \sqrt{\frac{2630 - (226)^2/20}{19}} = \sqrt{\frac{76.2}{19}}$$

$$= \sqrt{4.01} = 2.00$$

10. For symmetrical bell-shaped curves, three standard deviation units on either side of $\overline{X}$, for a total of 6, will typically encompass all or almost all the cases. An approximation of S can therefore be obtained by finding 1/6 of the value of R.   **(a)** R/6 = 48/6 = 8; calculated s of 8.5 is probably accurate.   **(b)** 21/6 = 3.5; calculated S = 7.2 is too large.   **(c)** 59/6 = 9.8; s = 9.3 is probably accurate.   **(d)** 46/6 = 7.7; S = 3.8 is too small.   **(e)** s was calculated to be -3.6, obviously wrong since s always takes a positive value.

11. **(a)**

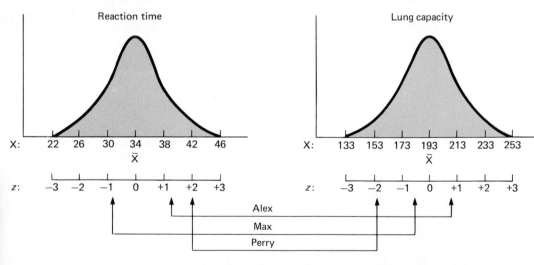

(b)

	z_{RT}		z_{LC}	
Alex	(39–34)/4 =	1.25	(210–193)/20 =	.85
Max	(31–34)/4 =	–.75	(183–193)/20 =	–.50
Perry	(42–34)/4 =	2.00	(155–193)/20 =	–1.90

(c) Alex and Max each had similar standings on the two tests, Alex being above average on both and Max being below average on both. Perry, however, was much above average on RT and much below average on LC. (d) Sam: $X_{RT} = z(S) + \overline{X} = 2.50(4) + 34 = 10 + 34 = 44$; Jim: $X_{RT} = -1.75(4) + 34 = (-7) + 34 = 27$; Boris: $X_{LC} = .25(20) + 193 = 5 + 193 = 198$.

12. (a) $z = \dfrac{(80 - 65)}{15} = 1.00$; $U = 10(1) + 50 = 60$

(b) $U = \dfrac{100}{15}(41) - \dfrac{100(65)}{15} + 500$

$= \dfrac{4100 - 6500}{15} + 500 = -160 + 500 = 360$

(c) $U = \dfrac{100}{15}(93) - \dfrac{100(65)}{15} + 500$

$= 186.67 + 500 = 686.67$

CHAPTER 6

1. (a) NME. A given crime may involve more than one type of offense and thus be assigned to more than one category. For example, a murder may be committed in the course of an armed robbery. (b) ME, if it is assumed that a student is permitted to be enrolled in only one college. If the university allows dual enrollment, the answer is NME. (c) ME. Each student receives only one course grade and thus can be assigned to only one of the five letter-grade categories.

2. (a) NI. Once one member of a pair has been assigned to the first condition, the other is automatically assigned to the second condition. Further, the pairs are likely to have similar growth patterns so that their scores on the experimental measures are likely to be correlated. (b) NI. The factors that lead an individual to earn good or poor grades in one semester tend to be present on successive semesters as well. (c) I. Assuming that the cards have been properly shuffled and dealt, the particular cards that the person is dealt in one hand do not influence the cards in successive hands.

3. (a) $p(A) = n_A/N = \frac{60}{200} = .30$. (b) $p(B) = .25; p(C) = .45; p(B \text{ or } C) = p(A) + p(B) = .25 + .45 = .70$. (c) $p(\overline{A})$ or complement of A. (d) $p(C, B) = p(C) \times p(B) = .45 \times .25 = .1125$. (e) $p(A, A, A) = .3 \times .3 \times .3 = .027$.

4. (a) $p(AL \text{ or } HI) = p(AL) + p(HI) = \frac{1}{50} + \frac{1}{50} = \frac{2}{50} = .04$. (b) $\frac{13}{50} = .26$. (c) Since the first prize winner has already been selected, 49 contestants remain for the second drawing. Therefore $p(CA) = \frac{1}{49}$. (d) $p(IA, ME, WY) = p(IA) \times p(ME|IA) \times p(WY|IA, ME) = \frac{1}{50} \times \frac{1}{49} \times \frac{1}{48} = .0000085$.

5. (a)

	Less	Same	More	Total
3-year-olds	.033	.067	.200	.300
5-year-olds	.000	.167	.167	.333
8-year-olds	.000	.300	.067	.367
Total	.033	.534	.434	1.000

Note: Except for rounding errors, the cell entries in each row and column should equal the row and column totals.

(b) p (same) $= \frac{16}{30} = .533$. (p can also be read directly from the table in (a).) Table has slight rounding error.

(c)

	Less	Same	More	Total
3-year-olds	.111	.222	.667	1.00
5-year-olds	.000	.500	.500	1.00
8-year-olds	.000	.818	.182	1.00

(d) p (same) $= \frac{5}{10} = .500$. (p can also be read directly from the table in (c).) (e) p (more) $= \frac{6}{9} = .667$. (p can also be read directly from the table.)

6. $P_N = N! = 4! = 4(3)(2)(1) = 24$.

7. (a) $P_r^N = \dfrac{N!}{(N - r)!} = \dfrac{10!}{(10 - 2)!} = 90$. (b) $C_r^N = \dfrac{N!}{r!(N - r)!} = \dfrac{10!}{2!(8!)} = 45$.

CHAPTER 7

1. (a) On each card, there are 4 equally possible arrangements of 1 winner and 3 losers. (That is, the winner is equally likely to appear on line 1, 2, 3, or 4.) The number of possible patterns over the three cards is therefore $4 \times 4 \times 4 = 64$ and the probability of each pattern is $(\frac{1}{4})^3$ or $\frac{1}{64}$. (b) $(p + q)^N = (\frac{1}{4} + \frac{3}{4})^3 = (\frac{1}{4})^3 + 3(\frac{1}{4})^2 (\frac{3}{4}) + 3(\frac{1}{4}) (\frac{3}{4})^2 + (\frac{3}{4})^3 = \frac{1}{64} + \frac{9}{64} + \frac{27}{64} + \frac{27}{64} = .0156 + .1406 + .4219 + .4219 = 1$. These values correspond, respectively, to the probability of 3, 2, 1 and 0 "winners." (c) $C_1^3 pq^2 = \dfrac{3!}{1!(3 - 1)!} (\frac{1}{4})(\frac{3}{4})^2 = 3(.25)(.5625) = .4219$. This is the same p value obtained in (b). (d) p (2 or 3 winners) $= p$ (2 winners) $+ p$ (3 winners) $= .1406 + .0156 = .1562$. (e) $\mu = Nq = 3(\frac{3}{4}) = \frac{9}{4} = 2.25$. $\sigma = \sqrt{Npq} = \sqrt{3(1/4)(3/4)} = \sqrt{9/16} = \frac{3}{4} = .75$.

2. (a) $z = (63 - 75)/12 = \frac{-12}{12} = -1.00$; from Table B, 34.13% of the cases in a normal distribution are between the mean and $z = -1.00$. Therefore $50 - 34.13 = 15.87\%$ score 63 or below. (b) The z for $X = 63$ was calculated in (a). For $X = 87$, $z = (87 - 75)/12 = +1.00$. The percentage lying between 63 and 87 is $34.13 + 34.13 = 68.26\%$. (c) 68.26% of 5000 $= 3413$ students. (d) For $X = 81$, $z = (81 - 75)/12 = +.5$; Table B shows that 19.15% of the cases lie between the mean and this point. For $X = 93$, $z = (93 - 75)/12 = +1.5$; 43.32% lie between the mean and this point. Therefore $43.32 - 19.15 = 24.17\%$ lie between these two z scores or between the raw scores of 81 and 93. (e) $z = (66 - 75)/12 = -.75$; 27.34% of the area lies between the mean and this point and $50 - 27.34 = 22.66\%$ below it. The percentile rank of $X = 66$ is therefore 22.66. (f) The z score at or below which 67% of the cases fall is first determined. Since 50% fall at or below the mean, look up $67 - 50 = 17\%$ in the body of Table B and determine the associated z score. This z is $+.44$. The raw-score equivalent of the 67th percentile is $X = .44(12) + 75 = 5.28 + 75 = 80.28$.

3. (a) $z = (62 - 58)/10 = +.4$; 15.54% lie between the mean and this point and 50% below the mean. The probability of $X = 62$ or below is therefore .6554. (b) $z = \pm 5/10 = \pm .50$; 19.15% of the cases lie between the mean and each of these z values and $50 - 19.15 = 30.85\%$ beyond each of them. The probability of a deviation this large or larger in either direction is therefore $.3085 + .3085 = .6170$. (c) From Table B, 47.5% lie between the mean and $z = \pm 1.96$ and 2.5% lie beyond each of these z values. $X = +1.96(10) + 58 = 77.6$ and $X = -1.96(10) + 58 = 38.4$. The extreme 5% had scores of 77.6 or more or 38.4 or less.

CHAPTER 8

1. **(a)** Sampling distribution of $\overline{X}$'s.   **(b)** 78, the value of μ for the population.   **(c)** Standard error of the mean. By Formula 8.1, $\sigma_{\overline{X}} = 10/\sqrt{25} = 2.0$.   **(d)** The mean would still be equal to μ(i.e., 78). $\sigma_{\overline{X}} = 10/\sqrt{49} = 1.43$.   **(e)** 1.00   **(f)** Without complex calculations, beyond the scope of this text, your representations cannot be exact. Your figures should have the major features of the following three curves.

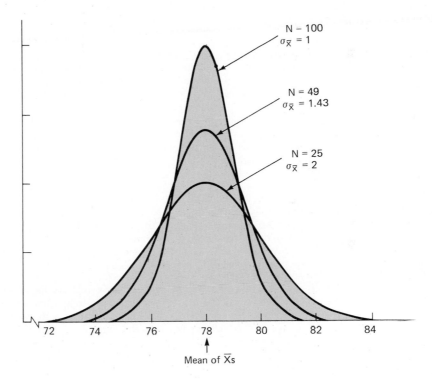

Sampling distribution of $\overline{X}$'s when $\mu = 78$, $\sigma = 10$, and sample N's are 25, 49, or 100.

(g) As N's increase, variability among $\overline{X}$'s decrease, as reflected in the decreasing value of $\sigma_{\overline{X}}$. The value of $\sigma_{\overline{X}}$ approaches 0 as the sample N's approach the population N.

2. **(a)** The sampling distribution of $\overline{X}$'s with N = 64 can be expected to have a mean of 150 and $\sigma_{\overline{X}} = 16/\sqrt{64} = 2.00$. The given $\overline{X}$ of 153 must first be converted to a z score: z = (153 − 150)/2 = 1.5. From Table B, 43.32% lie between the mean and this z and 6.68% beyond it. The probability of $\overline{X} = 153$ or greater is therefore .0668.   **(b)** $z = \pm 4/2 = \pm 2$. In a normal distribution, 2.28% of the cases fall at or above z = +2 and an equal percentage at or below z = −2. The probability of deviating ± 4 score units or more is therefore 2(.0228) = .0456. **(c)** From the body of Table B, it can be seen that 44.95 of the cases fall between the mean and a z of 1.64 and (approximately) 5% beyond this z. Converting this z into its corresponding $\overline{X}$, $\overline{X} = 1.64(2) + 150 = 153.28$.   **(d)** $s_{\overline{X}} = 17/\sqrt{64} = 2.125$. Through errors of random samplings, the estimate of σ was somewhat higher than the actual σ, and the estimate of the standard error of the mean was therefore also slightly higher than the true value.

3. (a) $s_{\overline{X}} = 1.2/\sqrt{144} = .10$.   (b) If there is no stereotype, the mean rating in the population would be 4 (any other value of μ would indicate some degree of stereotype). Therefore: H_0: $\mu = 4.00$; H_1: $\mu \neq 4.00$.   (c) $t = (4.15 - 4.00)/.10 = 1.50$. With a sample of this size, $t = 1.96$ at $\alpha = .05$ (two-tailed test).* We therefore retain the hypothesis that $\mu = 4.00$. We conclude that 16-year-old girls perceive that being a salesclerk is equally appropriate for men and women. (d) We could have made a Type II error.

CHAPTER 9

1. (a) Independent variable: type of therapy. Dependent variable: score on the test evaluating emotional status. H_0: The two therapy groups come from populations with the same mean on the test—that is, the population mean is the same after insight therapy as it is after cognitive therapy. (b) Independent variable: level of self-esteem. Dependent variable: ratings on attribution scale H_0: The μ's of the two self-esteem groups are equal; level of self-esteem is unrelated to attribution. (c) Independent variable: presence or absence of social experience given to infant monkeys. Dependent variable: amount of fear in response to a strange toy. H_0: The population mean of fear responses is the same in monkeys previously given social experience as in monkeys previously given no social experience.

2. (a) By Formula 8.1, $\overline{X}_{WWI} = 3/\sqrt{100} = .3$ and $\sigma_{\overline{X}_{WWII}} = 3/\sqrt{100} = .3$.   (b) The mean of the distribution of differences between pairs of $\overline{X}$'s ($\overline{X}_{WWII} - \overline{X}_{WWI}$) takes the same value as the difference between the μ's of the two populations. Thus $68 - 65 = 3$.   (c) Standard error of the difference between means ($\sigma_{\overline{X}_1 - \overline{X}_2}$). By Formula 9.1, $\sigma_{\overline{X}_{WWII} - \overline{X}_{WWI}} = \sqrt{(.3)^2 + (.3)^2} = .42$. (d) The mean of the distribution of differences between $\overline{X}$'s is 3 and its standard deviation is .42. The z score of $\overline{X}_{WWII} - \overline{X}_{WWI} = 4$ is therefore $(4 - 3)/.42 = 2.38$. From Table B, it can be determined that a z score of 2.38 or greater has a probability of only .0087.

3. (a) H_0: $\mu_{WWII} - \mu_{WWI} = 0$; H_1: $\mu_{WWII} - \mu_{WWI} \neq 0$. A specific value must be specified in H_0. Since the question is whether the two population μ's are the same or different, H_0 must specify that they are the same since this hypothesis specifies a value, zero, for the difference between μ's. (b) H_1: $\mu_{WWII} > \mu_{WWI}$. Better nutrition and other similar factors have resulted in systematic increases in people's height over the past century or more. We therefore expect that the average recruit in WWII would also be taller.   (c) $s_{\overline{X}_{WWII} - \overline{X}_{WWI}} = \sqrt{(3.1)^2/70 + (2.9)^2/70} = \sqrt{.137 + .120} = .51$; $t = (67.2 - 65.8)/.51 = 2.75$. For $\alpha = .01$, $t = 2.58$ for a two-tailed test. Since the calculated t is greater than this value, H_0 can be rejected at the .01 significance level. (d) It is concluded that inductees were taller in the Second than in the First World War.

4. Since the experimenter is uncertain about the direction of any difference that may occur, the H_1 must be bidirectional. Thus: H_0: $\mu_L - \mu_{NL} = 0$; H_1: $\mu_L - \mu_{NL} \neq 0$. $s_{\overline{X}_L - \overline{X}_{NL}} = \sqrt{(4.1)^2/20 + (3.6)^2/20} = 1.22$; $t = (43.2 - 47.7)/1.22 = -3.69$; $df = 20 + 20 - 2 = 38$. Calculated t is greater than 2.72, the t at $\alpha = .01$ for a two-tailed test. ($df = 35$ is used since $df = 38$ does not appear in Table C.) H_0 is rejected at $\alpha = .01$. It is concluded at the .01 significance level that on the average, lonely women students are lower in intimacy of self-disclosure than nonlonely women.

---

*In this and all subsequent problems in which H_1 is bidirectional, the critical value of t at $\alpha = .05$ or .01 is specified without sign. H_0 is rejected if the absolute value of the calculated t equals or exceeds the critical value at the specified α level. When H_1 is unidirectional, the sign (plus or minus) of the critical value of t must be specified and for H_0 to be rejected, the calculated t must have the same sign.

5. $H_0: \mu_E - \mu_S = 0; H_1: \mu_E - \mu_S \neq 0.$

$$s_{\bar{X}_E - \bar{X}_S} = \sqrt{\frac{4(5.6)^2 + 9(5.2)^2}{13}\left(\frac{1}{5} + \frac{1}{10}\right)} = \sqrt{8.51} = 2.92.$$

$t = (58.4 - 52.6)/2.92 = 1.99.$ For $df = 15 - 2 = 13; t = 2.16$ at $\alpha = .05$. The calculated t is below this value, so the null hypothesis cannot be rejected. With $\alpha = .05$, it cannot be concluded that the drugs have any differential effects.

6. (a) $t = (58.9 - 53.1)/1.53 = 3.79; df = 50 - 2 = 48.$ From Table C, $t = 2.014$ for $\alpha = .05$ and $df = 45.$ (48 df is not listed; 45 is the nearest df below this figure.) The calculated t is larger than this value and H_0 is rejected. H_0 could also be rejected at $\alpha = .01$ (for 45 df, $t_{.01} = 2.69$). (b) Three factors influence the power of the t test to detect a false H_0: the size of the difference between μ's (which is reflected in the sizes of the difference between pairs of $\bar{X}$'s), the magnitude of the population σ's (estimated by s), and the sample N's. In the two experiments, the difference between $\bar{X}$'s turned out to be the same and the s's were comparable. However, the sample N's were larger in the second experiment, which resulted in decreasing $s_{\bar{X}_E - \bar{X}_S}$ and thus in increasing t. We cannot conclude with absolute certainty that a Type II error was made in the first experiment or that the second experiment "proved" the new drug was more beneficial. However, in view of the near significance of t in problem 5, it seems reasonable to conclude that the drugs are differentially effective and that a significant difference was found in the second experiment but not the first because of the larger samples it employed.

7. (a) $\hat{\omega}^2 = \dfrac{(2.18)^2 - 1}{(2.18)^2 + 70 + 1} = \dfrac{4.75 - 1}{75.75} = .05$

Subjects shown positive words had higher ratings than those shown neutral words. Word type was estimated to account for only 5 percent of the variability in the ratings, a quite modest effect.

(b) $\hat{\omega}^2 = \dfrac{(2.98)^2 - 1}{(2.98)^2 + 28 + 1} = \dfrac{8.88 - 1}{37.88} = .20$

The rat pups given the special diet fed to their mothers ate more than the pups given the standard diet. Diet was estimated to account in 20 percent of the variability, a relatively strong effect.

CHAPTER 10

1. (a) Linear; negative r. Those who watch TV more tend to have poorer grades. (b) Curvilinear. The relationship is likely to take the form of an inverted U, women who are emaciated or who are obese tending to be in poorer health than those of intermediate weights. (c) Linear; positive r. Higher level of education is associated with higher incomes. (d) Little or no relationship is expected between the two variables; the correlation would be close to zero.

2. (a) In almost all pairs, the z's have the same sign so that their cross-product is positive, and within pairs, the z values tend to be quite similar. A high positive r is expected. (b) Inspection of the scatter plot, below, suggests that the relationship is linear.

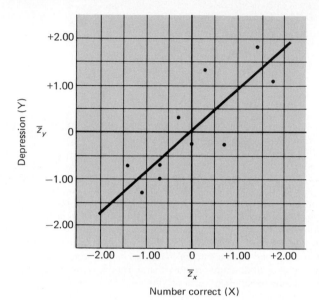

Scatter plot of z scores for number correct and depression scores and a straight line that comes close to the points.

Number correct (X)

(c) Obtain ΣXY by multiplying each X by its corresponding Y and summing the resulting cross-products. Then obtain $\overline{X}$ and $\overline{Y}$ by dividing ΣX and ΣY by N. All other values called for in Formula 10.2 are given in the problem. Entering these values into the formula,

$$r = \frac{841 - 10(5)(15)}{\sqrt{330 - 10(5^2)} \ \sqrt{2402 - 10(15^2)}}$$

$$= \frac{91}{\sqrt{80} \ \sqrt{152}} = \frac{91}{110.26} = .825.$$

(d) For $df = 10 - 2 = 8$, $r_{.01} = .765$. We reject H_0: $r = 0$ at $\alpha = .01$.

3.

Individual	R_1	R_2	d	d^2
A	6	8	−2	4
B	1	2	−1	1
C	5	5	0	0
D	8	7	1	1
E	2	1	1	1
F	4	6	−2	4
G	7	3	4	16
H	3	4	−1	1
			$\Sigma d^2 =$	28

$$r_S = 1 - \frac{6 \ \Sigma d^2}{N(N^2 - 1)}$$

$$= 1 - \frac{6(28)}{8(64 - 1)}$$

$$= 1 - .33$$

$$= .67$$

For N = 8 pairs, $r_S = .738$ at $\alpha = .05$. Our obtained r_S is not significant.

4. (a) The teacher assumes that lack of playmates causes lack of self-confidence, so that giving children the opportunity to make friends will raise their confidence. However, causality cannot be inferred

from the existence of a correlation. X may bring about Y, Y may bring about X, or both X and Y may be "caused" by a similar set of factors.   **(b)** $Y_{pred} = \{.50(1.4)/2.0\} (X) - \{.50(1.4)/2.0\} (16.8) + (5.2) = .35X - .68$.
(c) and (d)

X	Y_{pred}	Actual Y
14	4.22	2
17	5.27	4
19	5.97	7

The predictions correspond only modestly well to actual scores. Since r is not high, these errors in prediction are not surprising.   **(e)** With $r = .50$, $r^2 = .25$. Only 25 percent of the variability in one set of scores is explained by variations in the other set of scores.

5. **(a)** $X_{pred} = [(.94)(5.90)/5.64] (Y) - (.983)(58.75) + 47.90 = .983Y - 9.87$.   **(b)** For Y = 50, $X_{pred} = .983(50) - 9.87 = 39.30$. For Y = 70, $X_{pred} = .983(70) - 9.87 = 58.96$.

(c)

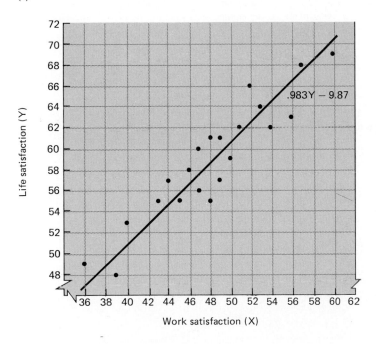

Scatter plot of work satisfaction and life scores and regression line of X on Y.

(d) $s_{est\,X} = s_X \sqrt{1 - r^2} = 5.9 \sqrt{1 - (.94)^2} = 5.9 \sqrt{.116} = 5.9(.341) = 2.01$. Thus the standard deviation of actual X points around the regression line at any given Y value should be about 2.01 score units. Inspection of the deviation of the points from the regression line at the various Y values (for example, Y = 57) reveals deviations consistent with this statement.

CHAPTER 11

1. **(a)** The moderate correlation suggests that the set of variables on which the pairs of patients were matched had some effect on performance. The matching was thus done on relevant variables. **(b)** H_0: $\mu_S - \mu_M = 0$; H_1: $\mu_S - \mu_M \neq 0$. $s_{\overline{X}_S - \overline{X}_M} = \sqrt{(2.3)^2 + (2.6)^2} = 3.47$; $t = (84.2 - 91.1)/3.47 = -1.99$. $df = 15 + 15 - 2 = 28$. For 28 df, $t_{.05} = 2.05$. H_0 cannot be rejected.

(c) $s_{\overline{X}_S - \overline{X}_M} = \sqrt{(2.3)^2 + (2.6)^2 - 2(.45)(2.3)(2.6)} = 2.58$.

$t = (84.2 - 91.1)/2.58 = -2.67$. $df = N - 1 = 15 - 1 = 14$. For 14 df, $t_{.05} = 2.14$. H_0 is rejected at $\alpha = .05$. It is concluded that schizophrenics do not perform as well on the task as medical patients. H_0 could be rejected because, with matched pairs whose performance is correlated, Formula 11.1 reduces $s_{\overline{X}_1 - \overline{X}_2}$ and permits a more powerful test of H_0. The conclusion that the groups differ significantly is the correct one to draw because it follows from the proper formula for a matched pairs design.

2. **(a)** H_0: $\mu_{Ch} - \mu_S = 0$; H_1: $\mu_{Ch} - \mu_S \neq 0$. When the differences (D) between pairs of scores and the square of each D are obtained, $\Sigma D = -26$, $\overline{D} = -26/10 = -2.6$, and $\Sigma D^2 = 186$. $s_D^2 = \{(186) - (-26)^2/10\}/10 - 1 = 13.16$. $s_{\overline{D}} = \sqrt{13.16/10} = 1.147$; $t = -2.6/1.147 = -2.27$. $df = 10 - 1 = 9$. For 9 df, $t_{.05} = 2.26$. H_0 is significant at the .05 level. It is concluded that after being made ill, the animals subsequently found the chocolate-flavored mash less palatable. **(b)** $A = 186/(26)^2 = .275$. This value is slightly smaller than the *maximum* A of .276 allowed at $\alpha = .05$ with $N - 1 = 9$. Therefore, H_0 is significant at the .05 level, the same conclusion reached in (b) with t.

3. **(a)** The population correlation is equal to 0. **(b)** For $df = 20 - 2 = 18$, $r_{.05} = .444$. Obtained r is not significantly different from 0. **(c)** For $df = 28$, $r_{.01} = .463$. Obtained r is significant. **(d)** For $df = 203$, $r_{.05} = .138$. Obtained r is significant. **(e)** For $N = 16$, $r_S = .665$ at $\alpha = .01$. Obtained r_S is not significant. **(f)** For $N = 25$, $r_S = .537$ at $\alpha = .01$. Obtained r_S is not significant.

CHAPTER 12

1. **(a)** $\overline{X}_1 = 16$, $\overline{X}_2 = 12.8$, $\overline{X}_3 = 10.2$. **(b)** H_0: $\mu_1 = \mu_2 = \mu_3$. The population mean reaction times are assumed to be equal for tilts of 45°, 90°, and 180°.

Mean reaction times for the three groups in object orientation study.

(c) $SS_{bg} = \dfrac{(80)^2}{5} + \dfrac{(64)^2}{5} + \dfrac{(51)^2}{5} - \dfrac{(195)^2}{15} = 2619 - 2535 = 84.$

$SS_{tot} = 1300 + 852 + 535 - \dfrac{(195)^2}{15} = 2687 - 2535 = 152.$

$SS_{wg} = 152 - 84 = 68.$

$df_{bg} = 3 - 1 = 2; \; df_{wg} = 15 - 3 = 12; \; df_{tot} = 15 - 1 = 14.$

$MS_{bg} = \dfrac{84}{2} = 42.0; \; MS_{wg} = \dfrac{68}{12} = 5.7; \; F = \dfrac{42.0}{5.7} = 7.37.$

For $df = 2$ and 12, $F_{.01} = 6.93$; calculated F is significant at $\alpha = .01$.

Source of Variation	SS	df	MS	F	p
Between groups	84	2	42.0	7.37	< .01
Within groups	68	12	5.7		
Total	152	14			

(d) There is a significant tendency for mean reaction times to differ as tilt changes. The observed trend is for means to be greatest with the least tilt of one member of a pair and smallest with the most tilt. (A multiple-comparison test such as the Tukey *hsd* test could indicate whether the specific trend observed is present in the populations as well.)

2. $\hat{\omega}^2 = \dfrac{84 - (3 - 1)(5.7)}{152 + 5.7} = \dfrac{72.6}{157.7} = .46.$ There is a strong effect of tilt on reaction time.

3. Being conservative since $q_{4,116}$ is not tabled for the .05 level, we find $q_{4,60} = 3.74$ for the .05 level. Then $hsd = 3.74 \sqrt{\dfrac{27.30}{30}} = 3.74\,(.9539) = 3.57.$

Absolute Difference between Pairs of Means

	$\overline{X}_1$	$\overline{X}_2$	$\overline{X}_3$
$\overline{X}_2$	1.2		
$\overline{X}_3$	6.8	8.0	
$\overline{X}_4$	4.4	5.6	2.4

The underlined differences exceed the *hsd* value of 3.57 at $\sigma = .05$. The significant F from the ANOVA leads to the conclusion that there are differences among the means. The follow-up *hsd* test indicates that the specific nature of the these differences are such that discussion groups 3 and 4 earned significantly better grades than did groups 1 and 2. Neither groups 1 and 2 nor groups 3 and 4 differ significantly.

4. (a) The sample means are all less than the medians, suggesting that non-normality may be present. (b) No apparent problem with non-normal data or unequal population variances. (c) Since the differences between upper and lower points in the ranges are 11, 22, and 30, respectively, we suspect that the population variances are unequal, contradicting the assumption of equal variances in the three populations.

CHAPTER 13

1. In each of the figures below, one variable was chosen to be represented on the baseline and the other to be represented in separate curves. Choice of which variable is to be shown on the baseline is more or less arbitrary, and you may have made the opposite choice.

(a) I.

(a)

II. Table of $\overline{X}$'s

	Group		
	Exp.	Control	Row $\overline{X}$
Assembly	35	25	30
Office	37	32	34.5
Col. $\overline{X}$	36	28.5	

III. Both variables appear to have main effects. Workers in the experimental flextime program are more satisfied than workers in the control group working set hours, and office workers are more satisfied than assembly line workers. There also appears to be an interaction between the variables, the difference in satisfaction between the two types of working conditions being greater for the assembly line workers.

(b) I.

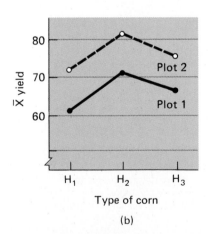

(b)

II. Table of $\overline{X}$'s

	Corn Type			
	H_1	H_2	H_3	Row $\overline{X}$
Plot 1	61	71	66	66
Plot 2	72	81	75	76
Col. $\overline{X}$	66.5	76	70.5	

III. Both variables appear to have main effects, plot 2 producing more than plot 1 and type of corn also producing different amounts in the order H_1, H_3, and H_2. Plot and type of corn appear to combine additively, the two curves being approximately parallel. Thus, the magnitude of the superiority of H_2 over H_3 and H_3 over H_1 is the same in each plot.

(c) I.

(c)

II. Table of $\overline{X}$'s

	Self-esteem		
	High	Low	Row $\overline{X}$
Success	63	58	60.5
Failure	57	64	60.5
Col. $\overline{X}$	60	61	

III. A crossover interaction between the variables can be observed in the graph. High self-esteem subjects work faster after failure than after success, whereas low self-esteem subjects work faster after success than after failure. These opposite effects cancel out any main effects of success and failure, the row means turning out to be identical. Similarly, self-esteem also has no main effect, the column means being nearly equal.

2. (a) In order to emphasize differences in ratings of the two tapes within each of the three groups of majors, the experimental conditions have been plotted along the baseline in the graph below. It would be acceptable, however, to indicate major along the baseline.

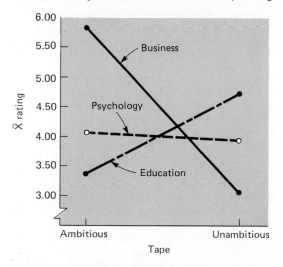

(b) 1. Main effect of tape. H_0: $\mu_A - \mu_U = 0$. Collapsing over raters' type of major, the population mean of the ratings of the tape of the ambitious man is the same as the mean of the ratings of the tape of the unambitious man. 2. Main effect of raters' major. H_0: $\mu_B = \mu_E = \mu_P$. Collapsing over the two tapes, the population means of the ratings of the three types of major are all equal. 3. Interaction between tape and major. H_0: the two variables combine additively. (c) $SS_{tot} = (703 + 299 + 387 + 212 + 499 + 358) - [(117 + 67 + 81 + 60 + 95 + 78)^2 / 120] = 2458$

$-2066.7 = 391.3.$ $SS_{bg} = (117^2/20) + (67^2/20) + (81^2/20) + (60^2/20) + (95^2/20) + (78^2/20) - 2066.7 = 2172.4 - 2066.7 = 105.7.$ $SS_{wg} = (703 - 117^2/20) + (212 - 60^2/20) + (299 - 67^2/20) + (499 - 95^2/20) + (387 - 81^2/20) + (358 - 78^2/20) = 285.6,$ or $SS_{wg} = SS_{tot} - SS_{bg} = 391.3 - 105.7 = 285.6.$ $SS_{Tape} = (117 + 67 + 81)^2/60 + (60 + 95 + 78)^2/60 - 2066.7 = 8.5.$ $SS_{Major} = (117 + 60)^2/40 + (67 + 95)^2/40 + (81 + 78)^2/40 - 2066.7 = 2071.35 - 2066.7 = 4.6.$ $SS_{Tape \times Maj} = SS_{bg} - SS_{Tape} - SS_{Major} = 92.6.$

Source	SS	df	MS	F	p*
Tape	8.5	1	8.5	3.40	>.05
Major	4.6	2	2.3	.92	>.05
Interaction	92.6	2	46.3	18.52	<.01
Within groups	285.6	114	2.5		
Total	391.3	119			

*For $df = 1$ and 114, $F_{.05} = 4.00$ and for $df = 2$ and 114, $F_{.05} = 3.15$ and $F_{.01} = 4.98$. (Note: when df is not tabled, the next lowest df in the table is used to find the critical F value.)

(d) Neither main effect was significant, but the interaction was highly significant, suggesting that type of tape did affect ratings, but not in the same way in all three majors. Inspection of the graph of $\overline{X}$'s in (a) shows how the significant interaction came about. The business majors rated the ambitious man much more favorably than the nonambitious man, whereas for the education majors, the difference was in the reverse direction. Compared to each of the other two groups, psychology majors gave moderately favorable ratings to both types of tapes. Apparently business majors like men more who are highly ambitious, education majors like men who are less ambitious, and psychology majors like both about equally.   (e) For $k = 6$ groups, $df = 114$ and $\alpha = .05$, $bsd = 4.16 \sqrt{2.5/20} = 1.47$. The difference between the means for the two business groups (2.85) exceeded this value and was thus significant. The difference between the means of the two education groups was 1.40 and therefore was close to being significant at the .05 level. The difference for the psychology majors was .15, far short of 1.47, and thus not significant.

(f) Tape: $\hat{\omega}^2 = \dfrac{8.5 - (1)(2.5)}{391.3 + 2.5} = .009$

Major: $\hat{\omega}^2 = \dfrac{4.6 - 2(2.5)}{391.3 + 2.5} = -.001.$ The true ω^2 cannot be less than 0. When $\hat{\omega}^2$ is negative, statisticians advise reporting effect size as 0.

Interaction: $\hat{\omega}^2 = \dfrac{92.6 - 2(2.5)}{391.3 + 2.5} = .22$

CHAPTER 14

1. (a) There is no guessing bias; the probability of guessing head is the same as guessing tail. H_0: $p(H) = p(T) = .50.$

(b)

	Guess H	Guess T	Total
Observed	118	82	200
Expected	100	100	200
O − E	+ 18	− 18	
$(O - E)^2$	324	324	
$(O - E)^2/E$	3.24	3.24	

$\chi^2 = 3.24 + 3.24 = 6.48$. For 1 df, $\chi^2_{.05} = 3.84$. H_0 can be rejected at $\alpha = .05$. It is concluded that there is a bias for guessing "heads."

2. **(a)**

	Club	Spade	Heart	Diamond	Total
Observed	43	51	54	52	200
Expected	50	50	50	50	200

$\chi^2 = (-7)^2/50 + (1)^2/50 + (4)^2/50 + (2)^2/50 = 1.40$. For $df = 3$, and $\alpha = .05$, $\chi^2 = 7.82$. Since the obtained χ^2 is less than this value, the hypothesis is retained. **(b)** It is concluded that in guessing the suit of a card, there is probably no bias.

3. **(a)** χ^2 test of independence, or test of homogeneity (significance of difference) between groups.

(b)

	Same		Different		
	O	E	O	E	Total
Physicians	14	13	6	7	20
Lawyers	12	13	8	7	20
Total	26		14		40

$\chi^2 = (1)^2/13 + (-1)^2/13 + (-1)^2/7 + (1)^2/7 = .44$. For 1 df, and $\alpha_{.05}$, $\chi^2 = 3.84$; the hypothesis is accepted. It is concluded that the proportion of those who would make the same choice again does not differ in the two professions.

(c) $\chi^2 = \dfrac{40\,[(14)(8) - (6)(12)]^2}{(14 + 6)(12 + 8)(14 + 12)(6 + 8)} = .44$

As it should be, the answer is the same as in (b).

4. Test of contingency. The H_0 is that there is no relationship between job status and plans to vote.

5. **(a)** $\chi^2 = (11 - 7.97)^2/7.97 + (4 - 7.03)^2/7.03 + (13 - 18.06)^2/18.06 + (21 - 15.94)^2/15.94 + (10 - 7.97)^2/7.97 + (5 - 7.03)^2/7.03 = 6.60$. **(b)** With $df = 2$, $\chi^2_{.05} = 5.99$ and $\chi^2_{.01} = 9.21$. If $\alpha = .05$ is selected, the hypothesis that age is independent of choice would be rejected; it would be concluded that whereas 3-year-olds choose small, medium, and large approximately equally on the test trial following training, 6-year-olds more often choose the medium size stimulus.

6. $df = (5 - 1)(10 - 1) = 36$. In order to evaluate χ^2 based on greater than 30 df, χ^2 must be converted into a z score and its probability determined from the normal curve table. By Formula 14.5, $z = \sqrt{2(55.05)} - \sqrt{2(36) - 1} = 2.06$. At $\alpha = .05$, $z = 1.96$. The obtained z is greater than this value so that the hypothesis is rejected at .05 significance level. It is concluded that the proportion of students choosing various fields is related to geographic region.

CHAPTER 15

1. **(a)** The assumptions of equal variance and normality appear to be violated. **(b)** $Mdn = 27.5$. $\chi^2 = 15.2$. Since a χ^2 of 9.21 is required with $df = 2$ and $\alpha = .01$, the null hypothesis of equal enjoyment of competition by the three groups is rejected. Apparently football players enjoy such competition much more than either of the other two groups.

2. $U_1 = 69$, $U_2 = 27$, $U_E = 48$, and $\sigma_U = 12.96$, making $z = 1.62$ with U_1 and $z = -1.62$ with U_2. Since the absolute value of z must exceed 1.96 when $\alpha = .05$, we accept the null hypothesis of no difference in recall for the two groups.

3. $R_1 = 33.5$, $R_2 = 38$, and $R_3 = 48.5$, making $H = 1.18$, which must be compared with a required χ^2 of 5.99 for $df = 2$ and $\alpha = .05$. Therefore H_0 is accepted, and we conclude that neither of the sucrose groups could detect its presence, at least enough to produce the expected increase in speed when sucrose is present as a reward.

4. $T = 3.0$, and $N_{S-R} = 9$. Since Table J shows that T must be less than or equal to 6 to be significant with this value of N_{S-R} and $\alpha = .05$, we reject H_0. We conclude that recognition is facilitated by presenting an associated word before the test word.

5. $\chi^2 = 5.20$, which is not significant with $df = 2$ and $\alpha = .05$, since a χ^2 of 5.99 is required in this situation.

CHAPTER 16

1. (a) Compute Pearson r. Test H_0 that $r = 0$, that is, that husbands' and wives' satisfaction is unrelated.
   (b) By direct difference t or Sandler's A for matched pairs, test H_0 that μ's for husbands' and wives' satisfaction scores are equal.

2. Compute Spearman r for the ranks found for each offense in 1970 and last year. The H_0 is that $r_S = 0$.

3. Compute independent groups t to test H_0: $\mu_1 = \mu_2$, that is, the brain lesion had no effect on memory.

4. Compute one-way ANOVA to test H_0: $\mu_1 = \mu_2 = \mu_3$, that is, the 3 feedback conditions result in equal performance on the second task.

5. Compute χ^2 testing H_0 that the proportion of guesses are equal for each of the 3 words, $\frac{1}{3}, \frac{1}{3}, \frac{1}{3}$.

6. Compute two-way ANOVA, testing 3 H_0's:
   H_0: μ's of the 3 reward groups are equal (i.e., their ratings of fairness are equal).
   H_0: μ's of the two methods of allocation (performance or chance) are equal.
   H_0: the effects of reward and method condition are additive.

7. Compute χ^2 testing H_0 that the two groups of students are homogeneous in the proportions choosing each alternative (career or family more important).

Index

Addition rule, 101
Alpha (α) levels, 146
Alternate hypothesis (H_1), 143
  bidirectional vs. unidirectional, 146
  one-tailed vs. two-tailed test, 149
Analysis of variance (ANOVA), one-way
  assumptions underlying, 255
  computational procedures for, 252–53, 258–59
  degrees of freedom, 255
  effect size, 260–61
  F-ratio, 257
  mean square, 256–57
  multiple comparison test following, 261–63
  purpose of, 242
  sums of squares, definitions of, 248–49
Analysis of variance (ANOVA), two-way
  computational procedures for, 278
  degrees of freedom, 282
  effect size, 286
  F-ratios, 283
  interaction in, 275–78
  main effects in, 273–75
  mean squares, computational procedures for, 282
  Tukey *hsd* test and, 285
  sum of squares, computational procedures for, 278–82
Arithmetic mean, *See* Mean
Asymptotic relative efficiency (ARE), 323–24
Average deviation, 70–72

Bar graph, 41
Bidirectional hypothesis, 146
Binomial expansion, 118
Binomial probability distribution
  mean and standard deviation, 121
  shape of, 122

Calculators, 12
Categorical data, 10
  mutually exclusive, 11
Central-limit theorem, 141
Central tendency, measures of
  comparison of measures of, 60–61
  mean, 50
  median, 58
  mode, 58
  when to use each measure, 61–63
Chi square
  a priori hypothesis and, 298
  as test of contingency, 303
  as test of homogeneity, 300

as test of independence, 300
  degrees of freedom, 302
  formula for, 297
  with more than 30 *df*, 306
  with one sample, 296
    degrees of freedom, 298
  restrictions on use of, 299–300
  table of, 365
  testing significance of difference, 300, 304
Class interval, 18
  midpoint of, 20
  real and apparent limits, 20
  width (*i*) of, 18
Coefficient of determination (r^2), 215
Coefficient of nondetermination ($1 - r^2$), 215
Combinations, 108
Computers
  programs for, 342–45
  types of, 341–42
  use in research, 12
Conditional probability
  independent events, 103
  joint events, 104
  and multiplication rule, 103
  nonindependent events, 103
Confidence intervals, 152
  95 percent, 153
  99 percent, 153
Continuous variables, 9
Control group, 2
Correlation
  and causation, 198–99
  linear and curvilinear, 203–05
  Pearson r (*See* Product-moment correlation)
    computational formula for, 203
  rank order (r_S), 217
  significance test for, 204
Cumulative frequency polygon, 37–39

Deciles, 40
Decision tree, 332
Degrees of freedom, 75
  chi square, 298, 302
  F-ratio, one-way analysis of variance, 255
  F-ratio, two-way analysis of variance, 283
  product-moment (Pearson) correlation, 205
  t of matched samples, 232
  t of pairs of independent samples, 177
  t of single sample, 149
Dependent variable, 166
Direct-difference method, 232
  formula for, 235
Discrete variables, 9

Effect size, *See* omega squared
Experimental group, 2

Factorial design, 272
F-ratio
  one-way analysis of variance, 257
  table of, 360
  two-way analysis of variance, 283
Frequency distributions
  cumulative, 37–39
  forms of, 36–37
  graphic representations of, 31–35
  grouped, 18
  simple, 17
  stem and leaf display, 22
Friedman two-way analysis of variance by ranks, 321–22

Graphic representations
  bar graph, 41
  cumulative frequency polygon, 37–39
  frequency polygon, 33
  histogram, 31
  line graph, 43

Histogram, 31
Honestly significant difference (*hsd*) test (*See* multiple comparison test)

Independent variable, 166
Interaction between variables, 275–78

Kruskal-Wallis one-way analysis of variance by ranks, 317–19

Line graph, 43–44

Magnitude data, 9
Mann-Whitney U test, 315–17
Matched pairs, 7
  advantages of, 8, 230
  t test with, 231–32
Mean
  computation of, with grouped data, 55–56
  computation of, with ungrouped data, 54–55
  definitions of, 50, 52
  population versus sample, 56–57
Mean square, concept of, 255

Mean squares, one-way analysis of
    variance
  degree of freedom for, 255
  formulas for, 256
Mean squares, two-way analysis of
    variance
  degrees of freedom for, 282
  formulas for, 282
Median, 40
  approximation from frequency
    distribution, 58–60
  computation from ungrouped data,
    60
  definitions of, 58, 60
Median test, 314–15
Mode, 58
Multiple comparison test
  following one-way ANOVA, 261
  following two-way ANOVA, 285
Multiplication rule, 102

Nominal data, 10
Nonparametric tests
  Friedman two-way analysis of
    variance by ranks for matched
    groups, 321–22
  Kruskal-Wallis one-way analysis of
    variance by ranks, 317–19
  median test, more than two groups,
    315
  median test, two independent
    groups, 314
  rank test for two independent
    samples (Mann-Whitney U),
    315–17
  relative efficiency of, 323–24
  versus parametric tests, 313
  Wilcoxon signed-ranks test for two
    matched groups, 319–21
Normal probability distribution
  characteristics of, 123
  inflection points, 124
  probabilities and percent area, 124
  table of, 355
  use of table, 125
Null hypothesis (H_0)
  about population mean, 143
  difference between means, 171
  choice of H_0, 172
Numerical data, 9

Ogive (*See* Cumulative frequency
    polygon)
Omega squared, estimated ($\hat{\omega}^2$)
  with one-way ANOVA, 260
  with t, 185
  with two-way ANOVA, 286
One-tailed vs. two-tailed test, 149

Parameters, 8
Pearson r (*See* Product-moment corre-
    lation coefficient)
Percentile ranks, 40
Percentiles, 39

Permutations, 107–8
Point estimation, 74
Polygon,
  cumulative frequency, 37–39
  frequency, 17
Population, 4
Power of test, 181
  factors affecting, 183
  parametric vs. nonparametric tests,
    313
Probability
  definition for equally likely events,
    100
  general definition, 101
  normal curve, 123
  principles of
    addition rule, 101
    conditional probability, 103
    joint events, 104
    multiplication rule, 102
Product-moment correlation coeffi-
    cient (Pearson r)
  assumptions in testing significance
    of, 205
  basic formula for, 200
  coefficient of determination, 215
  coefficient of nondetermination,
    215
  computational formula for, 203
  errors in prediction, 215
    standard error of estimate and,
    216
  interpretation of, 203
  range of possible values for, 202
  regression lines for, 210
  table of, 358
  testing the significance of, 204
  use in prediction, 206

Quartiles, 40

r, *See* Product-moment correlation
    coefficient
r_S, *See* Rank order correlation coeffi-
    cient
Random numbers
  table of, 6
Random samples, 5
  with replacement, 5
  without replacement, 6
Randomized samples, 7
Range, 18, 69
Rank order correlation coefficient (r_S),
    217
  formula for, 218
  interpretation of, 219
  table of, 359
  testing the significance of, 219
  tied ranks and, 219
Rank-order data, 10
Rank tests, *See* Nonparametric tests
Regression lines
  equations of, 212–13
  logic of, 206–7
  relationship between, 209–10
Rounding, 10

Sample
  definition of, 4
Sampling distribution
  of difference between means, 168
  of means, 138
  of proportions, 155
Sampling error, 140
Sandler's A statistic, 235
  table of, 364
Scatter plot, 195
Semi-interquartile range, 69–70
Sets
  elements of, 99
Sigma units, 81
Significance levels, 145
  choice of, 179
Skewness, 36
Spearman r, *See* Rank order corre-
    lation coefficient
Standard deviation
  basic formula for, 72
  calculated from frequency distribu-
    tion, 79
  derivation of raw score formula for,
    76
  estimate of population value from
    sample, 74
  population, 75
  raw score formula, population
    estimate, 78
  raw score formula, sample value, 76
  relation to range, 87
  sample, 72
  sample means, 142
  sample proportions, 155
Standard error of difference between
    means, 169
  formulas for estimating
    independent samples, equal N's,
    170
    independent samples, unequal
    N's, 176
    matched samples, 231
Standard error of estimate, 216–17
Standard error of mean
  estimate of, 142
  formula for, 140
  relation to N, 140
Standard error of proportion
  formula for, 155
Standard (U) scores, 86
  formulas for, 87
Statistical vs. experimental hypothesis,
    148
Stem and leaf display, 22
Studentized range statistic, 261
  table of, 362
Sum of squares, one-way analysis of
    variance
  between-groups, 249
  computational formulas for,
    252–53
  total, 248
  within-groups, 248
Sum of squares, two-way analysis of
    variance
  A × B interaction, 281–82
  between groups, 279

main effects of variables A and B,
280–81
total, 278–79
within-groups, 280
Summation (Σ), 51

Test of independence, chi square, 300
t-ratio
assumptions underlying, 178
with matched samples, 231
direct-difference method, 232
Sandler's *A* statistic, 235
table of, 356
testing hypothesis about difference
between μ's, 171
testing hypothesis about μ
with large sample, 143
with small sample, 149
use of table, 150, 177

T score, 86
Tukey *honestly significant difference test
(hsd)*, 261, 285
table for, *See* Studentized range
statistic, 360
Type I and Type II error, 151, 180
Types of data
comparison of, 11

U scores, 87
Unidirectional hypothesis, 146

Variability, measures of
average deviation, 70

need for index of, 68
range, 69
semi-interquartile range, 69
standard deviation and variance, 72
Variance, 72
estimate of population value from
sample, 73

Wilcoxon signed-ranks test for two
matched groups, 319–21
table of, 366

z scores, 81
formula for, 83
mean and variance of, 85

DIFFERENCE BETWEEN μ_1 AND μ_2 (MATCHED PAIRS)

$$H_0: \mu_1 - \mu_2 = 0$$

Direct difference t

$$s_D = \sqrt{\frac{\sum D^2 - \left(\sum D\right)^2 \big/ N}{N - 1}}$$

$$s_{\overline{D}} = \sqrt{\frac{s_D{}^2}{N}}$$

$$t = \frac{\overline{D}}{s_{\overline{D}}} \qquad \text{where } df = N - 1$$

Sandler's A

$$A = \frac{\sum D^2}{\left(\sum D\right)^2}$$

ONE-WAY ANOVA

$$H_0: \mu_1 = \mu_2 = \cdots = \mu_k$$

Sums of squares

$$SS_{tot} = \left(\sum_{tot} X^2\right) - \frac{\left(\sum_{tot} X\right)^2}{N_{tot}}$$

$$SS_{bg} = \sum_g \left[\frac{\left(\sum X_g\right)^2}{N_g'}\right] - \frac{\left(\sum_{tot} X\right)^2}{N_{tot}}$$

$$SS_{wg} = SS_{tot} - SS_{bg}$$

Mean squares and df's

$$MS_{bg} = \frac{SS_{bg}}{df_{bg}}$$

where $df_{bg} = k - 1$ and $k =$ number of groups

$$MS_{wg} = \frac{SS_{wg}}{df_{wg}}$$

where $df_{wg} = N_{tot} - k$

F ratio

$$F = \frac{MS_{bg}}{MS_{wg}}$$

Estimated omega squared

$$\hat{\omega}^2 = \frac{SS_{bg} - (k - 1) MS_{wg}}{SS_{tot} + MS_{wg}}$$

hsd follow-up test for pairs of $\overline{X}$'s

$$hsd = q_\alpha \sqrt{\frac{MS_{wg}}{N_g}}$$

TWO-WAY ANOVA

Sums of squares

SS_{tot}, SS_{bg}, SS_{wg} (see one-way ANOVA)

$$SS_A = \frac{\left(\sum X_{A1}\right)^2 + \left(\sum X_{A2}\right)^2 + \cdots + \left(\sum X_{Am}\right)^2}{N_A}$$

$$- \frac{\left(\sum_{tot} X\right)^2}{N_{tot}}$$

where $N_A =$ number in each A condition

$$SS_B = \frac{\left(\sum X_{B1}\right)^2 + \left(\sum X_{B2}\right)^2 + \cdots + \left(\sum X_{Bn}\right)^2}{N_B}$$

$$- \frac{\left(\sum_{tot} X\right)^2}{N_{tot}}$$

where $N_B =$ number in each B condition

$$SS_{A \times B} = SS_{bg} - SS_A - SS_B$$